20 CENTURIES OF
GREAT PREACHING

VOLUME THREE

WESLEY

to

FINNEY

1703–1875

20 CENTURIES OF GREAT PREACHING

An Encyclopedia of Preaching

VOLUME THREE

WESLEY

to

FINNEY

1703–1875

CLYDE E. FANT, JR.
WILLIAM M. PINSON, JR.

Donald E. Hammer
Research Associate

WORD BOOKS, Publisher
Waco, Texas

20 CENTURIES OF GREAT PREACHING. Volume Three:
WESLEY TO FINNEY

Library of Congress Catalog Card Number: 78-156697
Printed in the United States of America.

First Printing—November 1971
Second Printing—December 1974
Third Printing—July 1976

Special Thanks:

We are indebted to the Trustees of the Lane Theological Seminary for the portrait of Lyman Beecher. We are likewise grateful for the courteous assistance of Miss Gertrude Jacob of the Oberlin College Archives in supplying several excellent likenesses of Charles G. Finney.

Contents

Illustrations

Abbreviations of the Books of the Bible and Apocrypha

Old Testament	Authorized	Douay
Genesis	Gen.	Gen.
Exodus	Exod.	Exod.
Leviticus	Lev.	Lev.
Numbers	Num.	Num.
Deuteronomy	Deut.	Deut.
Joshua	Josh.	Josue
Judges	Judg.	Judges
Ruth	Ruth	Ruth
1 Samuel	1 Sam.	1 Kings
2 Samuel	2 Sam.	2 Kings
1 Kings	1 Kings	3 Kings
2 Kings	2 Kings	4 Kings
1 Chronicles	1 Chron.	1 Par.
2 Chronicles	2 Chron.	2 Par.
Ezra	Ezra	1 Esdras
Nehemiah	Neh.	2 Esdras
Esther	Esther	Esther
Job	Job	Job
Psalms	Ps.	Ps.
Proverbs	Prov.	Prov.
Ecclesiastes	Eccles.	Eccles.
Song of Solomon	Song of Sol.	Cant.
Isaiah	Isa.	Isa.
Jeremiah	Jer.	Jer.
Lamentations	Lam.	Lam.
Ezekiel	Ezek.	Ezech.
Daniel	Dan.	Dan.
Hosea	Hos.	Osee
Joel	Joel	Joel
Amos	Amos	Amos
Obadiah	Obad.	Abdias
Jonah	Jon.	Jon.
Micah	Mic.	Mich.

Old Testament	Authorized	Douay
Nahum	Nah.	Nah.
Habakkuk	Hab.	Hab.
Zephaniah	Zeph.	Soph.
Haggai	Hag.	Aggeus
Zechariah	Zech.	Zach.
Malachi	Mal.	Mal.

New Testament	Authorized and Douay	New Testament	Authorized and Douay
Matthew	Matt.	1 Timothy	1 Tim.
Mark	Mark	2 Timothy	2 Tim.
Luke	Luke	Titus	Titus
John	John	Philemon	Philem.
Acts of the Apostles	Acts	Hebrews	Heb.
Romans	Rom.	James	James
1 Corinthians	1 Cor.	1 Peter	1 Pet.
2 Corinthians	2 Cor.	2 Peter	2 Pet.
Galatians	Gal.	1 John	1 John
Ephesians	Eph.	2 John	2 John
Philippians	Phil.	3 John	3 John
Colossians	Col.	Jude	Jude
1 Thessalonians	1 Thess.	Revelation	Rev.(Apoc.)
2 Thessalonians	2 Thess.		

Apocrypha

The Wisdom of Solomon	Wisd.
Ecclesiasticus	Ecclus.

20 CENTURIES OF
GREAT PREACHING

VOLUME THREE

WESLEY
to
FINNEY

1703–1875

JOHN WESLEY

1703 - 1791

JOHN WESLEY by N. Hone, 1766, National Portrait Gallery, London.

JOHN BENJAMIN WESLEY

1703	*Born June 17 at Epworth, England*
1724	*Graduated from Oxford with B.A. degree*
1725	*Ordained a deacon*
1727	*Received M.A. degree and became curate at Epworth*
1729	*Returned to Oxford*
1735	*Departed for America*
1738	*Returned to England and experienced conversion in a Moravian devotional meeting on Aldersgate Street*
1739	*Joined Whitefield in open-air preaching*
1740	*Began direction of Methodist societies*
1751	*Married Mary Vazeille*
1778	*Founded* Arminian Magazine
1784	*Led Methodists to separation from Church of England*
1791	*Died on March 2 at Chapel House, City Road, London*

NO PREACHER OF THE EIGHTEENTH CENTURY exerted more influence than John Wesley. Some historians have insisted that had it not been for Wesley the horrors of revolution would have shaken British society. He led a religious and moral revival of such extent that the character and course of an entire nation were changed.

LIFE AND TIMES

John Benjamin Wesley was born at Epworth Rectory, Lincoln-shire, on June 17, 1703. The fifteenth of nineteen children, he was named for the tenth child, John, and the eleventh child,

Benjamin, who had died in infancy. His father, Samuel Wesley, was an Anglican priest who had been among the dissenters in England early in his career. In 1683, however, he renounced his nonconformity and entered the Church of England. He remained in his parish at Epworth for nearly forty years. Though a man of great learning and devotion he was a poor manager of money, and as a result, John Wesley remembered his childhood as a continuous state of poverty.

Susannah Annesley Wesley, John's mother, profoundly influenced his life. She was a devout woman who believed in strict regimentation of her family. She was herself the twenty-fifth child of her father. Accustomed to large families, she knew how to create order and discipline out of what could have been continual chaos. As a firm believer in education, Susannah Wesley created scholars of her children. On each child's fifth birthday, he was expected to recite the alphabet by memory. Then he was taught to spell out the first chapter of the Bible. When a child became six, he spent six hours each day in classes learning Christian theology.

Under this regimen John Wesley developed rapidly in both spiritual and academic matters. When he was ten he went to Charterhouse in London to begin his formal education. There he learned Latin and Greek as well as theology. The discipline of his home life continued to affect his life, and he rigidly adhered to a daily schedule which included meditation and prayer. He continued his education at Oxford and graduated with the B.A. degree in 1724. Under pressure from his father and others he was ordained a deacon in 1725. Deeply attracted to scholarship, Wesley received an appointment as a fellow in Lincoln College, Oxford, and studied logic. He was chosen to lecture in Greek and excelled in his studies. In 1727 he received the M.A. degree.

For a brief time he served as curate in his father's rectory. Soon he discovered that he had no taste for the pastor's role, and he returned to Oxford in 1729 to participate in the academic life where he remained until 1735. When Wesley returned to Oxford he found that his brother Charles had established a group of "Methodists." The nickname was not new. It was applied to any group of persons who tried to be methodical in their religious life. The group came to be known as the "Holy Club." Their activities included prayer and study as well as social outreach — visiting prisoners, almsgiving, and ministries for the poor and needy. Outwardly John Wesley was very religious, but inwardly there was a sense of emptiness and a longing for something better.

In his early thirties John was persuaded to go to Georgia in America as a missionary. He and his brother Charles left England on October 14, 1735. On the ship Wesley became acquainted with Moravians also traveling to America. Deeply influenced by their piety and courage in the face of danger, he sought more information about Moravian beliefs and experiences.

In Georgia, Wesley suffered failure and experienced deep religious doubt. His mission was interrupted by squabbles and a romance which turned sour. The anguish of his religious uncertainty is reflected in this entry in his *Journal*, January 24, 1738:

> I went to America to convert the Indians; but Oh! who shall convert me? Who, what is he that will deliver me from this evil heart of mischief? I have a fair summer religion. I can talk well; nay, and believe myself, while no danger is near; but let death look me in the face, and my spirit is troubled. Nor can I say, "To die is gain!"[1]

In 1737 he fled the colony and arrived back in England in February of the next year. Deeply depressed by his sense of failure, he sought spiritual help. Moravians again supplied spiritual guidance. A Moravian preacher, Peter Bohler, provided John Wesley with his concept of saving faith.

The religious experience which changed Wesley's life occurred on May 4, 1738. Participating in a Moravian devotional meeting on Aldersgate Street, he found assurance that Christ had taken away his sins. Never before had he experienced such spiritual certainty. Because of the experience a change came in Wesley's life. No longer was his religion merely formal and correct; he became excited about what the gospel could do for human life. He described this experience in his *Journal*:

> In the evening I went very unwillingly to a society in Aldersgate Street, where one was reading Luther's

---

1. Percy Livingstone Parker, ed., *The Journal of John Wesley* (Chicago: Moody Press, 1951), p. 53. Used by permission of Moody Press, Moody Bible Institute of Chicago.

preface to the Epistle to the Romans. About a quarter before nine, while he was describing the change which God works in the heart through faith in Christ, I felt my heart strangely warmed. I felt I did trust in Christ, Christ alone, for salvation; and an assurance was given me that He had taken away my sins, even mine, and saved me from the law of sin and death.[2]

George Whitefield was already engaged in open-air preaching when Wesley had his Aldersgate experience. In March of 1739 Wesley joined Whitefield in Bristol for an open-air preaching service. To Wesley, this was a distasteful experience. Nevertheless he continued to preach to masses of people in open-air meetings for the rest of his life.

The radical approach of Wesley and his plea for heart religion gained for him the hostility of many clergymen. Most pulpits were closed to him. Some preachers attacked him and urged the people not to hear him, but Wesley continued to preach. Though church pulpits were not open to him, he found his pulpits in open fields, on fences, in doorways, and even on tombstones.

In 1740 Wesley began to carve out for himself an independent course. He broke with the Moravians and with Whitefield. Wesley was a convinced Arminian and opposed the Calvinism of Whitefield. As people responded to Wesley's preaching, he organized them into societies. The remainder of Wesley's life was spent in developing these Methodist societies. He preached, wrote, and handled administrative matters. He was virtually a dictator over the societies but guided them with a tender and loving hand.

Wesley never favored leaving the Church of England; he only desired internal reform. But as the years rolled by it became evident that a break would finally become necessary. On February 28, 1784, he executed the "Deed of Declaration," which was enrolled in the courts, and which constitutes the charter of Wesleyan Methodism.

Early in his ministry John Wesley advocated a celibate clergy. Gradually he changed his mind and in 1751 he married Mary Vazeille. But the marriage was a catastrophe. Wesley's wife detested his dedication to work; she tampered with his notes and spread slander about him. In 1776 she finally left him, and he spent the remainder of his life alone.

---

2. Ibid., p. 64.

Domestic troubles were not the only problems that plagued Wesley. Frequent disputes broke out among the societies. Some of these were organizational; others swirled about personality conflicts. The more serious centered in theological matters—conflict between Arminian and Calvinistic theology finally led Wesley to found the *Arminian Magazine* and to give a great deal of his time to spreading Arminian doctrine.

Wesley directed his messages and the activities of his societies against the evils of his day. Many of the churches were cold and devoid of genuine religious experience. Religion was mere form. Wesley insisted that the gospel should bring men to real life and should generate excitement about Jesus Christ. While he did not encourage emotional excess, he believed that a relation to God in Christ should warm a man's heart.

Economically, in the eighteenth century England was entering the Industrial Revolution. The Industrial Revolution displaced labor, packed the cities with mobs of people—often without work—and created a wide gap between the wealthy and the poor. Wesley displayed great compassion for the poor. His journal carried notation after notation insisting that his societies were made up of both the rich and the poor. He preached to the poor and he counseled the poor. He pled their cause and labored to help them escape the grips of poverty.

Slavery drew from him nothing but condemnation. He abhorred the practice and made public his statements. He pled for abolition of the slave trade and the eradication of slavery from the British holdings. In his *Thoughts Upon Slavery* (1774) he rejected it by every law of nature and demand of justice and mercy. He wrote: "Give liberty to whom liberty is due, that is, to every child of man, to every partaker of human nature. Let none serve you but by his own act and deed, by his own voluntary choice. Away with all whips, all chains, all compulsion. Be gentle toward all men." When the Abolition Committee was formed in 1787, Wesley wrote a letter supporting it enthusiastically. One of his last letters (February 26, 1791) was to a prominent anti-slavery worker—probably Wilberforce— praising him for his activity against slavery. Wesley described slavery as "that execrable villainy, which is the scandal of religion, of England, and of human nature."

Politically Wesley was conservative—as a Tory, he sided with the monarchy. He insisted that commoners could not rule. He argued that representative forms of government were not practical because no real representation could take place. Naturally with such views he opposed the American colonists when they revolted against the British crown. Wesley's outspoken condemnation of the American struggle for independence created great opposition to Methodism in the early days of the United States.

Yet Wesley counseled his preachers to stay out of politics. He believed that more harm than good would come if they involved themselves in political disputes. Although he himself spoke on political matters from time to time, he refused to allow that privilege to others. In spite of his opposition, Methodists became more and more involved in political activity. Soon they were a force to be considered in the political life of England.

Wesley also preached against personal moral evils. Initially he was not a total abstainer, but he soon changed his mind and demanded that his followers do likewise. He looked upon alcohol as slow poison which sapped the very springs of life. Largely due to the influence of Wesley, between 1744 and 1784 the consumption of alcohol decreased remarkably.

In education, he was a pioneer in the area of popular public education. He even authored books in the field of education: *A Short English Grammar, Complete English Dictionary*, and *A Concise History of England.* He threw his support behind religious education, especially the Sunday School movement.

Wesley was a fiercely independent person. He believed that a man who had accepted the help of God did not need the help of the state. He led Methodism to be independent from state support and control, and he called for self-dependence and initiative on the part of those who led his societies.

The effectiveness of Wesley is irrefutable. At the end of his career, at least 70,000 Methodists lived in England alone; another 70,000 had probably died during his career. These Methodists were shepherded by 550 itinerant preachers, most of whom Wesley himself had called out and trained.

No man labored more intensely in the ministry than Wesley. He averaged 800 sermons a year—more than fifteen a week. For sixty years he preached to open-air throngs all over the British Isles. Wesley drew immense crowds: often 10,000 to 20,000 persons waited to hear him preach. He went wherever the population was the thickest. His missions took him into the mines, the fields, the streets, and the churches. He rode horseback 20,000 miles a year, reading out of his saddle bag as he rode. In his labors he covered more than 250,000 miles and preached more than 42,000 sermons. He produced more than 200 works.

His vast responsibilities left no time for careful editing or flowery phrasing; in fact, he detested such flourishes anyway. In the preface to a volume of sermons published in 1788 he wrote:

> I dare no more write in a *fine style* than wear a fine coat. But were it otherwise, had I time to spare, I should still write just as I do. I should purposely decline, what many admire, a highly ornamented style. I cannot admire French oratory: I despise it from my heart. Let those that please be in raptures at the pretty, elegant sentences of Massillon or Bourdaloue; but give me the plain, nervous style. . . .
>
> I think a preacher, or a writer of sermons, has lost his way, when he imitates any of the French orators; even the most famous of them; even Massillon or Bourdaloue.[3]

Blessed with robust health, Wesley carried on his intense work until the year of his death. He regretted that in his eighties he was usually only able to preach two sermons a day every day. Earlier he had often preached four or five times a day. In his *Journal* he wrote concerning his good health in old age:

> May we not impute it as inferior means,
> 1. To my constant exercise and change of air?
> 2. To my never having lost a night's sleep, sick or well, at land or at sea, since I was born?
> 3. To my having slept at command so that whenever I feel myself almost worn out I call it and it comes, day or night?
> 4. To my having constantly, for above sixty years, risen at four in the morning?
> 5. To my constant preaching at five in the morning, for above fifty years?
> 6. To my having had so little pain in my life; and so little sorrow, or anxious care?
>
> Even now, though I find pain daily, in my eye, or temple, or arm; yet it is never violent, and seldom lasts many minutes at a time. Whether or not this is sent to give me warning, that I am shortly to quit this tabernacle, I do not know; but be it one way or another, I have only to say,

---

3. John Wesley, *Sermons on Several Occasions*, vol. 2 (New York: Carlton & Porter, 1788), p. iv.

My remnant of days
I spend to His praise
Who died the whole world to redeem:
Be they many or few,
My days are His due,
And they all are devoted to Him![4]

On March 2, 1791, at Chapel House, City Road, London, John Wesley died after a brief illness. But his spirit and his movement live on. They live on not only in the Methodist churches of the world, but in numerous other denominations affected by his message and by his life. Wherever evangelism and ethics, proclamation and application, spiritual concern and social concern exist side by side, there dwells something of the spirit of John Wesley.

PREACHING AND SERMONS

One of the students who heard John Wesley preach at Saint Mary's, Oxford, was Benjamin Kennicott. He was neither a Methodist nor a friend of Wesley, so his description of Wesley's preaching is all the more interesting:

> When he mounted the pulpit, I fixed my eyes on him and his behavior. He is neither tall nor fat; for the latter would ill become a Methodist. His black hair quite smooth, and parted very exactly, added to a peculiar composure in his countenance, showed him to be an uncommon man. . . .
> And now he began to exalt his voice. . . . Under these three heads he expressed himself like a very good scholar, but a rigid zealot; and then he came to what he called his plain, practical conclusion. . . . And he fired his address with so much zeal and unbounded satire as quite spoiled what otherwise might have been turned to a great advantage.[5]

Nevertheless, that zeal and satire which so offended the young student likewise persuaded thousands to join the societies of Wesley.

In his *History of Preaching* Dargan gave one of the best brief statements of Wesley's preaching:

---

4. Parker, pp. 405–6.
5. Edward H. Sudgon, ed., *Standard Sermons of John Wesley* (London: Epworth Press, 1951), p. 89.

> Wesley's preaching was eminently characteristic of the man. As to contents it was Arminian in theology, evangelical in doctrine, and full of Scripture; in thought it was rich, logical, clear, and strong; in imagination not deficient, yet not especially marked; in feeling intense but not vehement; in style clear and sweet, without notable eloquence or passion; not so stilted as was the usual manner of his age, and yet to our taste lacking in ease and simplicity. In delivery he was calm, but there was a subdued intensity and glow that powerfully moved his hearers.[6]

In spite of Dargan's remarks, there is really some question whether Wesley was calm in his delivery. He named and rebuked the sins of the rich and the poor alike and called men to repentance. At times his sermons had the fervor of John the Baptist. Wesley sought to make his generation conscious of their sins, and his zeal frequently got him in trouble.

Poverty and ignorance had contributed to coarse conditions in the villages of England. Once when Wesley was preaching he ordered his crowd to part so he could see a man who was shouting insults at him. When the crowd separated Wesley looked his attacker in the face, and the man slunk away. Crude men often threw vegetables or rotten eggs at him. Once a man who brought a pocketful of overripe eggs to hurl at Wesley got a taste of his own medicine when the crowd mashed them in his pocket.

Preaching near the docks of Kellis, Wesley was berated by "a violence of the rabble" that "grew fiercer and fiercer, as their numbers increased." Wesley located the leader of the mob, fearlessly walked up to him and took him by the hand. Apparently the man was overwhelmed by Wesley's courage and said, "Sir, I will see you safe home. No man shall touch you." Then he turned to the crowd: "Stand off, I will knock the first man down who touches him." Wesley remarked in his *Journal*, "We walked on in great peace; my conductor every now and then stretching out his neck (he was a very tall man) to see if any behaved rudely, till we came to Mr. Hide's door. We then parted in much love."[7]

No mob ever prevented Wesley from preaching the gospel.

---

6. Edwin Charles Dargan, *A History of Preaching*, vol. 2 (Grand Rapids, Michigan: Baker Book House, 1954), p. 323.
7. *The Journal of the Rev. John Wesley*, 4 vols. (London: J. M. Dent & Co., n.d.), 2:23.

If they shouted, he spoke louder until he could be heard, or else he waited until they had finished. If they abused him physically, he took their abuse and returned it with love. Immense crowds heard him. Sometimes he spoke in meadows, sometimes upon walls or even tombstones. He preached in some places to as many as 20,000 persons. In one entry in his *Journal* he wrote: "What building except St. Paul's would contain such a congregation? And if it would, what human voice could have reached them there? By repeated observations I find I can command thrice the number in the open air that I can under a roof."

Wesley was not all fierce courage and vigorous attack upon sin; his major theme was the love of God. Far more of his sermons sought to impress men with the mercies of God than his terrors. He offered to men the promise of the redeeming love of God. He offered mercy to those made acutely aware of sin by his sermons.

Wesley's preaching was thoroughly biblical. In many of his sermons he devoted most of his time to an examination of the text or its background. He said:

> I have thought, I am a creature of a day, passing through life, as an arrow through the air. . . . I want to know one thing, the way to heaven: how to land safe on that happy shore. God himself has condescended to teach the way; for this very end he came from heaven. He hath written it down in a book! O give me that book! At any price, give me the book of God! I have it: here is knowledge enough for me.[8]

Perhaps the Bible supplied knowledge enough for his salvation, but his preaching was also marked by a learning of another sort: his sermons are filled with Greek and Latin quotations taken from his wide reading in literature.

There has been some misunderstanding at that point. Wesley is reputed by various sources to have taken his illustrations almost entirely from the Bible: "Rarely if ever do we find illustrative materials from his own experiences, and only occasionally do we observe illustrations from history and literature."[9] It is true that Wesley used more biblical illustrations than any other kind. McGraw counted 109 quotations from the Bible in Wesley's sermon "Scriptural Christianity" —

8. *The Works of the Rev. John Wesley, A.M.*, vol. 1 (New York: B. Waugh & T. Mason, 1835), p. xix.
9. James McGraw, *Great Evangelical Preachers of Yesterday* (New York: Abingdon Press, 1961), p. 59.

some from the Old Testament and many from the New Testament—not one of which was improperly or inaccurately quoted.

But Wesley did quote extensively from other literature. In his sermon "Human Life a Dream," Wesley cites nine separate pieces of poetry! It would be difficult to find another sermon in the history of Christian preaching that used more poetry in one sermon. The same sermon cites Moultray and relates the experience of the shooting of Charles XII, King of Sweden, at the siege of Fredrickssten. In another sermon "On the Omnipresence of God," Wesley quotes from two or three other poems. In the sermon "The Duty of Reproving Our Neighbour," Wesley quotes Richard Baxter and also uses an illustration about a drunkard taken from his own personal experience. Other examples could be given, but these are sufficient to show that Wesley was not at all unbalanced in his use of illustrative material. Biblical illustrations, poetry, literature, and personal illustrations—Wesley used them all.

Wesley gave some advice to young preachers who sought to follow in his ministry; quite likely this advice was taken from his own conduct in preaching:

> Let your whole deportment before the congregation be serious, weighty, and solemn. Always suit your subject to your audience. Choose the plainest texts you can. Take care not to ramble; but keep to your text, and make out what you take in hand. . . . Take care of anything awkward or affected, either in your gesture, phrase, or pronunciation. . . . Beware of clownishness, either in speech or dress. Wear no slouched hat.[10]

As might be expected, there was little wit or humor about the preaching of Wesley. The solemn preacher who complained in his *Journal* about the children "who play in the streets on Sunday" did not regard the pulpit as a place for humor. Although Wesley's serious sermons were unrelieved by wit, they were not tedious or dry; his lively style added spark to the solid substance of his sermons.

One of Wesley's most interesting sermons is "True Christianity Defended," apparently preached at the University of Oxford in June or July of 1741. Numerous references, particularly one in his *Journal* dated Thursday, June 18, seem to agree:

---

10. *Works of John Wesley*, vol. 7, pp. 224–25.

I . . . advised with Mr. Gambold concerning the subject
of my sermon before the University; but he seemed to
think it of no moment: "For (said he) all here are so
prejudiced, that they will mind nothing you say." I know
not that. However, I am to deliver my own soul, whether
they will hear, or whether they will forbear.[11]

In the sermon Wesley cited Tillitson (unfavorably) and Bishop
Bull (favorably). Numerous times in this sermon Wesley referred to a college setting: "We have public prayers, both morning and evening, in all our colleges." His own interest in education – and it might be added, his own intellect – is revealed by
the following remarks:

Know ye not then so much as this, you that are called
moral men, that all idleness is immorality? that there is
no grosser dishonesty than sloth? that every voluntary
blockhead is a knave? He defrauds his benefactors, his
parents, and the world, and robs both God and his own
soul. Yet how many of these are among us? . . . How
many whose ignorance is not owing to incapacity, but to
mere laziness?

How few (let it not seem immodest that even such an
one as I should touch on that point) of the vast number
who have it in their power, are truly learned men? Not
to speak of the other eastern tongues, who is there that
can be said to understand Hebrew? might I not say, or
even Greek? A little of Homer or Xenophon, we may still
remember; but how few can readily read or understand
so much as a page of Clemens Alexandrinus, Chrysostom, or Ephrem Syrus?

And as to philosophy (not to mention mathematics, or
the abstruser branches of it), how few do we find who
have laid the very foundation, who are masters even of
logic? who thoroughly understand so much as the rules
of syllogyzing! the very doctrine of the moods and
figures? Oh what is so scarce as learning, save religion?

The preaching of John Wesley is an excellent example of
both learning and religion. The following sermons reveal the
sermonic gifts of one of the truly significant figures in Christian history.

----

11. *The Journal of John Wesley,* vol. 1 (New York: E. P. Dutton & Co., 1906),
pp. 316–17.

Sermons

ON THE OMNIPRESENCE OF GOD

"Do I not fill heaven and earth? saith the Lord" (Jeremiah 23:24).

1. How STRONGLY and beautifully do these words express the omnipresence of God. And can there be, in the whole compass of nature, a more sublime subject? Can there be any, more worthy the consideration of every rational creature? Is there any, more necessary to be considered and understood, so far as our poor faculties will admit? How many excellent purposes may it answer? What deep instruction may it convey to all the children of men? And more directly to the children of God?

2. How is it, then, that so little has been written on so sublime and useful a subject? It is true, that some of our most eminent writers have occasionally touched upon it, and have several strong and beautiful reflections, which were naturally suggested by it. But which of them has published a regular treatise, or so much as a sermon, upon this head? Perhaps many were conscious of their inability to do justice to so vast a subject. It is possible, there may some such lie hid in the voluminous writings of the last century. But as they are hid even in their own country, if they are already buried in oblivion, it is the same, for any use they are of, as if they had never been written.

3. What seems to be wanting still, for general use, is a plain discourse on the omnipresence or ubiquity of God: first, in some manner explaining and proving that glorious truth – God is in this, and every place; and then applying it to the consciences of all thinking men, in a few practical inferences.

I. 1. Accordingly I will endeavour, by the assistance of his Spirit, first, a little to explain the omnipresence of God – To shew how we are to understand this glorious truth, God is in this, and every place. The psalmist, you may remember, speaks strongly and beautifully upon it, in Psalm 139 observing in the most exact order, first, God is in this place, and then God is in every place. He observes, first, "Thou art about my bed, and about my path, and spiest out all my ways"(v. 2).

Reprinted from John Wesley, *Sermons on Several Occasions,* vol. 2 (London: Fisher, Son, & Co., n.d.), pp. 496–501.

"Thou hast fashioned me behind and before, and laid thine hand upon me" (v. 4), although the manner thereof he could not explain: *how* it was he could not tell. "Such knowledge (says he) is too wonderful for me: I cannot attain unto it" (v. 5). He next observes, in the most lively and affecting manner, that God is in every place. "Whither shall I go (then) from thy Spirit, or whither shall I flee from thy presence? If I climb up into heaven, thou art there; if I go down to hell, thou art there also" (v.v. 6–7). If I could ascend, speaking after the manner of men, to the highest part of the universe, or could I descend to the lowest point, thou art alike present both in one and the other. "If I should take the wings of the morning, and remain in the utmost parts of the sea; even there thy hand would lead me." "Thy power and thy presence would be before me, "and thy right hand would hold me," seeing thou art equally in the length and breadth, and in the height and depth, of the universe. Indeed, thy presence and knowledge not only reach the utmost bounds of the creation, but

> Thine omnipresent sight
> Even to the pathless realms extends
> Of uncreated night.

In a word, there is no point of space, whether within or without the bounds of creation, where God is not.

2. Indeed, this subject is far too vast to be comprehended by the narrow limits of human understanding. We can only say, The great God, the eternal, the almighty Spirit, is as unbounded in his presence as in his duration and power. In condescension, indeed, to our weak understanding, he is said to "dwell in heaven": but, strictly speaking, the heaven of heavens cannot contain him; but he is in every part of his dominion. The universal God dwelleth in universal space; so that we may say,

> Hail, Father! whose creating call
> Unnumber'd worlds attend!
> Jehovah, comprehending all,
> Whom none can comprehend!

3. If we may dare attempt the illustrating this a little farther, what is the space occupied by the grain of sand, compared to that space which is occupied by the starry heavens? It is as a cipher: it is nothing: it vanishes away in the comparison. What is it then to the whole expanse of space, to which the whole creation is infinitely less than a grain of sand? And yet this space, to which the whole creation bears no proportion at all, is infinitely less, in comparison of the great God, than a grain of sand, yea, less than a millionth part of it is in comparison of that whole space.

II. 1. This seems to be the plain meaning of those solemn words which God speaks of himself, "Do not I fill heaven and earth?" And these sufficiently prove his omnipresence; which may be farther proved from this consideration, God acts everywhere, and, therefore, is everywhere: for it is an utter impossibility that any being, created or uncreated, should work where it is not. God acts in heaven, in earth, and under the earth, throughout the whole compass of his creation; by sustaining all things, without which everything would, in an instant, sink into its primitive nothing: by governing all, every moment superintending every thing that he has made; strongly and sweetly influencing all, and yet without destroying the liberty of his rational creatures. The very heathens acknowledged, that the great God governs the large and conspicuous parts of the universe: that he regulates the motions of the heavenly bodies, of the sun, moon, and stars . . . .

But they had no conception of his having a regard to the least things as well as the greatest; of his presiding over all that he has made, and governing atoms as well as worlds. This we could not have known, unless it had pleased God to reveal it unto us himself. Had he not himself told us so, we should not have dared to think, that "not a sparrow falleth to the ground without the will of our Father which is in heaven"; and much less affirm, that "even the very hairs of our head are all numbered!"

2. This comfortable truth, that God "filleth heaven and earth," we learn also from the words of the psalmist above recited. "If I climb up into heaven, thou art there: if I go down to hell, thou art there also. If I take the wings of the morning, and remain in the uttermost parts of the sea, even there thy hand shall lead me." The plain meaning is, If I remove to any distance whatever, thou art there, thou still besettest me, and layest thine hand upon me. Let me flee to any conceivable or inconceivable distance, above, beneath, or on any side, it makes no difference: thou art still equally there. In thee I still "live, and move, and have my being."

3. And where no creature is, still God is there. The presence or absence of any or all creatures, makes no difference with regard to him. He is equally in all, or without all. Many have been the disputes among philosophers, Whether there be any such thing as empty space in the universe? And it is now generally supposed, that all space is full. Perhaps it cannot be proved that all space is filled with matter. But the heathen himself will bear us witness, "All things are full of God." Yea, and whatever space exists beyond the bounds of creation, (for creation must have bounds, seeing nothing is boundless, nothing can be, but the great Creator,) even that space cannot exclude him who fills the heaven and the earth.

4. Just equivalent to this is the expression of the apostle, Ephesians 1:23 (not, as some have strangely supposed, concerning the church,

but concerning the head of it), "the fulness of him that filleth all in all," literally translated, "all things in all things:" the strongest expression of universality which can possibly be conceived. It necessarily includes the last and the greatest of all things that exist. So that if any expression could be stronger, it would be stronger than even that, the "filling heaven and earth."

5. Indeed, this very expression, "Do not I fill heaven and earth?" (the question being equal to the strongest affirmation) implies the clearest assertion of God's being present everywhere, and filling all space. For it is well known, the Hebrew phrase, *heaven and earth,* includes the whole universe, the whole extent of space, created or uncreated, and all that is therein.

6. Nay, and we cannot believe the omnipotence of God, unless we believe his omnipresence. For seeing (as was observed before) nothing can act where it is not; if there were any space where God was not present, he would not be able to do anything there: therefore, to deny the omnipresence of God, implies likewise the denial of his omnipotence. To set bounds to the one is, undoubtedly, to set bounds to the other also.

7. Indeed, wherever we suppose him not to be, there we suppose all his attributes to be in vain. He cannot exercise there either his justice or mercy, either his power or wisdom. In that extramundane space (so to speak), where we suppose God not to be present, we must, of course, suppose him to have no duration; but as it is supposed to be beyond the bounds of the creation, so it is beyond the bounds of the Creator's power. Such is the blasphemous absurdity which is implied in this supposition.

8. But to all that is or can be said of the omnipresence of God, the world has one grand objection: they cannot see him. And this is really at the root of all their other objections. This our blessed Lord observed long ago: "Whom the world cannot receive, because they see him not." But is it not easy to reply, "Can you see the wind? You cannot. But do you, therefore, deny its existence or its presence?" You say, No; for I can perceive it by my other senses. But by which of your senses do you perceive your soul? Surely you do not deny either the existence or the presence of this! And yet it is not the object of your sight, or of any of your other senses. Suffice it then to consider, that God is a spirit, as is your soul also. Consequently, "him no man hath seen nor can see" with eyes of flesh and blood.

III. 1. But allowing that God is here, as in every place, that he is "about our bed, and about our path," that he "besets us behind and before, and lays his hand upon us": what inference should we draw from hence? what use should we make of this awful consideration? Is it not meet and right to humble ourselves before the eyes of his majesty? Should we not labour continually to acknowledge his presence, "with reverence and godly fear?" Not, indeed, with the fear of devils, that believe and tremble, but with the fear of angels, with something similar to that which is felt by the inhabitants of heaven, when—

> Dark with excessive bright, his skirts appear,
> Yet dazzle heaven, that brightest seraphim
> Approach not, but with both wings veil their eyes.

2. Secondly, If you believe that God is about your bed and about your path, and spieth out all your ways, then take care not to do the least thing, not to speak the least word, not to indulge the least thought, which you have reason to think would offend him. Suppose that a messenger of God, an angel, to be now standing at your right hand, and fixing his eyes upon you, would you not take care to abstain from every word or action that you knew would offend him? Yea, suppose one of your mortal fellow-servants, suppose only a holy man, stood by you, would not you be extremely cautious how you conducted yourself, both in word and action? How much more cautious ought you to be, when you know, that not only a holy man, not an angel of God, but God himself, the Holy One, "that inheriteth eternity," is inspecting your heart, your tongue, your hand, every moment! and that he himself will surely bring you into judgment, for all you think, and speak, and act under the sun!

3. In particular: If there is not a word in your tongue, not a syllable you speak, but he "knoweth it altogether"; how exact should you be in "setting a watch before your mouth, and in keeping the door of your lips?" How wary does it behove you to be in all your conversation, being forewarned by your Judge, that, "by your words you shall be justified, or by your words you shall be condemned?" How cautious, lest "any corrupt communication," any uncharitable, yea, or unprofitable discourse, should "proceed out of your mouth": instead of "that which is good to the use of edifying," and meet to "minister grace to the hearers!"

4. Yea, if God sees our hearts, as well as our hands, and in all places; if he understandeth our thoughts long before they are clothed with words; how earnestly should we urge that petition, "Search me, O Lord, and prove me; try out my reins and my heart: look well if there be any way of wickedness in me, and lead me in the way everlasting!" Yea, how needful is it to work together with him, in "keeping our hearts with all diligence," till he hath "cast down imaginations, evil reasonings, and every thing that exalteth itself against the knowledge of God, and brought into captivity every thought to the obedience of Christ."

5. On the other hand, if you are already listed under the great Captain of your salvation, seeing you are continually under the eye of your Captain, how zealous and active should you be, "to fight the good fight

of faith, and lay hold on eternal life!—to endure hardship as good soldiers of Jesus Christ," to use all diligence, to "war a good warfare," and to do whatever is acceptable in his sight! How studious should you be to approve all your ways to his all-seeing eyes, that he may say to your hearts, what he will proclaim aloud in the great assembly of men and angels, "Well done, good and faithful servants."

6. In order to attain these glorious ends, spare no pains to preserve always, a deep, a continual, a lively, and a joyful sense of his gracious presence. Never forget his comprehensive word to the great father of the faithful, "I am the almighty [rather the all-sufficient] God, walk before me, and be thou perfect!" Cheerfully expect, that he, before whom you stand, will ever guide you with his eye, will support you by his guardian hand, will keep you from all evil. And "when you have suffered a while, will make you perfect, will establish, strengthen, and settle you": and then preserve you "unblameable, unto the coming of our Lord Jesus Christ."

Portsmouth, August 12, 1788.

TRUE CHRISTIANITY DEFENDED

"How is the faithful city become an harlot!" (Isaiah 1:21).

1. "WHEN I BRING A SWORD upon a land, saith the Lord, if the watchman blow the trumpet and warn the people, then whosoever heareth the sound of the trumpet, and taketh not warning, if the sword come and take him away, his blood shall be upon his own head. But if the watchman see the sword come, and blow not the trumpet, and the people be not warned; if the sword come and take any person from among them, he is taken away in his iniquity, but his blood will I require at the watchman's hand."

2. It cannot be doubted that word of the Lord is come unto every minister of Christ also. "So thou, O son of man, I have set thee a watchman unto the house of Israel: therefore thou shalt hear the word at

Reprinted from John Wesley, *Sermons on Several Occasions*, vol. 2 (London: Fisher, Son, & Co., n. d.), pp. 584-93.

my mouth, and warn them from me. When I say unto the wicked, O wicked man, thou shalt surely die: if thou dost not speak to warn the wicked from his way, that wicked man shall die in his iniquity; but his blood will I require at thine hand."

3. Nor ought any man therefore to be counted our enemy because he telleth us the truth: the doing of which is indeed an instance of love to our neighbour, as well as of obedience to God. Otherwise few would undertake so thankless a task; for the return they will find, they know already. The scripture must be fulfilled: "Me the world hateth," saith our Lord, "because I testify of it that the deeds thereof are evil."

4. It is from a full, settled conviction, that I owe this labour of love to my brethren, and to my tender parent (University of Oxford) by whom I have been nourished for now more than twenty years, and from whom, under God, I have received those advantages, of which, I trust, I shall retain a grateful sense, till my spirit returns to God who gave it: it is, I say, from a full conviction, that love and gratitude, as well as that dispensation of the gospel wherewith I am intrusted, require it of me, that even I have undertaken to speak on a needful, though unwelcome, subject. I would have wished that some more acceptable person would have done this; but should all hold their peace, the very stones would cry out, "How is the faithful city become an harlot!"

5. How faithful she once was to her Lord, to whom she had been betrothed as a chaste virgin, let not only the writings of her sons, which shall be had in honour through all generations, but also the blood of her martyrs, speak; a stronger testimony of her faithfulness than could be given by words, even

By all the speeches of the babbling earth.

But how is she now become an harlot! How hath she departed from her Lord! How hath she denied him, and listened to the voice of strangers, both

I. In respect of doctrine; and,

II. Of practice.

I. In respect of doctrine. 1. It cannot be said, that all our writers are setters forth of strange doctrines. There are those who expound the oracles of God by the same Spirit wherewith they were written, and who faithfully cleave to the solid foundation which our church hath laid agreeably thereto, touching which we have his word who cannot lie, "that the gates of hell shall not prevail against it." There are those also (blessed be the Author of every good gift), who, as wise master-builders, build thereon not hay or stubble, but gold and precious stones—but that charity which never faileth.

2. We have likewise cause to give thanks to the Father of lights, for that he hath not left himself without witness, but that there are those who now preach the gospel of peace, the truth as it is in Jesus: but how few are these in comparison of those who *adulterate* the word of God!

How little wholesome food have we for our souls, and what abundance of poison! How few are there, that, either in writing or preaching, declare the genuine gospel of Christ in the simplicity and purity wherewith it is set forth in the venerable records of our own church! and how are we enclosed on every side with those who, neither knowing the doctrines of our church, nor the scriptures, nor the power of God, have found out to themselves inventions wherewith they constantly corrupt others also!

3. I speak not now of those *first-born of Satan,* the Deists, Arians, or Socinians: these are too infamous among us to do any great service to the cause of their master. But what shall we say to those who are accounted the pillars of the church, and champions of our faith, who indeed betray that church, and sap the very foundation of the faith we are taught thereby?

4. But how invidious a thing it is to shew this! who is sufficient to bear the weight of prejudice which must necessarily follow the very mention of such a charge against men of so established a character? Nay, and who have, indeed, in many other respects, done great service to the church of God? Yet must every faithful minister say, "God forbid that I should accept any man's person. I dare not give any man flattering titles, nor spare any that corrupt the gospel. In so doing, my Maker would soon take me away."

5. Let me, however, be as short as may be upon this head; and I will instance only in two or three men of renown, who have endeavoured to sap the very foundation of our church, by attacking its fundamental, and indeed the fundamental doctrine of all the reformed churches, viz. justification by faith alone.

One of these, and one of the highest station in our church, hath written and printed before his death, several sermons, expressly to prove, that not *faith alone,* but *good works* also, are necessary in order to justification. The unpleasing task of quoting particular passages out of them is superseded by the very title of them, which is this, "The necessity of regeneration (which he at large proves to imply holiness both of heart and life), in order to justification."

6. It may appear strange to some, that an angel of the church of God (as the great Shepherd terms the overseers of it), and one so highly esteemed both in our own and many other nations, should coolly and calmly speak thus. But O! what is he, in comparison of the great Bishop Bull? Who shall be able to stand, if this eminent scholar, Christian, and prelate, in his youth wrote and published to the world, and in his riper years defended, the positions that follow.

"A man is said *to be justified by works,* because good works are the condition, according to the divine appointment, established in the gospel covenant, requisite and necessary to a man's justification; that is, to his obtaining remission of sins through Christ" (Bishop Bull's *Harmonica Apostolica,* p. 4).

A little after, being about to produce testimonies in proof of this proposition, he says, "The first class of these shall be those who speak of good works in a general sense, as the requisite and necessary condition of justification." Then follow certain texts of scripture, after which he adds, "Who does not believe that in these scriptures there is an abundance of good works required, which, if a man do not perform, he is altogether excluded from the hope of pardon, and remission of sins" (ibid. p. 6).

Having introduced some other things, he adds, "Besides *faith*, there is no one but may see that *repentance* is required as necessary to justification." Now, repentance is not one work alone, but is, as it were, a collection of many others; for in its compass the following works are comprehended: 1. Sorrow on account of sin. 2. Humiliation under the hand of God. 3. Hatred to sin. 4. Confession of sin. 5. Ardent supplication of the divine mercy. 6. The love of God. 7. Ceasing from sin. 8. Firm purpose of new obedience. 9. Restitution of ill-gotten goods. 10. Forgiving our neighbour his transgression against us. 11. Works of beneficence, or alms-giving. How much these things avail to procure remission of sins from God, is sufficiently evident from Daniel, 4:24, where the prophet gives this wholesome advice to Nebuchadnezzar, who was at that time cleaving to his sins; "Redeem your sins by almsgiving, and your iniquities by shewing mercy to the poor" (Dan. 4:27).

7. To instance in one point more. All the liturgy of the church is full of petitions for that holiness, without which, the scripture everywhere declares, no man shall see the Lord; and these are all summed up in those comprehensive words, which we are supposed to be so frequently repeating: "Cleanse the thoughts of our hearts by the inspiration of thy holy Spirit, that we may perfectly love thee, and worthily magnify thy holy name." It is evident, that in the last clause of this petition, all outward holiness is contained; neither can it be carried to a greater height, or expressed in stronger terms; and those words, "Cleanse the thoughts of our hearts," contain the negative branch of inward holiness, the height and depth of which is purity of heart, by the inspiration of God's holy Spirit: the remaining words, "that we may perfectly love thee," contain the positive part of holiness; seeing this love, which is the fulfilling of the law, implies the whole mind that was in Christ.

8. But how does the general stream of writers and preachers (let me be excused the invidious task of instancing in particular persons) agree with this doctrine? Indeed, none at all. Very few can we find who simply and earnestly enforce it; but very many who write and preach as if Christian holiness, or religion, was a purely negative thing; as if not to curse or swear, not to lie or slander, not to be a drunkard, a thief, or a whoremonger, not to speak or do evil, was religion enough to entitle a man to heaven! How many, if, they go something farther than

this, describe it only as an outward thing? – as if it consisted chiefly, if not wholly, in doing good (as it is called) and using the means of grace? Or, should they go a little farther still, yet what do they add to this poor account of religion? Why, perhaps, that a man should be orthodox in his opinions, and have a zeal for the constitution in church and state: and this is all; this is all the religion they can allow, without degenerating into enthusiasm! So true it is, that the faith of a devil, and the life of a heathen, make up what most men call a *good Christian!*

9. But why should we seek further witnesses of this? Are there not many present here who are of the same opinion? – who believe that a good moral man and a good Christian mean the same thing? that a man need not trouble himself any further, if he only practises as much Christianity as was written over the heathen emperor's gate; "Do as thou wouldst be done unto": especially, if he be not an infidel or an heretic, but believes all that the bible and the church says is true.

10. I would not be understood as if I despised these things, as if I undervalued right opinions, true morality, or a zealous regard for the constitution we have received from our fathers; yet, what are these things, being alone? What will they profit us in that day? What will it avail to tell the Judge of all, "Lord, I was not as other men were; not unjust, not an adulterer, not a liar, not an immoral man." Yea, what will it avail, if we have done all good, as well as done no harm? If we have given all our goods to feed the poor, and have not charity? How shall we then look on those who taught us to sleep on and take our rest, though *the love of the Father was not in us*? or who, teaching us to seek salvation by works, cut us off from receiving that faith freely, whereby alone the love of God could have been shed abroad in our hearts?

To these miserable corrupters of the gospel of Christ, and the poison they have spread abroad, is chiefly owing,

II. Secondly, the general corruption in practice as well as in doctrine. There is hardly to be found (O tell it not in Gath, publish it not in the streets of Askelon) either the form of godliness, or the power! So is the faithful city become an harlot!

1. With grief of heart I speak it, and not with joy, that scarce is the form of godliness seen among us. We are all indeed called to be saints, and the very name of Christian means no less; but who has so much as the appearance? Take anyone you meet; take a second, a third, a fourth, or the twentieth. Not one of them has even the appearance of a saint any more than of an angel. Observe his look, his air, his gesture! does it breathe nothing but God? does it bespeak a temple of the Holy Ghost? Observe his conversation: not an hour only, but day by day; can you gather from any outward sign that God dwelleth in his heart? that this is an everlasting spirit, who is going to God? Would you imagine that the blood of Christ was shed for that soul, and had purchased

everlasting salvation for it, and that God was now waiting till that salvation should be wrought out with fear and trembling.

2. Should it be said, Why, what signifies the form of godliness? We readily answer, Nothing, if it be alone; but the absence of form signifies much: it infallibly proves the absence of the power; for though the form may be without the power, the power cannot be without the form. Outward religion may be where inward is not; but if there is none without, there can be none within.

3. But it may be said, We have public prayers, both morning and evening, in all our colleges. It is true, and it were to be wished that all the members thereof, more especially the elder, those of note and character, would, by constantly attending them, shew how sensible they are of that invaluable privilege. But have all who attend them the form of godliness? Before those solemn addresses to God begin, does the behaviour of all who are present shew that they know before whom they stand? What impression seems to be left on their minds, when those holy offices are ended? And even during their continuance, can it be reasonably inferred, from the tenor of their outward behaviour, that their hearts are earnestly fixed on him who standeth in the midst of them? I much fear, were a heathen, who understood not our tongue, to come into one of these our assemblies, he would suspect nothing less than that we were pouring out our hearts before the Majesty of heaven and earth. What then shall we say, if indeed God is not mocked, but,—what a man soweth, that also shall he reap?

4. On Sundays, however, say some, it cannot be denied that we have the form of godliness, having sermons preached both morning and afternoon, over and above the morning and evening service; but do we keep the rest of the sabbath-day holy? Is there no needless visiting upon it? no trifling? no impertinence of conversation? Do neither you yourselves do any unnecessary work upon it, nor suffer others, over whom you have any power, to break the laws of God and man herein? If you do, even in this you have nothing whereof to boast; but herein also you are guilty before God.

5. But if we have the form of godliness on one day in a week, is there not on other days what is quite contrary thereto? Are not the best of our conversing hours spent in foolish talking and jesting, which are not convenient? nay, perhaps, in wanton talking too, such as modest ears could not bear? Are there not many among us found to eat and drink with the drunken? And if so, what marvel is it that our profaneness should also go up into the heavens, and our oaths and curses into the ears of the Lord of sabaoth?

6. And even as to the hours assigned for study, are they generally spent to any better purpose? Not if they are employed in reading (as is too common) plays, novels, or idle tales, which naturally tend to increase our inbred corruptions, and to heat the furnace of our unholy

desires seven times hotter than it was before! How little preferable is
the laborious idleness of those who spend day after day in gaming or
diversions, vilely casting away that time, the value of which they cannot know till they are passed through it into eternity?

7. Know ye not then so much as this, you that are called moral men,
that all idleness is immorality? that there is no grosser dishonesty
than sloth? that every voluntary blockhead is a knave? He defrauds
his benefactors, his parents, and the world, and robs both God and his
own soul. Yet how many of these are among us? How many lazy
drones, as if only *fruges consumere nati*? born to eat up the produce
of the soil. How many whose ignorance is not owing to incapacity, but
to mere laziness? How few (let it not seem immodest that even such
an one as I should touch on that point), of the vast number who have
it in their power, are truly learned men? Not to speak of the other
eastern tongues, who is there that can be said to understand Hebrew?
might I not say, or even Greek? A little of Homer or Xenophon, we may
still remember; but how few can readily read or understand so much
as a page of Clemens Alexandrinus, Chrysostom, or Ephrem Syrus?
And as to philosophy (not to mention mathematics, or the abstruser
branches of it), how few do we find who have laid the very foundation,
who are masters even of logic? who thoroughly understand so much as
the rules of syllogyzing! the very doctrine of the moods and figures?
O what is so scarce as learning, save religion?

8. And, indeed, learning will be seldom found without religion; for
temporal views, as experience shews, will very rarely suffice to carry
anyone through the labour required to be a thorough scholar. Can it
then be dissembled, that there is too often a defect in those to whom
the care of youth is intrusted? Is that solemn direction sufficiently considered, *Let the tutor diligently instruct those scholars committed
to his care in strict morality, and especially in the first principles
of religion, and the articles of doctrine* (Statutes, p. 7).

And do they to whom this important charge is given, labour diligently to lay this good foundation? to fix true principles of religion in
the minds of the youth intrusted to them, by their lectures? to recom-
mend the practice thereof by the powerful and pleasing influence of
their example? to enforce this by frequent private advice, earnestly
and strongly inculcated? to observe the progress, and carefully inquire into the behaviour, of every one of them? in a word, to watch
over their souls as they that must give account.

9. Suffer me, since I have begun to speak upon this head, to go a
little farther. Is there sufficient care taken that they should know and
keep the statutes which we are all engaged to observed? How then is
it that they are so notoriously broken every day? To instance only in a
few:

It is appointed, as to divine offices and preaching, "That all shall
publicly attend: — Graduates and scholars shall attend punctually, and

continue till all be finished, with due reverence from the beginning to the end"(p. 181).

It is appointed, "That scholars of every rank shall abstain from all kinds of play where money is contended for; such as cards, dice, and bowls; nor shall they be present at public games of this nature" (p. 157).

It is appointed, "That all (the sons of noblemen excepted) shall accustom themselves to black or dark-coloured clothing; and that they shall keep at the utmost distance from pomp and extravagance" (p. 157).

It is appointed, "That scholars of every rank shall abstain from alehouses, inns, taverns, and from every place within the city where wine or any other kind of liquor is ordinarily sold" (p. 164).

10. It will be objected, perhaps, "That these are but little things." Nay, but perjury is not a little thing; nor, consequently, the wilful breach of any rule which we have solemnly sworn to observe. Surely those who speak thus have forgotten those words, *Thou shalt pledge thy faith to observe all the statutes of this university. So help thee God, and the holy inspired Gospels of Christ* (p. 229).

11. But is this oath sufficiently considered by those who take it? or any of those prescribed by public authority? Is not this solemn act of religion, the calling God to record on our souls, commonly treated as a slight thing? in particular, by those who swear by the living God, *That neither entreaties nor reward, neither hatred nor friendship, neither hope nor fear, induce them to give a testimony to any unworthy person* (p. 88). And by those who swear, *I know this person to be meet and fit in morals and knowledge for that high degree to which he is presented?* (p. 114).

12. Yet one thing more. We have all testified before God, "That all and every the articles of our church, as also the book of common-prayer, and the ordaining of bishops, priests, and deacons, are agreeable to the word of God." And in so doing we have likewise testified, "That both the first and the second book of homilies doth contain godly and wholesome doctrine." But upon what evidence have many of us declared this? Have we not affirmed the things we know not? If so, however true they may happen to be, we are found false witnesses before God. Have the greater part of us ever used any means to know whether these things are so or not? Have we ever, for one hour, seriously considered the articles to which we have subscribed? If not, how shamefully do we elude the design of the very compilers who compiled them, "to remove difference of opinion, and to establish unanimity in the true religion?"

Have we half of us read over the book of common-prayer, and of ordaining bishops, priests, and deacons? If not, what is it we have so solemnly confirmed? In plain terms, we cannot tell; and as to the two books of homilies, it is well if a tenth part of those who have subscribed to them, I will not say, had considered them before they did this, but if they have even read them over to this day! Alas, my brethren, how shall we reconcile these things even to common honesty, to plain heathen morality? So far are those who do them, nay, and perhaps defend them too, from having even the form of Christian godliness!

13. But waving all these things, where is the power? Who are the living witnesses of this? Who among us (let God witness with our hearts) experimentally knows the force of inward holiness? Who feels in himself the workings of the Spirit of Christ drawing up his mind to high and heavenly things? Who can witness, – "The thoughts of my heart God hath cleansed by the inspiration of his holy Spirit?" Who knoweth that "peace of God which passeth all understanding?" Who is he that "rejoiceth with joy unspeakable and full of glory?" Whose "affections are set on things above, not on things of the earth?" Whose "life is hid with Christ in God?" Who can say, "I am crucified with Christ; yet I live, yet not I, but Christ liveth in me; and the life that I now live in the body, I live by the faith of the Son of God, who loved me, and gave himself for me?" In whose heart is the "love of God shed abroad, by the Holy Ghost which is given unto him?"

14. Is not almost the very notion of this religion lost? Is there not a gross overflowing ignorance of it? Nay, is it not utterly despised? Is it not wholly set at nought and trodden under foot? Were anyone to witness these things before God, would he not be accounted a madman, an enthusiast? Am not I unto you a barbarian who speak thus? My brethren, my heart bleeds for you. O that you would at length take knowledge, and understand that these are the words of truth and soberness! O that you knew, at least, in this your day, the things that make for your peace!

15. I have been a messenger of heavy tidings this day. But the love of Christ constraineth me: and to me it was the less grievous, because for you it was safe. I desire not to accuse the children of my people. Therefore neither do I speak thus in the ears of them that sit on the wall: but to you I endeavour to speak the truth in love, as a faithful minister of Jesus Christ. And I can now call you to record this day, that I am pure from the blood of all men; for I have not shunned to declare unto you all the counsel of God.

16. May the God of all grace, who is longsuffering, of tender mercy, and repenteth him of the evil, fix these things in your hearts, and water the seed he hath sown with the dew of Heaven! May he correct whatsoever he seeth amiss in us! May he supply whatsoever is wanting! May he establish, strengthen, and settle us, that this place may again be a faithful city to her Lord, yea, the praise of the whole earth!

June 24, 1741.

THE DUTY OF REPROVING OUR NEIGHBOUR

"Thou shalt not hate thy brother in thy heart; thou shalt in
any wise rebuke thy neighbour, and not suffer sin upon him"
(Leviticus 19:17).

A GREAT PART OF THE BOOK of Exodus, and almost the whole of the
book of Leviticus, relate to the ritual or ceremonial law of Moses,
which was peculiarly given to the children of Israel; but was such "a
yoke," says the apostle Peter, "as neither our fathers nor we are able
to bear." We are, therefore, delivered from it; and this is one branch
of "the liberty wherewith Christ hath made us free." Yet it is easy to
observe, that many excellent moral precepts are interspersed among
these ceremonial laws. Several of them we find in this very chapter.
Such as, "Thou shalt not gather every grape in thy vineyard; thou
shalt leave them for the poor and stranger. I am the Lord your God"
(v. 10). "Ye shall not steal, neither lie one to another" (v. 11). "Thou
shalt not defraud thy neighbour, neither rob him; the wages of him
that is hired shall not abide with thee til the morning" (v. 13). "Thou
shalt not curse the deaf, nor put a stumbling-block before the blind;
but shalt fear thy God; I am the Lord"(v. 14). As if he had said, I am
he whose eyes are over all the earth, and whose ears are open to their
cry. "Ye shall do no unrighteousness in judgment: thou shalt not
respect the person of the poor" (which compassionate men may be
tempted to do); nor honour the person of the mighty"; to which there
are a thousand temptations (v. 15). "Thou shalt not go up and down as
a tale-bearer among thy people"(v. 16), although this is a sin which
human laws have never yet been able to prevent. Then follows, "Thou
shalt not hate thy brother in thy heart; thou shalt, in any-wise, rebuke
thy neighbour, and not suffer sin upon him."

In order to understand this important direction aright, and to apply
it profitably to our own souls, let us consider,

I. What it is that we are to rebuke or reprove? What is the thing that
is here enjoined?

II. Who are they whom we are commanded to reprove? And,

III. How are we to reprove them?

I. 1. Let us consider, first, What is the duty that is here enjoined?
What is it we are to rebuke or reprove? And what is it, To reprove?

Reprinted from John Wesley, *Sermons on Several Occasions*, vol. 2 (London:
Fisher, Son, & Co., n. d.), pp. 102–9.

To tell any one of his faults, as clearly appears from the following words, "Thou shalt not suffer sin upon him." Sin is, therefore, the thing we are called to reprove, or rather him that commits sin. We are to do all that in us lies to convince him of his fault, and lead him in the right way.

2. Love, indeed, requires us to warn him not only of sin (although of this chiefly), but likewise of any error, which, if it were persisted in, would naturally lead to sin. If we do not hate him in our heart, if we love our neighbour as ourselves, this will be our constant endeavour, to warn him of every evil way, and of every mistake which tends to evil.

3. But if we desire not to lose our labour, we should rarely reprove any one for any thing that is of a disputable nature, that will bear much to be said on both sides. A thing may possibly appear evil to me; therefore, I scruple the doing of it. And if I were to do it while that scruple remains, I should be a sinner before God. But another is not to be judged by my conscience, to his own Master he standeth or falleth. Therefore, I would not reprove him, but for what is clearly and undeniably evil. Such, for instance, is profane cursing and swearing, which even those who practise it most, will not often venture to defend, if one mildly expostulates with them. Such is drunkenness, which even an habitual drunkard will condemn when he is sober. And such, in the account of the generality of people, is the profaning of the Lord's day. And if any who are guilty of these sins for a while attempt to defend them, very few will persist to do it, if you look them steadily in the face, and appeal to their own conscience in the sight of God.

II. 1. Let us, in the second place, consider, Who are those that we are called to reprove? It is the more needful to consider this, because it is affirmed by many serious persons, that there are some sinners whom the scripture itself forbids us to reprove. This sense has been put on that solemn caution of our Lord, in his sermon on the mount; "Cast not your pearls before swine, lest they trample them under foot, and turn again and rend you." But the plain meaning of these words is, Do not offer the pearls, the sublime doctrines or mysteries of the gospel, to those whom you know to be brutish men, immersed in sins, and having no fear of God before their eyes. This would expose those precious jewels to contempt, and yourselves to injurious treatment. — But even those whom we know to be, in our Lord's sense, dogs and swine, if we saw them do, or heard them speak, what they themselves know to be evil, we ought, in any-wise, to reprove them; else we "hate our brother in our heart."

2. The person intended by our neighbour is every child of man, every one that breathes the vital air, all that have souls to be saved. And if we refrain performing this office of love to any, because they

are sinners above other men, they may persist in their iniquity, but their blood will God require at our hands.

3. How striking is Mr. Baxter's reflection on this head, in his Saints' Everlasting Rest. "Suppose thou wert to meet one in the lower world, to whom thou hast denied this office of love, when ye were both together under the sun; what answer couldst thou make to his upbraiding? At such a time and place, while we were under the sun, God delivered me into thy hands. I then did not know the way of salvation, but was seeking death in the error of my life. And therein thou sufferedst me to remain, without once endeavouring to awake me out of sleep! Hadst thou imparted to me thy knowledge, and warned me to flee from the wrath to come, neither I nor thou need ever have come into this place of torment."

4. Every one, therefore, that has a soul to be saved, is entitled to this good office from thee. Yet this does not imply, that it is to be done in the same degree to every one. It cannot be denied, that there are some, to whom it is particularly due. Such, in the first place, are our parents, if we have any that stand in need of it; unless we should place our comforts and our children on an equal footing with them. Next to these we may rank our brothers and sisters, and afterwards our relations as they are allied to us in a nearer or more distant manner, either by blood or by marriage. Immediately after these, are our servants, whether bound to us for a term of years, or any shorter term. Lastly, such, in their several degrees, are our countrymen, our fellow-citizens, and the members of the same society, whether civil or religious; the latter have a particular claim to our service; seeing these societies are formed with that very design, to watch over each other for this very end, that we may not suffer sin upon our brother. If we neglect to reprove any of these, when a fair opportunity offers, we are undoubtedly to be ranked amongst those that "hate their brother in their heart." And how severe is the sentence of the apostle against those who fall under this condemnation! "He that hateth his brother," though it does not break out into words or actions, "is a murderer." "And ye know," continues the apostle, "that no murderer hath eternal life abiding in him." He hath not that seed planted in his soul, which groweth up unto everlasting life. In other words, he is in such a state, that if he die therein he cannot see life. It plainly follows, that to neglect this, is no small thing, but eminently endangers our final salvation.

III. We have seen what is meant by reproving our brother, and who those are that we should reprove. But the principal thing remains to be considered. How, in what manner, are we to reprove them?

1. It must be allowed that there is a considerable difficulty in performing this in a right manner. Although, at the same time, it is far less difficult to some than it is to others. Some there are, who are particularly qualified for it, whether by nature, or practice, or grace. They

are not encumbered either with evil shame, or that sore burden, the fear of man. They are both ready to undertake this labour of love, and skilful in performing it. To these, therefore, it is little or no cross; nay, they have a kind of relish for it, and a satisfaction therein, over and above that which arises from a consciousness of having done their duty. But be it a cross to us, greater or less, we know that hereunto we are called. And be the difficulty ever so great to us, we know in whom we have trusted; and that he will surely fulfil his word, "As thy day, so shall thy strength be."

2. In what manner, then, shall we reprove our brother, in order that our reproof may be most effectual? Let us first of all take care, that whatever we do, may be done in "the spirit of love," in the spirit of tender good-will to our neighbour, as for one who is the son of our common Father, and one for whom Christ died, that he might be a partaker of salvation. Then, by the grace of God, love will beget love. The affection of the speaker will spread to the heart of the hearer; and you will find, in due time, that "your labour hath not been in vain in the Lord."

3. Meantime, the greatest care must be taken, that you speak in the spirit of *humility*. Beware that you do not think of yourself more highly than you ought to think. If you think too highly of yourself, you can scarce avoid despising your brother. And if you shew, or even feel, the least contempt of those whom you reprove, it will blast your whole work, and occasion you to lose all your labour. In order to prevent the very appearance of pride, it will be often needful to be explicit on this head; to disclaim all preferring yourself before him; and at the very time you reprove that which is evil, to own and bless God for that which is good in him.

4. Great care must be taken, in the third place, to speak in the spirit of *meekness,* as well as *lowliness.* The apostle assures us, "that the wrath of man worketh not the righteousness of God." Anger, though it be adorned with the name of zeal, begets anger, not love or holiness. We should therefore avoid, with all possible care, the very appearance of it. Let there be no trace of it, either in the eyes, the gesture, or the tone of your voice; but let these concur in manifesting a loving, humble, and dispassionate spirit.

5. But all this time see that you do not trust in yourself. Put no confidence in your own wisdom, or address, or abilities of any kind. For the success of all you speak or do, trust not in yourself, but in the great Author of every good and perfect gift. Therefore, while you are speaking, continually lift up your heart to him that worketh all in all. And whatsoever is spoken in the spirit of *prayer* will not fall to the grounds.

6. So much for the *spirit* wherewith you should speak, when you reprove your neighbour. I now proceed to the outward *manner.* It has been frequently found, that the prefacing a reproof with a frank

profession of good-will, has caused what was spoken to sink deep into the heart. This will generally have a far better effect than the grand fashionable engine, flattery, by means of which the men of the world have often done surprising things. But the very same things, yea, far greater, have much oftener been effected, by a plain and artless declaration of disinterested love. When you feel God has kindled this flame in your heart, hide it not; give it full vent. It will pierce like lightning. The stout, the hard-hearted, will melt before you, and know that God is with you of a truth.

7. Although it is certain that the main point in reproving, is to do it with a right spirit; yet, it must also be allowed, there are several little circumstances with regard to the outward manner, which are by no means without their use, and, therefore, are not to be despised. One of these is, whenever you reprove, do it with great *seriousness;* so that, as you really are in earnest, you may likewise appear so to be. A ludicrous reproof makes little impression, and is soon forgot. Besides that, many times it is taken ill, as if you ridiculed the person you reprove. And, indeed, those who are not accustomed to make jests, do not take it well to be jested upon. One mean of giving a serious air to what you speak, is, as often as may be, to use the very words of scripture. Frequently we find the word of God, even in a private conversation, has a peculiar energy; and the sinner, when he expects it least, feels it "sharper than a two-edged sword."

8. Yet there are some exceptions to this general rule of reproving seriously. There are some exempt cases, wherein, as a good judge of human nature observes, a little well-placed raillery will pierce deeper than solid argument. But this has place chiefly when we have to do with those who are strangers to religion. And when we condescend to give a ludicrous reproof to a person of this character, it seems we are authorized so to do, by that advice of Solomon, "Answer a fool according to his folly, lest he be wise in his own eyes."

9. The manner of the reproof may in other respects too be varied, according to the occasion. Sometimes you may find it proper to use many words, to express your sense at large. At other times you may judge it more expedient to use few words, perhaps a single sentence. And at others, it may be advisable to use no words at all; but a gesture, a sigh, or a look. Particularly when the person you would reprove is greatly your superior. And frequently this silent kind of reproof will be attended by the power of God; and consequently have a far better effect than a long and laboured discourse.

10. Once more. Remember the remark of Solomon: "A word spoken in season, how good is it!" It is true, if you are providentially called to reprove anyone, whom you are not likely to see anymore, you are to snatch the present opportunity, and to speak "in season," or "out of season." But with them whom you have frequent opportunities of seeing, you may wait for a fair occasion. Here the advice of the poet

has place. You may speak – when he is in a good humour, or when he asks it of you. Here you may catch the times when his mind is in a soft, mild frame. And then God will both teach you how to speak, and give a blessing to what is spoken.

11. But here let me guard you against one mistake. It passes for an indisputable maxim, "Never attempt to reprove a man when he is intoxicated with drink." Reproof, it is said, is then thrown away, and can have no good effect. I dare not say so. I have seen not a few clear instances of the contrary. Take one. Many years ago, passing by a man in Moorfields, who was so drunk he could hardly stand, I put a paper into his hand. He looked at it, and said, "A Word – A Word to a Drunkard – that is me – Sir, Sir! I am wrong – I know I am wrong – pray let me talk a little with you." He held me by the hand a full half hour. And I believe he got drunk no more.

12. I beseech you, brethren, by the mercies of God, do not despise poor drunkards. Have compassion on them. Be instant with them, in season, and out of season! Let not shame, or fear of man, prevent your pulling these brands out of the burning; many of them are self-condemned: –

> Nor do they not discern the evil plight
> That they are in.

But they despair; they have no hope of escaping out of it. And they sink into it still deeper, because none else has any hope for them!

"Sinners of every other sort," said a venerable old clergyman, "have I frequently known converted to God. But an habitual drunkard I have never known converted." But I have known five hundred, perhaps five thousand. Ho! art thou one who readest these words? Then hear thou the words of the Lord! I have a message from God unto thee, O sinner! Thus saith the Lord, cast not away thy hope. I have not forgotten thee. He that tells thee, "There is no help," is a liar from the beginning. Look up! Behold the Lamb of God, who taketh away the sin of the world! This day is salvation come to thy soul; only see that thou despise not him that speaketh! Just now he saith unto thee, "Son, be of good cheer! Thy sins are forgiven thee!"

13. Lastly. You that are diligent in this labour of love, see that you be not discouraged, although, after you have used your best endeavours, you should see no present fruit. You have need of *patience,* and then, "after ye have done the will of God" herein, the harvest will come. Never be "weary of well-doing; in due time ye shall reap, if ye faint not." Copy after Abraham, who "against hope, still believed in hope. Cast thy bread upon the waters, and after many days thou shalt find it again."

14. I have now only a few words to add unto you, my brethren, who

are vulgarly called Methodists. I never heard or read of any considerable revival of religion, which was not attended with a spirit of reproving. I believe it cannot be otherwise; for what is faith, unless it
work by love? Thus it was in every part of England, when the present
revival of religion began about fifty years ago; all the subjects of that
revival, all the Methodists so called, in every place, were reprovers of
outward sin. And indeed so are all that, "being justified by faith, have
peace with God through Jesus Christ." Such they are at first: and if
they use that precious gift, it will never be taken away. Come, brethren!
In the name of God, let us begin again! Rich or poor, let us all arise as
one man! And in any-wise, let every man "rebuke his neighbour, and
not suffer sin upon him!" Then shall all Great Britain and Ireland
know, that we do not "go a warfare at our own cost." Yea, "God shall
bless us, and all the ends of the world shall fear him."

HUMAN LIFE A DREAM

"Even like a dream when one awaketh, so shalt thou make
their image to vanish out of the city" (Psalm 73:20).

1. ANYONE THAT CONSIDERS the foregoing verses, will easily observe
that the psalmist is speaking directly of the wicked that prosper in
their wickedness. It is very common for these utterly to forget that
they are creatures of a day; to live as if they were never to die; as if
their present state was to endure for ever; or at least, as if they were
indisputably sure that they "had much goods laid up for many years":
so that they might safely say, "Soul, take thine ease; eat, drink, and be
merry." But how miserable a mistake is this! How often does God say
to such a one, "Thou fool! this night shall thy soul be required of
thee!" Well then may it be said of them, "O, how suddenly do they
consume, perish, and come to a fearful end! Yea, even like a dream

Reprinted from John Wesley, *Sermons on Several Occasions*, vol. 2 (London:
Fisher, Son, & Co., n. d.), pp. 546–52.

when one awaketh, so shalt thou make their image to vanish out of the city."

2. But I would at present carry this thought farther; I would consider it in a general sense, and shew how near a resemblance there is between human life and a dream. An ancient poet carries the comparison farther still, when he styles life "the dream of a shadow." And so does Cowley, when he cries out,

> O Life, thou Nothing's younger brother,
> So like, that we mistake the one for th' other.

But setting these and all other flights of poetry aside, I would seriously inquire wherein this resemblance lies, wherein the analogy between the one and the other does properly consist.

3. In order to this, I would inquire, first, What is a dream? You will say, "Who does not know this?" Might you not rather say, Who *does* know? Is there any thing more mysterious in nature? Who is there that has not experienced it, that has not dreamed a thousand times? Yet he is no more able to *explain* the nature of it, than he is to grasp the skies. Who can give any clear, satisfactory account of the parent of dreams, sleep? It is true, many physicians have attempted this; but they have attempted it in vain. They have talked learnedly about it; but have left the matter at last just as dark as it was before. They tell us some of its properties and effects. But none can tell what is the *essence* of it.

4. However, we know the origin of dreams, and that with some degree of certainty. There can be no doubt but some of them arise from the present constitution of the body, while others of them are probably occasioned by the passions of the mind. Again, we are clearly informed in scripture, that some are caused by the operation of good angels; as others undoubtedly are owing to the power and malice of evil angels. (If we may dare to suppose that there are any such now, or at least that they have any thing to do in the world!) From the same divine treasury of knowledge we learn, that on some extraordinary occasions, the great Father of spirits has manifested himself to human spirits "in dreams and visions of the night." But which of all these arises from natural, which from supernatural influence, we are many times not able to determine.

5. And how can we certainly distinguish between our dreams and our waking thoughts? What criterion is there by which we shall surely know whether we are awake or asleep? It is true, as soon as we awake out of sleep, we know we have been in a dream, and are now awake. But how shall we know that a dream is such, while we continue therein? What is a dream? To give a gross and superficial, not a philosophical, account of it: It is a series of persons and things presented to our mind in sleep, which have no being but in our own imagination.

A dream, therefore, is a kind of digression from our real life; it seems to be an echo of what was said or done when we were awake. Or, may we say, a dream is a fragment of life, broken off at both ends, not connected either with the part that goes before or with that which follows after? And is there any better way of distinguishing our dreams from our waking thoughts, than by this very circumstance? It is a kind of parenthesis, inserted in life, as that is in a discourse, which goes on equally well, either with it or without it. By this then we may infallibly know a dream, by its being broken off at both ends; by its having no proper connexion with the real things which either precede or follow it.

6. It is not needful to *prove* that there is a near resemblance between these transient dreams and the dream of life. It may be of more use to *illustrate* this important truth, to place it in as striking a light as possible. Let us then seriously consider, in a few obvious particulars, the case of one that is just awaking out of life, and opening his eyes in eternity.

7. Let us then propose the case. Let us suppose we had now before us, one that was just passed into the world of spirits. Might not you address such a new-born soul in some such manner as this? You have been an inhabitant of earth forty, perhaps fifty or sixty years. But now God has uttered his voice, "Awake, thou that sleepest!" You awake, you arise; you have no more to do with these poor transient shadows. Arise, and shake thyself from the dust! See, all is *real* here! all is permanent and eternal! far more stable than the foundations of the earth; yea, than the pillars of that lower heaven. Now that your eyes are open, see how inexpressibly different are all the things that are now round about you! What a difference do you perceive in yourself? Where is your body? your house of clay? where are your limbs? your hands, your feet, your head? There they lie, cold, insensible!

> No anger, hereafter, or shame,
> Shall redden this innocent clay;
> Extinct is the animal flame,
> And passion is vanish'd away!

What a change is in the immortal spirit! You see every thing around you: but how? Not with eyes of flesh and blood! You hear: but not by a stream of undulating air, striking on an extended membrane. You feel: but in how wonderful a manner. You have no nerves to convey the ethereal fire to the common sensory: rather, are you not now all eye, all ear, all feeling, all perception? How different, now you are thoroughly awake, are all the objects round about you! Where are the houses, and gardens, and fields, and cities, which you lately saw? where are the rivers and seas, and everlasting hills? Was it then only a dream, that our poet discovered,

> Earth hath this variety from heaven,
> Of pleasure situate in hill and dale?

Nay, I doubt all these vanished away like smoke the moment you awoke out of the body.

8. How strange must not only the manner of existence appear, and the place wherein you are, if it may be called *place*, though who can define or describe the *place of spirits*, but the inhabitants of that unknown region? Whether they are of the number of those unhappy spirits that kept not their first estate, or of those holy ones that still minister to the heirs of salvation? How strange are the employments of those spirits with which you are now surrounded? How bitter are they to the taste of those that are still dreaming upon earth? "I have no relish (said one of these, a much-applauded wit, who has lately left the body) for sitting upon a cloud all day long, and singing praise to God." We may easily believe him; and there is no danger of his being put to that trouble. Nevertheless, this is no trouble to them that cease not day and night, but continually sing, "Holy, holy, holy, Lord God of sabaoth!"

9. Suppose this to be the case with any of you that are now present before God. It may be so tomorrow; perhaps tonight: perhaps this night your soul may be required of you. The dream of life may end, and *you* may wake into broad eternity. See, there lies the poor inanimate carcase, shortly to be sown in corruption and dishonour. But, where is the immortal, incorruptible spirit? There it stands naked before the eyes of God! Meantime, what is become of all the affairs which you have been eagerly engaged in under the sun! What profit have you reaped of all your labour and care? Does your money follow you? No, you have left it behind you; the same thing to you, as if it had vanished into air? Does your gay or rich apparel follow you? Your body is clothed with dust and rottenness. Your soul indeed is clothed with immortality.

But O! what immortality? Is it an immortality of happiness and glory? or, of shame and everlasting contempt? Where is the honour, the pomp, of the rich and the great? the applause that surrounded you? All are gone: all are vanished away, "like as a shadow that departeth." "The play is over," said Monsieur Moultray, when he saw the ball pierce the temple of his dying master. And what cared the courtier for this? No more than if it had been the conclusion of a farce or dance. But while the buffoon slept on and took his rest, it was not so with the monarch. Though he was not terrified with any thing on earth, he would be at the very gates of hell. Vain valour! In the very article of death he grasped the hilt of his sword! But where was he the next moment, when the sword dropped out of his hand, and the soul out of his body? Then ended the splendid dream of royalty, of destroying cities, and of conquering kingdoms!

10. "How are the mighty fallen, and the weapons of war perished!" What are the weapons that are so terrible among *us*, to the inhabitants of eternity? How are the wise, the learned, the poet, the critic, fallen, and their glory vanished away! How is the beauty fallen, the late idol of a gazing crowd? In how complete a sense are "the daughters of music brought low"; and all the instruments thereof forgotten? Are you not now convinced, that (according to the Hebrew proverb) "a living dog is better than a dead lion?" For the *living know*, yea, *must* know, unless they obstinately refuse, "that they shall die: but the dead know not any thing," that will avail, for the ease of their pain, or to lessen their misery. Also, "their hope and fear, and their desire," all are perished, all of them are fled; "they have not any portion in the things that are done under the sun!"

11. Where indeed is the *hope* of those who were lately laying deep schemes, and saying, "Today, or tomorrow, we will go to such a city, and continue there a year, and traffic, and get gain?" How totally had they forgotten that wise admonition, "Ye know not what shall be on the morrow; for, what is your life? It is a vapour that appeareth awhile, and then vanisheth away!" Where is all your business? where your worldly cares? your troubles or engagements? All these things are fled away like smoke, and only your soul is left; and how is it qualified for the enjoyment of this new world? Has it a relish for the objects and enjoyments of the invisible world? Are your affections loosened from things below, and fixed on things above? fixed on that place where Jesus sitteth at the right hand of God? Then happy are ye; and when he whom ye love shall appear, "ye shall also appear with him in glory."

12. But how do you relish the company that surrounds you? Your old companions are gone: a great part of them probably separated from you, never to return. Are your present companions angels of light? ministering spirits, that but now whispered, "Sister spirit, come away!" "We are sent to conduct thee over the gulf into Abraham's bosom." And what are those? Some of the souls of the righteous, whom thou didst formerly relieve with "the mammon of unrighteousness," and who are now commissioned by your common Lord to *receive*, to welcome you "into the everlasting habitations?" Then the angels of darkness will quickly discern they have no part in you. So they must either hover at a distance of flee away in despair. Are some of these happy spirits that take acquaintance with you, the same that travelled with you below, and bare a part in your temptations? – that, together with you, fought the good fight of faith, and laid hold on eternal life? As you then wept together, you may rejoice together, you and your guardian angels, perhaps, in order to increase your thankfulness for being "delivered from so great a death." They may give you a view of the realms below: those

> Regions of sorrow, doleful shades, where peace
> And rest can never dwell.

See, on the other hand, the mansions which were "prepared for you from the foundation of the world!" O what a difference between the dream that is past and the real scene that is now present with thee! Look up! See,

> No need of the sun in that day
>   Which never is follow'd by night!
> Where Jesus's beauties display
>   A pure and a permanent light.
> Look down! What a prison is there!
> 'Twixt upper, nether, and surrounding fire!

And what inhabitants! What horrid, fearful shapes, emblems of their rage against God and man; the envy, fury, despair fixed within, causing them to gnash their teeth at him they so long despised! Meanwhile, does it comfort them to see, across the great gulf, the righteous in Abraham's bosom? What a place is that! what "a house of God, eternal in the heavens!" Earth is only his footstool; yea,

> The spacious firmament on high
> And all the blue ethereal sky.

Well then may we say to its inhabitants,

> Proclaim the glories of the Lord,
>   Dispers'd through all the heavenly street;
> Whose boundless treasures can afford
>   So rich a pavement for his feet.

And yet how inconsiderable is the glory of that house, compared to that of its great inhabitant! – in view of whom all the first-born sons of light, angels, archangels, and all the company of heaven, full of light as they are full of love,

> Approach not, but with both wings veil their eyes.

13. How wonderful then, now the dream of life is over, now you are quite awake, do all these scenes appear! even such a sight as never entered or could enter into your hearts to conceive. How are all those that "awake up after his likeness, now satisfied with it!" They have now a portion, real, solid, incorruptible, "that fadeth not away." Meantime, how exquisitely wretched are they who (to wave all other considerations) have chosen for their portion those transitory shadows which now are vanished, and have left them in an abyss of real misery, which must remain to all eternity!

14. Now, considering that every child of man, who is yet upon earth,

must sooner or later wake out of this dream, and enter real life, how infinitely does it concern every one of us to attend to this before our great change comes! Of what importance is it to be continually sensible of the condition wherein we stand? How advisable, by every possible means, to connect the ideas of time and eternity? — so to associate them together, that the thought of one may never recur to your mind without the thought of the other! It is our highest wisdom to associate the ideas of the visible and invisible world, to connect temporal and spiritual, mortal and immortal being. Indeed, in our common dreams we do not usually know we are asleep, whilst we are in the midst of our dreams; as neither do we know it while we are in the midst of the dream which we call life: but you may be conscious of it now! God grant you may, before you awake in a winding-sheet of fire!

15. What an admirable foundation for thus associating the ideas of time and eternity, of the visible and invisible world, is laid in the nature of religion! For what is religion? (I mean scriptural religion, for all others is the vainest of all dreams.) What is the very root of this religion? It is Immanuel, God with us! God in man! heaven connected with earth! the unspeakable union of mortal with immortal. For "truly our fellowship (may all Christians say) is with the Father, and with his Son Jesus Christ. God hath given unto us eternal life; and this life is in his Son." What follows? "He that hath the Son, hath life; and he that hath not the Son of God, hath not life."

16. But how shall we retain a constant sense of this? I have often thought, in my waking hours, "Now, when I fall asleep, and see such and such things, I will remember it is but a dream." Yet I could not, while the dream lasted; and probably none else can. But it is otherwise with the dream of life, which we do remember to be such, even while it lasts; and if we do forget it (as we are indeed apt to do), a friend may remind us of it. It is much to be wished that such a friend were always near; one that would frequently sound in our ear, "Awake, thou that sleepest, and arise from the dead!" Soon you will awake into real life. You will stand a naked spirit, in the world of spirits, before the face of the great God! See that you now hold fast that "eternal life which he hath given you in his Son."

17. How admirably does this life of God branch out into the whole of religion! I mean scriptural religion. As soon as God reveals his Son in the heart of a sinner, he is enabled to say, "The life that I now live, I live by faith in the Son of God, who loved me, and gave himself for me." He then "rejoices in hope of the glory of God, even with joy unspeakable." And in consequence both of this faith and hope, the "love of God is shed abroad in his heart," which filling the soul with love to all mankind, "is the fulfilling of the law."

18. And how wonderfully do both faith and love connect God with

man, and time with eternity! In consideration of this we may boldly
say,

> Vanish then this world of shadows;
>   Pass the former things away;
> Lord, appear! appear to glad us
>   With the dawn of endless day!
> O conclude this mortal story:
>   Throw this universe aside:
> Come, eternal King of glory,
>   Now descend, and take thy bride!

FOR ADDITIONAL INFORMATION ABOUT JOHN WESLEY:

Bready, John Wesley. *England: Before and After Wesley.* New York:
Harper & Bros., 1938.

Burtner, Robert W., and Chiles, Robert E., eds. *A Compend of Wesley's Theology.* Nashville: Abingdon Press, 1954.

Doughty, William Lamplough. *John Wesley: Preacher.* London:
Epworth Press, 1955.

Ensley, Francis Gerald. *John Wesley, Evangelist.* Nashville: Methodist Evangelist Materials, 1958.

Fitchett, William Henry. *Wesley and His Century.* New York: Eaton
& Mains, 1912.

McGraw, James. "John Wesley." *Great Evangelical Preachers of
Yesterday.* Nashville: Abingdon Press, 1961.

Parker, Percy Livingstone, ed. *The Journal of John Wesley.* Chicago:
Moody Press, 1951.

Wesley, John. *John Wesley on Pulpit Oratory.* Revised and abridged
by Ross E. Price. Kansas City: Beacon Hill Press, 1955.

FOR OTHER SERMONS BY JOHN WESLEY:

The Marrow of Methodism: Twelve Sermons. Introduction and
Analysis by Benjamin Gregory. London: Methodist Publishing
House, n.d.

Standard Sermons of John Wesley. Edited by Edward H. Sudgon.
2 vols. London: Epworth Press, 1951.

Also: *Sermons on Several Occasions,* (1944).

JONATHAN EDWARDS

1703 - 1758

JONATHAN EDWARDS by Joseph Badger, Yale University Art Gallery, bequest of Eugene Phelps Edwards.

JONATHAN EDWARDS

1703   *Born on October 5 at Windsor Farms, Connecticut*
1716   *Entered Yale College*
1720   *Received B.A. from Yale*
1722   *Served a Presbyterian church in New York for eight months*
1724   *Began to tutor in Yale; continued until 1726*
1727   *Married Sarah Pierpont and became copastor (with grandfather) of the Congregational church in Northampton, Massachusetts*
1729   *Became pastor of the church in Northampton*
1741   *Preached the famous sermon, "Sinners in the Hands of an Angry God"*
1751   *Became pastor of the Congregational church in Stockbridge, Massachusetts, and missionary to the Indians*
1758   *Became president of Princeton, February 16, and died March 22*

HE PREACHED what is perhaps the most famous sermon of all time. He participated in the most dramatic single revival in American life. He is regarded as one of the world's great thinkers—and probably the greatest mind of early colonial America. He is widely regarded as the greatest preacher of his era in the American colonies. Without a doubt, Jonathan Edwards is one of the most significant names in the history of American preaching.

LIFE AND TIMES

Born the same year as John Wesley, 1703, Jonathan Edwards was destined to spend his life in New England. He was born at Windsor Farms, Connecticut, and educated at Yale. He pastored in Massachusetts and died while president of Princeton.

His father was a Congregational clergyman. His mother was the daughter of Solomon Stoddard, pastor of the Congregational church at Northampton, Massachusetts, for fifty-seven years. Edwards received superb guidance within his home. His mother was a woman of deep devotion who guided her son in spiritual development. His father, also a devout Christian, believed strongly in discipline, education, and excellence.

Edwards began his formal education under his father. His study of Latin began when he was six years of age. Before he was thirteen, he had a working knowledge of Latin, Greek, and Hebrew. When he was only twelve years old, he entered Yale College; he graduated in 1720 with highest honors. He remained at the college to engage in further study.

During the year of his graduation, Edwards had a religious experience which completely altered his life. While reading the Bible he suddenly sensed the presence of God in a unique way. This mystical experience became for him the focal point around which other experiences were placed. The possibility of union of soul with God became the guiding principle of his religious life. Convinced by his experience of the sovereignty of God, he accepted Calvinistic doctrines which had previously been unappealing to him.

In New York he experienced his first duties as a pastor; in the year 1722–1723 he served a Presbyterian church in that city. Probably he was called to a Presbyterian church because of his deep commitment to Calvinism and his ability to defend that theological system. Actually Edwards was not a Presbyterian, and for the rest of his life he was a pastor of Congregational churches.

In 1724 he returned to Yale to assume a position as tutor. For two years he enjoyed the academic community. He also courted his future wife, Sarah Pierpont; she was a splendid Christian and the daughter of a New Haven pastor. Their wedding in 1727 began a marriage which was to be marked by happiness and Christian service. Eight daughters and three sons were born to the Edwardses; they had seventy-five grandchildren.

Also in 1727 Edwards became co-pastor of the Congregational church in Northampton, Massachusetts, where his grandfather, Solomon Stoddard, was pastor. Two years later Stoddard died and left Edwards as the sole pastor of the church.

Edwards served the church with distinction. A zealous student, he spent long hours in his study preparing his sermons. He felt that he was ill-equipped for small talk and did not do much pastoral visitation, although he did do some counseling in his study. But preaching was his strong point, and soon it gained for him a wide reputation throughout New England.

Edwards participated in two unique spiritual awakenings, commonly called the Great Awakenings, during his ministry in Northampton. The first was in 1734 or 1735. But the major outburst of religious fervor took place in 1740–1741. The religious life of the New England area had degenerated into deplorable conditions. Under the impact of these awakenings, people came to center their attention upon God and his will. The revivals had many bizarre side effects — persons often fainted, shouted, quivered, and wept uncontrollably. But the results were not solely emotional; many social conditions were altered for the good.

Edwards was not only a preacher, he was also a philosopher and a writer. His writings were distributed throughout the English-speaking world; *On the Will* was especially significant. The book was a defense of the freedom of the will in the Calvinist system of theology. In England both Robert Hall and Thomas Chalmers were deeply influenced by this particular writing. Much of Edwards' writing was done after he had been dismissed from the Northampton church over a dispute concerning church membership and had begun work in Stockbridge, Massachusetts, as pastor and missionary to the Indians. Stockbridge was a smaller community, and he had more time for writing than he had had at Northampton.

In 1758, at the age of fifty-four, Edwards was elected president of the newly-established Princeton College. At first he was reluctant to leave his place of ministry which afforded him an excellent opportunity to think and to write. But he considered the influence over young ministers which the position would afford him and agreed to make the change. A smallpox epidemic was raging at the time, and as a precautionary measure he was inoculated; but something went wrong with the inoculation and he died from it.

A number of factors affected the direction of the life of Edwards. The religious degeneracy of New England caused him to inject a note of urgency and warning in his preaching. Normally his sermons were not highly emotional, but he did warn people about the results of turning from God. Deeply influenced by Calvinistic theology, Edwards placed strong emphasis upon the sovereignty of God. This theme determined the direction of his preaching and certainly the direction of his life. He was concerned at every turn to do God's will.

The winds of freedom were stirring in New England during Jonathan Edwards' time. Already the forces that were to erupt in the American Revolution were beginning to direct the course of the colonies. Edwards was a contemporary of such men as George Washington, Thomas Jefferson, and Benjamin Franklin. Though he was not associated with these famous figures, he shared something of the spirit of freedom which they so dramatically demonstrated a few years later in the Revolution.

Puritanism was the reigning religious outlook of New England, and Edwards was deeply influenced by it. His theology, his habits, and his way of life were Puritan. He also followed the basic patterns of preaching employed by most Puritan ministers.

Edwards was quite often ill, and his health affected his career. He was not strong physically, and although this weakness limited his activity it provided time for thought and study. His weak body combined with his brilliant mind resulted in spectacular religious and philosophical discourses.

The issues of his day certainly affected his life—and he affected the issues in return. He was not a man to withdraw into isolation. Though he spent hours in his study preparing sermons, his sermons were directed to the issues of his day. Theologically, many issues were controversial. One of the deepest rifts in church life was created by the conflict between Calvinist and Arminian theology. Edwards was deeply committed to Calvinism. At every turn he took opportunity to answer the charges of Arminianism. His book *On the Will* was a carefully developed work to defend the freedom of man while declaring the sovereignty of God.

The issue of church membership was also a significant question. In the early days of the New England colonies, many of the persons coming to America as immigrants were deeply religious; for them religion was a matter of heart and of life.

But as second and third generation Christians developed, their faith was cold and their lives showed little fruit of the Christian experience. Yet culture was church-centered. Many of these persons, even though they showed no signs of being Christian, were allowed to be members of the church and participate in the Lord's Supper. If a person's parents were church members, the individual himself would be a church member. There was little emphasis upon religious experience.

Edwards opposed this indifferent attitude toward church membership. He insisted that only Christians should be allowed to come to the Lord's table. He stressed religious experience. This stand deeply upset some of the defenders of the status quo in his community. He refused to alter his position, and the church members dismissed him from Northampton even though his ministry there had been distinguished.

During the Great Awakening of 1740–1741 a controversy raged as to whether the revivals were beneficial or harmful. Edwards admitted that some excess was present, but he argued that on the whole the revivals were accomplishing good. The debate over revivals intensified after the actual impact of the spiritual outburst was past. Ministers were divided, church members took different positions, and entire families were split over the controversy. One of the reasons for the founding of Princeton was to have a school of higher education that was firmly in the camp of the revivalists.

Theological issues were not all that attracted Edwards' attention; social concerns were also part of his ministry. He protested the vices of New England—as seen from the Puritan viewpoint—such as dancing, bundling, unfair business practices, and common dishonesty. In some of his views he varied sharply with the common norm. This is especially evident in his defense of the Indians.

When he was dismissed from the church in Northampton, he began to work in Stockbridge, Massachusetts, as a missionary to the Housatonic and other Indians. In his new work he realized more than ever before the mistreatment of the Indian by the white man. He strongly protested the exploitation of the Indians, and for this opinion he drew sharp criticism.

Jonathan Edwards deeply influenced many people. Not only did he touch hundreds with his preaching and revival leadership, but through his correspondence and writing he molded the lives of many others. Through personal contact he left his mark upon great men. He was partly responsible for establishing George Whitefield, the famous revival preacher from England, in his strongly Calvinistic position. Edwards no doubt encouraged and stimulated David Brainerd, the early American missionary to the Indians, in his mission work. Brainerd was engaged to Edwards' daughter; when the young missionary died of tuberculosis, Edwards preached his funeral sermon.

The enthusiastic evaluation of Jonathan Edwards by scholars seems almost excessive. The church historian W. W. Sweet has said, "In many respects Jonathan Edwards is the outstanding figure of colonial America and has been generally recognized as one of the greatest minds America has produced." A. M. Fairbairn exclaimed, "He is not only the greatest of all the thinkers that America has produced but also the highest speculative genius of the eighteenth century."[1]

But careful analysis only undergirds such praise: Edwards was a religious genius, a brilliant philosopher, a masterful preacher, and a devout Christian. Perhaps his chief fault was his inability to lead men and work well with others. Yet his leadership ability could not have been completely lacking; such a man is seldom selected to head a university.

Edwards' life proves that intellectual power can walk hand in hand with emotional fervor. He showed clearly that one does not have to shelve his intelligence in order to be a deeply committed Christian. He demonstrated that men of integrity do not walk away from conflict, even when it costs them position and security. He indicated by his life that great men are concerned about common people and their struggle with injustice and oppression — that religion and life, evangelism and ethics, preaching and social concern go together.

PREACHING AND SERMONS

Jonathan Edwards has been studied more as a theologian than as a preacher. But he was a preacher first and a theologian second. In a splendid article on Edwards as a speaker Orville A. Hitchcock has written:

> No one has undertaken to study Edwards as a speaker.
> Not one of the seven major biographies contains an ade-

---

1. Ralph G. Turnbull, *Jonathan Edwards the Preacher* (Grand Rapids: Baker Book House, 1958), p. 30.

quate treatment of his public speaking. Yet Edwards was
a speaker first and a writer afterwards. Most of his time
was employed in the preparation and delivery of sermons. These religious addresses were the most important things in his life, and toward them he directed most
of his energy.[2]

His best-known sermon is "Sinners in the Hands of an Angry
God," which may be the most famous sermon ever preached.
At least since biblical times there has not been another sermon
whose title has been so widely known. Strangely enough, this
blistering denunciation of wickedness came from the pen of a
quiet, sickly man who is regarded by some as the most original
thinker that America ever produced.

The sermon itself has been the object of much discussion.
Many have regarded it as medieval in its concept of eternal
punishment and an unfortunate mark upon the otherwise
distinguished record of a great thinker. Other commentators
remind us that Edwards was a stern Puritan, and that this
presentation of eternal damnation represents only one side of
Edwards' theology.

What is the nature of this sermon that has excited so much
comment? An understanding of the setting in which it was
delivered may help to evaluate it properly.

At Enfield, Massachusetts, where this sermon was delivered,
the people were apathetic and unconcerned about spiritual
matters. At one place in the sermon Edwards referred to Suffield, a town in the neighborhood where he had earlier preached,
and asked the people at Enfield if they were not equally concerned about entering the kingdom as were the people at Suffield, "where they are flocking from day to day to Christ?"
It seems that Edwards deliberately assumed an even sterner
stance than usual in order to awaken the people of Enfield out
of their spiritual indifference.

One fact about this sermon cannot be denied, whatever one
thinks of its theology or taste: the sermon exploded like a bomb-
shell in the congregation. That is all the more remarkable when
we remember that Edwards was frail and sickly, his voice thin
and weak, his eyesight dim. He preached with a full manuscript
held closely before his eyes, his manner almost passive, devoid

2. William Norwood Brigance, ed. *A History and Criticism of American Public
Address*, vol. 1 (New York: Russell & Russell, 1943), p. 214.

of gestures. Yet the response of the people was so profound and emotional that at one point in the sermon, according to one who was present, "The preacher was obliged to speak to the people and desire silence that he might be heard."[3] At another point in the sermon a minister sitting behind him became so overcome with distress at the severity of Edwards' presentation of God's judgment that he tugged upon his coat and cried, "Mr. Edwards! Mr. Edwards! Is not God merciful?"[4] Unfortunately, like most vignettes from history, we are never told what Edwards' response was, or even whether he gave sign of having heard.

Harwood Pattison in his *History of Christian Preaching* suggests that Edwards' physical presence may actually have added to the effect of the sermon:

> But who can estimate aright the feeling which they produced when the preacher stood calm in his pulpit, while the distressed and convicted multitude wept around him, his very self-repression significant of a reserve power, his wasted form and thin voice suggestive of a being coming from the gates of death, and his eye, when it was lifted, so piercing that it was profanely said on one occasion that it "looked off" the bell rope in the steeple, so that the bell fell with a crash into the church?[5]

A careful reading of this notable sermon reveals a number of interesting facts. In the first place, it is a stern Puritan sermon; the severity of the judgment of the critics upon its one-sided presentation of God is entirely justified. There are points at which Edwards seems satisfied that the last drop of love has gone out of God. His presentation of God's judgment is so careful and intense – in his usual style of doing things – that Edwards entirely overstates the case. At one point, for example, he asserts that God cares absolutely nothing for the sinners he is about to dispose of so handily. He entirely avoids the paradox of the loving God who is also righteous in his judgments. In this particular sermon, the Old Testament God of fierce anger stands as far removed from the Christ of Galilee as night from day.

---

3. T. Harwood Pattison, *The History of Christian Preaching* (Philadelphia: American Baptist Publication Society, 1903), p. 356.
4. Ibid., p. 357.
5. Ibid.

Other criticisms are not so valid. There is nothing medieval about the sermon. True, it talks about the "pit" and "the flames of hell" and "everlasting punishment." But the New Testament itself uses all of this imagery. There is nothing of fiendish invention, or hideous, gory description, or devilish tormentings in the sermon. Only in one place does Edwards' description become lurid ("He will crush out your blood, and make it fly, and it shall be sprinkled upon his garments"), and even there he is extending the imagery of Isaiah 63:3: "I will tread them in mine anger, and trample them in my fury; and their blood shall be sprinkled upon my garments, and I will stain all my raiment."

As for its virtues, the sermon is a masterpiece of imagery. Compare it with the other sermons of its time, or compare it with most modern sermons, and it is more vivid, plain, and fascinating. There is a power and vigor about the sermon which did not always characterize the preaching of Edwards. The sentences are direct: there is an ascending force about the sermon as Edwards meticulously and relentlessly turns from picture to picture, from description to description. Few sermons have ever excelled this one for direct application; in various places Edwards addresses the old men, the middle-aged, and the children in his congregation. He repeatedly says "you," "this congregation," and "today."

Notice also that Edwards' principal concern was not in describing the fate of the wicked as is usually supposed, but in urging the unconverted to accept God's mercy. That theme is unmistakable throughout the sermon. Edwards showed real sympathy with those who were about to receive—as he firmly believed—the logical and just outworkings of God's righteous anger. At one point he pled earnestly with the congregation to consider how terrible it would be if only one person came into such a fate; yet he felt that many in his congregation probably faced condemnation. Edwards made it plain that no man need suffer alienation from God, but that some would do so because they scorned God's offer of mercy: "they have no interest in any Mediator."

The entire subject of judgment in general, and especially any suggestion of hell or eternal damnation, has fallen into disfavor in modern times. (It obviously wasn't too popular in Edwards' time!) Nevertheless, "Sinners in the Hands of an Angry God" simply represents the usual detailed and logical handling that Edwards gave to scriptural texts which he took strictly and seriously. It does not lean upon medieval allegories or torture chamber scenes, nor does it delight in the writhings of the damned. Instead, Edwards sought to convince the congregation at Enfield that salvation was urgently at hand:

> And now you have an extraordinary opportunity, a day wherein Christ has thrown the door of mercy wide open, and stands in calling and crying with a loud voice to poor sinners; a day wherein many are flocking to him, and pressing into the kingdom of God. Many are daily coming from the east, west, north, and south; many that were very lately in the same miserable condition that you are in, are now in a happy state, with their hearts filled with love to him who has loved them, and washed them from their sins in his own blood, and rejoicing in hope of the glory of God.

Describing any other of Edwards' sermons seems almost anticlimactic. But the two other sermons included in this study are notable examples of his various skills. The sermon "God Glorified in Man's Dependence" is another example of the brilliant mind of Edwards as it meticulously examines a scriptural theme. The other sermon, "Charity and Its Fruits," is a splendid study from 1 Corinthians 13. This sermon stands as a worthy counterbalance to "Sinners in the Hands of an Angry God," for it shows that Edwards could be equally thorough in his discussion of the workings of love.

As a matter of fact, wrath was by no means the central theme of the preaching of Edwards. Alexander Whyte referred to one writer who claimed "sweetness" as the favorite and most frequently recurring word in Edwards' writing and to another who would pick "light" as his favorite term, while Whyte himself chose "beauty" as Edwards' most popular theme. This evaluation is probably correct since Edwards had worked out a deeply philosophical concept of beauty.

His sermon themes varied widely. Edwards could preach against such comparatively trivial practices of his day as dancing and such strange customs as bundling; yet his indignation could be turned even more severely against unfair business practices and exploitation of the Indians.

All in all, Edwards never gained the popularity of his contemporary, George Whitefield. Perhaps his sermons were too carefully worked, too logical, too meticulous in their expression, too intellectually superior. But this profoundly logical thinker, who frequently wept while he delivered his great sermons, made an unforgettable impression upon American preaching.

Sermons

SINNERS IN THE HANDS
OF AN ANGRY GOD

"Their foot shall slide in due time" (Deuteronomy 32:35).

IN THIS VERSE IS THREATENED the vengeance of God on the wicked unbelieving Israelites, who were God's visible people, and who lived under the means of grace; but who, notwithstanding all God's wonderful works towards them, remained (Deut. 32:28) void of counsel, having no understanding in them. Under all the cultivations of heaven, they brought forth bitter and poisonous fruit; as in the two verses next preceding the text. – The expression I have chosen for my text, *Their foot shall slide in due time*, seems to imply the following things, relating to the punishment and destruction to which these wicked Israelites were exposed.

1. That they were always exposed to *destruction*; as one that stands or walks in slippery places is always exposed to fall. This is implied in the manner of their destruction coming upon them, being represented by their foot sliding. The same is expressed, Psalm 73:18. "Surely thou didst set them in slippery places; thou castedst them down into destruction."

2. It implies, that they were always exposed to sudden unexpected destruction. As he that walks in slippery places is every moment liable to fall, he cannot foresee one moment whether he shall stand or fall the next; and when he does fall, he falls at once without warning: Which is also expressed in Psalm 73:18–19. "Surely thou didst set them in slippery places; thou castedst them down into destruction: How are they brought into desolation as in a moment!"

3. Another thing implied is, that they are liable to fall *of themselves*, without being thrown down by the hand of another; as he that stands or walks on slippery ground needs nothing but his own weight to throw him down.

Reprinted from *Puritan Sage: Collected Writings of Jonathan Edwards*, ed. Vergilius Ferm (New York: Library Publishers, 1953), pp. 365–78. Preached at Enfield, July 8, 1741, at a time of great awakenings and attended with remarkable impressions on many of the hearers.

4. That the reason why they are not fallen already, and do not fall now, is only that God's appointed time is not come. For it is said, that when that due time, or appointed time comes *their foot shall slide.* Then they shall be left to fall, as they are inclined by their own weight. God will not hold them up in these slippery places any longer, but will let them go; and then, at that very instant, they shall fall into destruction; as he that stands on such slippery declining ground, on the edge of a pit, he cannot stand alone, when he is let go he immediately falls and is lost.

The observation from the words that I would now insist upon is this. — "There is nothing that keeps wicked men at any one moment out of hell, but the mere pleasure of God" — By the *mere* pleasure of God, I mean his *sovereign* pleasure, his arbitrary will, restrained by no obligation, hindered by no manner of difficulty, any more than if nothing else but God's mere will had in the least degree, or in any respect whatsoever, any hand in the preservation of wicked men one moment. — The truth of this observation may appear by the following considerations.

1. There is no want of *power* in God to cast wicked men into hell at any moment. Men's hands cannot be strong when God rises up. The strongest have no power to resist him, nor can any deliver out of his hands. — He is not only able to cast wicked men into hell, but he can most easily do it. Sometimes an earthly prince meets with a great deal of difficulty to subdue a rebel, who has found means to fortify himself, and has made himself strong by the numbers of his followers. But it is not so with God. There is no fortress that is any defence from the power of God. Though hand join in hand, and vast multitudes of God's enemies combine and associate themselves, they are easily broken in pieces. They are as great heaps of light chaff before the whirlwind; or large quantities of dry stubble before devouring flames. We find it easy to tread on and crush a worm that we see crawling on the earth; so it is easy for us to cut or singe a slender thread that any thing hangs by: thus easy is it for God, when he pleases, to cast his enemies down to hell. What are we that we should think to stand before him, at whose rebuke the earth trembles, and before whom the rocks are thrown down?

2. They *deserve* to be cast into hell; so that divine justice never stands in the way, it makes no objection against God's using his power at any moment to destroy them. Yea, on the contrary, justice calls aloud for an infinite punishment of their sins. Divine justice says of the tree that brings forth such grapes of Sodom, "Cut it down, why cumbereth it the ground?" (Luke 13:7). The sword of divine justice is every moment brandished over their heads, and it is nothing but the hand of arbitrary mercy, and God's mere will, that holds it back.

3. They are already under a sentence of *condemnation* to hell.

They do not only justly deserve to be cast down thither, but the sentence of the law of God, that eternal and immutable rule of righteousness that God has fixed between him and mankind, is gone out against them, and stands against them; so that they are bound over already to hell. "He that believeth not is condemned already" (John 3:18). So that every unconverted man properly belongs to hell; that is his place; from thence he is, "Ye are from beneath": (John 8:23). And thither he is bound; it is the place that justice, and God's word, and the sentence of his unchangeable law assign to him.

4. They are now the objects of that very same *anger* and wrath of God, that is expressed in the torments of hell. And the reason why they do not go down to hell at each moment, is not because God, in whose power they are, is not then very angry with them; as he is with many miserable creatures now tormented in hell, who there feel and bear the fierceness of his wrath. Yea, God is a great deal more angry with great numbers that are now on earth; yea, doubtless, with many that are now in this congregation, who it may be are at ease, than he is with many of those who are now in the flames of hell.

So that it is not because God is unmindful of their wickedness, and does not resent it, that he does not let loose his hand and cut them off. God is not altogether such an one as themselves, though they may imagine him to be so. The wrath of God burns against them, their damnation does not slumber; the pit is prepared, the fire is made ready, the furnace is now hot, ready to receive them; the flames do now rage and glow. The glittering sword is whet, and held over them, and the pit hath opened its mouth under them.

5. The *devil* stands ready to fall upon them, and seize them as his own, at what moment God shall permit him. They belong to him; he has their souls in his possession, and under his dominion. The scripture represents them as his goods, Luke 11:21. The devils watch them; they are ever by them at their right hand; they stand waiting for them, like greedy hungry lions that see their prey, and expect to have it, but are for the present kept back. If God should withdraw his hand, by which they are restrained, they would in one moment fly upon their poor souls. The old serpent is gaping for them; hell opens its mouth wide to receive them; and if God should permit it, they would be hastily swallowed up and lost.

6. There are in the souls of wicked men those hellish *principles* reigning, that would presently kindle and flame out into hell fire, if it were not for God's restraints. There is laid in the very nature of carnal men, a foundation for the torments of hell. There are those corrupt principles, in reigning power in them, and in full possession of them, that are seeds of hell fire. These principles are active and powerful, exceeding violent in their nature, and if it were not for the restraining hand of God upon them, they would soon break out, they

would flame out after the same manner as the same corruptions, the same enmity does in the hearts of damned souls, and would beget the same torments as they do in them. The souls of the wicked are in scripture compared to the troubled sea (Isa. 57:20). For the present, God restrains their wickedness by his mighty power, as he does the raging waves of the troubled sea, saying, "Hitherto shalt thou come, but no further"; but if God should withdraw that restraining power, it would soon carry all before it. Sin is the ruin and misery of the soul; it is destructive in its nature; and if God should leave it without restraint, there would need nothing else to make the soul perfectly miserable. The corruption of the heart of man is immoderate and boundless in its fury; and while wicked men live here, it is like fire pent up by God's restraints, whereas if it were let loose, it would set on fire the course of nature; and as the heart is now a sink of sin, so if sin was not restrained, it would immediately turn the soul into a fiery oven, or a furnace of fire and brimstone.

7. It is no security to wicked men for one moment, that there are no visible means of death at hand. It is no security to a natural man, that he is now in health, and that he does not see which way he should now immediately go out of the world by any accident, and that there is no visible danger in any respect in his circumstances. The manifold and continual experience of the world in all ages, shows this is no evidence, that a man is not on the very brink of eternity, and that the next step will not be into another world. The unseen, unthought-of ways and means of persons going suddenly out of the world are innumerable and inconceivable. Unconverted men walk over the pit of hell on a rotten covering, and there are innumerable places in this covering so weak that they will not bear their weight, and these places are not seen. The arrows of death fly unseen at noon-day; the sharpest sight cannot discern them. God has so many different unsearchable ways of taking wicked men out of the world and sending them to hell, that there is nothing to make it appear, that God had need to be at the expence of a miracle, or go out of the ordinary course of his providence, to destroy any wicked man, at any moment. All the means that there are of sinners going out of the world, are so in God's hands, and so universally and absolutely subject to his power and determination, that it does not depend at all the less on the mere will of God, whether sinners shall at any moment go to hell, than if means were never made use of, or at all concerned in the case.

8. Natural men's prudence and care to preserve their own lives, or the care of others to preserve them, do not secure them a moment. To this, divine providence and universal experience do also bear testimony. There is this clear evidence that men's own wisdom is no security to them from death; that if it were otherwise we should see some difference between the wise and politic men of the world,

and others, with regard to their liableness to early and unexpected death: but how is it in fact? "How dieth the wise man? even as the fool" (Eccles. 2:16).

9. All wicked men's pains and *contrivance* which they use to escape hell, while they continue to reject Christ, and so remain wicked men, do not secure them from hell one moment. Almost every natural man that hears of hell, flatters himself that he shall escape it; he depends upon himself for his own security; he flatters himself in what he has done, in what he is now doing, or what he intends to do. Every one lays out matters in his own mind how he shall avoid damnation, and flatters himself that he contrives well for himself, and that his schemes will not fail. They hear indeed that there are but few saved, and that the greater part of men that have died heretofore are gone to hell; but each one imagines that he lays out matters better for his own escape than others have done. He does not intend to come to that place of torment; he says within himself, that he intends to take effectual care, and to order matters so for himself as not to fail.

But the foolish children of men miserably delude themselves in their own schemes, and in confidence in their own strength and wisdom; they trust to nothing but a shadow. The greater part of those who heretofore have lived under the same means of grace, and are now dead, are undoubtedly gone to hell; and it was not because they were not as wise as those who are now alive: it was not because they did not lay out matters as well for themselves to secure their own escape. If we could speak with them, and inquire of them, one by one, whether they expected, when alive, and when they used to hear about hell, ever to be the subjects of that misery: we doubtless, should hear one and another reply, "No, I never intended to come here: I had laid out matters otherwise in my mind; I thought I should contrive well for myself: I thought my scheme good. I intended to take effectual care; but it came upon me unexpected; I did not look for it at that time, and in that manner; it came as a thief: Death outwitted me: God's wrath was too quick for me. Oh, my cursed foolishness! I was flattering myself, and pleasing myself with vain dreams of what I would do hereafter; and when I was saying, Peace and safety, then suddenly destruction came upon me."

10. God has laid himself under *no obligation*, by any promise to keep any natural man out of hell one moment. God certainly has made no promises either of eternal life, or of any deliverance or preservation from eternal death, but what are contained in the covenant of grace, the promises that are given in Christ, in whom all the promises are yea and amen. But surely they have no interest in the promises of the covenant of grace who are not the children of the covenant, who do not believe in any of the promises, and have no interest in the Mediator of the covenant.

So that, whatever some have imagined and pretended about promises made to natural men's earnest seeking and knocking, it is plain and manifest, that whatever pains a natural man takes in religion, whatever prayers he makes, till he believes in Christ, God is under no manner of obligation to keep him a moment from eternal destruction.

So that, thus it is that natural men are held in the hand of God, over the pit of hell; they have deserved the fiery pit, and are already sentenced to it; and God is dreadfully provoked, his anger is as great towards them as to those that are actually suffering the executions of the fierceness of his wrath in hell, and they have done nothing in the least to appease or abate that anger, neither is God in the least bound by any promise to hold them up one moment; the devil is waiting for them, hell is gaping for them, the flames gather and flash about them, and would fain lay hold on them, and swallow them up; the fire bent up in their own hearts is struggling to break out: and they have no interest in any Mediator, there are no means within reach that can be any security to them. In short, they have no refuge, nothing to take hold of; all that preserves them every moment is the mere arbitrary will, and uncovenanted, unobliged forbearance of an incensed God.

APPLICATION

The use of this awful subject may be for awakening unconverted persons in this congregation. This that you have heard is the case of every one of you that are out of Christ. — That world of misery, that lake of burning brimstone, is extended abroad under you. There is the dreadful pit of the glowing flames of the wrath of God; there is hell's wide gaping mouth open; and you have nothing to stand upon, nor any thing to take hold of; there is nothing between you and hell but the air; it is only the power and mere pleasure of God that holds you up.

You probably are not sensible of this; you find you are kept out of hell, but do not see the hand of God in it; but look at other things, as the good state of your bodily constitution, your care of your own life, and the means you use for your own preservation. But indeed these things are nothing; if God should withdraw his hand, they would avail no more to keep you from falling, than the thin air to hold up a person that is suspended in it.

Your wickedness makes you as it were heavy as lead, and to tend downwards with great weight and pressure towards hell; and if God should let you go, you would immediately sink and swiftly descend and plunge into the bottomless gulf, and your healthy constitution, and your own care and prudence, and best contrivance, and all your righteousness, would have no more influence to uphold you and keep you out of hell, than a spider's web would have to stop a fallen rock. Were it not for the sovereign pleasure of God, the earth would not bear you one moment; for you are a burden to it; the creation groans with you; the creature is made subject to the bondage of your corruption, not willingly; the sun does not willingly shine upon you to give you light to serve sin and Satan; the earth does not willingly yield her increase to satisfy your lusts; nor is it willingly a stage for your wickedness to be acted upon; the air does not willingly serve you for breath to maintain the flame of life in your vitals, while you spend your life in the service of God's enemies. God's creatures are good, and were made for men to serve God with, and do not willingly subserve to any other purpose, and groan when they are abused to purposes so directly contrary to their nature and end. And the world would spew you out, were it not for the sovereign hand of him who hath subjected it in hope. There are black clouds of God's wrath now hanging directly over your heads, full of the dreadful storm, and big with thunder; and were it not for the restraining hand of God, it would immediately burst forth upon you. The sovereign pleasure of God, for the present, stays his rough wind; otherwise it would come with fury, and your destruction would come like a whirlwind, and you would be like the chaff of the summer threshing floor.

The wrath of God is like great waters that are dammed for the present; they increase more and more, and rise higher and higher, till an outlet is given; and the longer the stream is stopped, the more rapid and mighty is its course, when once it is let loose. It is true, that judgment against your evil works has not been executed hitherto; the floods of God's vengeance have been withheld; but your guilt in the mean time is constantly increasing, and you are every day treasuring up more wrath; the waters are constantly rising, and waxing more and more mighty; and there is nothing but the mere pleasure of God, that holds the waters back, that are unwilling to be stopped, and press hard to go forward. If God should only withdraw his hand from the flood-gate, it would immediately fly open, and the fiery floods of the fierceness and wrath of God, would rush forth with inconceivable fury, and would come upon you with omnipotent power; and if your strength were ten thousand times greater than it is, yea, ten thousand times greater than the strength of the stoutest, sturdiest devil in hell, it would be nothing to withstand or endure it.

The bow of God's wrath is bent, and the arrow made ready on the string, and justice bends the arrow at your heart, and strains the bow, and it is nothing but the mere pleasure of God, and that of an angry God, without any promise or obligation at all, that keeps the arrow one moment from being made drunk with your blood. Thus all you that never passed under a great change of heart, by the mighty power of the Spirit of God upon your souls; all you that were never born again, and made new creatures, and raised from being dead in sin, to a state of new, and before altogether unexperienced light and life, are in the hands of an angry God. However you may have reformed your life in many things, and may have had religious affections, and may keep up a form of religion in your families and closets, and in the house of God, it is nothing but his mere pleasure that keeps you from being this moment swallowed up in everlasting destruction. However unconvinced you may now be of the truth of what you hear, by and by you will be fully convinced of it. Those that are gone from being in the like circumstances with you, see that it was so with them; for destruction came suddenly upon most of them; when they expected nothing of it, and while they were saying, Peace and safety: now they see, that those things on which they depended for peace and safety, were nothing but thin air and empty shadows.

The God that holds you over the pit of hell, much as one holds a spider, or some loathsome insect over the fire, abhors you, and is dreadfully provoked: his wrath towards you burns like fire; he looks upon you as worthy of nothing else, but to be cast into the fire; he is of purer eyes than to bear to have you in his sight; you are ten thousand times more abominable in his eyes, than the most hateful venomous serpent is in ours. You have offended him infinitely more than ever a stubborn rebel did his prince; and yet it is nothing but his hand that holds you from falling into the fire every moment. It is to be ascribed to nothing else, that you did not go to hell the last night; that you were suffered to awake again in this world, after you closed your eyes to sleep. And there is no other reason to be given, why you have not dropped into hell since you arose in the morning, but that God's hand has held you up. There is no other reason to be given why you have not gone to hell, since you have sat here in the house of God, provoking his pure eyes by your sinful wicked manner of attending his solemn worship. Yea, there is nothing else that is to be given as a reason why you do not this very moment drop down into hell.

O sinner! Consider the fearful danger you are in: it is a great furnace of wrath, a wide and bottomless pit, full of the fire of wrath, that you are held over in the hand of that God, whose wrath is provoked and incensed as much against you, as against many of the damned in hell. You hang by a slender thread, with the flames of divine wrath flashing about it, and ready every moment to singe it, and burn it asunder; and you have no interest in any Mediator, and nothing to lay hold of to save yourself, nothing to keep off the flames of wrath, nothing of your own, nothing that you ever have done, nothing that you can do, to induce God to spare you one moment. — And consider here more particularly,

1. *Whose* wrath it is: it is the wrath of the infinite God. If it were only the wrath of man, though it were of the most potent prince, it would be comparatively little to be regarded. The wrath of kings is very much dreaded, especially of absolute monarchs, who have the possessions and lives of their subjects wholly in their power, to be disposed of at their mere will. "The fear of a king is as the roaring of a lion: Whoso provoketh him to anger, sinneth against his own soul" (Prov. 20:2). The subject that very much enrages an arbitrary prince, is

liable to suffer the most extreme torments that human art can invent, or human power can inflict. But the greatest earthly potentates in their greatest majesty and strength, and when clothed in their greatest terrors, are but feeble, despicable worms of the dust, in comparison of the great and almighty Creator and King of heaven and earth. It is but little that they can do, when most enraged, and when they have exerted the utmost of their fury. All the kings of the earth, before God, are as grasshoppers; they are nothing, and less than nothing: both their love and their hatred is to be despised. The wrath of the great King of kings, is as much more terrible than theirs, as his majesty is greater. "And I say unto you, my friends, Be not afraid of them that kill the body, and after that, have no more that they can do. But I will forewarn you whom you shall fear: fear him, which after he hath killed, hath power to cast into hell; yea, I say unto you, Fear him" (Luke 12:4–5).

2. It is the *fierceness* of his wrath that you are exposed to. We often read of the fury of God; as in Isaiah 59:18. "According to their deeds, accordingly he will repay fury to his adversaries." So Isaiah 66:15, "For behold, the Lord will come with fire, and with his chariots like a whirlwind, to render his anger with fury, and his rebuke with flames of fire." And in many other places. So Revelation 19:15, we read of "the wine press of the fierceness and wrath of Almighty God." The words are exceeding terrible. If it had only been said, "the wrath of God," the words would have implied that which is infinitely dreadful: but it is "the fierceness and wrath of God." The fury of God! the fierceness of Jehovah! Oh, how dreadful must that be! Who can utter what such expressions carry in them! But it is also "the fierceness and wrath of *Almighty* God." As though there would be a very great manifestation of his almighty power in what the fierceness· of his wrath should inflict, as though omnipotence should be as it were enraged, and exerted, as men are wont to exert their strength in the fierceness of their wrath. Oh! then, what will be the consequence! What will become of the poor worms that shall suffer it! Whose hands can be strong? And whose heart can endure? To what a dreadful, inexpressible, inconceivable depth of misery must the poor creature be sunk who shall be the subject of this!

Consider this, you that are here present, that yet remain in an unregenerate state. That God will execute the fierceness of his anger, implies that he will inflict wrath without any pity. When God beholds the ineffable extremity of your case, and sees your torment to be so vastly disproportioned to your strength, and sees how your poor soul is crushed, and sinks down, as it were, into an infinite gloom; he will have no compassion upon you, he will not forbear the executions of his wrath, or in the least lighten his hand; there shall be no moderation or mercy, nor will God then at all stay his rough wind; he will have no regard to your welfare, nor be at all careful lest you should suffer too much in any other sense, than only that you shall *not suffer beyond what strict justice requires.* Nothing shall be withheld, because it is so hard for you to bear. "Therefore will I also deal in fury: mine eye shall not spare, neither will I have pity; and though they cry in mine ears with a loud voice, yet I will not hear them" (Ezek. 8:18). Now God stands ready to pity you; this is a day of mercy; you may cry now with some encouragement of obtaining mercy. But when once the day of mercy is past, your most lamentable and dolorous cries and shrieks will be in vain; you will be wholly lost and thrown away of God, as to any regard to your welfare. God will have no other use to put you to, but to suffer misery; you shall be continued in being to no other end; for you will be a vessel of wrath fitted to destruction; and there will be no other use of this vessel, but to be filled full of wrath. God will be so far from pitying you when you cry to him, that it is said he will only "laugh and mock" (Prov. 1:25–26), &c.

How awful are those words, Isaiah 63:3, which are the words of the great God. "I will tread them in mine anger, and will trample them in my fury, and their blood shall be sprinkled upon my garments, and I will stain all my raiment." It is perhaps impossible to conceive of words that carry in them greater manifestations of these three things, *viz.* contempt, and hatred, and fierceness of indignation. If you cry to God to pity you, he will be so far from pitying you in your doleful case, or showing you the least regard or favour, that instead of that, he will only tread you under foot. And though he will know that you cannot bear the weight of omnipotence treading upon you, yet he will not regard that, but he will crush you under his feet without mercy; he will crush out your blood, and make it fly, and it shall be sprinkled on his garments, so as to stain all his raiment. He will not only hate you, but he will have you, in the utmost contempt: no place shall be thought fit for you, but under his feet to be trodden down as the mire of the streets.

3. The *misery* you are exposed to is that which God will inflict to that end, that he might show what that wrath of Jehovah is. God hath had it on his heart to show to angels and men, both how excellent his love is, and also how terrible his wrath is. Sometimes earthly kings have a mind to show how terrible their wrath is, by the extreme punishments they would execute on those that would provoke them. Nebuchadnezzar, that mighty and haughty monarch of the Chaldean empire, was willing to show his wrath when enraged with Shadrach, Meshech, and Abednego; and accordingly gave orders that the burning fiery furnace should be heated seven times hotter than it was before; doubtless, it was raised to the utmost degree of fierceness that human art could raise it. But the great God is also willing to show his wrath, and magnify his awful majesty and mighty power in the extreme

sufferings of his enemies. "What if God, willing to show his wrath, and to make his power known, endure with much long-suffering the vessels of wrath fitted to destruction?" (Rom. 9:22). And seeing this is his design, and what he has determined, even to show how terrible the unrestrained wrath, the fury and fierceness of Jehovah is, he will do it to effect. There will be something accomplished and brought to pass that will be dreadful with a witness. When the great and angry God hath risen up and executed his awful vengeance on the poor sinner, and the wretch is actually suffering the infinite weight and power of his indignation, then will God call upon the whole universe to behold that awful majesty and mighty power that is to be seen in it. "And the people shall be as the burnings of lime, as thorns cut up shall they be burnt in the fire. Hear ye that are far off, what I have done; and ye that are near, acknowledge my might. The sinners in Zion are afraid; fearfulness hath surprised the hypocrites" (Isa. 33:12–14), &c.

Thus it will be with you that are in an unconverted state, if you continue in it; the infinite might, and majesty, and terribleness of the omnipotent God shall be magnified upon you, in the ineffable strength of your torments. You shall be tormented in the presence of the holy angels, and in the presence of the Lamb; and when you shall be in this state of suffering, the glorious inhabitants of heaven shall go forth and look on the awful spectacle, that they may see what the wrath and fierceness of the Almighty is; and when they have seen it, they will fall down and adore that great power and majesty. "And it shall come to pass, that from one new moon to another, and from one sabbath to another, shall all flesh come to worship before me, saith the Lord. And they shall go forth and look upon the carcasses of the men that have transgressed against me; for their worm shall not die, neither shall their fire be quenched, and they shall be an abhorring unto all flesh" (Isa. 66:23–24).

4. It is *everlasting* wrath. It would be dreadful to suffer this fierceness and wrath of Almighty God one moment; but you must suffer it to all eternity. There will be no end to this exquisite horrible misery. When you look forward, you shall see a long for ever, a boundless duration before you, which will swallow up your thoughts, and amaze your soul; and you will absolutely despair of ever having any deliverance, any end, any mitigation, any rest at all. You will know certainly that you must wear out long ages, millions of millions of ages, in wrestling and conflicting with this almighty merciless vengeance; and then when you have so done, when so many ages have actually been spent by you in this manner, you will know that all is but a point to what remains. So that your punishment will indeed be infinite. Oh, who can express what the state of a soul in such circumstances is! All that we can possibly say about it, gives but a very feeble, faint representation of it; it is inexpressible and inconceivable: For "who knows the power of God's anger?"

How dreadful is the state of those that are daily and hourly in the danger of this great wrath and infinite misery! But this is the dismal case of every soul in this congregation that has not been born again, however moral and strict, sober and religious, they may otherwise be. Oh that you would consider it, whether you be young or old! There is reason to think, that there are many in this congregation now hearing this discourse, that will actually be the subjects of this very misery to all eternity. We know not who they are, or in what seats they sit, or what thoughts they now have. It may be they are now at ease, and hear all these things without much disturbance, and are now flattering themselves that they are not the persons, promising themselves that they shall escape. If we knew that there was one person, and but one, in the whole congregation, that was to be the subject of this misery, what an awful thing would it be to think of! If we knew who it was, what an awful sight would it be to see such a person! How might all the rest of the congregation lift up a lamentable and bitter cry over him! But, alas! instead of one, how many is it likely will remember this discourse in hell? And it would be a wonder, if some that are now present should not be in hell in a very short time, even before this year is out. And it would be no wonder if some persons, that now sit here, in some seats of this meeting-house, in health, quiet and secure, should be there before to-morrow morning. Those of you that finally continue in a natural condition, that shall keep out of hell longest will be there in a little time! your damnation does not slumber; it will come swiftly, and, in all probability, very suddenly upon many of you. You have reason to wonder that you are not already in hell. It is doubtless the case of some whom you have seen and known, that never deserved hell more than you, and that heretofore appeared as likely to have been now alive as you. Their case is past all hope; they are crying in extreme misery and perfect despair; but here you are in the land of the living and in the house of God, and have an opportunity to obtain salvation. What would not those poor damned hopeless souls give for one day's opportunity such as you now enjoy!

And now you have an extraordinary opportunity, a day wherein Christ has thrown the door of mercy wide open, and stands in calling and crying with a loud voice to poor sinners; a day wherein many are flocking to him, and pressing into the kingdom of God. Many are daily coming from the east, west, north and south; many that were very lately in the same miserable condition that you are in, are now in a happy state, with their hearts filled with love to him who has loved them, and washed them from their sins in his own blood, and rejoicing in hope of the glory of God. How awful is it to be left behind at such a day! To see so many others feasting, while you are pining and perishing! To see so many rejoicing and singing for joy of heart, while you have cause to mourn for sorrow of heart, and howl for vexation of spirit! How can you rest one moment in such a condition? Are not your souls as precious as the souls of the people at Suffield, where they are flocking from day to day to Christ?

Are there not many here who have lived long in the world, and are not to this day born again? and so are aliens from the commonwealth of Israel, and have done nothing ever since they have lived, but treasure up wrath against the day of wrath? Oh, sirs, your case, in an especial manner, is extremely dangerous. Your guilt and hardness of heart is extremely great. Do you not see how generally persons of your years are passed over and left, in the present remarkable and wounderful dispensation of God's mercy? You had need to consider yourselves, and awake thoroughly out of sleep. You cannot bear the fierceness and wrath of the infinite God. – And you, young men, and young women, will you neglect this precious season which you now enjoy, when so many others of your age are renouncing all youthful vanities, and flocking to Christ? You especially have now an extraordinary opportunity; but if you neglect it, it will soon be with you as with those persons who spent all the precious days of youth in sin, and are now come to such a dreadful pass in blindness and hardness. – And you, children, who are unconverted, do not you know that you are going down to hell, to bear the dreadful wrath of that God, who is now angry with you every day and every night? Will you be content to be the children of the devil when so many other children in the land are converted, and are become the holy and happy children of the King of kings?

And let every one that is yet of Christ, and hanging over the pit of hell, whether they be old men and women, or middle aged, or young people, or little children, now hearken to the loud calls of God's word and providence. This acceptable year of the Lord, a day of such great favours to some, will doubtless be a day of as remarkable vengeance to others. Men's hearts harden, and their guilt increases apace at such a day as this, if they neglect their souls; and never was there so great danger of such persons being given up to hardness of heart and blindness of mind. God seems now to be hastily gathering in his elect in all parts of the land; and probably the greater part of adult persons that ever shall be saved, will be brought in now in a little time, and that it will be as it was on the great out-pouring of the Spirit upon the Jews in the apostles' days; the election will obtain, and the rest will be blinded. If this should be the case with you, you will eternally curse this day, and will curse the day that ever you were born, to see such a season of the pouring out of God's Spirit, and will wish that you had died and gone to hell before you had seen it. Now undoubtedly it is, as it was in the days of John the Baptist, the axe is in an extraordinary manner laid at the root of the trees, that every tree which brings not forth good fruit, may be hewn down and cast into the fire.

Therefore, let every one that is out of Christ, now awake and fly from the wrath to come. The wrath of Almighty God is now undoubtedly hanging over a great part of this congregation: Let every one fly out of Sodom: "Haste and escape for your lives, look not behind you, escape to the mountain, lest you be consumed."

GOD GLORIFIED IN MAN'S DEPENDENCE

"That no flesh should glory in his presence. But of him are ye in Christ Jesus, who of God is made unto us wisdom, and righteousness, and sanctification, and redemption: That according as it is written, He that glorieth, let him glory in the Lord" (1 Corinthians 1:29–31).

THOSE CHRISTIANS to whom the apostle directed this epistle dwelt in a part of the world where human wisdom was in great repute; as the apostle observes in the 22d verse of this chapter, "The Greeks seek after wisdom." Corinth was not far from Athens, that had been for many ages the most famous seat of philosophy and learning in the world.

The apostle therefore observes to them, how that God, by the gospel, destroyed and brought to nought their human wisdom. The learned Grecians, and their great philosophers, by all their wisdom did not know God: they were not able to find out the truth in divine things. But after they had done their utmost to no effect, it pleased God at length to reveal himself by the gospel, which they accounted foolishness. He "chose the foolish things of the world to confound the wise, and the weak things of the world to confound the things which are mighty, and the base things of the world, and things that are despised, yea, and things which are not, to bring to nought the things that are." And the apostle informs them why he thus did, in the verse of the text; *That no flesh should glory in his presence.*

In which words may be observed,

1. What God aims at in the disposition of things in the affair of

Reprinted from Jonathan Edwards, *The Works of President Edwards,* vol. 4, 8th ed. in 4 vols. (New York: Leavitt & Allen, n. d.), pp. 169–78. This was the first piece the author published, 1731.

redemption, viz., that man should not glory in himself, but alone in God; *That no flesh should glory in his presence,—that, according as it is written, He that glorieth, let him glory in the Lord.*

2. How this end is attained in the work of redemption, viz., by that absolute and immediate dependence which men have upon God in that work for all their good. Inasmuch as,

First. All the good that they have is in and throught Christ; *He is made unto us wisdom, righteousness, sanctification, and redemption.* All the good of the fallen and redeemed creature is concerned in these four things, and cannot be better distributed than into them; but Christ is each of them to us, and we have none of them any otherwise than in him. *He is made of God unto us wisdom:* in him are all the proper good and true excellency of the understanding. Wisdom was a thing that the Greeks admired; but Christ is the true light of the world, it is through him alone that true wisdom is imparted to the mind. It is in and by Christ that we have righteousness: it is by being in him that we are justified, have our sins pardoned, and are received as righteous into God's favor. It is by Christ that we have sanctification: we have in him true excellency of heart as well as of understanding; and he is made unto us inherent, as well as imputed righteousness. It is by Christ that we have redemption, or actual deliverance from all misery, and the bestowment of all happiness and glory. Thus we have all our good by Christ, who is God.

Secondly. Another instance wherein our dependence on God for all our good appears, is this, That it is God that has given us Christ, that we might have these benefits through him; he *of God is made unto us wisdom, righteousness,* &c.

Thirdly. It is of him that we are in Christ Jesus, and come to have an interest in him, and so do receive those blessings which he is made unto us. It is God that gives us faith whereby we close with Christ.

So that in this verse is shown our dependence on each person in the Trinity for all our good. We are dependent on Christ the Son of God, as he is our wisdom, righteousness, sanctification, and redemption. We are dependent on the Father, who has given us Christ, and made him to be these things to us. We are dependent on the Holy Ghost, for it is *of him that we are in Christ Jesus*; it is the Spirit of God that gives faith in him, whereby we receive him, and close with him.

Doctrine

"God is glorified in the work of redemption in this, that there appears in it so absolute and universal a dependence of the redeemed on him."

Here I propose to show, 1st, That there is an absolute and universal dependence of the redeemed on God for all their good. And 2dly, That God hereby is exalted and glorified in the work of redemption.

I. There is an absolute and universal dependence of the redeemed on God. The nature and contrivance of our redemption is such, that the the redeemed are in every thing directly, immediately, and entirely dependent on God: they are dependent on him for all, and are dependent on him every way.

The several ways wherein the dependence of one being may be upon another for its good, and wherein the redeemed of Jesus Christ depend on God for all their good, are these, viz., that they have all their good of him, and that they have all through him, and that they have all in him: that he is the cause and original whence all their good comes, therein it is *of* him; and that he is the medium by which it is obtained and conveyed, therein they have it *through* him; and that he is that good itself that is given and conveyed, therein it is *in* him.

Now those that are redeemed by Jesus Christ do, in all these repects, very directly and entirely depend on God for their all.

First. The redeemed have all their good of God; God is the great author of it; he is the first cause of it, and not only so, but he is the only proper cause.

It is of God that we have our Redeemer: it is God that has provided a Saviour for us. Jesus Christ is not only of God in his person, as he is the only begotten Son of God, but he is from God, as we are concerned in him, and in his office of Mediator; he is the gift of God to us: God chose and anointed him, appointed him his work, and sent him into the world.

And as it is God that gives, so it is God that accepts the Saviour. As it is God that provides and gives the Redeemer to buy salvation for us, so it is of God that salvation is bought: he gives the purchaser, and he affords the thing purchased.

It is of God that Christ becomes ours, that we are brought to him, and are united to him: it is of God that we receive faith to close with him, that we may have an interest in him. "For by grace ye are saved, through faith; and that not of yourselves, it is the gift of God" (Eph. 2:8). It is of God that we actually do receive all the benefits that Christ has purchased. It is God that pardons and justifies, and delivers from going down to hell, and it is his favor that the redeemed are received into, and are made the objects of, when they are justified. So it is God that delivers from the dominion of sin, and cleanses us from our filthiness, and changes us from our deformity. It is of God that the redeemed do receive all their true excellency, wisdom, and holiness; and that two ways, viz., as the Holy Ghost, by whom these things are immediately wrought, is from God, proceeds from him, and is sent by him; and also as the Holy Ghost himself is God, by whose operation and indwelling, the knowledge of divine things, and a holy disposition, and all grace, are conferred and upheld.

And though means are made use of in conferring grace on men's souls, yet it is of God that we have these means of grace, and it is God that makes them effectual. It is of God that we have the holy Scriptures; they are the word of God. It is of God that we have ordinances, and their efficacy depends on the immediate influence of the Spirit of God. The ministers of the gospel are sent of God, and all their sufficiency is of him. "We have this treasure in earthen vessels, that the excellency of the power may be of God, and not of us" (2 Cor. 4:7). Their success depends entirely and absolutely on the immediate blessing and influence of God. The redeemed have all,

1. Of the grace of God. It was of mere grace that God gave us his only begotten Son. The grace is great in proportion to the dignity and excellency of what is given: the gift was infinitely precious, because it was a person infinitely worthy, a person of infinite glory; and also because it was a person infinitely near and dear to God. The grace is great in proportion to the benefit we have given us in him: the benefit is doubly infinite, in that in him we have deliverance from an infinite, because an eternal misery; and do also receive eternal joy and glory. The grace in bestowing this gift is great in proportion to our unworthiness to whom it is given; instead of deserving such a gift, we merited infinitely ill of God's hands. The grace is great according to the manner of giving, or in proportion to the humiliation and expense of the method and means by which way is made for our having the gift. He gave him to us dwelling amongst us; he gave him to us incarnate, or in our nature; he gave him to us in our nature, in the like infirmities, in which we have it in our fallen state, and which in us do accompany, and are occasioned by the sinful corruption of our nature. He gave him to us in a low and afflicted state; and not only so, but he gave him to us slain, that he might be a feast for our souls.

The grace of God in bestowing this gift is most free. It was what God was under no obligation to bestow: he might have rejected fallen man, as he did the fallen angels. It was what we never did any thing to merit; it was given while we were yet enemies, and before we had so much as repented. It was from the love of God that saw no excellency in us to attract it; and it was without expectation of ever being requited for it.

And it is from mere grace that the benefits of Christ are applied to such and such particular persons. Those that are called and sanctified are to attribute it alone to the good pleasure of God's goodness, by which they are distinguished. He is sovereign, and hath mercy on whom he will have mercy, and whom he will, he hardens.

Man hath now a greater dependence on the grace of God than he had before the fall. He depends on the free goodness of God for much more than he did then: then he depended on God's goodness for conferring the reward of perfect obedience: for God was not obliged to promise and bestow that reward: but now we are dependent on the grace of God for much more: we stand in need of grace, not only to bestow glory upon us, but to deliver us from hell and eternal wrath. Under the first covenant we depended on God's goodness to give us the reward of righteousness; and so we do now. And not only so, but we stand in need of God's free and sovereign grace to give us that righteousness; and yet not only so, but we stand in need of his grace to pardon our sin, and release us from the guilt and infinite demerit of it.

And as we are dependent on the goodness of God for more now than under the first covenant, so we are dependent on a much greater, more free and wonderful goodness. We are now more dependent on God's arbitrary and sovereign good pleasure. We were in our first estate dependent on God for holiness: we had our original righteousness from him; but then holiness was not bestowed in such a way of sovereign good pleasure as it is now. Man was created holy, and it became God to create holy all the reasonable creatures he created: it would have been a disparagement to the holiness of God's nature, if he had made an intelligent creature unholy. But now when a man is made holy, it is from mere and arbitrary grace; God may forever deny holiness to the fallen creature if he pleases, without any disparagement to any of his perfections.

And we are not only indeed more dependent on the grace of God, but our dependence is much more conspicuous, because our own insufficiency and helplessness in ourselves is much more apparent in our fallen and undone state, than it was before we were either sinful or miserable. We are more apparently dependent on God for holiness, because we are first sinful, and utterly polluted, and afterwards holy: so the production of the effect is sensible, and its derivation from God more obvious. If man was ever holy and always was so, it would not be so apparent, that he had not holiness necessarily, as an inseparable qualification of human nature. So we are more apparently dependent on free grace for the favor of God, for we are first justly the objects of his displeasure and afterwards are received into favor. We are more apparently dependent on God for happiness, being first miserable, and afterwards happy. It is more apparently free and without merit in us, because we are actually without any kind of excellency to merit, if there could be any such thing as merit in creature excellency. And we are not only without any true excellency, but are full of, and wholly defiled with, that which is infinitely odious. All our good is more apparently from God, because we are first naked and wholly without any good, and afterwards enriched with all good.

2. We receive all of the power of God. Man's redemption is often spoken of as a work of wonderful power as well as grace. The great power of God appears in bringing a sinner from his low state, from the depths of sin and misery, to such an exalted state of holiness and happiness. "And what is the exceeding greatness of his power to usward who believe, according to the working of his mighty power" (Eph. 1:19).

We are dependent on God's power through every step of our redemption. We are dependent on the power of God to convert us, and give faith in Jesus Christ, and the new nature.

It is a work of creation: "If any man be in Christ, he is a new creature" (2 Cor. 5:17). "We are created in Christ Jesus" (Eph. 2:10). The
fallen creature cannot attain to true holiness, but by being created
again. "And that ye put on the new man, which after God is created in
righteousness and true holiness." (Eph. 4:24). It is a raising from the
dead. "Wherein ye also are risen with him, through the faith of the
operation of God, who hath raised him from the dead" (Col. 2:12–13).
Yea, it is a more glorious work of power than mere creation, or raising
a dead body to life, in that the effect attained is greater and more excellent. That holy and happy being, and spiritual life which is reached
in the work of conversion, is a far greater and more glorious effect,
than mere being and life. And the state from whence the change is
made, of such a death in sin, and total corruption of nature, and depth
of misery, is far more remote from the state attained, than mere death
or nonentity.

It is by God's power also that we are preserved in a state of grace.
"Who are kept by the power of God through faith unto salvation."
(1 Pet. 1:5). As grace is at first from God, so it is continually from him,
and is maintained by him, as much as light in the atmosphere is all
day long from the sun, as well as at first dawning, or at sunrising.

Men are dependent on the power of God, for every exercise of grace,
and for carrying on the work of grace in the heart, for the subduing of
sin and corruption, and increasing holy principles, and enabling to
bring forth fruit in good works, and at last bringing grace to its perfection, in making the soul completely amiable in Christ's glorious
likeness, and filling of it with a satisfying joy and blessedness; and for
the raising of the body to life, and to such a perfect state, that it shall
be suitable for a habitation and organ for a soul so perfected and
blessed. These are the most glorious effects of the power of God, that
are seen in the series of God's acts with respect to the creatures.

Man was dependent on the power of God in his first estate, but he
is more dependent on his power now; he needs God's power to do more
things for him, and depends on the more wonderful exercise of his
power. It was an effect of the power of God to make man holy at the
first; but more remarkably so now, because there is a great deal of
opposition and difficulty in the way. It is a more glorious effect of power
to make that holy that was so depraved, and under the dominion of
sin, that to confer holiness on that which before had nothing of the
contrary. It is a more glorious work of power to rescue a soul out of the
hands of the devil, and from the powers of darkness, and to bring it
into a state of salvation, than to confer holiness where there was no
prepossession or opposition. "When a strong man armed keepeth his
palace, his goods are in peace; but when a stronger than he shall come
upon him, and overcome him, he taketh from him all his armor wherein
he trusted, and divideth his spoils" (Luke 11:21–22). So it is a more

glorious work of power to uphold a soul in a state of grace and holiness, and to carry it on till it is brought to glory, when there is so much sin remaining in the heart resisting, and Satan with all his might opposing, than it would have been to have kept man from falling at first, when Satan had nothing in man.

Thus we have shown how the redeemed are dependent on God for all their good, as they have all of him.

Secondly. They are also dependent on God for all, as they have all through him. It is God that is the medium of it, as well as the author and fountain of it. All that we have, wisdom, and the pardon of sin, deliverance from hell, acceptance in God's favor, grace and holiness, true comfort and happiness, eternal life and glory, we have from God by a Mediator; and this Mediator is God, which Mediator we have an absolute dependence upon as he through whom we receive all. So that here is another way wherein we have our dependence on God for all good. God not only gives us the Mediator, and accepts his mediation, and of his power and grace bestows the things purchased by the Mediator, but he is the Mediator.

Our blessings are what we have by purchase; and the purchase is made of God, the blessings are purchased of him, and God gives the purchaser; and not only so, but God is the purchaser. Yea, God is both the purchaser and the price; for Christ, who is God, purchased these blessings for us, by offering up himself as the price of our salvation. He purchased eternal life by the sacrifice of himself. "He offered up himself" (Heb. 7:27) and "He hath appeared to take away sin by the sacrifice of himself" (Heb. 9:26). Indeed it was the human nature that was offered; but it was the same person with the divine, and therefore was an infinite price; it was looked upon as if God had been offered in sacrifice.

As we thus have our good through God, we have a dependence on God in a respect that man in his first estate had not. Man was to have eternal life then through his own righteousness; so that he had partly a dependence upon what was in himself; for we have a dependence upon that through which we have our good, as well as that from which we have it; and though man's righteousness that he then depended on was indeed from God, yet it was his own, it was inherent in himself; so that his dependence was not so immediately on God. But now the righteousness that we are dependent on is not in ourselves, but in God. We are saved through the righteousness of Christ: he *is made unto us righteousness;* and therefore is prophesied of under that name, "the Lord our righteousness" (Jer. 23:6). In that the righteousness we are justified by is the righteousness of Christ, it is the righteousness of God: "That we might be made the righteousness of God in him" (2 Cor. 5:21).

Thus in redemption we have not only all things of God, but by and through him: "But to us there is but one God, the Father, of whom are all things, and we in him; and one Lord Jesus Christ, by whom are all things, and we by him." (1 Cor. 8:6).

Thirdly. The redeemed have all their good in God. We not only have it of him, and through him, but it consists in him; he is all our good.

The good of the redeemed is either objective or inherent. By their objective good, I mean that extrinsic object, in the possession and enjoyment of which they are happy. Their inherent good is that excellency or pleasure which is in the soul itself. With respect to both of which the redeemed have all their good in God, or, which is the same thing, God himself is all their good.

1. The redeemed have all their objective good in God. God himself is the great good which they are brought to the possession and enjoyment of by redemption. He is the highest good, and the sum of all that good which Christ purchased. God is the inheritance of the saints; he is the portion of their souls. God is their wealth and treasure, their food, their life, their dwelling place, their ornament and diadem, and their everlasting honor and glory. They have none in heaven but God; he is the great good which the redeemed are received to at death, and which they are to rise to at the end of the world. The Lord God, he is the light of the heavenly Jerusalem; and is the "river of the water of life," that runs, and "the tree of life that grows, in the midst of the paradise of God." The glorious excellencies and beauty of God will be what will for ever entertain the minds of the saints, and the love of God will be their everlasting feast. The redeemed will indeed enjoy other things; they will enjoy the angels, and will enjoy one another; but that which they shall enjoy in the angels, or each other, or in any thing else whatsoever that will yield them delight and happiness, will be what will be seen of God in them.

2. The redeemed have all their inherent good in God. Inherent good is twofold; it is either excellency or pleasure. These the redeemed not only derive from God, as caused by him, but have them in him. They have spiritual excellency and joy by a kind of participation of God. They are made excellent by a communication of God's excellency: God puts his own beauty, i.e., his beautiful likeness, upon their souls: they are made partakers of the divine nature, or moral image of God (2 Pet. 1:4). They are holy by being made partakers of God's holiness (Heb. 12:10). The saints are beautiful and blessed by a communication of God's holiness and joy, as the moon and planets are bright by the sun's light. The saint hath spiritual joy and pleasure by a kind of effusion of God on the soul. In these things the redeemed have communion with God; that is, they partake with him and of him.

The saints have both their spiritual excellency and blessedness by the gift of the Holy Ghost, or Spirit of God, and his dwelling in them. They are not only caused by the Holy Ghost, but are in the Holy Ghost as their principle. The Holy Spirit becoming an inhabitant, is a vital principle in the soul: he, acting in, upon, and with the soul, becomes a fountain of true holiness and joy, as a spring is of water, by the exertion and diffusion of itself. "But whosoever drinketh of the water that I shall give him, shall never thirst; but the water that I shall give him, shall be in him a well of water springing up into everlasting life" (John 4:14). Compared with chapter 8:38–39, "He that believeth on me, as the Scripture hath said, out of his belly shall flow rivers of living water; but this spake he of the Spirit, which they that believe on him should receive." The sum of what Christ has purchased for us, is that spring of water spoken of in the former of those places, and those rivers of living water spoken of in the latter. And the sum of the blessings, which the redeemed shall receive in heaven, is that river of water of life that proceeds from the throne of God and the Lamb (Rev. 22:1). Which doubtless signifies the same with those rivers of living water, explained, John 7:38–39, which is elsewhere called the "river of God's pleasures." Herein consists the fullness of good, which the saints receive by Christ. It is by partaking of the Holy Spirit, that they have communion with Christ in his fullness. God hath given the Spirit, not by measure unto him, and they do receive of his fullness, and grace for grace. This is the sum of the saints' inheritance; and therefore that little of the Holy Ghost which believers have in this world, is said to be the earnest of their inheritance. "Who hath also sealed us, and given us the Spirit in our hearts" (2 Cor. 1:22). And chapter 5:5, "Now he that hath wrought us for the self-same thing, is God, who also hath given unto us the earnest of the Spirit." And Ephesians 1:13–14, "Ye were sealed with that Holy Spirit of promise, which is the earnest of our inheritance, until the redemption of the purchased possession."

The Holy Spirit and good things are spoken of in Scripture as the same; as if the Spirit of God communicated to the soul, comprised all good things: "How much more shall your heavenly Father give good things to them that ask him?" (Matt. 7:11). In Luke it is, chapter 11:13, "How much more shall your heavenly Father give the Holy Spirit to them that ask him?" This is the sum of the blessings that Christ died to procure, and that are the subject of gospel promises: "He was made a curse for us, that we might receive the promise of the Spirit through faith" (Gal. 3:13–14). The Spirit of God is the great promise of the Father: "Behold, I send the promise of my Father upon you" (Luke 24:49). The Spirit of God therefore is called "the Spirit of promise" (Eph. 1:13). This promised thing Christ received, and had given into his hand, as soon as he had finished the work of our redemption, to bestow on all that he had redeemed: "Therefore, being by the right hand of God exalted, and having received of the Father the promise of the Holy Ghost, he hath shed forth this, which ye both see and hear" (Acts 2:33). So that all the holiness and happiness of the redeemed is in God. It is in the communications, indwelling, and acting of the Spirit of God. Holiness and happiness are in the fruit, here and hereafter, because God dwells in them, and they in God.

Thus it is God that has given us the Redeemer, and it is of him that our good is purchased: so it is God that is the Redeemer, and the price; and it is God also that is the good purchased. So that all that we have is of God, and through him, and in him: "For of him, and through him, and to him, or in him, are all things" (Rom. 11:36). The same in the Greek that is here rendered *to him*, is rendered *in him* (1 Cor. 7:6).

II. God is glorified in the work of redemption by this means, viz., By there being so great and universal a dependence of the redeemed on him.

1. Man hath so much the greater occasion and obligation to take notice and acknowledge God's perfections and all-sufficiency. The greater the creature's dependence is on God's perfections, and the greater concern he has with them, so much the greater occasion has he to take notice of them. So much the greater concern any one has with, and dependence upon, the power and grace of God, so much the greater occasion has he to take notice of that power and grace. So much the greater and more immediate dependence there is on the divine holiness, so much the greater occasion to take notice of, and acknowledge that. So much the greater and more absolute dependence we have on the divine perfections, as belonging to the several persons of the Trinity, so much the greater occasion have we to observe and own the divine glory of each of them. That which we are most concerned with, is surely most in the way of our observation and notice; and this kind of concern with any thing, viz., dependence, does especially tend to command and oblige the attention and observation. Those things that we are not much dependent upon, it is easy to neglect; but we can scarce do any other than mind that which we have a great dependence on. By reason of our so great dependence of God, and his perfections, and in so many respects, he and his glory are the more directly set in our view, which way soever we turn our eyes.

We have the greater occasion to take notice of God's all-sufficiency, when all our sufficiency is thus every way of him. We have the more occasion to contemplate him as an infinite good, and as the fountain of all good. Such a dependence on God, demonstrates God's all-sufficiency. So much as the dependence of the creature is on God, so much the greater does the creature's emptiness in himself appear to be; and so much the greater the creature's emptiness, so much the greater must the fullness of the Being be who supplies him. Our having all of God shows the fullness of his power and grace: our having all through him shows the fullness of his merit and worthiness; and our having all in him demonstrates his fullness of beauty, love, and happiness.

And the redeemed, by reason of the greatness of their dependence on God, have not only so much the greater occasion, but obligation to contemplate and acknowledge the glory and fullness of God. How unreasonable and ungrateful should we be if we did not acknowledge that sufficiency and glory that we do absolutely, immediately, and universally depend upon!

2. Hereby is demonstrated how great God's glory is considered comparatively, or as compared with the creature's. By the creature's being thus wholly and universally dependent on God, it appears that the creature is nothing, and that God is all. Hereby it appears that God is infinitely above us; that God's strength, and wisdom, and holiness, are infinitely greater than ours. However great and glorious the creature apprehends God to be, yet if he be not sensible of the difference between God and him, so as to see that God's glory is great, compared with his own, he will not be disposed to give God the glory due to his name. If the creature, in any respect, sets himself upon a level with God, or exalts himself to any competition with him, however he may apprehend that great honor and profound respect may belong to God from those that are more inferior, and at a greater distance, he will not be so sensible of its being due from him. So much the more men exalt themselves, so much the less will they surely be disposed to exalt God. It is certainly a thing that God aims at in the disposition of things in the affair of redemption (if we allow the Scriptures to be a revelation of God's mind), that God should appear all, and man nothing. It is God's declared design that others should not "glory in his presence"; which implies that it is his design to advance his own comparative glory. So much the more man "glories in God's presence," so much the less glory is ascribed to God.

3. By its being thus ordered, that the creature should have so absolute and universal a dependence on God, provision is made that God should have our whole souls, and should be the object of our undivided respect. If we had our dependence partly on God, and partly on something else, man's respect would be divided to those different things on which he had dependence. Thus it would be if we depended on God only for a part of our good, and on ourselves, or some other being for another part: or if we had our good only from God, and through another that was not God, and in something else distinct from both, our hearts would be divided between the good itself, and him from whom, and him through whom we received it. But now there is no occasion for this, God being not only he from or of whom we have all good, but also through whom and one that is that good itself, that we have from him and through him. So that whatsoever there is to attract our respect, the tendency is still directly towards God, all unites in him as the centre.

USE

1. We may here observe the marvellous wisdom of God, in the work of redemption. God hath made man's emptiness and misery, his low, lost and ruined state into which he sunk by the fall, an occasion of

the greater advancement of his own glory, as in other ways, so particularly in this, that there is now a much more universal and apparent dependence of man on God. Though God be pleased to lift man out of that dismal abyss of sin and woe into which he was fallen, and exceedingly to exalt him in excellency and honor, and to a high pitch of glory and blessedness, yet the creature hath nothing in any respect to glory of; all the glory evidently belongs to God, all is in a mere, and most absolute and divine dependence on the Father, Son, and Holy Ghost.

And each person of the Trinity is equally glorified in this work: there is an absolute dependence of the creature on every one for all: all is of the Father, all through the Son, and all in the Holy Ghost. Thus God appears in the work of redemption as all in all. It is fit that he that is, and there is none else, should be the Alpha and Omega, the first and the last, the all, and the only, in this work.

2. Hence those doctrines and schemes of divinity that are in any respect opposite to such an absolute and universal dependence on God, do derogate from God's glory, and thwart the design of the contrivance for our redemption. Those schemes that put the creature in God's stead, in any of the forementioned respects, that exalt man into the place of either Father, Son, or Holy Ghost, in any thing pertaining to our redemption; that, however they may allow of a dependence of the redeemed on God, yet deny a dependence that is so absolute and universal; that own an entire dependence on God for some things, but not for others; that own that we depend on God for the gift and acceptance of a Redeemer, but deny so absolute a dependence on him for the obtaining of an interest in the Redeemer; that own an absolute dependence on the Father for giving his Son, and on the Son for working out redemption, but not so entire a dependence on the Holy Ghost for conversion, and a being in Christ, and so coming to a title to his benefits; that own a dependence on God for means of grace, but not absolutely for the benefit and success of those means; that own a partial dependence on the power of God, for the obtaining and exercising holiness, but not a mere dependence on the arbitrary and sovereign grace of God, that own a dependence on the free grace of God for a reception into his favor, so far that it is without any proper merit, but not as it is without being attracted, or moved with any excellency; that own a partial dependence on Christ, as he through whom we have life, as having purchased new terms of life, but still hold that the righteousness through which we have life is inherent in ourselves, as it was under the first covenant; and whatever other way any scheme is inconsistent with our entire dependence on God for all, and in each of those ways, of having all of him, through him, and in him, it is repugnant to the design and tenor of the gospel, and robs it of that which God accounts its lustre and glory.

3. Hence we may learn a reason why faith is that by which we come to have an interest in this redemption; for there is included in the nature of faith, a sensibleness and acknowledgement of this absolute dependence on God in this affair. It is very fit that it should be required of all, in order to their having the benefit of this redemption, that they should be sensible of, and acknowledge their dependence on God for it. It is by this means that God hath contrived to glorify himself in redemption; and it is fit that God should at least have this glory of those that are the subjects of this redemption, and have the benefit of it.

Faith is a sensibleness of what is real in the work of redemption; and as we do really wholly depend on God, so the soul that believes doth entirely depend on God for all salvation, in its own sense and act. Faith abases men, and exalts God, it gives all the glory of redemption to God alone. It is necessary in order to saving faith, that man should be emptied of himself, that he should be sensible that he is "wretched, and miserable, and poor, and blind, and naked." Humility is a great ingredient of true faith: he that truly receives redemption, receives it as a little child. "Whosoever shall not receive the kingdom of heaven as a little child, he shall not enter therein" (Mark 10:15). It is the delight of a believing soul to abase itself and exalt God alone: that is the language of it, "Not unto us, O Lord, not unto us, but to thy name give glory" (Ps. 115:1).

4. Let us be exhorted to exalt God alone, and ascribe to him all the glory of redemption. Let us endeavor to obtain, and increase in a sensibleness of our great dependence on God, to have our eye to him alone, to mortify a self-dependent, and self-righteous disposition. Man is naturally exceeding prone to be exalting himself and depending on his own power or goodness, as though he were he from whom he must expect happiness, and to have respect to enjoyments alien from God and his Spirit, as those in which happiness is to be found.

And this doctrine should teach us to exalt God alone, as by trust and reliance, so by praise. *Let him that glorieth, glory in the Lord.* Hath any man hope that he is converted, and sanctified, and that his mind is endowed with true excellency and spiritual beauty, and his sins forgiven, and he received into God's favor, and exalted to the honor and blessedness of being his child, and an heir of eternal life; let him give God all the glory; who alone makes him to differ from the worst of men in this world, or the miserablest of the damned in hell. Hath any man much comfort and strong hope of eternal life, let not his hope lift him up, but despose him the more to abase himself, and reflect on his own exceeding unworthiness of such a favor, and to exalt God alone. Is any man eminent in holiness, and abundant in good works, let him take nothing of the glory of it to himself, but ascribe it to him whose workmanship we are, "created in Christ Jesus unto good works."

CHRISTIAN LOVE AS MANIFESTED
IN THE HEART AND LIFE

"Though I speak with the tongues of men and of angels, and have not charity, I am become as sounding brass, or a tinkling cymbal. And though I have the gift of prophecy, and understand all mysteries, and all knowledge; and though I have all faith, so that I could remove mountains, and have not charity, I am nothing. And though I bestow all my goods to feed the poor, and though I give my body to be burned, and have not charity, it profiteth me nothing" (1 Corinthians 13:1–3).

IN THESE WORDS we observe — *First,* that something is spoken of as of special importance, and as peculiarly essential in Christians, which the Apostle calls "charity." And this charity, we find, is abundantly insisted on in the New Testament by Christ, and his apostles, — more insisted on, indeed, than any other virtue.

But, then, the word "charity," as used in the New Testament, is of much more extensive signification, than as it is used generally in common discourse. What persons very often mean by "charity," in their ordinary conversation, is a disposition to hope and think the best of others, and to put a good construction on their words and behavior; and sometimes the word is used for a disposition to give to the poor. But these things are only certain particular branches, or fruits of that great virtue of charity which is so much insisted on throughout the New Testament. The word properly signifies *love,* or *that disposition or affection whereby one is dear to another*; and the original ("agape"), which is here translated "*charity*," might better have been rendered "*love*," for that is the proper English of it: so that by charity in the New Testament, is meant the very same thing as Christian love; and though it be more frequently used for love to men, yet sometimes it is used to signify not only love to men, but love to God. So it is manifestly used by the Apostle in this epistle, as he explains himself in chapter 8:1 — "Knowledge puffeth up, but charity edifieth," &c. Here the comparison is between knowledge and charity — and the preference is given to charity, because knowledge puffeth up, but charity edifieth. And then, in the next two verses, it is more particularly explained how knowledge usually puffs up, and why charity edifieth; so that what is called *charity* in the first verse, is called *loving God* in the third, for the very same thing is evidently spoken of in the two places. And doubtless the apostle means the same thing

Reprinted from *Puritan Sage: Collected Writings of Jonathan Edwards,* ed. Vergilius Ferm (New York: Library Publishers, 1953), pp. 333–54.

by charity in this thirteenth chapter, that he does in the eighth; for he is here comparing the same two things together that he was there, viz.: knowledge and charity. "Though I have all knowledge and have not charity, I am nothing"; and again, "charity never faileth, but— knowledge, it shall vanish away." So that by charity here, we are doubtless to understand *Christian love* in its full extent, and whether it be exercised toward God, or our fellow-creatures.

And this charity is here spoken of, as that which is, in a distinguishing manner, the great and essential thing: which will appear more fully when we observe, *Secondly,* what things are mentioned as being in vain without it, viz.: the most excellent things that ever belong to natural men; the most excellent privileges, and the most excellent performances. *First,* the most excellent privileges, such as preaching with tongues, the gift of prophecy, understanding all mysteries, faith to remove mountains, &c.; and *secondly,* the most excellent performances, such as giving all one's goods to feed the poor, and the body to be burned, &c. Greater things than these, no natural man ever had or did, and they are the kind of things in which men are exceedingly prone to trust; and yet the apostle declares that if we have them all, and have not charity, we are nothing. The doctrine taught, then, is this:

That all the virtue that is saying, and that distinguishes true Christians from others, is summed up in Christian love. This appears from the words of the text, because so many other things are mentioned that natural men may have, and the things mentioned are of the highest kind it is possible they should have, both of privilege and performance, and yet it is said they all avail nothing without this, whereas if any of them were saving, they would avail something without it.

And by the apostle's mentioning so many and so high things, and then saying of them all that they profited nothing without charity, we may justly conclude, that there is nothing at all that avails anything without it. Let a man have what he will, and do what he will, it signifies nothing without charity, which surely implies that charity is the great thing, and that everything which has not charity in some way contained or implied in it is nothing, and that this charity is the life and soul of all religion, without which all things that wear the name of virtues are empty and vain.

In speaking to this doctrine, I would first notice the nature of this divine love, and then show the truth of the doctrine respecting it. And,

I. *I would speak of the nature of a truly Christian love.* And here I would observe

1. *That all true Christian love is one and the same in its principle.* It may be various in its forms and objects, and may be exercised either toward God or men, but it is the same principle in the heart that is the

foundation of every exercise of a truly Christian love, whatever may be its object. It is not with the holy love in the heart of the Christian, as it is with the love of other men. Their love toward different objects, may be from different principles and motives, and with different views; but a truly Christian love is different from this. It is one as to its principle, whatever the object about which it is exercised; it is from the same spring or fountain in the heart, though it may flow out in different channels and diverse directions, and therefore it is all fitly comprehended in the one name of charity, as in the text. That this Christian love is one, whatever the objects toward which it may flow forth, appears by the following things: —

First, It is all *from the same Spirit* influencing the heart. It is from the breathing of the same Spirit that true Christian love arises, both toward God and man. The Spirit of God is a Spirit of love, and when the former enters the soul, love also enters with it. God is love, and he that has God dwelling in him by his Spirit, will have love dwelling in him also. The nature of the Holy Spirit is love; and it is by communicating himself, in his own nature, to the saints, that their hearts are filled with divine charity. Hence we find that the saints are partakers of the divine nature, and Christian love is called the "love of the Spirit." Romans 15:30, and "love in the Spirit" (Col. 1:8), and the very bowels of love and mercy seem to signify the same thing with the fellowship of the Spirit (Phil. 2:1). It is that Spirit, too, that infuses love to God (Rom. 5:5), and it is by the indwelling of that Spirit, that the soul abides in love to God and man (1 John, 14:12-13; and 3:23-24). And,

Second, Christian love both to God and man, is *wrought in the heart by the same work of the Spirit.* There are not two works of the Spirit of God, one to infuse a spirit of Love to God, and the other to infuse a spirit of love to men, but in producing one, the Spirit produces the other also. In the work of conversion, the Holy Spirit renews the heart by giving it a divine temper (Eph. 4:23); and it is one and the same divine temper thus wrought in the heart, that flows out in love both to God and man. And,

Third, When God and man are loved with a truly Christian love, they are both loved *from the same motives.* When God is loved aright, he is loved for his excellency, and the beauty of his nature, especially the holiness of his nature; and it is from the same motive that the saints are loved, for holiness' sake. And all things that are loved with a truly holy love, are loved from the same respect to God. Love to God is the foundation of gracious love to men; and men are loved, either because they are in some respect like God in the possession of his nature and spiritual image, or because of the relation they stand in to him as his children or creatures — as those who are blessed of him, or to whom his mercy is offered, or in some other way from regard to him. Only remarking that though Christian love be one in its principle, yet it is distinguished and variously denominated in two ways, with respect to its objects, and the kinds of its exercise, as for example, its degrees, &c. I now proceed,

II. *To show the truth of the doctrine, that all virtue that is saving or distinguishing of true Christians, is summed up in Christian love.* And,

1. *We may argue this from what reason teaches of the nature of love.* And if we duly consider its nature, two things will appear.

First, That love will *dispose to all proper acts of respect to both God and man.* This is evident because a true respect to either God or man *consists* in love. If a man sincerely loves God, it will dispose him to render all proper respect to him; and men need no other incitement to show each other all the respect that is due, than love. Love to God will dispose a man to honor him, to worship and adore him, and heartily to acknowledge his greatness, and glory, and dominion. And so it will dispose to all acts of obedience to God; for the servant that loves his master, and the subject that loves his sovereign, will be disposed to proper subjection and obedience. Love will dispose the Christian to behave toward God, as a child to a father; amid difficulties to resort to him for help, and put all his trust in him; just as it is natural for us, in case of need or affliction, to go to one that we love for pity and help. It will lead us, too, to give credit to his word, and to put confidence in him; for we are not apt to suspect the veracity of those we have entire friendship for. It will dispose us to praise God for the mercies we receive from him, just as we are disposed to gratitude for any kindness we receive from our fellow-men that we love. Love, again, will dispose our hearts to submission to the will of God, for we are more willing that the will of those we love should be done, than of others. We naturally desire that those we love should be suited, and that we should be agreeable to them; and true affection and love to God will dispose the heart to acknowledge God's right to govern, and that he is worthy to do it, and so will dispose to submission. Love to God will dispose us to walk humbly with him, for he that loves God will be disposed to acknowledge the vast distance between God and himself. It will be agreeable to such an one, to exalt God, and set him on high above all, and to lie low before him. A true Christian delights to have God exalted on his own abasement, because he loves him. He is willing to own that God is worthy of this, and it is with delight that he casts himself in the dust before the Most High, from his sincere love to him.

And so a due consideration of the nature of love will show that it disposes men to all duties toward their neighbors. If men have a sincere love to their neighbors, it will dispose them to all acts of justice toward those neighbors—for real love and friendship always dispose us to give those we love their due, and never to wrong them. "Love worketh no ill to his neighbor" (Rom. 13:10). And the same love will dispose to truth toward neighbors, and will tend to prevent all lying, and fraud, and deceit. Men are not disposed to exercise fraud and treachery toward those they love; for thus to treat men is to treat them like enemies, but love destroys enmity. Thus the aspostle makes use of the oneness that there ought to be among Christians, as an argument to induce them to truth between man and man (Eph. 4:25). Love will dispose to walk humbly amongst men, for a real and true love will incline us to high thoughts of others, and to think them better than ourselves. It will dispose men to honor one another, for all are naturally inclined to think highly of those they love, and to give them honor; so that by love are fulfilled those precepts. "Honor all men" (1 Pet. 11:17), and "Let nothing be done through strife or vain glory, but in lowliness of mind, let each esteem other better than themselves" (Phil. 2:3). Love will dispose to contentment in the sphere in which God hath placed us, without coveting any things that our neighbor possesses, or envying him on account of any good thing that he has. It will dispose men to meekness and gentleness in their carriage toward their neighbors, and not to treat them with passion, or violence, or heat of spirit, but with moderation, and calmness, and kindness. It will check and restrain everything like a bitter spirit; for love has no bitterness in it, but is a gentle and sweet disposition and affection of the soul. It will prevent broils and quarrels, and will dispose men to peaceableness, and to forgive injurious treatment received from others; as it is said in Proverbs 10:12, "Hatred stirreth up strifes, but love covereth all sins."

Love will dispose men to all acts of mercy toward their neighbors when they are under any affliction or calamity, for we are naturally disposed to pity those that we love when they are afflicted. It will dispose men to give to the poor, to bear one another's burdens, and to weep with those that weep, as well as to rejoice with those that do rejoice. It will dispose men to the duties they owe to one another in their several places and relations. It will dispose a people to all the duties they owe to their rulers, and to give them all that honor and subjection which are their due. And it will dispose rulers to rule the people over whom they are set, justly, seriously and faithfully, seeking their good, and not any by-ends of their own. It will dispose a people to all proper duty to their ministers, to hearken to their counsels and instructions, and to submit to them in the house of God, and to support and sympathize with and pray for them as those that watch for their souls; and it will dispose ministers faithfully and ceaselessly to seek the good of the souls of their people, watching for them as those that must give account. Love will dispose to suitable carriage between superiors and inferiors: it will dispose children to honor their parents, and servants to be obedient to their masters, not with eye service, but in singleness of heart; and it will dispose masters to exercise gentleness and goodness toward their servants.

Thus love would dispose to all duties both toward God, and toward man. And if it will thus dispose to all duties, then it follows, that it is the root, and spring, and, as it were, a comprehension of all virtues. It is a principle, which if it be implanted in the heart, is alone sufficient to produce all good practice; and every right disposition toward God and man is summed up in it, and comes from it, as the fruit from the tree, or the stream from the fountain.

Second, Reason teaches that *whatever performances or seeming virtues there are without love, are unsound and hypocritical.* If there be no love in what men do, then there is no true respect to God or men in their conduct; and if so, then certainly there is no sincerity. Religion is nothing without proper respect to God. The very notion of religion among mankind, is, that it is the creature's exercise and expression of such respect toward the creator. But if there be no true respect or love, then all that is called religion is but a seeming show, and there is no real religion in it, but it is unreal and vain. Thus if a man's faith be of such a sort that there is no true respect to God in it, reason teaches that it must be in vain; for if there be no love to God in it, there can be no true respect to him. From this it appears that love it always contained in a true and living faith, and that it is its true and proper life and soul, without which, faith is as dead as the body is without its soul; and that it is that which especially distinguishes a living faith from every other: but of this more particularly hereafter. Without love to God, again, there can be no true honor to him. A man is never hearty in the honor he seems to render to another whom he does not love; so that all the seeming honor or worship that is ever paid without love, is but hypocritical. And so reason teaches that there is no sincerity in the obedience that is performed without love, for if there be no love, nothing that is done can be spontaneous and free, but all must be forced. So without love, there can be no hearty submission to the will of God, and there can be no real and cordial trust and confidence in him. He that does not love God will not trust him: he never will, with true acquiescence of soul, cast himself into the hands of God, or into the arms of his mercy.

And so whatever good carriage there may be in men toward their neighbors, yet reason teaches that it is all unacceptable and in vain if at the same time there be no real respect in the heart toward those neighbors; if the outward conduct is not prompted by inward love. And from these two things taken together, viz., that love is of such a nature that it will produce all virtues, and dispose to all duties to God and men, and that without it there can be no sincere virtue, and no duty at all properly performed, the truth of the doctrine follows, that all true and distinguishing Christian virtue and grace may be summed up in love.

1. *The act which is the matter of the duty, which is, doing good to others.* — There are many ways in which persons may do good to others, and in which they are obliged so to do, as they have opportunity. And,

First, Persons may do good *to the souls of others,* which is the most excellent way of doing good. Men may be, and oftentimes are the instruments of spiritual and eternal good to others; and wherein any are so, they are the instruments of greater good to them than if they had given them the riches of the universe. And we may do good to the souls of others, by taking pains to instruct the ignorant, and to lead them to the knowledge of the great things of religion; and by counselling and warning others, and stirring them up to their duty, and to a seasonable and thorough care for their soul's welfare; and so again, by Christian reproof of those that may be out of the way of duty; and by setting them good examples, which is a thing the most needful of all, and commonly the most effectual of all for the promotion of the good of their souls. Such an example must accompany the other means of doing good to the souls of men, such as instructing, counselling, warning and reproving, and is needful to give force to such means, and to make them take effect; and it is more likely to render them effectual, than anything else whatsoever; and without it, they will be likely to be in vain.

Men may do good to the souls of vicious persons, by being the means of reclaiming them from their vicious courses; or to the souls of neglecters of the sanctuary, by persuading them to go to the house of God; or to the souls of secure and careless sinners, by putting them in mind of their misery and danger; and so may be the instruments of awakening them, and the means of their conversion, and of bringing them home to Christ. Thus they may be of the number of those, of whom we read Dan. 12:3, "that turn many to righteousness," and who "shall shine as stars forever and ever." Saints, too, may be the instruments of comforting and establishing one another, and of strengthening one another in faith and obedience; of quickening, and animating, and edifying one another; of raising one another out of dull and dead frames, and helping one another out of temptations, and onward in the divine life; of directing one another in doubtful and difficult cases; of encouraging one another under darkness or in trial; and generally, of promoting each other's spiritual joy and strength, and thus being mutually fellow-helpers on their way to glory.

Second, Persons may do good to others *in outward things, and for this world.* They may help others in their external difficulties and calamities; for there are innumerable kinds of temporal calamities to which mankind are liable, and in which they stand much in need of the help of their neighbors and friends. Many are hungry, or thirsty, or strangers, or naked, or sick, or in prison (Matt. 25:35–36), or in suffering of some other kind; and to all such we may minister. We may do good to others, by furthering their outward estate or substance; or in aiding their good name, and thus promoting their esteem and acceptance among men; or by anything that may truly add to their comfort and happiness in the world, whether it be in the kind word, or the considerate and benevolent deed. And by endeavoring thus to do good to them externally, we are under the greater advantage to do good to their souls; for when our instructions, counsels, warnings, and good examples are accompanied with such outward kindness, the latter tends to open the way for better effect of the former, and to give them their full force, and to lead such persons to appreciate our efforts when we seek their spiritual good. And we may thus contribute to the good of others, in three ways: by *giving to them,* of those things that they need and we possess; by *doing for them,* and taking pains to help them and promote their welfare; and by *suffering for them,* and aiding them to bear their burdens, and doing all in our power to make those burdens light. In each of these ways, Christianity requires us to do good to others. It requires us to *give* to others, "Give and it shall be given unto you" (Luke 6:38). It requires us to *do* for others, and to labor for them, "For ye remember, brethren, our labor and travail; for laboring night and day, because we would not be chargeable unto any of you, we preached unto you the gospel of God" (1 Thess. 2:9); and "For God is not unrighteous to forget your work and labor of love, &c." (Heb. 6:10). And it requires us, if need be, to *suffer* for others, "Bear ye one another's burdens, and so fulfill the law of Christ" (Gal. 6:2); and "Hereby perceive we the love of God, because he laid down his life for us; and we ought to lay down our lives for the brethren" (1 John 3:16). So that in all these ways the Scriptures require us to do good to all. I pass, then, to speak,

2. *Of the objects of this act, or of those to whom we should do good.* These are often spoken of in the Scriptures, by the expression, "our neighbor"; for the duty before us, is implied in the command, that we love our neighbor as ourselves. But here, perhaps, we may be ready with the young lawyer that came to Christ (Luke 11:29, &c.), to ask, "who is our neighbor?" – And as Christ's answer taught him that the Samaritan was neighbor to the Jew, though the Samaritans and Jews were each esteemed by the other vile, and accursed, and as bitter enemies, so we may be taught who those are to whom we are to do good, in three respects: –

First, We are to do good both to the *good* and to the *bad.* This we are to do, as we would imitate our heavenly Father, for "he (Matt. 5: 45) maketh his sun to rise on the evil and the good, and sendeth rain on the just and on the unjust." The world is full of various kinds of persons; some good, and some evil; and we should do good to all. We should, indeed, especially, "do good to them that are of the household of faith," or that we have reason, in the exercise of charity, to regard as saints. But though we should most abound in beneficence to them, yet our doing good should not be confined to them, but we should do good to all men as we have opportunity. While we live in the world, we must expect to meet with some men of very evil properties, and hateful dispositions and practices. Some are proud, some immoral,

some covetous, some profane, some unjust or severe, and some de-
spisers of God. But any or all these bad qualities should not hinder
our beneficence, or prevent our doing them good as we have opportunity. On this very account we should the rather be diligent to benefit
them, that we may win them to Christ; and especially should we be
diligent to benefit them in spiritual things.

Second, We should do good both to *friends* and *enemies.* We are
obliged to do good to our friends, not only from the obligation we
are under to do good to them as our fellow-creatures, and those that are
made in the image of God, but from the obligations of friendship, and
gratitude, and the affection we bear them. And we are also obliged to
do good to our enemies; for our Saviour says: "But I say unto you, love
your enemies; bless them that curse you; do good to them that hate
you; and pray for them that despitefully use you, and persecute you"
(Matt. 6:44). To do good to those that do ill to us, is the only retaliation
that becomes us as Christians; for we are taught to "recompense to
no man evil for evil," but on the contrary to "overcome evil with
good" (Rom. 12:17-21); and again it is written: "See that none render
evil for evil unto any man, but ever follow that which is good, both
among yourselves and to all men" (1 Thess. 6:15) and still again:
"Not rendering evil for evil, or railing for railing, but contrariwise,
blessing; knowing that ye are thereunto called, that ye should inherit
a blessing" (1 Pet. 3:9). And,

Third, We should do good both to the *thankful* and the *unthankful.*
This we are obliged to do by the example of our heavenly Father, for
he "is kind unto the unthankful and to the evil (Luke 6: 35); and the
command is, that we "be merciful as he also is merciful." Many make
an objection against doing good to others, saying, "If I do, they will
never thank me for it; and for my kindness, they will return abuse and
injury": and thus they are ready to excuse themselves from the
exercise of kindness, especially to those who may have shown themselves ungrateful. But such persons do not sufficiently look at Christ;
and they either show their want of acquaintance with the rules of
Christianity, or their unwillingness to cherish its spirit. Having thus
spoken of the duty of doing good, and the persons to whom we are to
do it, I pass, as proposed, to speak,

3. *Of the manner in which we should do good to others.* – This is
expressed in the single word *"freely."* This seems implied in the words
of the text; for to be kind, is to have a disposition freely to do good.
Whatever good is done, there is no proper kindness in the doer of it,
unless it be done freely. And this doing good freely, implies three
things: –

First, That our doing good *be not in a mercenary spirit.* We are not
to do it for the sake of any reward received or expected from the one to
whom we do the good. The command is: "Do good, and lend, hoping

for nothing again" (Luke 6:35). Oftentimes men will do good to others, expecting to receive as much again; but we should do good to the poor and needy from whom we can expect nothing in return. The command of Christ is: "When thou makest a dinner or a supper, call not thy friends, nor thy brethren, neither thy kinsmen, nor thy rich neighbors; lest they also bid thee again, and a recompense be made thee. But when thou makest a feast, call the poor, the maimed, the lame, the blind; and thou shalt be blessed; for they cannot recompense thee; for thou shalt be recompensed at the resurrection of the just" (Luke 14:12–14). That our doing good be free, and not mercenary, it is necessary that what we do, be done, not for the sake of any temporal good, or to promote our temporal interest, or honor, or profit, but from the spirit of love.

Second, That our doing good be free, it is requisite that we do it *cheerfully or heartily,* and with real good-will to the one we would benefit. What is done heartily, is done from love; and what is done from love, is done with delight, and not grudgingly or with backwardness and reluctance of spirit. "Use hospitality," says the Apostle (1 Pet. 4:9): "one to another, without grudging"; and says Paul: "Every man, according as he purposeth in his heart, so let him give; not grudgingly, or of necessity: for God loveth a cheerful giver" (2 Cor. 9:7). This requisite or qualification for our doing good, is much insisted on in the Scriptures. "He that giveth," says the Apostle (Rom. 12: 8) "let him do it with simplicity; he that ruleth, with diligence; he that showeth mercy, with cheerfulness." And God gives a strict charge: "that we shall not be grieved in our heart when we give to our neighbor" (Deut. 15:10). And in a word, the very idea of giving acceptably, is presented throughout the Bible, as implying that we give with a cordial and cheerful spirit. Doing good freely also implies,

Third, That we do it *liberally and bountifully.* We are not to be scant and sparing in our gifts or efforts, but to be open-hearted and openhanded. We are to "abound to every good work" (2 Cor. 9:8, 11), "being enriched in everything, to all bountifulness." Thus God requires that when we give to the poor, we should "open our hand wide unto him" (Deut. 15:8); and we are told (Prov. 11:25), that "the liberal soul shall be made fat"; and the Apostle would have the Corinthians be bountiful in their contributions for the poor saints in Judea, assuring them that "he that soweth sparingly, shall reap also sparingly, and he that soweth bountifully, shall reap also bountifully" (2 Cor. 9: 6).

In dwelling on this thought, I would show, 1, What is the nature of an envious spirit; 2, Wherein a Christian spirit is the opposite of such a spirit; 3, The reason and evidence of the doctrine. And,

I. *The nature of envy.* — Envy may be defined to be a spirit of dissatisfaction with and opposition to the prosperity and happiness of others as compared with our own. The thing that the envious person is opposed to and dislikes, is, the comparative superiority of the state of honor, or prosperity or happiness, that another may enjoy; over that which he possesses. And this spirit is especially called envy, when we dislike and are opposed to another's honor or prosperity, because, in general, it is greater than our own, or because, in particular, they have some honor or enjoyment that we have not. It is a disposition natural in men, that they love to be uppermost; and this disposition is directly crossed, when they see others above them. And it is from this spirit, that men dislike and are opposed to the prosperity of others, because they think it makes those who possess it, superior, in some respect, to themselves. And from this same disposition, a person may dislike another's being equal to himself in honor or happiness, or in having the same sources of enjoyment that he has; for as men very commonly are, they cannot bear a rival, much, if any better than a superior, for they love to be singular and alone in their eminence and advancement. Such a spirit is called envy in the Scriptures. Thus Moses speaks of Joshua's envying for his sake, when Eldad and Medad were admitted to the same privilege with himself in having the spirit of prophecy given them, saying "Enviest thou for my sake? (Num. 11:29). Would God that all the Lord's people were prophets, and that the Lord would put his spirit upon them." And Joseph's brethren, we are told (Gen. 27:11), envied him when they had heard his dream, which implied that his parents and brethren were yet to bow down before him, and that he was to have power over them. From such a spirit, persons are not only unwilling that others should be above them or equal to them, but that they should be near them; for the desire to be distinguished in prosperity and honor, is the more gratified just in proportion as they are elevated and others are below them, so that their comparative eminence may be marked and visible to all. And this disposition may be exercised, either in reference to the prosperity that others may obtain and of which they are capable, or in reference to that which they actually have obtained. In the latter form, which is the most common, the feeling of envy will be manifest in two respects, first, in respect to their prosperity, and next in respect to themselves. And,

1. It will be manifest in an *uneasiness and dissatisfaction with the prosperity* of others. Instead of rejoicing in the prosperity of others, the envious man will be troubled with it. It will be a grievance to his spirit to see them rise so high, and come to such honors and advancement. It is no comfortable feeling to him to hear of their having obtained such and such advantages and honors and preferments, but on the contrary very uncomfortable. He is very much of the spirit of Haman, who in view of all "the glory of his riches, and the multitude of his children, and all the things wherein the king had promoted him," still could say, "yet all this availeth me nothing, so long as I see Mor-

decai the Jew sitting in the king's gate" (Esther 5:13). From such a
spirit, the envious person stands ready to rejoice at anything that
happens to diminish the honor and comfort of others. He is glad to see
them brought down, and will even study how to lower their estate, as
Haman did how to humble and bring down Mordecai. And often, like
Haman, he will show his uneasiness, not only by planning and schem-
ing, but by actual endeavors of one kind or another, to bring them
down; and the very first opportunity of pulling them down that offers,
he will gladly embrace. And it is from this disposition, that the sight
even of others' prosperity, often sets the envious on talking against
them and speaking evil of them, even when perhaps they do not know
them. Envying them the prominence they have obtained, they hope,
by speaking evil of them, in some measure to diminish their honors,
and lower them in the esteem of men. This suggests, again,

2. That the opposition of the envious to the prosperity of others
will be manifest *in a dislike of their persons for it.* Seeing how others
prosper, and what honors they attain, the envious dislike, and even
hate them, on account of their honor and prosperity. They entertain
and cherish an evil spirit toward them, for no other reason but that
they are prospered. They are embittered against them in spirit, only
because they are eminent in name or fortune. Thus Haman, it is said
(Esther 5: 9), "Was full of indignation against Mordecai," because he
saw him "in the king's gate," and because "he stood not up, nor moved
for him;" and Joseph's brethren (Gen. 37:4–5) "hated him and could
not speak peaceably unto him," because his father loved him; and
when he had dreamed a dream implying their inferiority, "they hated
him yet the more." And so the envious generally resent the prosperity
of others and their coming to honor, as if in it they were guilty of some
injury to themselves. Sometimes there is a settled hatred toward
others upon this account, leading as in the case of Joseph's brethren
(Gen. 37: 19–28), to acts of the greatest cruelty and wickedness.

First, Humility doth primarily and chiefly consist in *a sense of our
meanness as compared with God,* or a sense of the infinite distance
there is between God and ourselves. We are little, despicable creatures,
even worms of the dust, and we should feel that we are as nothing and
less than nothing in comparison with the majesty of heaven and earth.
Such a sense of his nothingness Abraham expressed, when he said,
"Behold now, I have taken upon me to speak unto the Lord, which am
but dust and ashes" (Gen. 18:27). There is no true humility without
somewhat of this spirit; for however sensible we may be of our meanness as compared with some of our fellow-creatures, we are not truly
humble, unless we have a sense of our nothingness as compared with
God. Some have a low thought of themselves as compared with other
men, from the meanness of their circumstances, or from a melancholy
and despondent temperament which is natural to them, or from some

other cause, while still they know nothing of the infinite distance there is between them and God; and though they may be ready to look upon themselves as humble-spirited, yet they have no true humility. That which above all other things it concerns us to know of ourselves, is, what we are in comparison with God, who is our creator, and the one in whom we live, and move, and have our being, and who is infinitely perfect in all things. And if we are ignorant of our meanness as compared with him, then the most essential thing, and that which is indispensable in true humility, is wanting. But where this is truly felt, there arises from it,

Secondly, A sense of our own meanness as compared with many of our fellow-creatures. For man is not only a mean creature in comparison with God, but he is very mean as compared with multitudes of creatures of a superior rank in the universe; and most men are mean in comparison with many of their fellow-men. And when a sense of this comparative meanness arises from a just sense of our meanness as God sees it, then it is of the nature of true humility. He that has a right sense and estimate of himself in comparison with God, will be likely to have his eyes open to see himself aright in all respects. Seeing truly how he stands with respect to the first and highest of all beings, will tend greatly to help him to a just apprehension of the place he stands in among creatures. And he that does not rightly know the first and greatest of beings, who is the fountain and source of all other beings, cannot truly know anything aright; but so far as he has come to a knowledge of the former, so far is he prepared for and led unto the knowledge of other things, and so of himself as related to others, and as standing among them.

Having thus shown what is that angry or wrathful spirit, to which charity or a Christian spirit is contrary, I pass, as proposed, to show,

II. *How charity, or a Christian spirit, is contrary to it.* And this I would do by showing, first, that charity or love, which is the sum of the Christian spirit, is directly, and in itself, contrary to the anger that is sinful; and secondly, that the fruits of charity which are mentioned in the context, are all contrary to it. And,

1. *Christian charity or love, is directly, and in itself, contrary to all undue anger.* — Christian love is contrary to anger which is undue in its nature, and that tends to revenge, and so implies ill-will, for the nature of love is good-will. It tends to prevent persons from being angry without just cause, and will be far from disposing anyone to be angry for but little faults. Love is backward to anger, and will not yield to it on trivial occasions, much less where there is no cause for being angry. It is a malignant and evil, and not a loving spirit, that disposes persons to be angry without cause. Love to God is opposite to a disposition in men to be angry at other's faults, chiefly as they them-

selves are offended and injured by them: it rather disposes them to look at them chiefly as committed against God. If love be in exercise, it will tend to keep down the irascible passions, and hold them in subjection, so that reason and the spirit of love may regulate them and keep them from being immoderate in degree or of long continuance. And not only is charity, or Christian love, directly, and in itself, contrary to all undue anger, but,

2. *All the fruits of this charity which are mentioned in the context, are also contrary to it.* — And I shall mention only two of these fruits, as they may stand for all, viz.: those virtues that are contrary to pride and selfishness. And,

First, Love or charity is contrary to all undue and sinful anger, as, *in its fruits, it is contrary to pride.* Pride is one chief cause of undue anger. It is because men are proud, and exalt themselves in their own hearts, that they are revengeful, and are apt to be excited, and to make great things out of little ones that may be against themselves. Yea, they even treat as vices things that are in themselves virtues, when they think their honor is touched, or when their will is crossed. And it is pride that makes men so unreasonable and rash in their anger, and raises it to such a high degree, and continues it so long, and often keeps it up in the form of habitual malice. But, as we have already seen, love or Christian charity is utterly opposed to pride. And so,

Secondly, Love or charity is contrary to all sinful anger, as, *in its fruits, it is contrary to selfishness.* It is because men are selfish and seek their own, that they are malicious and revengeful against all that oppose or interfere with their own interests. If men sought not chiefly their own private and selfish interests, but the glory of God and the common good, then their spirit would be a great deal more stirred up in God's cause, than in their own; and they would not be prone to hasty, rash, inconsiderate, immoderate, and long-continued wrath, with any who might have injured or provoked them, but they would, in a great measure, forget themselves for God's sake, and from their zeal for the honor of Christ. The end they would aim at, would be, not making themselves great, or getting their own will, but the glory of God, and the good of their fellow-beings. But love, as we have seen, is opposed to all selfishness.

1. A censorious spirit appears *in a forwardness to judge evil of the state of others.* It often shows itself in a disposition to think the worst of those about us, whether they are men of the world, or professing Christians. In respect to the latter class, it often leads persons to pass censure on those who are professors of religion, and to condemn them as being hypocrites. Here, however, extremes are to be avoided. Some persons are very apt to be positive, from little things that they observe in others, in determining that they are godly men;

and others are forward, from just as little things, to be positive in condemning others as not having the least degree of grace in their hearts,
and as being strangers to vital and experimental religion. But all
positiveness in an affair of this nature, seems to be without warrant
from the word of God. God seems there to have reserved the positive
determination of men's state to himself, as a thing to be kept in his
own hands, as the great and only searcher of the hearts of the children
of men.

Persons are guilty of censoriousness in condemning the state of
others, when they will do it from things that are no evidence of their
being in a bad estate; or when they will condemn others as hypocrites
because of God's providential dealings with them, as Job's three friends
condemned him as a hypocrite on account of his uncommon and
severe afflictions. And the same is true, when they condemn them for
the failings they may see in them, and which are no greater than are
often incident to God's children, and it may be no greater, or not so
great as their own, though notwithstanding just such things they
think well of themselves as Christians. And so persons are censorious,
when they condemn others as being unconverted and carnal men,
because they differ from them in opinion on some points that are not
fundamental; or when they judge ill of their state from what they
observe in them, for want of making due allowances for their natural
temperament, or for their manner or want of education, or other
peculiar disadvantages under which they labor—or when they are
ready to reject all as irreligious and unconverted men, because their
experiences do not, in everything, quadrate with their own; setting
up themselves, and their own experience, as a standard and rule to
all others; not being sensible of that vast variety and liberty which the
Spirit of God permits and uses in his saving work on the hearts of men,
and how mysterious and inscrutable his ways often are, and especially
in this great work of making men new creatures in Christ Jesus. In all
these ways, men often act, not only censoriously, but as unreasonably,
in not allowing any to be Christians who have not their own experiences, as if they would not allow any to be men, who had not just their
own stature, and the same strength, or temperament of body, and the
very same features of countenance with themselves. In the next place,

2. A censorious spirit appears in *a forwardness to judge evil of the
qualities of others.* It appears in a disposition to overlook their good
qualities, or to think them destitute of such qualities when they are
not, or to make very little of them; or to magnify their ill qualities, and
make more of them than is just; or to charge them with those ill qualities that they have not. Some are very apt to charge others with
ignorance and folly, and other contemptible qualities, when they
in no sense deserve to be esteemed thus by them. Some seem very apt
to entertain a very low and despicable opinion of others, and so to

represent them to their associates and friends, when a charitable disposition would discern many good things in them, to balance or more than balance the evil, and would frankly own them to be persons not to be despised. And some are ready to charge others with those morally evil qualities that they are free from, or to charge them with such qualities in a much higher degree than they at all deserve. Thus some have such a prejudice against some of their neighbors, that they regard them as a great deal more proud sort of persons, more selfish, or spiteful, or malicious, than they really are. Through some deep prejudice they have imbibed against them, they are ready to conceive that they have all manner of bad qualities, and no good ones. They seem to them to be an exceeding proud, or covetous, or selfish, or, in some way, bad sort of men, when it may be that to others they appear well. Others see their many good qualities, and see perhaps many palliations of the qualities that are not good; but the censorious see only that which is evil, and speak only that which is unjust and disparaging as to the qualities of others. And,

3. A censorious spirit appears *in a forwardness to judge evil of the actions of others.* By actions, here, I would be understood to mean, all the external voluntary acts of men, whether consisting in words or deeds. And a censorious spirit in judging evil of others' actions, discovers itself in two things: —

First, In judging them to be guilty of evil actions, *without any evidence that constrains them to such a judgment.* A suspicious spirit, which leads persons to be jealous of others, and ready to suspect them of being guilty of evil things when they have no evidence of it whatever, is an uncharitable spirit, and contrary to Christianity. Some persons are very free in passing their censures on others with respect to those things that they suppose they do out of their sight. They are ready to believe that they commit this, and that, and the other evil deed, in secret, and away from the eyes of men, or that they have done or said thus and so among their associates, and in the circle of their friends, and that, from some design or motive, they keep these things hid from others that are not in the same interest with themselves. These are the persons chargeable with the "evil surmisings," spoken of and condemned by the Apostle (1 Tim. 6:4), and which are connected with "envy, strife and railings." Very often, again, persons show an uncharitable and censorious spirit with respect to the actions of others, by being forward to take up, and circulate evil reports about them. Merely hearing a flying and evil rumor about an individual, in such a thoughtless and lying world as this is, is far from being sufficient evidence against any one, to make us believe he has been guilty of that which is reported; for the devil, who is called "the god of this world," is said to be "a liar, and the father of it," and too many, alas! of his children are like him in their speaking of falsehoods. And yet it is a very common thing for persons to pass a judgment on others, on no better ground or foundation, than that they have heard that somebody has said this, or that, or the other thing, though they have no evidence that what is said is true. When they hear that another has done or said so and so, they seem at once to conclude that it is so, without making any further inquiry, though nothing is more uncertain, or more likely to prove false, than the mutterings or whispers of common fame. And some are always ready to catch up all ill-report, that it seems to be pleasing to them to hear evil of others. Their spirit seems greedy of it; and it is, as it were, food to the hunger of their depraved hearts, and they feed on it, as carrion birds do on the worst of flesh. They easily and greedily take it in as true, without examination, thus showing how contrary they are in character and conduct to him of whom the Psalmist speaks, Psalm 15:1-3, as dwelling in God's tabernacle and abiding in his holy hill, and of whom he declares, that "he taketh not up a reproach against his neighbor"; and showing, also, that they are rather like "the wicked doer," that "giveth heed to false lips," and as the "liar," who "giveth ear to a naughty tongue" (Prov. 17: 4). A censorious spirit in judging evil of the actions of others, also, discovers itself.

Second, In a disposition *to put the worst constructions on their actions*. The censorious are not only apt to judge others guilty of evil actions without sufficient evidence, but they are also prone to put a bad construction on their actions, when they will just as well, and perhaps better admit of a good construction. Very often the moving design and end in the action, is secret, confined to the recesses of the actor's own bosom; and yet persons are commonly very forward to pass their censure upon the act, without reference to these: and this is a kind of censoriousness and uncharitable judging, as common, or more common than any other. Thus it is very common with men, when they are prejudiced against others, to put bad constructions on their actions or words that are seemingly good, as though they were performed in hypocrisy; and this is especially true in reference to public offices and affairs. If anything be said or done by persons, wherein there is a show of concern for the public good, or the good of a neighbor, or the honor of God, or the interest of religion, some will always be ready to say, that all this is in hypocrisy, and that the design really is, only to promote their own interest, and to advance themselves; and that they are only flattering and deluding others, having all the time some evil design in their hearts.

But here it may be inquired, "Wherein lies the evil of judging ill of others, since it is not true that all judging ill of others is unlawful? And where are the lines to be drawn?" To this, I reply,

First, There are some persons *that are appointed on purpose to be judges,* in civil societies, and in churches, who are impartially to judge of others that properly fall under their cognizance, whether good or bad, and to pass sentence according to what they are; to approve the good, and condemn the bad, according to the evidence, and the nature of the act done, and its agreement or disagreement with the law which is the judges' rule.

Second, Particular persons in their private judgments of others, *are not obliged to divest themselves of reason,* that they may thus judge well of all. This would be plainly against reason; for Christian charity is not a thing founded on the ruins of reason, but there is the most sweet harmony between reason and charity. And therefore we are not forbidden to judge all persons when there is plain and clear evidence that they are justly chargeable with evil. We are not to blame, when we judge those to be wicked men, and poor Christless wretches, e.g. who give flagrant proof that they are so by a course of wicked action. "Some men's sins," says the Apostle, "are open beforehand, going before to judgment, and some men they follow after." That is, some men's sins are such plain testimony against them, that they are sufficient to condemn them as wicked men in full sight of the world, even before the coming of that final day of judgment that shall disclose the secrets of the heart to all. And so some men's actions give such clear evidence of the evil of their intentions, that it is no judging the secrets of the heart, to judge that their designs and ends are wicked. And therefore it is plain, that all judging as to others' states, or qualifications, or actions, is not an uncharitable censoriousness. But the evil of that judging wherin censoriousness consists, lies in two things: —

It lies, *first,* in judging evil of others when evidence does not oblige to it, or in thinking ill of them when the case very well allows of thinking well of them; when those things that seem to be in their favor are overlooked, and only those that are against them are regarded, and when the latter are magnified, and too great stress laid on them. And the same is the case, when persons are hasty and rash in judging and condemning others, though both prudence and charity oblige them to suspend their judgment till they know more of the matter, and all the circumstances are plain before them. Persons may often show a great deal of uncharitableness and rashness, in freely censuring others before they have heard what they have to say in their defence. And hence it is said, "He that answereth a matter before he heareth it, it is folly and shame unto him" (Prov. 18:13).

And the evil of that judging which is censorious, lies, in the *second* place, in a well-pleasedness in judging ill of others. Persons may judge ill of others, from clear and plain evidence that compels them to it, and yet it may be to their grief that they are obliged to judge as they do; just as when a tender parent hears of some great crime of a child with such evidence that he cannot but think it true. But very often judgment is passed against others, in such a manner as shows that the individual is well pleased in passing it. He is so forward in judging evil, and judges on such slight evidence, and carries his judgment to such extremes, as shows that his inclination is in it, and that he loves to think the worst of others. Such a well-pleasedness in judging ill of others, is also manifested in our being forward to declare our judgment, and to speak, as well as think evil of others. It may be in speaking of them with ridicule, or an air of contempt, or in bitterness, or maliciousness of spirit, or with manifest pleasure in their deficiencies or errors. When to judge ill of others, is against the inclination of persons, they will be very cautious in doing it, and will go no further in it than evidence obliges them, and will think the best that the nature of the case will admit, and will put the best possible construction on the words and actions of others. And when they are obliged, against their inclination, to think evil of another, it will be no pleasure to declare it, but they will be backward to speak of it to any, and will only do so when a sense of duty leads them to it.

2. *In view of this subject let all examine themselves, whether their grace is real and sincere.* — Let every one diligently and prayerfully ask, whether their graces all tend to practice, and are seen from day to day in the life and conduct. But here even some truly godly persons may be ready to say, that if they judge themselves by their practice, they must condemn themselves, for they fail so much and so frequently, and are so often wandering out of the way, that at times it scarcely seems that they can be the children of God. But to such I answer, that persons who try themselves by their practice, may find that they greatly fail every day, and are often wandering out of the way, and yet they may really see no just cause in their practice to condemn themselves. For when we speak of a life of Christian practice, and when the Scriptures speak of the course of life as Christian, the meaning is not, that the life is a perfect and sinless life. On the contrary, a Christian's life may be attended with many and exceeding great imperfections, and yet be a holy life, or a truly Christian life. It may be such a life as to clearly, and even necessarily show, that the grace which the individual has, is of the kind which has a tendency to holy practice. His fruits may be such as to be good evidence of the good nature of the tree, and his works such as to show his faith. And if you ask for still further light, then I would say, whatever your imperfections and failings may be, examine yourself whether you find the following evidences of your grace being of that kind which tends to holy practice.

First, Has your supposed grace such influence, *as to render those things in which you have failed of holy practice, loathsome, grievous and humbling to you?* Has it such an influence in your mind as to render your past sinful practices hateful in your eyes, and has it led you to mourn before God for them? And does it render those things in your conduct that since your supposed conversion have been contrary to Christian practice, odious in your eyes? And is it the great burden of your life, that your practice is no better? Is it really grievous to you, that you have fallen, or do fall into sin; and are you ready, after the example of holy Job, to abhor yourself for it, and repent in dust and ashes, and like Paul to lament your wretchedness, and pray to be delivered from sin, as you would from a body of death?

Second, Do you carry about with you, habitually, a dread of sin? Do you not only mourn, and humble yourself for sins that are past, but have you a dread of sin for the future? And do you dread it because in itself it is evil, and so hurtful to your own soul, and offensive to God? Do you dread it as a terrible enemy that you have often suffered by, and feel that it has been a grievous thing to you heretofore? And do you dread it as something that has hurt, and wounded, and stung you, so that you would see it no more? Do you stand on your watch against it, as a man would keep watch against something that he dreads, with such a dread as led Joseph to say, "How can I do this great wickedness, and sin against God?" (Gen. 39:9).

Third, Are you sensible of the beauty and pleasantness of the ways of holy practice? Do you see the beauty of holiness, and the loveliness of the ways of God and Christ? It is said in the text that "charity rejoiceth in the truth"; and it is given as the character of the truly godly, that "he rejoiceth and worketh righteousness," which is the same as saying that "he rejoices to work righteousness." And how often does the Psalmist speak of the law of God as being his delight, and of his love to the divine commandments!

Fourth, Do you find that you do particularly esteem and delight in those practices that may, by way of eminence, be called Christian practices, in distinction from mere worldly morality? And by Christian practices are meant such as are implied in a meek, humble, prayerful, self-denying, self-renouncing, heavenly walk and behavior. Some of the heathen have been eminent for many of the moral virtues, and wrote excellently about them, as for example, of justice, and generosity, and fortitude, &c.; but they were far from a Christian poverty of spirit and lowliness of mind. They sought their own glory, and gloried exceedingly in their outward virtues, and seemed to know nothing of such a walk as the gospel commands, a walk of self-emptiness, and poverty of spirit, and self-distrust, and self-renunciation, and prayerful reliance on God. They were strangers to meekness, and did not allow, or even dream that the forgiveness and love of enemies was a virtue. Such virtues as these, are peculiarly Christian by way of distinction and eminence, and of these it is, that I ask, if you hold them in special esteem, for your Saviour's sake, and because they are fraught with his spirit? If you are essentially distinguished and different in your spirit from the mere moralist, or the heathen sage or philosopher, you will have a spirit of special esteem for and delight in these virtues that do especially belong to the gospel.

Fifth, Do you hunger and thirst after a holy practice? Do you long to live a holy life, to be conformed to God, to have your conduct, day by day, better regulated, and more spiritual, more to God's glory, and more such as becometh a Christian? Is this what you love, and pray for, and long for, and live for? This is mentioned by Christ, as belonging to the character of true Christians, that they "hunger and thirst after righteousness." Does this trait belong to you?

Sixth, Do you make a business of endeavoring to live holily, and as God would have you, in all respects? Not only can be said to endeavor after holiness, but do you make *a business* of endeavoring after it? Is it a matter that lies with weight upon your mind. A true and faithful Christian does not make holy living a mere incidental thing, but it is his great concern. As the business of the soldier is to fight, so the business of the Christian is to be like Christ, to be holy as he is holy. Christian practice is the great work that he is engaged in, just as the race was the great work of the racers. Is this so with you? And is it your great aim and love to keep *all* God's commandments, and so far as known to neglect none? "Then," says the Psalmist, "I shall not be ashamed when I have respect unto all thy commandments." Is this your serious, constant, and prayerful aim, that you may be faithful in every known duty? And once more,

Seventh, Do you greatly desire that you may know all that is your duty? And do you desire to know it that you may do it? With the patriarch Job, can you, and do you pray to the Almighty, "That which I see not, teach thou me," adding, as he added, to the great searcher of hearts, "If I have done iniquity, I will do no more?"

If you can honestly meet these tests, then you have the evidence that your grace is of the kind that tends to holy practice, and to growth in it. And though you may fall, through God's mercy you shall rise again. He that hath begun a good work in you, will carry it on until the day of Jesus Christ. Though you may be, at times, faint, yet if pursuing, you shall be borne on from strength to strength, and kept, and kept by the power of God, through faith, unto salvation. . . .

FOR ADDITIONAL INFORMATION ABOUT JONATHAN EDWARDS:

Aldridge, Alfred O. *Jonathan Edwards.* New York: Washington Square Press, 1966.

Brigance, William Norwood, ed. "Jonathan Edwards." *A History and Criticism of American Public Address,* vol. 1. New York: Russell & Russell, 1943.

Ferm, Vergilius, ed. *Puritan Sage: Collected Writings of Jonathan Edwards.* New York: Library Publishers, 1953.

Gerstner, John H. *Steps to Salvation: The Evangelistic Message of Jonathan Edwards.* Philadelphia: Westminster Press, 1959.

Hoyt, Arthur S. "Jonathan Edwards." *The Pulpit and American Life.* New York: Macmillan Co., 1921.

Parkes, Henry Bamford. *Jonathan Edwards: The Fiery Puritan.* New York: Minton, Balch & Co., 1930.

Turnbull, Ralph G. *Jonathan Edwards: The Preacher.* Grand Rapids: Baker Book House, 1958.

Walker, Williston. "Jonathan Edwards." *Great Men of the Christian Church.* Chicago: University of Chicago Press, 1908.

FOR OTHER SERMONS BY JONATHAN EDWARDS:

The Works of President Edwards. 4 vols. New York: Leavitt & Allen, 1843.

Selected Sermons of Jonathan Edwards. Edited by H. Norman Gardiner. New York: Macmillan Co., 1904.

Also: *Edward's Sermon Outlines* (1958), *Selected Sermons of President Edwards* (1834), *Charity and Its Fruits* (1851).

GEORGE WHITEFIELD

1714 - 1770

GEORGE WHITEFIELD, engraving after Hone, by F.
Halpin from United Methodist Missions, New York.

GEORGE WHITEFIELD

1714   *Born in Gloucester, England, December 16*
1733   *Entered Oxford University*
1736   *Granted B.A. degree from Oxford and ordained a deacon*
1739   *Ordained a priest in the Church of England*
1741   *Married Mrs. Elizabeth Majes*
1743   *Started Calvinistic Methodist Society*
1770   *Died September 30, in Newbury Port, Massachusetts*

IF RESULTS ARE ANY CRITERION for judging preaching, George Whitefield was second to none. On one occasion, near Glasgow, Scotland, he preached to nearly 100,000 persons; after an hour and a half the converts numbered 10,000. Often in the open fields he addressed crowds numbering 25,000.

LIFE AND TIMES

Born in Gloucester, England, December 16, 1714, George Whitefield was the son of a wine merchant who died when George was just two years old. His grandfather was a preacher. As a boy, George was a typical "bad boy" in many ways, full of mischief and pranks at home and school. The influence of life around the tavern which his mother ran led him into profanity and drinking. He was not above stealing money from his mother. He often quarreled with his family, and after one of these quarrels Whitefield left home and lived with his brother in Bristol.

Later his life was transformed by a deep religious experience. He describes his conversion as follows:

About the end of the seventh week, after having undergone innumerable buffetings of Satan and many months' inexpressible trials by night and day under the spirit of bondage, God was pleased at length to remove the heavy load, to enable me to lay hold on His dear Son by a living faith, and by giving me the spirit of adoption, to seal me, as I humbly hope, even to the day of everlasting redemption.[1]

At twelve, he was placed in the School of Saint Mary de Crypt, Gloucester, where he displayed an interest in rhetoric and drama which he was to fulfill in his preaching. Upon entering Oxford, he met John and Charles Wesley and joined the Holy Club. The Holy Club was devoted to methodically carrying out religious duties: each week the members attended communion; they also arose early each morning for prayer, studied religious literature, and ministered to the needy around them in the name of Christ.

Whitefield was ordained a deacon in 1736 and received the B.A. degree from Oxford in the same year. His deep religious experience intensified his concern for preaching, and he proved to be an effective and enthusiastic preacher from the beginning of his ministry. A compulsive desire to lead men to faith in Jesus Christ drove him from sermon to sermon, wherever he could find any place to preach.

Because of his pulpit excess, many ministers of the Church of England refused to allow him to preach in their churches. Whitefield promptly went to the fields and preached there. Not content to confine his ministry to England, he sailed for America in 1737. This was to be the first of thirteen journeys across the Atlantic to the colonies. His preaching in America stimulated the religious revival known as the Great Awakening. He preached throughout the colonies and at first was greeted everywhere with great enthusiasm.

In his *Autobiography,* Benjamin Franklin comments on the effect of Whitefield's visit to Philadelphia:

> It was wonderful to see the Change soon made in the Manners of our Inhabitants; from being thoughtless or indifferent about Religion, it seem'd as if all the World were growing Religious; so that one could not walk thro' the Town in an Evening without Hearing Psalms sung in different Families of every Street.

---

1. Edwin Charles Dargan, *A History of Preaching,* vol. 2 (Grand Rapids: Baker Book House, 1954), p. 309.

And it being found inconvenient to assemble in the open Air, subject to its Inclemencies, the Building of a House to meet in was no sooner propos'd and Persons appointed to receive Contributions, but sufficient Sums were soon receiv'd to procure the Ground and erect the Building which was 100 feet long and 70 broad, about the Size of Westminster-hall; and the Work was carried on with such Spirit as to be finished in a much shorter time than could have been expected.[2]

Benjamin Franklin also confessed that he himself was moved by Whitefield's persuasive powers. In his tours through Georgia, Whitefield had discovered scores of helpless children left orphaned. He desired to build an orphanage in Georgia and so proposed to raise money in Philadelphia and other northern colonies, purchase materials, transport them to Georgia, and build the orphanage. Benjamin Franklin insisted that it would be more practical to build the orphanage in Philadelphia and move the children to it. Whitefield refused to change his plans and Franklin refused to contribute. After this disagreement had taken place, Franklin attended one of Whitefield's sermons. This is Franklin's account of what happened:

I happened soon after to attend one of his Sermons, in the Course of which I perceived he intended to finish with a Collection, and I silently resolved that he should get nothing from me. I had in my Pocket a Handful of Copper Money, three or four silver Dollars, and five Pistoles in Gold. As he proceeded I began to soften, and concluded to give the Coppers. Another Stroke of his Oratory made me asham'd of that, and determin'd me to give the Silver; and he finish'd so admirably, that I empty'd my Pocket wholly into the Collector's Dish, Gold and all.[3]

In addition to the orphanage, Whitefield established Kingswood School, wrote many journals and printed numerous sermons. In the colonies, these were printed by Benjamin Franklin. In his various encounters with Franklin, Whitefield often urged him to become a Christian. Of this Franklin said: "He

---

2. Leonard W. Labaree, Ralph L. Ketcham, Helen C. Boatfield, and Helene H. Fineman, eds., *The Autobiography of Benjamin Franklin* (New Haven: Yale University Press, 1964), pp. 175–76. Used by permission of University of California Press.
3. Ibid., p. 177.

us'd indeed sometimes to pray for my Conversion, but never had the Satisfaction of believing that his Prayers were heard. Ours was a mere civil Friendship, sincere on both Sides, and lasted to his Death."[4]

Though an ordained priest of the Church of England, Whitefield was basically nondenominational in his approach. He lived most of his life under the Methodist label and was buried in a Presbyterian church which he had helped found. On one occasion he declared:

> Father Abraham, whom have you in heaven? Any Episcopalians? No! Any Presbyterians? No! Have you any Independents or Seceders? No! Have you any Methodists? No! No! No! Whom have you there? We don't know those names here! All who are here are Christians.[5]

An indefatigable worker, he preached over 18,000 sermons in his ministry—an average of over 500 per year, or ten a week. In addition he was an extensive letter writer and traveler. He made a preaching tour of England almost every year. He traveled to Scotland fourteen times and visited Wales repeatedly. He toured Ireland three times, traveled to Spain and to Holland once each, and crossed the Atlantic thirteen times.

He lacked Wesley's administrative skills. He left his converts without organization and frequently the results of his work were of short duration. He also differed with Wesley in theology. Wesley was a confirmed Arminian. Whitefield, who always had Calvinist tendencies, was confirmed in his Calvinism by persons in the colonies—among them, Jonathan Edwards. He broke with Wesley over theological matters and established the Calvinistic Methodist Society in 1743. He particularly challenged Wesley's concepts of election, perseverance of the believer, and perfection over sin.

Approximately one-third of Whitefield's ministry was spent in the colonies; he died in one of them, Massachusetts. After preaching a particularly strenuous sermon, he retired to bed and died on September 30, in Newbury Port, Massachusetts.

Theological differences did not blind Wesley to Whitefield's significant service to Christ. At the time of Whitefield's death, Wesley paid the famous evangelist a great tribute:

4. Ibid., p. 178.
5. Albert David Beldon, *George Whitefield, The Awakener,* 2d ed. (London: Rockliff Pub. Corp., 1953), p. 240.

Have we read or heard of any person who called so many thousands, so many myriads of sinners to repentance? Above all, have we read or heard of anyone who has been the blessed instrument of bringing so many sinners from darkness to light, and from the power of Satan unto God?[6]

PREACHING AND SERMONS

George Whitefield must have had one of the greatest speaking voices the world has ever known. Benjamin Franklin said that Whitefield's voice had perfect modulation, emphasis and action, and gave the effect of "an excellent piece of music."[7] He was called the Demosthenes of the pulpit. His voice was described by another writer as resembling "an organ, a flute, a harp, all in one" — what *that* might sound like is not certain, but supposedly it was meant as a compliment.

During Whitefield's lifetime there were widespread reports that his voice could be heard for more than a mile. Benjamin Franklin doubted the report that 25,000 people at one gathering were able to hear Whitefield preach. Franklin then made a personal study of the matter and recorded the results in his *Autobiography*:

He had a loud and clear Voice, and articulated his Words and Sentences so perfectly that he might be heard and understood at a great Distance, especially as his Auditories, however numerous, observ'd the most exact Silence. He preach'd one Evening from the Top of the Court House Steps, which are in the Middle of Market Street, and on the West Side of Second Street which crosses it at right angles. Both Streets were fill'd with his Hearers to a considerable Distance. Being among the hindmost in Market Street, I had the Curiosity to learn how far he could be heard, by retiring backwards down the Street towards the River, and I found his Voice distinct till I came near Front-Street, when some Noise in that Street obscur'd it. Imagining then a Semi-Circle, of which my Distance should be the Radius, and that it were fill'd with Auditors, to each of whom I allow'd two square feet, I computed that he might well be heard by

---

6. J. C. Ryle and R. Eliot, [comps.], *Select Sermons of George Whitefield* (London: Banner of Truth Trust, 1951), p. 23.
7. Labaree, p. 180.

more than Thirty-Thousand. This reconcil'd me to the Newspaper Accounts of his having preach'd to 25,000 People in the Fields, and to the ancient Histories of Generals haranguing whole Armies, of which I had sometimes doubted.[8]

Franklin's calculation is actually faulty; but in *Poor Richard,* 1749, in discussing the same matter he pointed out more accurately that 45,000 persons might easily have heard Whitefield.

Whitefield's preaching was filled with emotion. Cornelius Winter, a friend who accompanied him on many of his preaching journeys, said Whitefield seldom preached without weeping at some point in the sermon. His sermons were also notable for vigorous denunciation of sin, frightening declarations of judgment, and beautiful descriptions of the spiritual life. Unlike Wesley, the preaching of Whitefield was highlighted by many passages of humor. He delighted in mocking imaginary opponents or poking fun at pompous churchgoers.

Whitefield preached without a manuscript. He spent long hours in the study preparing his sermons, and at times he did attempt to use a manuscript; but Whitefield felt that he was at his best preaching freely to an audience. Because of the success of his unorthodox style of delivery, Whitefield reformed the habits of as many preachers in the pulpit as he did laymen in the pews.

Whitefield's gestures were expressive. His entire manner was vigorous and active. The transcripts of his sermons show that he did not attempt to maintain his dignity as Wesley did but rather threw himself energetically into his preaching.

Most of Whitefield's sermons are notable for their clear development and smooth transitions between ideas. Occasionally his interpretation of Scripture is strained, and some critics have accused him of lifting some texts out of their proper settings to prove his point. But a careful study of his sermons indicates that such errors must have been rare. It is true that Whitefield was exceptionally free in his approach to the Scripture, sometimes digressing from his theme rather badly; nevertheless, whatever faults he had in interpretation were due to presuppositions in his theology rather than carelessness in his use of the Bible.

---

8. Ibid., p. 179.

In the case of Whitefield — as in the case of many great preachers of the past — many false impressions of his preaching have been given by the poor editing of his sermons. Sometimes these editions have become obsolete with the passing of years; but in other collections of Whitefield's sermons, his racy, natural prose has suffered "polishing" of the sorriest sort.

For example, read his sermon "The Burning Bush"; then read "Walking with God." Do they sound like the same preacher? They do not. "The Burning Bush" was stenographically recorded and reproduced exactly as Whitefield spoke it; the other sermon has been edited out of its style by someone who was obviously embarrassed by Whitefield's roughness. Some editions of Whitefield's works make him sound cold and intellectually sterile. Whitefield himself wouldn't recognize his sermons in that form. No doubt many interpreters of Christian preaching have been deceived by such miserable alterations of what was once great preaching. (See notation on the editing of the sermons of George Truett, volume 8, pp. 137–39.)

In those sermons that were faithfully recorded the real Whitefield comes through. His lively sense of humor is unmistakable. In "The Burning Bush," he wrote: "I will assure you, Moses was a Methodist, a very fine one, a very strong one too. . . ." In the same sermon he wrote:

> "O," says one, "I never felt the devil"; I am sure thou mayst feel him now; thou are *dadda's* own child; thou art speaking the very language of the devil, and he is teaching thee to deny thy own father; therefore graceless child of the devil, you never felt the devil's fiery darts, it is because the devil is sure of thee. . . .[9]

Or notice his use of popular language:

> Some, who it is to be hoped are God's children, if you tell them that God has loved them with an everlasting love, they are afraid to suck it in, and especially if you pop out the word election, or that hard word predestination, they will be quite frightened; but talk to them in another way, their dear hearts will rejoice.

9. Quotation marks, paragraphing, capitalization, and italics have been added to this passage and to the following ones from "The Burning Bush" and "All Men's Place."

Whitefield used the same explicit language to describe various occasions when he was persecuted:

> I know we had more comfort in Moorfields, on Kennington Common, and especially when the rotten eggs, the cats and dogs were thrown upon me, and my gown was filled with clods of dirt that I could scarce move it; I have had more comfort in this burning bush than when I have been at ease.
>
> I remember when I was preaching at Exeter, a stone came and made my forehead bleed, I found at that very time the word came with double power to a laborer that was gazing at me, who was wounded at the same time by another stone. I felt for the lad more than for myself, went to a friend, and the lad came to me. "Sir," says he, "the man gave me a wound but Jesus healed me; I never had my bonds broke til I had my head broke."
>
> I appeal to you whether you were not better when it was colder than now, because your nerves were braced up; you have a day like a dog-day, now you are weak, and are obliged to fan yourselves: thus it is prosperity lulls the soul, and I fear Christians are spoiled by it.

The many writers who have called the preaching of Whitefield dull and tedious must never have read such a passage as that one.

The zealous earnestness of Whitefield is apparent in this passage from "All Men's Place":

> When I saw you from my study crowding to come in, when I saw you pushing forward, some to go up to the tabernacle, or into the vestry, some to fill the area, and others to stand at the door, I thought, "how shall I manage with myself tonight? Shall I endeavor to make these weep and cry? Shall I not earnestly address so many precious souls in a practical way, to bring them not to the preacher, but to the preacher's master?" Knowing the terrors of the Lord, we would fain persuade all to flee from this wrath to come.

Some older commentators have claimed that the preaching of Whitefield was not "learned"; but they must have had strange standards by which to judge learning. His sermons are filled with illustrative quotations from learned men: for example,

"Walking with God" makes reference to Luther, Bowen, Bishop Hall, Henry, Bishop Beveridge, Arndt, and Watts; in addition there are countless scriptural references and citations, Latin and Greek phrases—all arranged in a careful outline and following a detailed exposition.

Unlike Wesley, who seldom used personal illustrations, nearly every one of Whitefield's sermons relates several lengthy personal experiences. His early life is revealed in this citation from "All Men's Place":

> When I was sixteen years of age, I began to fast twice a week for thirty-six hours together, prayed many times a day, received the sacrament every Lord's Day, fasted myself almost to death all the forty days of Lent, during which, I made it a point of duty never to go less than three times a day to public worship, besides seven times a day to my private prayers, yet I knew no more that I was to be born again in God, born a new creature in Christ Jesus, than if I was never born at all.
>
> I had a mind to be upon the stage, but then I had a qualm of conscience; I used to ask people, "Pray can I be a player, and yet go to the sacrament and be a Christian?" "O," say they, "such a one, who is a player, goes to the sacrament; though according to the law of the land, no player should receive the sacrament, unless they give proof that they repent; that was Archbishop Tilotson's doctrine"; "well then, if that be the case," said I, "I will be a player," and I thought to act my part for the devil as well as any body; but, blessed be God, he stopped me in my journey. I must bear testimony to my old friend, Mr. Charles Wesley; he put a book into my hands, called *The Life of God in the Soul of Man*, whereby God showed me, that I must be born again or be damned. I know the place; it may be superstitious, perhaps, but whenever I go to Oxford, I cannot help running to that place where Jesus Christ first revealed himself to me, and gave me the new birth.

Less inspiring, but no less revealing of the personality of Whitefield, is this comical conclusion to the same fine sermon:

> The world thinks I am very rich; a man the other day, was so persuaded of my riches, that he sent me word, if I did not lay thirty pounds in such a place, I should

be killed as sure as I am alive; but, blessed be God, I am alive yet; I do not fear dying suddenly. . . .

You may think, perhaps, I get a great deal by preaching here; and now I am going away, what do you think my stated allowance is for preaching at the Tabernacle? I have no more from this place than one hundred pounds a year; and I asked but last night how it stood, and instead of having a single sixpence, I was told there were fifty pounds arrears; well, said I, ungrateful as it is to me, I will make a collection tonight that all may be left free; and if others are left to make an advantage of it, may God make it a blessing.

There are not six people in this place that I have had the value of a guinea of from January to August; nor have I had a guinea from all these ordinances towards bearing the expenses of my voyage. When I come my brethren, to heaven, you shall then know with what a spirit I have served you; you shall then know that all I have done is to build places for others, where I hope God will meet you and your children when I am dead and gone.

All these passages and many others reveal a genuine human being and a great orator.

Sermons

ALL MEN'S PLACE

"Do not all go to one place?" (Ecclesiastes 6:6).

I REMEMBER an ingenious writer, who had been very copious in his publications, observed, that the best and most profitable were written after he was fifty years of age: It is supposed, then the judgment is ripened, and the genius is as it were advanced to maturity and knowledge; and experiences gathered when young, will be more useful in the decline of life, when grey hairs are seen here and there upon them. It is said indeed, that old men are twice children; but there are some whose geniuses are so very low that they cannot be twice children, because they are no better than children from their cradle to their grave; but this is not the case with God's children, for upon a reflection of the wrong steps they have taken, if it proceeds from the sanctified sense of afflictions, they serve to make them more instructive in their latter day.

This was the case of Solomon, though highly favored when young, for the Lord appeared unto him twice, yet he fell most awfully, and had we not read of his recovery again, the doctrine of the final perseverance of the saints, must seem to fall to the ground; but we have reason to think that he was restored, and gave evidence of his recovery by writing in such a manner, that none could but one that knew much of God and himself; witness the book of Ecclesiastes, which in all ages of the church has been received with a peculiar respect. Ecclesiastes signifies a preacher; such Solomon was from his own experience, and exceeded by none but him "who spake as no man ever did."

The chapter in which is the text, describes the vanity and misery of our present state, if unsanctified. "There is an evil," saith he, "that I have seen under the sun, and it is common among men": though he is going about to describe a monster, yet it is a monster that walks and stalks abroad, a man to whom God hath given riches, wealth and honor, so that he wanteth nothing for his soul of all that he desireth, though

Reprinted from George Whitefield, *Eighteen Sermons,* rev. Andrew Gifford (Boston: n. p., 1820), pp. 227–43.

God gives him not power to eat; this is vanity and a great disease. Was there ever a more striking description of an old covetous miser, who leaves his wealth to some person that spends it faster than the poor wretch got it? He goes on and says, "If a man beget an hundred children, and live many years, so that the days of his years be many, and his soul be not filled with good, and also that he have no burial, I say, that an untimely birth is better than he, for he cometh in with vanity, and departeth in darkness, and his name shall be covered with darkness. Moreover, he hath not seen the sun, nor known any thing; this hath more rest than the other." And then though this creature should be supposed to live a thousand years twice told, why, saith he, yet hath he seen no good; he has never been possessed of real good to make him happy here or hereafter; for, adds he, do not all go, both the abortive and the aged, young and old, high and low, rich and poor, whether blessed with children, or have no children, whether like Lazarus, that beg their bread, or Dives, clothed in purple and fine linen, and fare sumptuously every day, "Do not all go to one place?"

An important question! shall I propose it to you tonight? Do you know what the wise man means when he offers this question to your consideration, "Do not all go to one place?" What can be the design of this? the thing, no doubt, here spoken of, is death; the place here spoken of, no doubt is the grave. An amazing consideration! part of the first sentence that the great and holy God ever denounced against fallen man, to one and all, "Dust thou art, and unto dust thou shalt return." On account of our first parents' transgression, it is appointed unto all men, all sorts of men, all the inhabitants under heaven, once to die; and therefore the apostle saith, "Death hath passed upon all men, even upon those who have not sinned after the similitude of the transgression of Adam," that is, who have not been guilty of actual sin. Can there be a stronger proof of the imputation of Adam's guilt, of original sin, or a more cutting trial that a tender father and nursing mother can undergo, than to see a dear little child just born, or but lent to the loving parents for a few months, taken away often in the greatest agonies that we can conceive? and if God, my dear hearers, has ever suffered your dear children suddenly to be seized with convulsions, and continue in anguish and agonizing pains for many days together, you have had sufficient proof of it.

A friend of mine in London, about thirty-two years ago, that was doatingly fond of every child he had, to whom I wrote a letter from Georgia, beginning with these words: Is your idol dead yet? for I thought it was such an idol that would soon go. The account he gave me the first time I saw him was, that the day before my letter was received, the child died in such agony and torture, that its excrements came out of his mouth, which made the fond and too indulgent parent wish to have rather died a thousand deaths himself, than that his child should die in such a way; and added, I was obliged to go to God, and desire him to take my darling away. What an awful proof are there sufferings, that children come into the world with a corruption that renders them liable to God's wrath and damnation; but the blood, the precious blood of Jesus Christ, it is to be hoped cleanses them from the guilt and filth of sin. So any of you that have got children dead in infancy, O may you improve what I shall say by and by from the text, and pray endeavor to go to that place, where I hope you will see your children making a blessed constellation in the firmament of heaven: in this respect all go to the same place, some at the beginning of life, some at the middle, and some at the decline; and happy, happy they who go to bed soonest, if their souls are saved!

But, my dear hearers, in another case we may venture to contradict even Solomon; for if we consider the words of our text in another view, all do not go to one place; it is true, all are buried in the grave either of earth or water, but then after death comes judgment; death gives the decisive, the separating blow. Suppose then in our enlarging on the text, we should confine the word to all the unregenerate, and to those who are not born of God; these ideeed, die when they will, all go to one place. If you should ask me, for I love dearly to have an inquisitive auditory, who I mean by unregenerate? who I mean by those that are not born of God? I answer, I do not mean all that only bear the name of Jesus Christ; I mention this, because a great many people think that all that are baptized, either when they are adult or when they are young, whether sprinkled or put under water, I believe a great many people think that all these go to heaven.

I remember when I began to speak against baptismal regeneration in my first sermon, printed when I was about twenty-two years old, or a little more; the first quarrel many had with me was, because I did not say that all people who were baptized, were born again; I would as soon believe the doctrine of transubstantiation. Can I believe that a person who gives no evidence of being a saint, from the time of his baptism to the time perhaps of his death, that never fights against the world, the flesh, and the devil, and never minds one word of what his god-fathers and god-mothers promised for him, can I believe that person is a real Christian! no, I can as soon believe, that a little water in the priest's hand, about a quarter of an inch long, is the very blood and bones of Jesus Christ, who was hung upon the cross without the gates of Jerusalem. I do believe baptism to be an ordinance of Christ; but at the same time, no candid person can be angry for my asserting, that there are numbers that have been baptized when grown up, or when very young, that are not regenerated by God's Spirit, who will all go to one place, and that place is where there will be no water to quench that dreadful fire that will parch them with thirst. I am speaking out of a book which contains the lively oracles of God, and in the name of one who is truth itself, who knowing very well what he spoke, is pleased in the most solemn and awful manner to say, and that to a master in Israel, that "if a man be not born again of water and the Spirit, he cannot see the kingdom of God"; he can have no idea, no proper, no adequate notion of it, much less is he to expect to be happy eternally with God hereafter; and therefore as our Lord spoke to this man, give me leave to observe to you.

I don't mean the Deists only by unregenerate sinners; I don't mean the profane mocker who is advanced to the scorner's chair, nor your open profligate adulterers, fornicators, abusers of themselves with mankind; these have damnation as it were written upon their foreheads with a sun beam; and they may know that God is not mocked, for if they die without repenting of these things, they show they are in an unregenerate state, and will go to one place; if any of you are going thither, may God stop you this night.

But, my brethren, I will come closer; there are more unbelievers within the pale than without the pale of the church; let me repeat it again, you may think of it when I am tossing upon the mighty waters, there are more unbelievers within the pale of the church than without; all are not possessors that are professors; all have not got the thing promised; all are not partakers of the promise, that talk and bless God they have got the promised Saviour: I may have him in my mouth and upon my tongue, without having the thing promised, or the blessed promise in my heart. A moral man that can walk touching the law blameless, a person that thinks he is righteous, because he does not know why a person who has got no other religion than to go to a particular place of worship, values himself upon being a churchman or a dissenter; he is such a bigot that he thinks no man will go to heaven but himself; these, however they may think themselves safe, will ere long go to one place, whether they think so or no; they will be soon summoned to one bar, and the voice of the archangel sounding "arise, ye dead, and come to judgment," will be the great alarm; the dead shall arise and appear before the Son of God as Judge of all mankind; these, as well as the infidels would gladly be excused; and as they once said, I pray have me excused from coming to Christ, so they will fain be excused from appearing before and being condemned by him, but they must all go to one place: and as they know not God, and are unacquainted with the divine life, they must hear and suffer the dreadful sentence, "Depart ye cursed, into everlasting fire, prepared for the devil and his angels."

This is a thought, that if our hearts my dear hearers, were properly awakened, would make our blood run cold: to be in a place of absence from God, a place where damned souls will be forever cursing God and one another: give me leave to dwell upon it a little, and may it be blessed, under God, to awaken some careless person, who, perhaps, may be taking a walk tonight, and just step in to hear what the babbler has to say while he is about to take his leave of the people.

When I saw you from my study crowding to come in, when I saw you pushing forward, some to go up to the tabernacle, or into the vestry, some to fill the area, and others to stand at the door, I thought how shall I manage with myself tonight? shall I endeavor to make these weep and cry? shall I not earnestly address so many precious souls in a practical way, to bring them not to the preacher, but to the preacher's master? knowing the terrors of the Lord, we would fain persuade all to flee from this wrath to come.

O awful thought! and yet it is a certain truth, all on earth must go to one place: if we live like and are devils here, we must go and be with them when we die forever! A blessed minister of Christ in Scotland, told me a story he knew for truth, of a dreadful answer a poor creature gave on her death bed (for the Scotch, except the people of New England, are the most knowing people in religious matters, perhaps any where); this person when dying was asked by a minister, where do you hope to go when you die? says she, I don't care where I go; what, says he, don't you care whether you go to heaven or hell? no, says she, I don't care whither I go; but, says he, if you was put to your choice where would you go? says she, to hell; to that he replied are you mad, will you go to hell? yes, says she, I will; why so? says he; why, says she, all my relations are there. The dear minister of Christ preached after her death, told the story, and asked is it not shocking to hear a woman say she would go to hell because her relations were there: why, you that are unregenerate must go to hell, for all your unregenerate relations are there; your father the devil is there; all damned angels and damned spirits are there; your brothers and sisters are there; as they went one way here, so they must be banished from Jesus Christ to one place hereafter.

But I must close this mournful theme; it is too gloomy to dwell upon; blessed be God, I have another place to tell you of, and another sort of people to speak of, who shall all, as well as those I have spoken of, go to one place; perhaps, here are some of them; blessed is it to live in God. When death closes the eyes, an actual separation is made, and instead of hearing, "Depart, ye cursed," they will hear, "Come, ye blessed of my Father, inherit the kingdom prepared for you from the foundation of the world." Our blessed master, and who speaks like him, gives us an awful view of Dives and Lazarus, the one feasting and fattening his body to the grave, not keeping one fast day in a year, and the other starving at his gate, perhaps buried in the ditch, denied a grave by the parish, while this vile wretch, who died also, had a pompous funeral; there he was carried to one place; he was, perhaps, laid in state, two mutes attending round the coffin, while damned devils were gnawing his soul; he lift up his eyes in torment. Hark! don't you hear him; I will stop a little that you may; you ungodly ones, do not you hear your brother cry? he would not pray while alive, but hell makes him pray, not to God, but to Abraham; "Father Abraham," says he, "send Lazarus to dip the tip of his finger in water, and cool my tongue"; and I verily believe, the damned will have a sight of those that are in heaven, to let them know what a heaven, what a Christ, what a glory they have lost: God grant this may be none of your case, it will not be if you are of the number of those who are born from above, that are made new creatures in Christ Jesus; for by being born again from above, I mean receiving a principle of new life, imparted to our hearts by the Holy Ghost, changing you, giving you new thoughts, new words, new actions, new views, so that old things pass away, and all things become new in our souls.

I know very well that the doctrine of a divine influence is exploded: I have often told you, and I tell you again, now I am about going to another clime for a while, that the grand quarrel that our Lord Jesus Christ has with England, and I do not speak it as a prophet, or the son of a prophet, but as the Lord God liveth, in whose name I speak, and for whose glory I am going abroad, and in whose fear I desire to die, if the Spirit of God and his divine influence is not more regarded in this land than it has been, woe, woe, woe to those that despise it; they may by and by, one day or other, wonder and perish. Blessed be God, there are a happy few who do regard it, and I am persuaded in my very soul, that a number in England, in Scotland, in Ireland, in Wales, and in America, does, and I pray it may still greatly increase. Yet notwithstanding the word of God does run and is glorified, how many are there at this day that wilfully do despite to the Spirit of God, that hate the doctrine of the Spirit's divine influences; that if it were in their power, but we live under revolution principles, and are blessed with toleration which is the bulwark of liberty of conscience, otherwise the street would run with the blood of both churchmen and dissenters; but whether the world will hear of forbear, blessed be God, when we speak of the new birth, we do not speak of a cunningly devised fable; what our eyes have seen, our hands have handled, and what our hearts have felt of the word of life, that declare we unto you.

When I was sixteen years of age, I began to fast twice a week for thirty-six hours together, prayed many times a day, received the sacrament every Lord's day, fasting myself almost to death all the forty days of Lent, during which, I made it a point of duty never to go less than three times a day to public worship, besides seven times a day to my private prayers, yet I knew no more that I was to be born again in God, born a new creature in Christ Jesus, than if I was never born at all. I had a mind to be upon the stage, but then I had a qualm of conscience; I used to ask people, pray can I be a player, and yet go to the sacrament and be a Christian? O say they, such a one, who is a player, goes to the sacrament; though according to the law of the land, no player should receive the sacrament, unless they give proof that they repent; that was Archbishop Tilotson's doctrine; well then, if that be the case, said I, I will be a player, and I thought to act my part for the devil as well as any body; but blessed be God, he stopped me in my journey.

I must bear testimony to my old friend, Mr. Charles Wesley; he put a book into my hands, called, *The Life of God in the Soul of Man*, whereby God shewed me, that I must be born again or be damned. I know the place; it may be superstitious, perhaps, but whenever I go to Oxford, I cannot help running to that place where Jesus Christ first revealed himself to me, and gave me the new birth. As a good writer says, a man may go to church, say his prayers, receive the sacrament, and yet, my brethren, not be a Christian. How did my heart rise, how did my heart shudder, like a poor man that is afraid to look into his account books, lest he should find himself a bankrupt; yet shall I burn that book, shall I throw it down, shall I put it by, or shall I search into it? I did, and holding the book in my hand, thus addressed the God of heaven and earth: Lord, if I am not a Christian, if I am not a real one, God, for Jesus Christ's sake, show me what Christianity is, that I may not be damned at last. I read a little further, and the cheat was discovered; O, says the author, they that know any thing of religion, know it is a vital union with the Son of God, Christ formed in the heart; O what a ray of divine life did then break in upon my poor soul; I fell a writing to all my brethren, to my sisters, talked to the students as they came in my room, put off all trifling conversation, put all trifling books away, and was determined to study to be a saint, and then to be a scholar; and from that moment God has been carrying on his blessed work in my soul; and as I am now fifty-five years of age, going towards sixty, I tell you, my brethren, as I shall leave you in a few days, I am more and more convinced that this is the truth of God, and without it you never can be saved by Jesus Christ: all those born of God, whether when young or old, at the sixth, ninth, or eleventh hour, however separated from one another, through the grace of God they shall all go to one place.

If you ask where that place is? I answer, blessed be God, to heaven: if you ask to whom they shall go? I answer, to the spirits of just men made perfect; and, what will be best of all, to Jesus Christ, the heavenly inheritance. If we were not to go to him, what would heaven be? if we were not to see him, what would glory be? I know some people think heaven is a fine place, so it is; but what makes it so, but the presence and joy of the God of glory?

I would rather die a thousand deaths, than sacrifice my affections as I have done: after I had taken leave of all my friends some years ago at Deptford, I burst out into tears and said, Lord, I would not suffer all I feel for my friends but for thee; then returned to my friends and said, now the bitterness of death is passed, I am going to be executed, God's will be done. Blessed be God, after death there are no separations; we shall all go to one place; ministers that could not preach in one pulpit, and Christians that could not agree with one another, blessed be God, shall bye and bye go to one heaven; whether they go to one place or no in this world, does not signify: says one, I go to the dissenters; another, I go to church; and a great many Christians judge of one another as infidels, because they are not of one sentiment.

A good woman came to me some years ago, just as I had done preaching – some people love to be impertinent – what do you think, says she, of Cotton Mather and another minister? one said, I ought to receive the sacrament before my experience was given in; the other said not, and I believe the angels were glad to carry them both to heaven. I said, good woman, I believe they have not talked about it since, for they will no more talk about these things. We have but one Father, one Holy Ghost, we have lived in one communion of faith; blessed be the living God, ere long the angels shall come and call the elect from the east, the west, the north, and the south, to be at home with the Lord.

If this be the case, my brethren, it may support us under all the changes and partings of this mortal state. As I have been in a public character, I suppose I may venture to say, that no one has been called to such frequent partings from God's people as I have: I am going now the thirteenth time over the water; yes, I find what is said of Saint Paul is true, he could bear a whipping, not a weeping: what mean you, says he, to weep and break my heart; he never said, whip me and break my back, no, no. All get to one place: what a blessed state! to see one's spiritual father, to see one's spiritual children, and hear them say, such and such a time God begat me to himself by your ministry! what a blessing will it be to hear them say, blessed be God, next to the Spirit I owe my coming here to that servant of thine! and with what ravishment will the minister say, behold me and the children thou hast given me! with what holy triumph will they all then cast their crowns at the foot of the Lamb! with what joy will they cry, grace, grace, when the top stone is brought forth, and how will they then try who shall praise redeeming love and rich free grace in the highest strain! The difference here is you know, that we sing in parts, some sing treble, some tenor, and some bass; what then? each part helps the other, were all to sing alike the harmony would not be compleat; however shocking it is in this world, all the differences that have been among the people of God, will only make us sing and unite us the better in a future state.

Well, my dear hearers, by this time then I hope you have began to ask, to what place am I going; suppose now you reason thus; I have heard tonight that all unregenerate persons go to hell, and dwell among the damned; I have heard that all that are born again of God, and all that believe in Jesus Christ, whether Jew or Gentile, whether bond or free, all go to dwell with God, with angels, and the spirits of just men made perfect; I have heard the minister say, though he seems sometimes to ramble in his discourse, that we all go to one place, that is, the grave: I am hastening there, autumn is coming on, the fall of the leaf is approaching, a blast, occasioned by the sudden change of the weather, or a surfeit, by feasting too luxuriantly on the fruits of God's bounty; another illness may take me to my long home. I hear of such a one's dying, and of such a one, perhaps in an apoplectic, perhaps in a paralytic fit: I am lusty and strong, I am glorying in my strength, but who knows but that may be only making me food for a fever; one would stand it better that was more emaciated than I am.

If I should be taken this night, am I going the way to hell, or the way to heaven. Adrian, the emperor, cried out upon a time, "my trembling, dear departing soul, whether art thou going?" these were his words. Won't you hear an emperor preach, preach on his dying bed, when the silver cords of life are loosed? Conscience, conscience, conscience, thou candle of the Lord, may he help thee to light a poor sinner into a knowledge of himself. I charge thee in the name of our Lord Jesus Christ, in the name of that Saviour, in whose name and by whose power, I trust I now preach; O conscience! thou faithful monitor, let every one hear their own. Come, if conscience was to speak what would it say? why, that if you are not acquainted with yourself and Christ, you are lost forever.

The Americans are the most hospitable people under heaven, they love to entertain strangers, who may be hereby kindly provided for without going to an inn: I always endeavored to drop a word for Christ when I came to their houses. I remember Mr. Seeward and some other good friends were with me; when I first got into the house, I began to talk of Christ; the master of it said, sir, I believe you are right; I can't open a leaf in my Bible, but I find I am no Christian: would to God all here minded the same leaf! May be, many here say, sir, I scorn your words; well, don't I? don't God tell you that won't do? you are a moral man, but don't love God; you don't get drunk, because it will make your head ache; you don't commit fornication and adultery, which is common among the great, and therefore they think God will not punish them for it; perhaps you are not a fornicator, lest you should stand in a sheet, though we have no discipline among us now; you don't do these things for fear of maintaining the bastard, or being taken up; but does your obedience proceed from love to God, to Christ, if not, may God convince you of your miserable state before you go hence.

But, blessed be God, there are numbers of dear souls here, that I hope e'er long to live in one place and to eternal ages with. All hail, my fellow Christians; all hail, my dear brethren and friends; all hail, ye that are children of one parent, born of one Spirit, and bring forth the fruits of the Holy Ghost in your conversation; yet a little while, and we must part; whether I die, or you die, blessed be God, one place shall e'er long hold us; in yonder blessed world we shall e'er long meet, and praise free grace; my brethren we shall be then forever with the Lord, forever one with Christ; and if this be the case, let us comfort one another with these things; and if we are all going to one place, God, of his infinite mercy, keep us from falling out by the way.

Don't say, I am of the Foundery; don't say, I am of the Tabernacle; don't spend your time in talking against John Wesley and George Whitefield; don't say, you go to the Tabernacle, I'll go to the Chapel; no, don't speak of Paul and Cephas; God unite us more and more to Jesus Christ; and if you are going to heaven, God help you to travel a little farther than we do. My brethren, let us press forward toward the mark of the prize of our high calling in Christ Jesus. O that the God of love may fill us with such peace and such joy, that every storm, every trial, every temptation we meet with may be overruled to good for us; all our afflictions, all our temptations, are to make heaven more desirable, and earth more loathsome.

If this is not the case with some of you, God convert you tonight. Help me, my dear Tabernacle and London hearers, help me, help me, help me for Jesus Christ's sake. You was once going to hell yourselves for God's sake endeavor to stop those that are going there: pray for your uncoverted friends. Young people, young people, that are going to hell giddily, may God stop you this night: was I to talk to you seriously, you would say as a young gentleman did, when I desired he would not swear; he turned to me and said, Doctor (I was no more a doctor then than now, and but young too) it is very hard you will not let a man go to hell his own way; if any of you are of this stamp, God grant he may not let you go to hell your own way, but go to heaven in God's way, in Christ's way. I am sure you are not happy; the devil never had a happy child in the world: O that God may turn your feet into the way of peace tonight: O that it may be with you as with a young man one night formerly: I remember I had about two hundred notes then; I came into Moorfields this morning at six o'clock, says he, to meet my sweetheart, but, blessed be God, I met with Jesus Christ, my sweetheart: would to God you may do so, young men, tonight: when you have gone on to that place, O that it may be with you as it was with good Mr. Crane, who is appointed steward of the Orphan-house; he went once to see a play at Drury-lane, but that being full he went to Covent-garden, and that was so full he could not put his head in; well, says he, he told it me himself, and he is an Israelite indeed, one of the most honest men, perhaps, in the world, I will go and hear doctor Whitefield; there God reached his heart, and now he shines. I had letters yesterday or the day before from Georgia, that made my heart leap for joy; honest Mr. Wright, that ingenious, indefatigable man, and Mr. Crane, have gone on so well, and have managed the Orphan-house so well, that all letters from all parts give me a pleasure: would to God, one says, you could send ten thousand such people as Mr. Wright, and Mr. Crane; would to God you could send a thousand such over, and an hundred preachers to preach Christ among us.

O that curiosity may be overruled for good to some of you tonight: but I forgot myself, and can you blame me if I should detain you a little, though I am really afraid of unfitting myself for the voyage, if I tire myself before I go: tomorrow I am to go to see where I am to sleep. I intend, God willing, to have a sacrament here tomorrow, and another next Sabbath day morning. I intend, God willing, to give you a parting word on Sunday evening, and give you notice of taking my last farewell in the week, for I must get a day or two to dispatch my private business, and be ready to go where my God calleth me.

I shall, I think, be called to do something which I would, if possible, have avoided; and that is as this place has been repaired, you see 'tis fresh done, which is expensive, and I am willing to leave every thing clear before I go, a collection must be made for defraying the charge. The world thinks I am very rich; a man the other day, was so persuaded of my riches, that he sent me word, if I did not lay thirty pounds in such a place, I should be killed as sure as I am alive; but, blessed be God, I am alive yet; I do not fear dying suddenly, or being dispatched by a poignard, or a pistol to make a passage for my soul to flee to God. You may think, perhaps, I get a great deal by preaching here; and now I am going away, what do you think my stated allowance is for preaching at the Tabernacle? I have no more from this place than one hundred pounds a year; and I asked but last night how it stood, and instead of having a single sixpence, I was told there were fifty pounds arrears; well, said I, ungrateful as it is to me, I will make a collection tonight that all may be left free; and if others are left to make an advantage of it, may God make it a blessing. There are not six people in this place that I have had the value of a guinea of from January to August; nor have I had a guinea from all these ordinances towards bearing the expences of my voyage. When I come my brethren, to heaven, you shall then know with what a spirit I have served you; you shall then know that all I have done is to build places for others, where I hope God will meet you and your children when I am dead and gone.

O that we may meet in one place, when God calls me hence: the Lord quicken you, the Lord strengthen you, the Lord Jesus Christ be with you, and grant that ere long we may be where there shall be no more sorrow, but we shall dwell with God and one another forever; even so, Lord Jesus Christ. Amen.

THE BURNING BUSH

"And he looked, and, behold, the bush burned with fire, and the bush was not consumed. And Moses said, I will now turn aside, and see this great sight, why the bush is not burnt" (Exodus 3:2–3).

IT IS A COMMON SAYING, and common sayings, are generally founded on matter of fact, that it is always darkest before break of day; and I am persuaded, that if we do justice to our own experience, as well as consider God's dealings with his people in preceding ages, we shall find that man's extremity has been usually made God's opportunity, and that "when the enemy has broke in like a flood, the spirit and providence of God has lifted up a standard against him": and I believe at the same time, that however we may dream of a continued scene of prosperity in church or state, either in respect to our bodies, souls, or temporal affairs, we shall find this life to be chequered, that the clouds return after the rain, and the most prosperous state attended with such cloudy days, as may make even the people of God sometimes cry, "all men are liars, and God has forgotten to be gracious."

The chapter in which is our text, is an instance of this. What a glorious day of the son of man was that when Joseph sent for his father to Egypt; and the good old patriarch, after he had thought his son had been dead many years, agreeably surprized by a message from him to come to him, with all his family, and are by him comfortably settled in Goshen; where the good old patriarch, after many a stormy day, died in peace, and was highly honored at his funeral by Pharoah and his servants, and attended to the sepulchre of his fathers in Canaan by all his sons. After which, Joseph continued to live in splendor, lord of all the land of Egypt; and his brethren, doubtless, in the height of prosperity: but how sadly did the scene change at Pharaoh's death, soon after which, "another king arose that knew not Joseph," verifying the observation, New lords, new laws, by whom the descendants of Jacob, instead of reigning in Goshen, were made bond slaves; many, many long years, employed in making bricks, and in all probability, had what we call their bibles taken from them, by being forced to conform to the idolatry of Egypt, and so were in a worse state than the unhappy Negroes in America are at this day.

No doubt, numbers of them either wondered that ever they had been prospered at all, or that God had forgot them now; but what a mercy it is that "a thousand years in God's sight are but as one day," and therefore when God's time is come, the set time that he has appointed, he

Reprinted from George Whitefield, *Eighteen Sermons,* rev. Andrew Gifford (Boston: n. p., 1820), pp. 167–80.

will maugre all the opposition of men and devils, he will come down and deliver his people, and in such a manner, that the enemy shall know, as well as friends, it is the Lord's doing. A deliverer is born and bred in Pharaoh's court, a Moses is brought up in all the learning of the Egyptians, for Pharaoh intended him for a high and exalted post: but when offers of the highest preferment are made to him, he did not catch at them as some folks now do, who are very good and humble till something occurs to take them from God. Young as he was, he refused the highest dignity, and spurned at it with an holy contempt; and chooses rather to suffer affliction with the people of God, than enjoy all the grandeur and pleasures of, perhaps, one of the greatest courts on earth.

Forty years continued he in this state of obscurity, in which time he acquired such a competent degree, and variety of knowledge, as qualified him for every thing God intended him for: the occasion of this was his kind attempt to compose a difference between two of his brethren, one of whom accused him of murder, on which he that was to be king in Jeshurun, is forced to fly into a strange land; there he submits to the humble office of a servant, marries, and lives in a state of subjection for forty years, as was said before.

At length when he was eighty years old, dreaming of no such thing, behold God calls, and commands him to go and deliver his people: as he himself informs us, who is the author of this book, verse 1. "Now Moses kept the flock of Jethro his father-in-law, priest of Midian": he might have said, what such a scholar as I keep a parcel of sheep! such a learned man as I am employed in such a menial service! some proud hearts would break first, but you never knew a truly great man but would stoop; some that are called great men, swell till they burst; like sturdy oaks, they think they can stand every wind, till some dreadful storm comes and blows them up by the roots, while the humble reed bends and rises again. Moses was one of the latter, he keeps the flock of Jethro his father-in-law, and leads them to the mountain of God, even to Horeb. This shows how persons ought to methodize their time; but however the name of a Methodist is despised, they will never be bad servants and masters; you would be only weathercocks, unless you took care to order things in proper seasons: the devotion and business of Methodist go hand in hand; I will assure you, Moses was a Methodist, a very fine one, a very strong one too; he kept his flock, but that did not hinder his going to Horeb, he took them to the desert and being thus employed in his lawful business, God met him. Some say, we encourage people in idleness; I deny it; we say, people ought to be industrious; and I defy any one to say, a person is called by God that is negligent in his calling. "The angel of the Lord appeared to him in a flame of fire out of the bush": some think this angel was Gabriel, but most agree, and I believe with the greatest probability, that it was Jesus Christ, "the angel of the everlasting covenant"; and an expositor tells you, that the eternal *Logos,* longing to become man, often visited this earth in that form, as an evidence of his coming by and by, and dying a cursed death for man.

The manner of this angel's appearing is taken particular notice of, it was to Moses when nobody was with him: I do not hear he had so much as a boy, or one companion; and I mention this, because I believe we have often found that we are never less alone than when with God; we often want this and that companion, but happy they that can say, Lord, thy company is enough. Moses was startled at the sight, and I don't know that he is to be discommended for it, it was not to gratify a bare curiosity, but seeing a bush burning it engaged his attention, and made him think that something was uncommon; "the bush burned with fire and yet was not consumed": this startled him, as it was intended to do; for where God designs to speak, he will first gain attention from the person spoken to; Moses therefore says, "I will now turn aside and see this great sight, why the bush is not burned"; he did not know but the bush might take fire by some accident; he saw no fire come from above, he saw no fire round the bush, yet that did not so much startle him, as to see, though it did burn, it was not consumed, or in the least diminished; it was a strange sight, but it was, my brethren, a glorious one; a sight which, I pray God, you and I may behold with faith and comfort this evening; for, my dear hearers, this bush, and the account of it, was given for our learning; and I will venture to say, could Moses arise from the dead, he would not be angry with me for telling you, this is of no private interpretation, but is intended as a standing lesson, as a significant emblem of the church, and every individual child of God, till time itself shall be no more. I would therefore observe to you, that this bush,

In the first place, is typical of the church of God in all ages; the bush was burning, why might it not be a tall cedar, why might it not be some large or some glorious tree, why should the great God choose a bush, a little bush of briars and thorns, above any other thing? but because the church of Christ generally consists of poor, mean, despicable creatures: though it is all glorious within, yet it is all despicable without. It is observable, that when the church came to prosper when Constantine smiled on it, it was soon hugged to death; and that great poet, Milton, observes, that when that emperor gave ministers rich vestments, high honors, great livings, and golden pulpits, there was a voice heard from heaven, saying, this day there is poison come into the church; and I have sometimes said in discourse, I don't doubt but if any one made an experiment, and left 100,000*l.* or 200,000*l.* only among the Methodists, there would be hundreds and thousands that would not be reckoned Methodists now, that would turn Methodists presently, that would buy an hymn book, because a part of the legacy would pay for the hymn book and would wish to have a living into the bargain: but though "not many mighty men, not many noble are called," yet some are; if any of you are rich here, and are Christians, thank God for it, you ought to be doubly thankful for it; God's people are but like a little bramble bush. I remember an eminent minister said once, when I heard him preach upon Christmas day, "Christ personal is very rich, but Christ mystical is very poor"; and Jesus Christ does this on purpose to confound the world. When he comes to judgment, millions that have their thousands now, will be damned and burnt to all eternity, and Christ's church will be rich to all eternity, that is now like a bramble all on fire.

"The bush burned," what is that for? it shewed that Christ's church while in this world, will be a bush burning with fiery trials and afflictions of various kinds; this was a lively emblem of the state of religion, and liberty of Israel at that time: they were busy making of brick, and there consequently were burning continually; as though the Lord had said, this bush is burning with fire, so my people are burning with slavery. Ah, but say you, that was only the case of the Israelites when they were under Pharaoh; pray is not that the case of the church in all ages? yes, it has been; read your Bibles, and you may instantly see that it is little else than an historical account of a burning bush; and though there might be some periods wherein the church had rest, yet these periods have been of a short date; and if God's people have "walked in the comforts of the Holy Ghost," it is only like a calm that precedes an earthquake. If you remember, before the last earthquake, it was a fine morning, and who when they arose in the morning, would have thought the earth should shake under them before night; and so with the church when they are in a calm, and all seems safe there, then comes a storm: God prepare us for it.

But this is not the only case with the church of Christ collected, but also it is so with individual believers, especially those that God intends to make great use of as prophets in his church. I know very well that 'tis said, that now the case is altered: modern commentators therefore, and our great Dr. Young, calls them downy Doctors; they tell us, now we have got a Christian king and governor, and are under the toleration act, we shall have no persecution; and, blessed be God, we have had none since this family has been on the throne: May God continue it till time shall be no more. Yet, my dear hearers, we shall find, if God's word is true, whether we are born under a despotic power, or a free government, that they that will live godly in Christ Jesus must suffer persecution. You have heard of that saying, "Wonder not at the fiery trial wherewith you are to be tried"; and God saith, "I have chosen thee," which is applicable to every believer, "in the furnace of affliction." Now the furnace is a hot place, and they that are tried in the furnace must be burnt surely. Now what must the Christian burn with? with tribulation and persecution.

I heard a person not long ago say, I have no enemies. Bishop Latimer came to a house one day, and the man of the house said, he had not met with a cross in all his life; give me my horse, says the good bishop, I am sure God is not here where no cross is.

But suppose we are not persecuted by the world, is there one Christian but is persecuted by his friends; if there is an Isaac in the family, I warrant there is an Ishmael to mock at him. "Woe is me," says David, "that I must dwell with Mesheck, and in Kedar": and in one's own family, one's own brothers and sisters, one's own dependants, though they wait for our death, and perhaps, long to have us gone, that they may run away with our substance, to have these persons mock at us, and if they dare not speak out, yet let us see they hate the God we worship; if this be thy case, why, God knows, poor soul, thou art a burning bush: but if we have no such things as mocking, yet if we are surrounded with afflictions, domestic trials, the loss of dear and near friends, the bad conduct of our children, the dreadful misconduct of those that are dependant upon us; O there is many a parent here that is a burning bush; burning with what? with family afflictions; some don't care what becomes of their children; O, I thank God, I have left my boy so much, and my daughter a coach, perhaps; ah! well your son and daughter may ride in that coach post to the devil: but the godly man says, I want an eternal inheritance for my son; I want God's blessing for him; this is the poor man's prayer, while the poor deluded youth mocks him: or, supposing this is not the case, a person may burn with inward temptation; you have heard of the fiery darts, of the devil, and were you to feel them, I believe you would find them fiery darts indeed! and you have great reason to suspect your experience, your having any interest in the love of the Son of God at all, if you never found the fiery darts of the devil.

O, says one, I never felt the devil; I am sure thou mayst feel him now; thou art dadda's own child; thou art speaking the very language of the devil, and he is teaching thee to deny thy own father; therefore graceless child of the devil, you never felt the devil's fiery darts, it is because the devil is sure of thee; he has got thee into a damnable slumber; may the God of love wake thee before real damnation comes! The fiery darts of Satan are poisoned, and wherever they stick they fill the persons with tormenting pain like fire; this I mention, because there are some poor souls perhaps here tonight, whom the devil tells, thou hast committed the unpardonable sin; you are afraid to come to sacrament, you are afraid to go to prayer, because at these seasons the devil disturbs thee most, and tempts you to leave these seasons; and there are some go on thus burning a great while. My brethren the time would fail, and I shall draw this discourse to too great a length, and hinder you from your families, if I was to mention but a few more of those thousands that the believer burns with, the trials without, and what is still worse, their trials within.

Why, says one, it is very strange you talk thus tonight; I am sorry it is strange to any of you; sure you are not much acquainted with your bibles, and less with your hearts, if you know not this. Why, sure, say some, you make God a tyrant; no, but having made ourselves devils incarnate, we are now in a state of preparation, and these various trials are intended by the great God to train us up for heaven; and therefore, that you may not think I am drawing a picture without any life, give me leave to observe, that it is particularly remarkable, that though "the bush burned, it was not consumed": it was this struck Moses, he looked to see why the bush was not consumed. But the burning I have been here painting forth to you is not a consuming but a purifying fire; is not that enough to answer the shade that has been already drawn; it is true the bush burns, the Christian is persecuted, the Christian is oppressed, the Christian is burned with inward trials, he is perplexed at times, he is "cast down but" blessed be God, "he is not destroyed," he is not in despair.

Who is that, that says he has got into such an estate that nothing disturbs him? vain man! he discovers an ignorance of Christ; are you greater than the apostle Paul? some people think that the apostles had no trials; so they think, perhaps, of some ministers, that they are always on the mount, while, perhaps, they have been in the burning to get that sermon for them. We that are to speak for others, must expect to be tempted in all things like to our brethren, or we should be only poor whip syllabub preachers, and not rich men's hearts. But whether ministers or people burn, the great God, the angel of the everlasting covenant, spoke to Moses out of the bush; he did not stand at a distance from the bush, he did not speak to him so much as one yard or foot from the bush, but he spoke to him out of the bush; he said, Moses, Moses, my people shall burn in this bush to the end of time, but be not afraid, I will succour them; when they burn, I will burn too. There is a scripture vastly strong to this purpose, in which it is not said, "the good will of him that" was "in the bush," but "the good will of him that" dwelt "in the bush."

Amazing! I thought God dwelt in heaven; but as a poor woman who was once in darkness fourteen years, before she was brought out of it, said, God has two homes, one in heaven, the other in the lowest heart. He dwells in the bush, and I am sure if he did not, the devil and their own cursed hearts would burn the bush to ashes. How is it that it is not consumed? why, it is because God has declared it shall not be consumed; he has made an everlasting covenant, and I pity those that are not acquainted with an interest in God's covenant; and it would be better that people would pity them, than dispute with them: I really believe a disputing devil is one of the worst devils that can be brought into God's church, for he comes with his gown and book in his hand, and I should always suspect the devil when he comes in his gown and band, and this is the cause they agree and disagree. Some, who it is to be hoped are God's children, if you tell them that God has loved them with an everlasting love, they are afraid to suck it in, and especially if you pop out the word election, or that hard word predestination, they will be quite frightened; but talk to them another way, their dear hearts will rejoice.

God has said, "As the waters of Noah shall cease forever, so he will not forget the covenant of his peace: nothing shall pluck them out of his hand." Ah! say some, the apostle has said, "that neither things present, nor things to come, shall separate us from the love of Christ": but he has not said an evil heart shall not; I fancy that is one of the "present things." The bush is not consumed, because if the devil is in the bush, God is in the bush too; if the devil acts one way, the Lord, the Spirit, acts another to balance it, and the Spirit of God is engaged to train up the souls of his people; and God has determined the bush shall not be consumed; his Spirit stands near believers to support and guide, and make them more than conquerors: all that are given to Jesus Christ shall come, he will not lose one of them; this is food for the children of God; a bad mind will turn every thing to poison; and if it was not for this, that God had promised to keep them, my soul within these thirty years would have sunk a thousand times over.

Come then, O suffering saints, to you the word of this salvation is sent. I don't know who of you are the followers of the Lamb; may the Spirit of the living God point them out, may every one be enabled to say, I am the man. O, says one, I have been watching and very attentive tonight, but you have not mentioned my burnings; what do you think of my burning lusts? what do you think of my burning corruptions? what do you think of my burning pride? O, perhaps some of you will say, thank God, I have no pride at all; like the bishop of Cambray, as mentioned by Dr. Watts, who said, he had received many sins from his father Adam, but, thank God, he had no pride. Alas! alas! we are all as proud as the devil. Pray, what do you think of passion, that burns not only themselves but all around them? what do you think of enmity? what do you think of jealousy, is not this something that burns the bush? and there are some people that pride themselves, they have not got so much of the beast about them, they never got drunk, scorn to commit murder, and at the same time are full of enmity, of envy, malice, and pride, as the devil: the Lord God help such to see their condition.

Happy is it, Christ can dwell in the bush when we cannot dwell ourselves there; there are few Christians can live together, very few relations can live together under one roof; we can take that from other people that we can't bear from our own flesh and blood; and if God did not bear with us more than we bear with one another, we should all have been destroyed every day. Does the devil make you say, that you will give all up; I will go to the Tabernacle no more; I will lay on my couch and take my ease; Oh! if this is the case of any tonight, thus tempted by satan, may God rescue their souls. O poor dear soul, you never will have such sweet words from God as when you are in the bush; our suffering times will be our best times.

I know we had more comfort in Moorfields, on Kennington Common, and especially when the rotten eggs, the cats and dogs were thrown upon me, and my gown was filled with clods of dirt that I could scarce move it; I have had more comfort in this burning bush than when I have been in ease. I remember when I was preaching at Exeter, a stone came and made my forehead bleed, I found at that very time the word came with double power to a laborer that was gazing at me, who was wounded at the same time by another stone, I felt for the lad more than for myself, went to a friend, and the lad came to me, Sir, says he, the man gave me a wound, but Jesus healed me; I never had my bonds broke till I had my head broke. I appeal to you whether you were not better when it was colder than now, because your nerves were braced up; you have a day like a dog-day, now you are weak, and are obliged to fan yourselves: thus it is prosperity lulls the soul, and I fear Christians are spoiled by it.

Whatever your trails are, let this be your prayer, Lord, though the bush is burning, let it not be consumed. I think that is too low, let it be thus; Lord, when the bush is burning, let me not burn lower as the fire does, but let me burn higher and higher: I thank thee my God, for trouble; I thank thee, my God, for putting me into these afflictions one after another; I thought I could sing a requiem to myself, that I should have a little rest, but trouble came from that very quarter where I might reasonably expect the greatest comfort: I thank thee for knocking my hands off from the creature; Lord, I believe, help my unbelief; and thus you will go on blessing God to all eternity: by and by the bush shall be translated to the paradise of God; no burning bush in heaven, except the fire of love, wonder, and gratitude; no trials there; troubles are limited to this earth; above our enemies can't reach us.

Perhaps there are some of you here are saying, "burning bush, a bush burn't and not consumed!" I don't know what to make of this nonsense: come, come, go on, I am used to it, and I guess what are the thoughts of your hearts: I pray God, that every one of you here may be afraid of comfort, lest they should be tossed about by the devil. What is it I have said? how have I talked in such an unintelligible manner? why, say you, what do you mean by a burning bush? why, thou art the very man, how so? why, you are burning with the devil in your hearts; you are burning with foppery, with nonsense, with "the lust of the flesh," with "the lust of the eye, and pride of life"; and if you do not get out of this state as Lot said to his sons-in-law, e'r long you shall be burning in hell, and not consumed: the same angel of the covenant who spake to Moses out of the bush, he shall e'er long descend, surrounded with millions of the heavenly host, and sentence you to everlasting burnings.

O you frighten me! did you think I did not intend to frighten you? would to God I might frighten you enough! I believe it will be no harm for you to be frightened out of hell, to be frighted out of an unconverted state: O go and tell your companions that the madman said, that wicked men are as firebrands of hell: God pluck you as brands out of that burning. Blessed be God, that there is yet a day of grace: Oh! that this might prove "the accepted time"; Oh! that this might prove "the day of salvation"; Oh! angel of the everlasting covenant, come down; thou blessed, dear comforter, have mercy, mercy, mercy upon the unconverted, upon our unconverted friends, upon the unconverted part of this auditory; "speak, and it shall be done: command, O Lord, and it shall come to pass": turn the burning bushes of the devil into burning bushes of the Son of God: who knows but God may hear our prayer, who knows but God may hear this cry, "I have seen, I have seen the afflictions of my people: the cry of the children of Israel is come up to me, and I am come down to deliver them": God grant this may be his word to you under all your trouble; God grant he may be your comforter.

The Lord awaken you that are dead in sin, and though on the precipice of hell, God keep you from tumbling in: and you that are God's burning bushes, God help you stand to keep this coat of arms, to say when you go home, blessed be God, "the bush is burning but not consumed." Amen! even so, Lord Jesus. Amen!

REPENTANCE AND CONVERSION

"Repent ye therefore, and be converted, that your sins may be blotted out, when the times of refreshing shall come from the presence of the Lord" (Acts 3:19).

WHAT A PITY it is that modern preachers attend no more to the method those took who were first inspired by the Holy Ghost, in preaching Jesus Christ! The success they were honored with, gave a sanction

Reprinted from George Whitefield, *Eighteen Sermons*, rev. Andrew Gifford (Boston: n. p., 1820), pp. 77–92.

to their manner of preaching, and the divine authority of their discourses, and energy of their elocution, one would think, should have
more weight with those that are called to dispense the gospel, than all
modern schemes whatever. If this was the case, ministers would
then learn first to sow, and then to reap; they would endeavour to
plough up the fallow ground, and thereby prepare the people for God's
raining down blessings upon them.

Thus Peter preached when under a divine influence, as I mentioned
last Wednesday night: he charged the audience home, though many of
them were learned and high and great, with having been the murderers of the Son of God. No doubt but the charge entered deep into
their conscience, and that faithful monitor beginning to give them a
proper sense of themselves, the apostle lets them know that great as
their sin was, it was not unpardonable; that though they had been concerned in the horrid crime of murdering the Lord of Life, notwithstanding they had thereby incurred the penalty of eternal death, yet
there was a mercy for them, the way to which he points out in the text;
"Repent ye therefore," says he, "and be converted," and adds, "that
your sins may be blotted out." Though they are but few words, they are
weighty; a short sentence this, but sweet: may God make it a blessed
sweetness to every one of your hearts!

But must we preach conversion to a professing people? Some of you
perhaps are ready to say go to America; go among the savages and
preach repentance and conversion there; or, if you must be a field-
preacher, go to the highways and hedges; go to the colliers; go ramble
up and down, as you used to do, preach conversion to the drunkards:
would to God my commission might be renewed, that I might have
strength and spirit to take the advice!

Possibly others will say, do not preach it to us; pray who are you?
I answer, one sent to call you to repentance; and although I might,
yet I will not come so close to you at present, as to inquire in my
turn, who are you; yet permit me to pray, that while I am preaching
God's Spirit may find you out; and not only let you know who you are,
but what you are; and then you will not be easy with yourselves,
nor angry with a minister of Jesus Christ for preaching conversion
to your souls.

Repentance and conversion are nearly the same. The expression in
the text is complex, and seems to include both what goes before and
follows "turning to God": and if the Lord is pleased to honor me so far
tonight to be useful to sinners, as well as saints, I will endeavour to
shew you,

First, what it is not to be converted; secondly, what it is to be truly
converted: thirdly, offer some motives why you should repent and be
converted: and fourthly, answer some objections that have been made
against persons repenting and being converted, and yet at the same
time, if you come and examine them, they know not so much as spec-
ulatively what real conversion is; the general notion many have of it

is, a person's being a convert from the Church of Rome to the Church of England.

There is a particular office in the large prayer book, to be used when any one publicly renounces popery in the great congregation. When this is done, that prayer read, and the person said Amen to the collects upon the occasion, every body wishes him joy, and thanks God he is converted; whereas, if this is all, he is as much unconverted to God as ever; he has in words renounced popery, but never took leave of the sins of his heart. Well, after this he looks into the church, and does not like that white thing called a surplice; he looks, and thinks there are some rags of the whore of Babylon left still: now, says he, I will be converted; how? I will turn Dissenter: so after he is converted from the Church of Rome to the Church of England, he goes to the dissenting church: maybe, curiosity may bring him to the Methodists, those monstrous troublesome creatures, and, perhaps, he may then be converted a third time, like their preaching, like their singing; O dear, I must have a Tabernacle-ticket, I must have a Psalm-book, I will come as often as there is preaching, or at least as often as I can; and there he sits down, and becomes an outside converted Methodist, as demure as possible: this is going a prodigious way, and yet all this is conversion from one party only to another. If the minister gives a rub or two he will take miff perhaps, and be converted to some other persuasion, and all the while Jesus Christ is left unthought of; but this is conversion only from party to party, not real, and that which will bring a soul to heaven.

Possibly, a person may go further, and be converted from one set of principles to another; he may, for instance, be born an Arminian, which all men naturally are; and one reason why I think Calvinism right, is, because proud nature will not stoop to be saved by grace. You that are brought up in an orthodox belief, under an orthodox ministry, cannot easily make an allowance for thousands that have nothing ringing in their ears but Arminianism; you have sucked in orthodoxy with your mother's milk, and that makes so many sour and severe professors. I knew a rigid man that would beat Christianity into his wife; and so many beat people with their Bibles, that they are likely, by their bitter proceeding, to hinder them from attending to the means God has designed for conversion. What is this but being converted from one set of principles to another; and I may be very zealous for them, without being transformed by them into the image of God.

But some go further, they think they are converted because they are reformed: they say, "a reformed rake makes a good husband," but I think a renewed rake will make a better. Reformation is not renovation: I may have the outside of the platter washed; I may be turned from prophaneness to a regard for morality; and because I do not swear, nor go to the play as I used to do; have left off cards, and perhaps put on a plain dress; and so believe, or rather fancy, that I am converted; yet the old man remains unmortified, and the heart is unrenewed still. Comparing myself with what I once was, and looking on my companions with disdain, I may there stick faster in self, and get into a worse and more dangerous state than I was before.

If any of you think me too severe, remember you are the person I mean; for you think me so only because I touch your case. The drunkards and sabbath-breakers, cursers and swearers, say to us, you can never preach but you preach against us: as a good man once replied to a person, who complained against us ministers for this preaching; I will put you to a way, said he, that we shall never preach against you; how is that? why, leave off cursing and swearing, &c. Then your consciences will be clear, and the minister will look over your heads: happy they that are convinced of it!

You have not heard me, I hope, speak a word against reformation; you have not heard me speak a word against being converted from the Church of Rome; against being converted to the Church of England; or against being good: no; all these are right in their place; but all these conversions you may have, and yet never be truly converted at all. What is conversion then? I will not keep you longer in suspence, my brethren: man must be a new creature, and converted from his own righteousness to the righteousness of the Lord Jesus Christ; conviction will always precede spiritual conversion: and therefore the Protestant divines make this distinction, you may be convinced and not converted, but you cannot be converted without being convinced; and if we are truly converted we shall not only be turned and converted from sinful self, but we shall be converted from righteous self; that is the devil of devils: for righteous self can run and hide itself in its own doings, which is the reason self-righteous people are so angry with gospel preachers; there are no such enemies to the gospel as these: "there were Jews who trusted in themselves that they were righteous," that set all in an uproar, and raised the mob on the apostles.

Our Lord denounced dreadful woes against the self-righteous Pharisees; so ministers must cut and hack them, and not spare; but say wo, wo, wo to all those that will not submit to the righteousness of Jesus Christ! I could almost say this is the last stroke the Lord Jesus gave Paul. I mean in turning him to real Christianity; for having given him a blow as a persecutor and injurious, he then brought him out of himself by revealing his person and office as a Saviour. "I am Jesus." Hence says the apostle, "I count all things but loss—that I may win Christ, and be found in him; not having my own righteousness, which is of the law, but that which is through the faith of Christ; the righteousness which is of God by faith." You hear him not only speak of himself as injurious, as a blasphemer, but also as a Pharisee; and in vain we may talk of being converted till we are brought out of ourselves; to come as poor lost undone sinners, to the Lord Jesus Christ; to be washed in his blood; to be clothed in his glorious imputed righteousness: the consequence of this imputation, or application of a Mediator's righteousness to the soul, will be a conversion from sin to holiness. I am almost tempted to say, it is perverseness in people to preach against the doctrine of imputed righteousness, because they love holiness, and charge the Calvinists with being enemies to it: how can they be charged with being enemies to Sanctification, who so strenuously insists on its being the genuine fruit, and unquestionable proof of the imputation of the righteousness of Christ, and application of it by the Spirit of grace? They that are truly converted to Jesus, and are justified by faith in the Son of God, will take care to evidence their conversion, not only by the having grace implanted in their hearts, but by that grace diffusing itself through every faculty of the soul, and making an universal change in the whole man.

I am preaching from a Bible that saith, "He that is in Christ is a new creature, old things", not "will" be, but "are passed away, all things", not only "will", but "are become new." As a child when born has all the several parts of a man, it will have no more limbs than it has now, if it lives to fourscore years and ten; so when a person is converted to God, there are all the features of the new creature and growth, till he becomes a young man and a father in Christ; till he becomes ripe in grace, and God translates him to glory. Any thing short of this is but the shadow instead of the substance; and however persons may charge us with being enthusiasts, yet we need not be moved either to anger or sorrow, since Paul says, "I travel in birth till Christ be formed in your hearts."

The author of this conversion is the Holy Ghost: it is not their own free will; it is not moral suasion; nothing short of the influence of the Spirit of the living God can effect this change in our hearts; therefore we are said to "be born again, born of God, of the Spirit, not of water only, but of the Holy Ghost; that which is born of the flesh, is flesh, but that which is born of the Spirit is Spirit": and though there is and will be a contest between these two opposites, flesh and spirit, yet if we are truly converted, the spirit will get the ascendency; and though for a while nature and grace may struggle in the womb of a converted soul, like Jacob and Esau, yet the elder shall serve the younger, Jacob shall supplant and turn out Esau, or at least keep him under: God grant we may all thus prove that we are converted. This conversion, however it begins at home, will soon walk abroad; as the Virgin Mary was soon found out to be with child, so it will be soon found out whether Christ is formed in the heart. There will be new principles, new ways, new company, new works; there will be a thorough change in the heart and life; this is conversion: at first it begins with terror and legal sorrow, afterwards it leads to joyfulness; first we work for spiritual life, afterwards from it: first we are in bondage, afterwards we receive the Spirit of adoption to long and thirst for God, because he has been pleased to let us know that he will take us to heaven.

Conversion means a being turned from hell to heaven, from the world to God. We have not so much as asked a person to sell his all, to leave his shop, to lay any thing at our feet: when we talk of being converted from the world, we mean being converted from the love of it: the heart once touched with the magnet of divine love, ever after turns to the pole. I think it is said of a sun-flower, though I question whether it will always hold true, that it turns to the sun; I am sure it is true of the Redeemer's flower that grow in his garden, they not only look to the sun, but they find fresh life, warmth, and transforming influence from him who is their all in all. Here Christianity appears in its glory; here the work done is worthy the Son of God. To be converted only to a party, is that worth Christ's coming from heaven to earth for; that we might have a set of principles without having them affect the heart? For to be baptized when young, or as some to come out of the water at age, and turn out as bad as ever, is a plain proof of the necessity of being baptized by the Holy Ghost.

What say you to this change, my dear souls? Is it not God-like, is it not divine, is it not heaven brought down to the soul; have you felt it, have you experienced it? I begin to catechize you already, for I could spend a whole sermon in speaking of conversion: but I am afraid those that sit under the gospel have more need of heart than light: would to God we had as much warmth in our hearts, as light in our understandings! But if there be any of you here that are not yet converted, upon what grounds do you hope for conversion? Give me leave to say, that you ought to repent and be converted, for till then you never can, never will, never shall find true rest for your souls. What wrong notions have people got of conversion! They think it is a wretched thing, and dread being converted; not knowing what it is, they think it is a frightful thing. I knew one sometime ago, that came to some Methodists; dear, says the person, you are cheerful, I could be glad if I was a Methodist too, if there was a majority of them in the land: but God help us to go to heaven with the minority, if the majority will not follow. But my dear hearers, there is not a single soul of you all that are satisfied in your stations: is not the language of your hearts when apprentices, we think we shall do very well when journeymen; when journeymen, that we should do very well when masters: when single, that we shall do well when married; and to be sure you think you shall do well when you keep a carriage.

I have heard of one who began low; he first wanted a house, then, says he, I want two, then four, then six; and when he had them, he said, I think I want nothing else; yes, says his friend, you will soon want another thing, that is, a hearse and six to carry you to your grave; and that made him tremble. O if you are Christians, if the Lord loves you, he will put a thorn in your flesh. I have often thought of what a good man says in his Diary, the Lord put a thorn in my flesh. Among politicians, when they find a man ambitious, they say, kick him up, that he may fall and break his neck: so it is in every condition; there is not one of you fifty years old, but have had many changes: have not you found thorns even on the rose that smelt so sweet, and thorns perhaps that pricked you so closely, that you have forgot the scent of the rose by it? And what is all this for, but to teach you that happiness is only to be found in the Lord. If a soul is truly converted, there will be a battle, and an awful chasm that will never be filled up but with the love of God; and therefore when we say, Repent and be converted, it is no more than saying, repent and be happy. Indeed we shall never be completely happy till we get to heaven. O that every man could see the good of every thing of a sublunary nature drop off like leaves in autumn: God grant this may be known by every one of you.

If it is asked, why you should repent and be converted? I answer, because else you can never be happy hereafter. What do you think heaven is? Why, says the covetous man, I think it is a place full of gold; so you think to steal some of the gold do you? Others would like heaven very well if there was a good gaming-table in heaven; if there was card-playing in heaven. I have heard of a lady that was so fond of gaming, that tho' she had the pangs of death upon her, yet when in the midst of her fits, or just coming out of one, instead of asking after Jesus, where he was to be found, she asked, what is trumps? So the gamster will ask, where is the backgammon table? Where is the box? He will want to shake his ungodly hand in heaven; he will say, let us have a gaming-table in heaven, where, as he will find, he has lost the game; that God has damned him without an interest in Christ. "Can two walk together unless they are agreed?" If you die and do not love God here, if you cannot love praying to God here, and cannot watch one hour, suppose you were to be struck by death and be taken to heaven, there is no such language and amusement there, what would you do? Why, say you, these Methodists are presumptuous people; they can tell us whether we are to go to heaven or no. Good Mr. Rogers, a Welsh Boanerges, preaching in the mountains, said, Christ is heaven, if I worship God here, and do all to God, and for God, without any hopes of reward upon the earth. My dear brethren, the devils would never be troubled with such a wretch in hell, he would set all hell in an uproar; if a true Methodist was to go to hell, the devil would say, turn that Methodist out, he is come to torment us: therefore you must be converted if you will go to heaven. Dr. Scott says, if a natural man was to be put into heaven it would be such a hell to him, that he would be glad to go to hell for shelter: angels they hate,

God they hate; and as Adam was afraid to meet with God when he first fell from him, so his sons hate God and flee away.

I mention one thing more, which is, that you must be converted, or be damned, and that is plain English, but not plainer than my Master made use of, "He that believeth not, shall be damned." I did not speak that word strong enough that says, "He that believeth not shall be damned"; that is the language of our Lord; and it is said of one of the primitive preachers, that used to speak the word damned so that it struck all his auditory. We are afraid of speaking the word damned for fear of offending such and such a one; at the same time they despise the minister for not being honest to his master. Some have said, and stand to it, that hell is only a temporary punishment: Who told them so? A temporary punishment! Nothing but a guilty conscience. O go to Bedlam! Do ask a child of God what he feels when his Lord is absent? Ask the spouse what she feels when she cries, "Saw ye him whom my soul loveth?" Ask a child of God when he is using this plaintive language, "Why standest thou afar off, O Lord?" and he will tell you, it is hell to my soul to be but one moment without the presence of my beloved.

And if his absence for a quarter of an hour can scarce be borne by a child of God, what must that soul undergo that is commanded to depart from him forever? and yet these very words were said to those that thought they bid fair for heaven; to these Jesus says, "I know ye not." God grant you may never know the meaning of these words by awful experience! Now, what say you? I could make a hundred heads more, but I choose to make as few as possible, that you may remember them. I say, conversion makes you happy hereafter, and without it you are damned forever.

"Are these things so?" why then, my dear hearers, do you think there can be any objection raised against conversion, do you think there can be any argument raised against turning to God directly? Is there any person here that will give himself time to consider a moment that will not say, though you speak in a rough, incoherent manner, yet there is some truth in what you say; I believe men ought to be converted, but the common saying is, I don't care to be converted yet; we think it is time enough to be converted. Is not this acting like the cardinal, when told he was elected pope, and desired to come that night and have the honor of pope conferred on him; because it was pretty late said, it is not a work of darkness, I will put it off till the morning; before which they chose another pope, and he lost his triple crown. You may think to put it off till the morning, though before the morning you may be damned. Pray why will you not be converted now? If you was in prison, and a person would take you out, you would choose to be let out tonight before morning, that you might sleep the better; why will you not do that for your soul you would for your body?

Well, I would be converted, but I shall be laughed at: suppose you was to have it promised, you should have a ten thousand pound lottery ticket, but you must be laughed at all your life time; there is none but would say, give me ten thousand pounds, and call me Methodist as long as I live: so if you loved God and your souls, you would say, give me God and call me what you will. You are afraid of being laughed at and nicknamed, and skulk into this and that place, because it does not stink so much of Methodism as this. Put your cockades in your hats, and let the world see that you are not ashamed of God's badge: let the devil and his agents preach to you; they can proclaim their sin like Sodom; they are not ashamed of going to balls and assemblies, to parties of pleasure, and subscribing to horse races. Is the gospel the glory of the land, and are you ashamed of the gospel? What think you, if you had given a hundred pounds to learn such a trade, would you say, I shall never attain it! No, you will persevere, and by giving diligence make an excellent mechanic, an admirable tradesman; and do you think to go to heaven without some trouble? Do you think the leopard can change his spots, the Ethiopian put his skin entirely off? Can we have any thing to nourish our bodies without the labour of particular persons? And therefore we are commanded "to work out our salvation with fear and trembling." Remember our Redeemer "will not quench the smoking flax, nor break the bruised reed; he will gently lead those that are with young." We are like poor swimmers; some people will put one foot in and cry oh! and then another, but a good swimmer plunges in at once, and comes out braced up: would to God we could do so, plunge into God at once, and God will bear up our souls indeed.

But say you, all in good time, I do not choose to be converted yet; why, what age are you now? I will come down to a pretty moderate age; suppose you are fourteen: and do not you think it time to be converted? And yet there are a great many here, I dare say, twenty years old, and not converted. Some are of opinion, that most people that are converted, are so before thirty. There was a young man buried last night at Tottenham Court but seventeen, an early monument of free grace! Are you forty, or fifty, is not that time? Is it time for the poor prisoners to be converted that are to be hanged tomorrow morning? If it is time for them, it is time for you, for you may be dead before them. There was a poor woman, but two or three days ago, that was damning and cursing most shockingly, now she is a dead corpse, was taken suddenly, and died away. God grant that may not be the case with any of you; the only way to prevent it is, to be enabled to think that "now is an accepted time, that now is the day of salvation."

Let me look round, and what do you suppose I was thinking? Why, that it is a mercy we have not been in hell a thousand times. How many are there in hell that used to say, Lord convert me, but not now? One of the good old Puritans says, hell is paved with good intentions. Now can you blame me, can you blame the ministers of Christ if this is the case, can you blame us for calling after you, for spending and being spent for your souls? It is easy for you to come to hear the gospel, but you do not know what nights and days we have; what pangs we have in our hearts, and "how we travel in birth till Jesus Christ be formed in your souls," Men, brethren, and fathers, hearken, God help you, save, save, "save yourselves from an untoward generation."

Tonight somebody sits up with the prisoners; if they find any of them asleep or no sign of their being awake, they knock and call, and the keepers cry, awake! and I have heard that the present ordinary sits up with them all the night before their execution: therefore, don't be angry with me if I knock at your doors, and cry, poor sinners, awake! awake! and God help thee to take care thou dost not sleep in an unconverted state tonight. The court is just sitting, the executioner stands ready, and before tomorrow, long before tomorrow, Jesus may say of some of you, "Bind him hand and foot." The prisoners tomorrow will have their hands tied behind them, their thumb strings must be put on, and their fetters knocked off; they must be tied fast to the cart, the cap put over their faces, and the dreadful signal given: if you were their relations would not you weep? Don't be angry then with a poor minister for weeping over them that will not weep for themselves.

If you laugh at me, I know Jesus smiles. I cannot force a cry when I will; the Lord Jesus Christ be praised, "I am free from the blood of you all": if you are damned for want of conversion, remember you are not damned for want of warning. Thousands that have not the gospel preached to them, may say, Lord, we never heard what conversion is; but you are gospel-proof; and if there is any deeper place in hell than other, God will order a gospel despising Methodist to be put there. You will have dreadful torments; to whom so much is given, much will be required. How dreadful to have minister after minister, preacher after preacher, say, "Lord God, I preached, but they would not hear." Think of this, professors, and God make you possessors!

You that do possess a little, and are really converted, God convert you and me every hour in the day; for there is not a believer in the world, but has got something in him that he should be converted from; the pulling down of the old house, and building up the new one, will be a work till death. Do not think I am speaking to the unconverted only, but to you that are converted. God convert you from lying a bed in the morning; God convert you from your conformity to the world; God convert you from lukewarmness; God convert us from ten thousand things which our own hearts must say we want to be converted from; then you will have the Spirit of the living God. Do not get into a cursed Antinomian way of thinking, and say, I thank God, I have the root of the matter in me: I thank God, that I was converted twenty or thirty years ago; and once in Christ always in Christ; and though I can go to a public house and play at cards, or the like yet, I bless God, I am converted. Whether you were converted formerly or not, you are perverted now; and may God convert you all to close Christianity with God!

You that are old professors, don't draw young ones back from God, by saying, ah! You will come down from the mount by and by; you will not always be so hot; and instead of encouraging poor souls, you will pull them down, because you have left your first love: would you have Jesus Christ catch you napping, with your lamps untrimmed?

O ye servants of the most high God, if any of you are here tonight, though I am the chief of sinners, and the least of all saints, suffer the word of exhortation. I am sure I preach feelingly now; God knows I seldom sleep after three in the morning; I pray every morning, Lord, convert me, and make me more a new creature today. I know I want to be converted from a thousand things, and from ten thousand more: Lord God, confirm me; Lord God, revive his work.

You young people, I charge you to consider; God help you to repent and be converted, who woos and invites you. You middle aged people, O that you would repent and be converted. You old grey-headed people, Lord make you repent and be converted, that you may thereby prove that your sins are blotted out. O I could preach till I preached myself dead; I could be glad to preach myself dead, if God would convert you! O God bless his work on you, that you may blossom and bring forth fruits unto God. Amen and Amen.

WALKING WITH GOD

"And Enoch walked with God: and he was not; for God took him" (Genesis 5:24).

VARIOUS ARE THE PLEAS and arguments which men of corrupt minds frequently urge against yielding obedience to the just and holy commands of God. But, perhaps, one of the most common objections that

---

Reprinted with permission from *Select Sermons of George Whitefield,* [comp.] J. C. Ryle and R. Elliot (London: Banner of Truth Trust, 1958), pp. 98–109.

they make is this, that our Lord's commands are not practicable, because contrary to flesh and blood; and consequently, that he is "an hard master, reaping where he has not sown, and gathering where he has not strewed."

These we find were the sentiments entertained by that wicked and slothful servant mentioned in the twenty-fifth chapter of Matthew; and are undoubtedly the same with many which are maintained in the present wicked and adulterous generation. The Holy Ghost foreseeing this, hath taken care to inspire holy men of old, to record the examples of many holy men and women; who, even under the Old Testament dispensation, were enabled cheerfully to take Christ's yoke upon them, and counted his service perfect freedom. The large catalogue of saints, confessors, and martyrs, drawn up in the eleventh chapter to the Hebrews, abundantly evidences the truth of this observation. What a great cloud of witnesses have we there presented to our view? All eminent for their faith, but some shining with a greater degree of lustre than do others.

The proto-martyr Abel leads the van. And next to him we find Enoch mentioned, not only because he was next in order of time, but also on account of his exalted piety. He is spoken of in the words of the text in a very extraordinary manner. We have here a short but very full and glorious account, both of his behaviour in this world, and the triumphant manner of his entry into the next. The former is contained in these words, "And Enoch walked with God." The latter in these, "and he was not: for God took him." He was not; that is, he was not found, he was not taken away in the common manner, he did not see death; for God had translated him (Heb. 11:5). Who this Enoch was, does not appear so plainly. To me, he seems to have been a person of public character; I suppose, like Noah, a preacher of righteousness. And, if we may credit the apostle Jude, he was a flaming preacher. For he quotes one of his prophecies, wherein he saith, "Behold, the Lord cometh with ten thousands of his saints, to excute judgment upon all, and to convince all that are ungodly among them, of all their ungodly deeds which they have ungodly committed, and of all their hard speeches, which ungodly sinners have spoken against him." But whether a public or private person, he has a noble testimony given him in the lively oracles. The author of the epistle to the Hebrews saith, that before his translation he had this testimony, "that he pleased God": and his being translated, was a proof of it beyond all doubt. And I would observe, that it was wonderful wisdom in God to translate Enoch and Elijah under the Old Testament dispensation, that hereafter, when it should be asserted that the Lord Jesus was carried into heaven, it might not seem a thing altogether incredible to the Jews; since they themselves confessed that two of their own prophets had been translated several hundred years before. But it is not my design to detain you any longer, by enlarging, or making observations, on Enoch's short but comprehensive character: the thing I have in view being to give a discourse, as the Lord shall enable, upon a weighty and a very important subject; I mean, *walking with God*. "And Enoch walked with God." If so much as this can be truly said of you and me after our decease, we shall not have any reason to complain that we have lived in vain.

In handling my intended subject, I shall,

First, Endeavour to shew what is implied in these words, *walked with God.*

Secondly, I shall prescribe some means, upon the due observance of which, believers may keep up and maintain their *walk with God.* And,

Thirdly, Offer some motives to stir us up, if we never walked with God before, to come and walk with God now. The whole shall be closed with a word or two of application.

First, I am to shew what is implied in these words, "walked with God"; or, in other words, what we are to understand by *walking with God.*

And *First, Walking with God* implies, that the prevailing power of the enmity of a person's heart be taken away by the blessed Spirit of God. Perhaps it may seem a hard saying to some, but our own experience daily proves what the scriptures in many places assert, that the carnal mind, the mind of the unconverted natural man, nay, the mind of the regenerate, so far as any part of him remains unrenewed, is enmity, not only an enemy, but enmity itself, against God; so that it is not subject to the law of God, neither indeed can it be. Indeed, one may well wonder that any creature, especially that lovely creature man, made after his Maker's own image, should ever have any enmity, much less a prevailing enmity, against that very God in whom he lives, and moves, and hath his being. But alas! so it is. Out first parents contracted it when they fell from God by eating the forbidden fruit, and the bitter and malignant contagion of it hath descended to, and quite overspread, their whole posterity.

This enmity discovered itself in Adam's endeavouring to hide himself in the trees of the garden. When he heard the voice of the Lord God, instead of running with an open heart, saying Here am I; alas! he now wanted no communion with God; and still more discovered his lately contracted enmity, by the excuse he made to the Most High: "The woman (or, this woman) thou gavest to be with me, she gave me of the tree, and I did eat." By saying thus, he in effect lays all the fault upon God; as though he had said, If thou hadst not given me this woman, I had not sinned against thee, so thou mayest thank thyself for my transgression. In the same manner this enmity works in the hearts of Adam's children. They now and again find something rising

against God, and saying even unto God, What doest thou? "It scorns
any meaner competitor (says the learned Dr. Owen, in his excellent
treatise on indwelling sin) than God himself." Its command is like that
of the Assyrians in respect to Ahab—shoot only at the king. And it
strikes against every thing that has the appearance of real piety, as the
Assyrians shot at Jehoshaphat in his royal clothes. But the opposition
ceases when it finds that it is only an appearance, as the Assyrians left
off shooting at Jehoshaphat, when they perceived it was not Ahab
they were shooting at. This enmity discovered itself in accursed Cain;
he hated and slew his brother Abel, because Abel loved, and was peculiarly favoured by, his God. And this same enmity rules and prevails
in every man that is naturally engendered of the offspring of Adam.
Hence that averseness to prayer and holy duties which we find in
children, and very often in grown persons, who have notwithstanding
been blessed with a religious education. And all that open sin and
wickedness, which like a deluge has overflowed the world, are only so
many streams running from this dreadful contagious fountain; I mean
the enmity of man's desperately wicked and deceitful heart. He that
cannot set his seal to this, knows nothing yet, in a saving manner, of
the Holy Scriptures, or of the power of God. And all that do know this,
will readily acknowledge, that before a person can be said to walk with
God, the prevailing power of this heart-enmity must be destroyed: for
persons do not use to walk and keep company together, who entertain
an irreconcilable enmity and hatred against one another.

Observe me, I say, the prevailing power of this enmity must be taken
away; for the in-being of it will never be totally removed, till we bow
down our heads, and give up the ghost. The apostle Paul, no doubt,
speaks of himself, and that, too, not when he was a Pharisee, but a
real Christian; when he complains, "that when he would do good, evil
was present with him"; not having dominion over him, but opposing
and resisting his good intentions and actions, so that he could not do
the things which he would, in that perfection which the new man
desired. This is what he calls sin dwelling in him. "And this is that
Φρόνημα σαρκος, which (to use the words of the ninth article of our
church), some do expound the wisdom, some sensuality, some the
affectation, some the desire, of the flesh, which doth remain, yea, in
them that are regenerated." But as for its prevailing power, it is destroyed in every soul that is truly born of God, and gradually more and
more weakened as the believer grows in grace, and the Spirit of God
gains a greater and greater ascendancy in the heart.

But *Secondly,* Walking with God not only implies, that the prevailing power of the enmity of a man's heart be taken away, but also that a
person is actually reconciled to God the Father, in and through the all-
sufficient righteousness and atonement of his dear Son. "Can two talk
together (says Solomon), unless they are agreed?" Jesus is our peace

as well as our peace-maker. When we are justified by faith in Christ, then, but not till then, we have peace with God; and consequently cannot be said till then to walk with him, walking with a person being a sign and token that we are friends to that person, or at least, though we have been at variance, yet that now we are reconciled and become friends again. This is the great errand that gospel ministers are sent out upon. To us is committed the ministry of reconciliation; as ambassadors for God, we are to beseech sinners, in Christ's stead, to be reconciled unto God, and when they comply with the gracious invitation, and are actually by faith brought into a state of reconciliation with God, then, and not till then, may they be said so much as to begin to walk with God.

Further, *Thirdly,* Walking with God implies a settled abiding communion and fellowship with God, or what in scripture is called, "The Holy Ghost dwelling in us." This is what our Lord promised when he told his disciples that "the Holy Spirit should be in and with them"; not to be like a wayfaring man, to stay only for a night, but to reside and make his abode in their hearts. This, I am apt to believe, is what the apostle John would have us understand, when he talks of a person abiding in him, in Christ, and walking as he himself also walked." And this is what is particularly meant in the words of our text. "And Enoch walked with God," that is, he kept up and maintained a holy, settled, habitual, though undoubtedly not altogether uninterrupted communion and fellowship with God, in and through Christ Jesus. So that to sum up what has been said on this part of the first general head, *walking with God* consists especially in the fixed habitual bent of the will for God, in an habitual dependence upon his power and promise, in an habitual voluntary dedication of our all to his glory, in an habitual eyeing of his precept in all we do, and in an habitual complacence in his pleasure in all we suffer.

Fourthly, Walking with God implies our making progress or advances in the divine life. *Walking,* in the very first idea of the word, seems to suppose a progressive motion. A person that walks, though he move slowly, yet he goes forward, and does not continue in one place. And so it is with those that walk with God. They go on, as the Psalmist says, "from strength to strength;" or, in the language of the apostle Paul, "they pass from glory to glory, even by the Spirit of the Lord." Indeed, in one sense, the divine life admits of neither increase nor decrease. When a soul is born of God, to all intents and purposes he is a child of God; and though he should live to the age of Methuselah, yet he would then be only a child of God after all. But in another sense, the divine life admits of decays and additions. Hence it is, that we find the people of God charged with backslidings and losing their first love. And hence it is that we hear of babes, young men, and fathers in Christ. And upon this account it is that the apostle exhorts Timothy, "to let his progress be made known to all men." And what is here required of Timothy in particular, by St. Peter is enjoined on all Christians in general, "But grow in grace (says he), and in the knowledge of our Lord and Saviour Jesus Christ." For the new creature increases in spiritual stature; and though a person can but be a new creature, yet there are some that are more conformed to the divine image than others, and will after death be admitted to a greater degree of blessedness. For want of observing this distinction, even some gracious souls, that have better hearts than heads (as well as men of corrupt minds, reprobates concerning the faith), have unawares run into downright Antinomian principles, denying all growth of grace in a believer, or any marks of grace to be laid down in the scriptures of truth. From such principles, and more especially from practices naturally consequent on such principles, may the Lord of all lords deliver us!

From what then has been said, we may now know what is implied in the words, "walked with God," viz. Our having the prevailing enmity of our hearts taken away by the power of the Spirit of God; our being actually reconciled and united to him by faith in Jesus Christ; our having and keeping up a settled communion and fellowship with him; and our making a daily progress in this fellowship, so as to be conformed to the divine image more and more.

How this is done, or, in other words, by what means believers keep up and maintain their walk with God, comes to be considered under our second general head.

And, *First*, Believers keep up and maintain their walk with God by reading of his holy word. "Search the scriptures," says our blessed Lord, "for these are they that testify of me." And the royal Psalmist tells us "that God's word was a light unto his feet, and a lanthorn unto his paths"; and he makes it one property of a good man, "that his delight is in the law of the Lord, and that he exercises himself therein day and night." "Give thyself to reading" (says Paul to Timothy), "And this book of the law (says God to Joshua) shall not go out of thy mouth." For whatsoever was written aforetime was written for our learning. And the word of God is profitable for reproof, for correction, and for instruction in righteousness, and every was sufficient to make every true child of God thoroughly furnished unto every good work.

If we once get above our Bibles, and cease making the written word of God our sole rule both as to faith and practice, we shall soon lie open to all manner of delusion, and be in great danger of making shipwreck of faith and a good conscience. Our blessed Lord, though he had the Spirit of God without measure, yet always was governed by, and fought the devil with, "It is written." This the apostle calls the "sword of the Spirit." We may say of it, as David said of Goliath's sword, "None like this." The scriptures are called the lively oracles of God: not only because they are generally made use of to beget in us a new life, but also to keep up and increase it in the soul. The apostle Peter, in his second epistle, prefers it even to seeing Christ transfigured upon the mount. For after he had said, chapter 1:18, "This voice which came from heaven we heard, when we were with him in the holy mount"; he adds, "We have also a more sure word of prophecy; whereunto ye do well that ye take heed, as unto a light shining in a dark place, until the day dawn, and the day-star arise in your hearts": that is, till we shake off these bodies, and see Jesus face to face. Till then we must see and converse with him through the glass of his word. We must make his testimonies our counsellors, and daily, with Mary, sit at Jesus' feet, by faith hearing his word. We shall then by happy experience find, that they are spirit and life, meat indeed and drink indeed, to our souls.

Secondly, Believers keep up and maintain their walk with God by secret prayer. The spirit of grace is always accompanied with the spirit of supplication. It is the very breath of the new creature, the fan of the divine life, whereby the spark of holy fire, kindled in the soul by God, is not only kept in, but raised into a flame. A neglect of secret prayer has been frequently an inlet to many spiritual diseases, and has been attended with fatal consequences. Origen observed, "That the day he offered incense to an idol, he went out of his closet without making use of secret prayer." It is one of the most noble parts of the believer's spiritual armour. "Praying always," says the apostle, "with all manner of supplication." "Watch and pray," says our Lord, "that ye enter not into temptation." And he spake a parable, that his disciples should pray, and not faint. Not that our Lord would have us always upon our knees, or in our closets, to the neglect of our other relative duties. But he means, that our souls should be kept in a praying frame, so that we might be able to say, as a good man in Scotland once said to his friends on his death-bed, "Could these curtains, or could these walls speak, they would tell you what sweet communion I have had with my God here."

O prayer! prayer! It brings and keeps God and man together. It raises man up to God, and brings God down to man. If you would therefore, O believers, keep up your walk with God; pray, pray without ceasing. Be much in secret, set prayer. And when you are about the common business of life, be much in ejaculatory prayer, and send, from time to time, short letters post to heaven upon the wings of faith. They will reach the very heart of God, and return to you again loaded with spiritual blessings.

Thirdly, Holy and frequent meditation is another blessed means of keeping up a believer's walk with God. "Prayer, reading, temptation, and meditation," says Luther, "make a minister." And they also make and perfect a Christian. Meditation to the soul, is the same as digestion to the body. Holy David found it so, and therefore he was frequently employed in meditation, even in the night season. We read also of

Isaac's going out into the fields to meditate in the evening; or, as it is in the margin, to pray. For meditation is a kind of silent prayer, whereby the soul is frequently as it were carried out of itself to God, and in a degree made like unto those blessed spirits, who by a kind of immediate intuition always behold the face of our heavenly Father. None but those happy souls that have been accustomed to this divine employ, can tell what a blessed promoter of the divine life, meditation is. "Whilst I was musing," says David, "the fire kindled." And whilst the believer is musing on the works and word of God, especially that work of works, that wonder of wonders, that mystery of godliness, "God manifest in the flesh," the Lamb of God slain for the sins of the world, he frequently feels the fire of divine love kindle, so that he is obliged to speak with his tongue, and tell of the loving-kindness of the Lord to his soul. Be frequent therefore in meditation, all ye that desire to keep up and maintain a close and uniform walk with the most high God.

Fourthly, Believers keep up their walk with God, by watching and noting his providential dealings with them. If we believe the scriptures, we must believe what our Lord hath declared therein, "That the very hairs of his disciples' heads are all numbered; and that a sparrow does not fall to the ground (either to pick up a grain of corn, or when shot by a fowler), without the knowledge of our heavenly Father." Every cross has a call in it, and every particular dispensation of divine providence has some particular end to answer in those to whom it is sent. If it be of an afflictive nature, God does thereby say, "My son, keep thyself from idols": if prosperous, he does, as it were by a small still voice, say, "My son, give me thy heart." If believers, therefore, would keep up their walk with God, they must from time to time hear what the Lord has to say concerning them in the voice of his providence. Thus we find that Abraham's servant, when he went to fetch a wife for his master Isaac, eyed and watched the providence of God, and by that means found out the person that was designed for his master's wife. "For a little hint from providence," says pious Bishop Hall, "is enough for faith to feed upon." And as I believe it will be one part of our happiness in heaven, to take a view of, and look back upon, the various links of the golden chain which drew us there; so those that enjoy most of heaven below, I believe, will be the most minute in remarking God's various dealings with them, in respect to his providential dispensations here on earth.

Fifthly, In order to walk closely with God, his children must not only watch the motions of God's providence without them, but the motions also of his blessed Spirit in their hearts. "As many as are the sons of God, are led by the Spirit of God," and give up themselves to be guided by the Holy Ghost, as as little child gives its hand to be led by a nurse or parent. It is no doubt in this sense that we are to be converted, and become like little children. And though it is the quintessence of enthusiasm, to pretend to be guided by the Spirit without the written word; yet it is every Christian's bounden duty to be guided by the Spirit in conjunction with the written word of God. Watch, therefore, I pray you, O believers, the motions of God's blessed Spirit in your souls, and always try the suggestions or impressions that you may at any time feel, by the unerring rule of God's most holy word: and if they are not found to be agreeable to that, reject them as diabolical and delusive. By observing this caution, you will steer a middle course between the two dangerous extremes many of this generation are in danger of running into; I mean, *enthusiasm,* on the one hand, and *deism,* and *downright infidelity,* on the other.

Sixthly, They that would maintain a holy walk with God, must walk with him in ordinances as well as providences, &c. It is therefore recorded of Zachary and Elizabeth, that "they walked in all God's ordinances, as well as commandments, blameless." And all rightly informed Christians, will look upon ordinances, not as beggarly elements, but as so many conduit-pipes, whereby the infinitely condescending Jehovah conveys his grace to their souls. They will look upon them as children's bread, and as their highest privileges. Consequently they will be glad when they hear others say, "Come, let us go up to the house of the Lord." They will delight to visit the place where God's honour dwelleth, and be very eager to embrace all opportunities to shew forth the Lord Christ's death till he come.

Seventhly and *lastly,* If you would walk with God, you will associate and keep company with those that do walk with him. "My delight," says holy David, "is in them that do excel" in virtue. They were, in his sight, the excellent ones of the earth. And the primitive Christians, no doubt, kept up their vigour and first love, by continuing in fellowship one with another. The apostle Paul knew this full well, and therefore exhorts the Christians to see to it, that they did not forsake the assembling of themselves together. For how can one be warm alone? And has not the wisest of men told us, that, "As iron sharpeneth iron, so doth the countenance of a man his friend?" If we look, therefore, into church history, or make a just observation of our own times, I believe we shall find, that as the power of God prevails, Christian societies, and fellowship meetings prevail proportionably. And as one decays, the other has insensibly decayed and dwindled away at the same time. So necessary is it for those that would walk with God, and keep up the life of religion, to meet together as they have opportunity, in order to provoke one another to love and good works.

Proceed we now to the third general thing proposed: to offer some motives to excite all to come and walk with God.

And, *First,* walking with God is a very honourable thing. This generally is a prevailing motive to persons of all ranks, to stir them up to any important undertaking. O that it may have its due weight and influence with you in respect to the matter now before us! I suppose you would all think it a very high honour to be admitted into an earthly prince's privy council, to be trusted with his secrets, and to have his ear at all times and at all seasons. It seems Haman thought it so, when he boasted (Esther 5:11), that besides his being "advanced above the princes and servants of the king; yea, moreover, Esther the queen did let no man come in with the king unto the banquet that she had prepared, but myself; and tomorrow am I invited unto her also with the king." And when afterwards a question was put to this same Haman, "What shall be done unto the man whom the king delighteth to honour?" (Esther 6:6). He answered, verse 8, "Let the royal apparel be brought which the king useth to wear, and the horse that the king rideth upon, and the crown royal which is set upon his head; and let this apparel and horse be delivered to the hand of one of the king's most noble princes, that they may array the man withal whom the king delighteth to honour, and bring him on horseback through the street of the city and proclaim before him, Thus shall it be done to the man whom the king delighteth to honour." This was all then, it seems, that an ambitious Haman could ask, and the most valuable thing that he thought Ahasuerus, the greatest monarch upon earth, could give. But, alas, what is this honour in comparison of that which the meanest of those enjoy, that walk with God! Think ye it a small thing, sirs, to have the secret of the Lord of lords with you, and to be called the friends of God? and such honour have all God's saints. The secret of the Lord is with them that fear him: and "Henceforth (says the blessed Jesus) call I you no longer servants, but friends; for the servant knoweth not the will of his master." Whatever you may think of it, holy David was so sensible of the honour attending a walk with God, that he declares, "he had rather be a door-keeper in his house, than to dwell even in the tents of ungodliness." O that all were like-minded with him!

But, *Secondly*, As it is an honourable, so it is a pleasing thing, to walk with God. The wisest of men has told us, that "wisdom's ways are ways of pleasantness, and all her paths peace." And I remember pious Mr. Henry, when he was just about to expire, said to a friend, "You have heard many men's dying words, and these are mine: A life spent in communion with God, is the pleasantest life in the world."

I am sure I can set to my seal that this is true. Indeed, I have been listed under Jesus's banner only for a few years; but I have enjoyed more solid pleasure in one moment's communion with my God, than I should or could have enjoyed in the ways of sin, though I had continued to have gone on in them for thousands of years. And may I not appeal to all you that fear and walk with God, for the truth of this? Has not one day in the Lord's courts been better to you than a thousand? In keeping God's commandments, have you not found a present, and very great reward? Has not his word been sweeter to you than the honey or the honeycomb? O what have you felt, when, Jacob-like, you have been wrestling with your God? Has not Jesus often met you when meditating in the fields, and been made known to you over and over again in breaking of bread? Has not the Holy Ghost frequently shed the divine love abroad in your hearts abundantly, and filled you with joy unspeakable, even joy that is full of glory? I know you will answer all these questions in the affirmative, and freely acknowledge the yoke of Christ to be easy, and his burden light; or (to use the words of one of our collects), "His service is perfect freedom." And what need we then any further motive to excite us to walk with God?

But methinks I hear some among you say, "How can these things be? For, if walking with God, as you say, is such an honourable and pleasant thing, whence is it that the name of the people of this way is cast out as evil, and every where spoken against? How comes it to pass that they are frequently afflicted, tempted, destitute, and tormented? Is this the honour, this the pleasure, that you speak of?" I answer, Yes. Stop a while; be not over hasty. Judge not according to appearance, but judge righteous judgment, and all will be well. It is true, we acknowledge the "people of this way," as you, and Paul before you, when a persecutor, called them, have their names cast out as evil, and are a sect every where spoken against. But by whom? Even by the enemies of the most high God. And do you think it a disgrace to be spoken evil of by them? Blessed be God, we have not so learned Christ. Our royal Master has pronounced those "blessed, who are persecuted, and have all manner of evil spoken against them falsely." He has commanded them "to rejoice and be exceeding glad," for it is the privilege of their discipleship, and that their reward will be great in heaven. He himself was thus treated. And can there be a greater honour put upon a creature, than to be conformed to the ever-blessed Son of God? And further, it is equally true that the people of this way are frequently afflicted, tempted, destitute, and tormented.

But what of all this? Does this destroy the pleasure of walking with God? No, in no wise; for those that walk with God are enabled, through Christ strengthening them, to joy even in tribulation, and to rejoice when they fall into divers temptations. And I believe I may appeal to the experience of all true and close walkers with God, whether or not their suffering times have not frequently been their sweetest times, and that they enjoyed most of God when most cast out and despised by men? This we find was the case of Christ's primitive servants, when threatened by the Jewish sanhedrim, and commanded to preach no more in the name of Jesus; they rejoiced that they were accounted worthy to suffer shame for the sake of Jesus. Paul and Silas sang praises even in a dungeon; and the face of Stephen, that glorious proto-martyr of the Christian church, shone like the face of an angel.

And Jesus is the same now as he was then, and takes care so to sweeten sufferings and afflictions with his love, that his disciples find, by happy experience, that as afflictions abound, consolations do much more abound. And therefore these objections, instead of destroying, do only enforce the motives before urged, to excite you to walk with God.

But supposing the objections were just, and walkers with God were as despicable and unhappy as you would represent them to be; yet I have a third motive to offer, which if weighed in the balance of the sanctuary, will over-weigh all objections, viz. That there is a heaven at the end of this walk. For, to use the words of pious bishop Beveridge, "Though the way be narrow, yet it is not long: and though the gate be strait, yet it opens into everlasting life." Enoch found it so. He walked with God on earth, and God took him to sit down with him for ever in the kingdom of heaven. Not that we are to expect to be taken away as he was: no, I suppose we shall all die the common death of all men. But after death, the spirits of those who have walked with God shall return to God that gave them; and at the morning of the resurrection, soul and body shall be for ever with the Lord; their bodies shall be fashioned like unto Christ's glorious body, and their souls filled with all the fullness of God. They shall sit on thrones; they shall judge angels. They shall be enabled to sustain an exceeding and eternal weight of glory, even that glory which Jesus Christ enjoyed with the Father before the world began. "*O gloriam quantam et qualem,*" said the learned and pious Arndt, just before he bowed down his head, and gave up the ghost. The very thought of it is enough to make us "wish to leap our seventy years," as good Dr. Watts expresses himself, and to make us break out into the earnest language of the royal Psalmist, "My soul is athirst for God, yea, for the living God. When shall I come to appear in the presence of my God?" I wonder not that a sense of this, when under a more than ordinary irradiation and influx of divine life and love, causes some persons to faint away, and even for a time lose the power of their senses. A less sight than this, even the sight of Solomon's glory, made Sheba's queen astonished; and a still lesser sight than that, even a sight of Joseph's waggons, made holy Jacob to faint, and for a while, as it were, die away. Daniel, when admitted to a distant view of this excellent glory, fell down at the feet of the angel as one dead. And if a distant view of this glory be so excellent, what must the actual possession of it be? If the first fruits are so glorious, how infinitely must the harvest exceed in glory?

And now, what shall I, or, indeed, what can I well say more to excite you, even you that are yet strangers to Christ, to come and walk with God? If you love honour, pleasure, and a crown of glory, come, seek it where alone it can be found. Come, put ye on the Lord Jesus. Come, haste ye away and walk with God, and make no longer provision for the flesh, to fulfil the lust thereof. Stop, stop, O sinner! turn ye, turn ye, O ye unconverted men, for the end of that way you are now walking in, however right it may seem in your blinded eyes, will be death, even eternal destruction both of body and soul. Make no longer tarrying, I say: at your peril I charge you, step not one step further on in your present walk. For how knowest thou, O man, but the next step thou takest may be into hell? Death may seize thee, judgment find thee, and then the great gulf will be fixed between thee and endless glory for ever and ever. O think of these things, all ye that are unwilling to walk with God. Lay them to heart. Shew yourselves men, and in the strength of Jesus say, Farewell, lust of the flesh, I will no more walk with thee! farewell, lust of the eye, and pride of life! Farewell, carnal acquaintance and enemies of the cross, I will no more walk and be intimate with you! Welcome Jesus, welcome thy word, welcome thy ordinances, welcome thy Spirit, welcome thy people, I will henceforth walk with you.

O that there may be in you such a mind! God will set his almighty fiat to it, and seal it with the broad seal of heaven, even the signet of his holy Spirit. Yes, he will, though you have been walking with, and following after, the devices and desires of your desperately wicked hearts ever since you have been born. "I, the high and lofty One," says the great Jehovah, "that inhabiteth eternity, will dwell with the humble and contrite heart, even with the man that trembleth at my word." The blood, even the precious blood of Jesus Christ, if you come to the Father in and through him, shall cleanse you from all sin.

But the text leads me to speak to you that are saints as well as to you that are open and unconverted sinners. I need not tell you, that walking with God is not only honourable, but pleasant and profitable also; for ye know it by happy experience, and will find it more and more so every day. Only give me leave to stir up your pure minds by way of remembrance, and to beseech you by the mercies of God in Christ Jesus, to take heed to yourselves, and walk closer with your God than you have in days past: for the nearer you walk with God, the more you will enjoy of him whose presence is life, and be the better prepared for being placed at his right hand, where are pleasures for evermore. O do not follow Jesus afar off! O be not so formal, so dead and stupid, in your attendance on holy ordinances! Do not so shamefully forsake the assembling yourselves together, or be so niggardly or indifferent about the things of God. Remember what Jesus says of the church of Laodicea, "Because thou art neither hot nor cold, I will spew thee out of my mouth." Think of the love of Jesus, and let that love constrain you to keep near unto him; and though you die for him, do not deny him, do not keep at a distance from him in any wise.

One word to my brethren in the ministry that are here present, and I have done. You see, my brethren, my heart is full; I could almost say it is too big to speak, and yet too big to be silent, without dropping a word to you. For does not the text speak in a particular manner to those who have the honour of being styled the ambassadors of Christ, and stewards of the mysteries of God. I observed at the beginning of this discourse, that Enoch in all probability was a public person, and a flaming preacher. Though he be dead, does he not yet speak to us, to quicken our zeal, and make us more active in the service of our glorious and ever-blessed Master? How did Enoch preach! How did Enoch walk with God, though he lived in a wicked and adulterous generation! Let us then follow him, as he followed Jesus Christ, and ere long, where he is there shall we be also. He is now entered into his rest: yet a little while and we shall enter into ours, and that too much sooner than he did. He sojourned here below three hundred years; but blessed be God, the days of man are now shortened, and in a few days our walk will be over. The Judge is before the door: he that cometh will come, and will not tarry: his reward is with him. And we shall all (if we are zealous for the Lord of hosts) ere long shine as the stars in the firmament, in the kingdom of our heavenly Father, for ever and ever. To Him, the blessed Jesus, and eternal Spirit, be all honour and glory, now, and to all eternity. *Amen*, and *Amen*.

SOUL PROSPERITY

"Beloved, I wish above all things that thou mayest prosper and be in health, even as thy soul prospereth" (3 John 2).

WHAT A HORRID BLUNDER has one of the famous, or rather infamous, deistical writers made, when he says that the gospel cannot be of God, because there is no such thing as friendship mentioned in it. Surely if he ever read the gospel, "having eyes he saw not, having ears he heard not": but I believe the chief reason is, his heart being waxen gross, he could not understand; for this is so far from being the case, that the world never yet saw such a specimen of steady and disinterested

Reprinted from George Whitefield, *Eighteen Sermons*, rev. Andrew Gifford (Boston: n. p., 1820), pp. 44–57.

friendship, as was displayed in the life, example, and conduct of Jesus Christ of Nazareth.

John, the writer of this epistle, had the honor of leaning on his bosom, and of being called, by way of emphasis, "the disciple whom Jesus loved"; and that very disciple, which is very remarkable concerning him, though he was one of those whom the Lord himself named Sons of Thunder (Mark 4:17), and was so suddenly, as bishop Hall observes, turned into a son of lightning, that he would have called down fire from heaven to consume his master's enemies: consequently, though he was of a natural fiery temper, yet the change in his heart was so remarkable, that if a judgment may be formed by his writings, he seems as full of love, if not fuller, than any of his fellow apostles. He learned pity and benevolence of the father of mercies; and, to show how christian friendship is to be cultivated, he not only wrote letters to churches in general, even to those he never saw in the flesh, but private letters to particular saints, friends to whom he was attached, and wealthy rich friends, whom God had, by his Spirit, raised up to be helpers of the distressed. Happy would it be for us, if we could all learn this one rule, never to write a letter without something of Jesus Christ in it; for, as Mr. Henry observes, if we are to answer for idle words, much more for idle letters; and if God has given us our pens, especially if he has given us "the pen of a ready writer," it will be happy if we can improve our literary correspondence for his glory and one another's good. But what an unfashionable style if compared to our modern ones, is that of the apostle to Gaius. The superscription "from the elder to the well-beloved Gaius whom I love in the truth"; there is fine language for you! Many who call themselves Christ's disciples, would be ashamed to write so now. "I send this, and that, and the other; I send my compliments." Observe what he styles himself, not as the pope; but he styles himself the elder. A judicious expositor is of opinion, that all the other apostles were dead, and only poor John left behind. I remember a remark of his, "the taller we grow, the lower we shall stoop." The apostle puts himself upon a level with the common elders of a church that he might not seem to take stare upon him, not to rule as a lion, but with a rod of love: "the elder to the well-beloved Gaius, whom I love in the truth." This Gaius seems to be in our modern language, what we call a gentleman, particularly remarkable for his hospitality, "Gaius mine host"; and this Gaius was well-beloved, not only beloved, but well-beloved; that is, one whom I greatly esteem and am fond of; but then he shows likewise upon what this fondness is founded, "whom I love in the truth." There are a great many people in writing say, "dear sir" or "good sir," and subscribe "your humble servant, sir"; and not one word of truth either in the beginning or end; but John and Gaius's love was in truth, not only in words, "but in deed and in truth"; as if he had said, my heart goes along with my hand while I am writing, and it gives me pleasure in such a correspondence as this, or "whom I love for the truth's sake," that is, whom I love for being particularly attached to the truth; and then our friendship has a proper foundation, when the Love of God and the Spirit of the Lord Jesus, is the basis and bond of it. One would think this was enough now; the epistles originally were not divided into verses as now, that people may the better find out particular places, though perhaps not altogether so properly as they might. The apostle's saying "beloved" is not needless tautology, but proves the strength of his affection; "I wish that thou mayest prosper and be in health, even as thy soul prospereth."

Gaius it seems at this time felt a weak constitution, or a bad habit of body; this may show, that the most useful persons, the choicest favourites of heaven, must not expect to be without the common infirmities of the human frame; so far from this that it is often found that a thousand useful Christians have weakly constitutions. That great and sweet singer of Israel, Dr. Watts, I remember about two and thirty years ago told me that he had got no sleep for three months, but what was procured by the most exquisite art of the most eminent physicians; and my dear hearers, none but those that have such habits of body can sympathize with those that are under them. When we are in high spirits we think people might do if they would, but when brought down ourselves we cannot: but notwithstanding his body was in this condition, his soul prospered so eminently, so very eminently, that the apostle could not think it a greater mercy, or the church a greater blessing, than that this bodily health might be as vigorous as the health of his soul. I remember the great colonel Gardiner, who had the honor of being killed in his country's cause, closes one of his last letters to me, with wishing I might enjoy a thriving soul in a healthy body; but this is peculiar to the followers of Jesus, they find the soul prospers most when the body is worst; and observe, he wishes him a prospering body above all things, that he might have joy and health with a prosperous soul; for if we have a good heart, and good health at the same time, and our hearts are alive to God, we go on with a fresh gale.

I observe, that the soul of man in general must be made a partaker of a divine life before it can be said to prosper at all. The words of our text are particularly applicable to a renewed heart, to one that is really alive to God. When a tree is dead we don't so much as expect leaves from it, nor to see any beauty at all in a plant or flower that we know is absolutely dead; and therefore the foundation of the apostle's wish lies here, that the soul of Gaius, and consequently the souls of all true believers, have life communicated to them from the Spirit of the living God. Such a life may God of his infinite mercy impart to each of us! and I think if I am not mistaken, and I believe I may venture to say that I am not, that where the divine life is implanted by the Spirit of the living God, that life admits of decrease and increase, admits of dreadful decays, and also of some blessed revivings. The rays of the divine life being once implanted, it will grow up to eternal life; the new creation is just like the old when God said "let there be light, and there was light," which never ceased since the universe was made, and the favorite creature man was born. Upon a survey of his own works, God pronounced "every thing good, and entered into his rest"; so it will be with all those who are made partakers of the divine nature. "The water that I shall give him, shall be a well of water springing up into everlasting life."

My brethren, from our first coming into the world, till our passing out of it to "the spirits of just men made perfect," all the Lord's Children have found, some more, and others less, that they have had dreadful as well as blessed times, and all has been overruled to bring them nearer to God: but I believe, I am sure, I speak to some this night, that if it was put to their choice, had rather know that their souls prospered, than to have ten thousand pounds left them: and it is supposed that we may not only know it ourselves, but that others may know it, "that their profiting," as Paul says, "may appear to all." Because John says, "I wish above all things, that thy body may be in health, as thy soul prospers." O may all that converse with us see it in us! We may frequently sit under the gospel, but if we do not take a great deal of care, however orthodox we are, we shall fall into practical Antinomianism, and be contented that we were converted twenty or thirty years ago, and learn, as some Antinomians, "to live by faith." Thank God, say some, we met with God so many months ago, but are not at all solicitous whether they met with him any more; and there is not a single individual here that is savingly acquainted with Jesus Christ, but wishes his soul prospered more than his body.

The great question is, how shall I know that my soul prospers? I have been told that there is such a thing as knowing this, and that I can be conscious of it myself, and others too. It may not be misspending an hour, to lay down some marks whereby we may know whether our souls prosper or no. If there be any of you of an Antinomian turn of mind (I don't know there are any of you), I don't know but you will be of the same mind of the man that came to me in Leadenhall twenty-five years ago: Sir, says he, you preached upon the marks of the birth. Marks, says I, yes, sir: O thank God, says he, I am above marks, I don't mind marks at all: and you may be assured persons are upon the brink of Antinomianism, that say away with your legal preaching. I wonder they don't say as they go along the streets, away with your dials, away with your dials, we don't want marks, we know what it is o'clock without any. If the marks upon the soul of a believer are like the sundial, there are marks to prove that we are upon the right foundation; if the sun does not shine on the sundial, there is no knowing what o'clock it is: but let it shine, and instantaneously you know the time of the day; this is not known when it is cloudy; and who dare to say but that a child of God, for want of the sun of righteousness shining upon his heart, may write bitter things against himself.

A good man may have the vapours, as one Mr. Brown had, that wrote a book of good hymns, who was so vapourish, that no body could make him believe he had a soul at all. Let the sun shine, the believer can see whether the sun is in the meridian at the sixth, ninth, or twelfth hour. O that there might be great searching of heart. I have been looking up to God for direction; I hope the preaching of this may be to awaken some, to call back some backsliders, to awaken some sinners that don't care whether their souls prosper or no. I don't mean the Tabernacle comers, or the Foundery comers, or the church, or dissenters, but I speak to all of you, of whatever denomination you are; God of his infinite mercy give you his Spirit. You that are believers, come, let us have that common name among us all; if we have got it we go off well. If you want to know whether your souls prosper, that is, whether they are healthy; you know what a person means when he wishes your body to prosper; let me ask you how it is between you and God, with respect to a secret prayer? Good Mr. Bunyan says, if we are prayerless, we are Christless. None of God's people, says he, come into the world still-born. Good Mr. Birket (whose commentary has gone through five or six-and-twenty editions; and yet I think if he was now alive, and to preach once or twice a day, they would cry, Away with his commentary, and preaching and all) speaks to the same purpose.

"Come into the world still-born!" what language is that in a preacher's mouth? but it will do for those that like to use marks and signs. "I will pour out a Spirit of grace and supplication," says the Lord; and I will venture to say, if the Spirit of grace resides in the heart, the Spirit of supplication will not be wanting. Persons under their first love dare not go without God; they go to God, not as the formalist does, not for fear of going to hell, or being damned. It is a mercy any thing drives to prayer; and a person under the spirit of bondage, that has been just brought to the liberty of the sons of God, goes freely to his heavenly father, under the discoveries and constraints of divine love. Come I will appeal to yourselves; did not you, like a dear, fond mother, if the child, the beloved child, made but the least noise in the world, O, says the mother, the dear child cries, I must go and hush it: so time was, when many hearkened to the call of God, and could no more keep from the presence of God in secret, than a fond mother from the presence of her dear child. No if your souls do prosper, this connection between you and God will be kept up; I do not say that you will always have the same fervour as when you first set out; I do not say your will always be carried up into the third heavens; the animal spirits possibly will not admit of such solace; but you should inquire with yourselves, whether you would be easy to be out of God's company? Steal from behind your counter, and go and converse with God. Sir Thomas Abney, who was observable for keeping up constant prayer in his family, being asked how he kept up prayer that night he was sworn in Lord-Mayor? Very well, says he, I got the company into my room, and entertained them, and when the time came, I told them, I must leave them a little, while I went and prayed with my family, and returned again. God grant we may have many such Lord-Mayors.

If our souls prosper the same principle will reign in us, and make us conscientiously attend on the means of grace. It is a most dreadful mark of an enthusiastic turn of mind, when persons think they are so high in grace, that they thank God they have no need of ordinances. Our being the children of God is so far from being the cause of our wanting no ordinances, that, properly speaking, the ordinances are intended for the nourishing of the children of God; not only for the awakening the soul at first, but for the feeding of the soul afterwards. If the same nourishment the child receives before, feeds it after it is born; and as the manna never failed, but the children of Israel partook of it daily while in the wilderness, till they came to Canaan, so we shall want our daily bread, we shall want the God of grace and mercy to convey his divine life into our hearts, till we get into the heavenly Canaan. There faith will be turned into vision, and then we shall not want ordinances; and let people say what they will, if our souls prosper we shall be glad of ordinances, we shall love the place where God dwells; we shall not say, "such a one preaches and I will not go," but if we are among them we shall be glad of a good plain country dish, as well as a fine garnished desert; and if our souls prosper, we shall be fond of the messengers as well as the message; we shall admire as much to hear a good ram's-horn, such as blowed down the walls of Jericho, as a fine silver trumpet. So in all the ordinances of the Lord, and that of the Lord's-supper for example; if the soul does not attend thereon, it is an evidence that it does not prosper. It is a wonder if that soul has not done something to make it afraid to meet God at his table. "Adam where art thou?" says the eternal Logos to his fallen creature; and every time we miss, whether we think of it or no, the Redeemer puts it down; but if our souls prosper, how shall we run to the table of the Lord, and be glad to come often to the commemoration of his death.

I will venture to affirm farther, that if your souls prosper, you will grow downwards. What is that; why you will grow in the knowledge of yourselves. I heard, when I was at Lisbon, that some people there began at the top of the house first. It is odd kind of preaching that will do for the Papists, resting merely in externals. The knowledge of ourselves is the first thing God implants. "Lord, let me know myself," was a prayer that one of the Fathers put up for sixteen years together;

and if you have high thoughts of yourselves, you may know you are light-headed, you forget what poor silly creatures you are. As our souls prosper we shall be more and more sensible, not only of the outside, but of the inside; we first battle with the outward man, but as we advance in the divine life, we have nearer views of the chambers of imagery that are in our hearts; and one day after another we shall find more and more abomination there, and consequently we shall see more of the glory of Jesus Christ, the wonders of that Immanuel, who daily delivers us from this body of sin and death; and I mention this; because there is nothing more common, especially with young Christians. I used formerly to have at least a hundred or two hundred in a day, who would come and say, O dear, I am so and so, I met with God; ah! that is quite well: a week after they would come and say, O, sir it is all delusion, there was nothing in it; what is the matter? O never was such a wretch as I am, I never thought I had such a wicked heart. Oh! God cannot love me; now, sir, all my fervour, and all that I felt is gone; and what then? does a tree never grow but when it grows upward? some trees I fancy grow downward; and the deeper you grow in the knowledge of yourself, the deeper you grow in the knowledge of God and his grace, that discovers the corruptions of your hearts.

Do not you find that aged men look back upon some former states. I know some people can't look back to see how many sins they have been guilty of, but if grace helps us to a sight of our inherent corruptions, it will make us weary of it, and lead us to the blood of Christ to cleanse us from it; consequently, if your souls prosper, the more you will fall in love with the glorious Redeemer, and with his righteousness. I never knew a person in my life that diligently used the word, and other means, but as they improved in grace, saw more and more of the necessity of depending upon a better righteousness than their own. Generally when we first set out, we have got better hearts than heads; but if we grow in the divine life, our heads will grow as well as our hearts, and the Spirit of God leads out of abominable self, and causes us to flee more and more to that glorious and complete righteousness that Jesus Christ wrought out.

The more your souls prosper, the more you will see of the freeness and distinguishing nature of God's grace, that all is of grace. We are all naturally free-willers, and generally young ones say, O we have found the Messiah, of whom Moses and the Prophets spoke; which is right, except that word *we* have found; for the believer a little after learns, that the *Messiah* had found him. I mention this, because we ought not to make persons offenders for a word; we should bear with young Christians, and not knock a young child's brains out because he cannot speak in blank verse.

Let it not be forgotten also, that the more your souls prosper, the more you will get above the world. You cannot think that I mean you should be negligent about the things of this life. Nothing tries my temper more, than to see any about me idle; an idle person tempts the devil to tempt him. In the state of paradise Adam and Eve were to dress the garden, and not to be idle there; after the fall they were to till the ground; but if anybody says that the Methodists think to be idle, they injure them. We tell people to rise and be at their work early and late, that they may redeem time to attend the word. If all that speak against the Methodists were as diligent, it would be better for their wives and families. What, do you think a true Methodist will be idle? No, he will be busy with his hands, he knows time is precious, and therefore he will work hard that he may have to give to them that need, and at the same time he will live above the world; and you know the earth is under your feet, so is the world. When he goes to sleep he will say, I care not whether I awake more.

I can look back, and tell you of hundreds and hundreds that once seemed alive to God, and have been drawn away with a little filthy, nasty dirt. How many places are there empty here, that have been filled with persons that once were zealous in their attendance? As a person the other day, to whose having a place it was objected, that he was a Methodist; no, says he, I have not been a Methodist these two years. I do not, for my part, wish people joy when they get money; only take care it does not get into, and put your eyes out; if your money increases, let your zeal for good works increase. Perhaps some stranger will say, I thought you were against good works. I tell you the truth, I am against good works, don't run away before I have finished my sentence; we are against good works being put in the room of Christ, as the ground of our acceptance; but we look upon it, if we have a right faith, our faith will work by love.

Ever since I was a boy, I remember to have heard a story of a poor indigent beggar, who asked a clergyman to give him his alms, which being refused, he said, will you please, sir, to give me your blessing; says he, God bless you; O, replied the beggar, you would not give me that if it was worth any thing. There are many who will talk very friendly to you, but if they suppose you are come for any thing, they will run away as from a pick-pocket; whereas, if our souls prospered, we should "count it more blessed to give than to receive." When we rise from our beds this would be our question to ourselves, what can I do for God today? what can I do for the poor? have I two, or five, or ten talents? God help me to do for the poor as much as if I knew I was to live only this day.

In a word, if your souls prosper, my dear hearers, you will grow in love. There are some good souls, but very narrow souls; they are so afraid of loving people that differ from them, that it makes me uneasy to see it. Party spirits creep in among Christians, and whereas it was formerly said, "see how these Christians love one another!" how it it may be said, "see how these Christians hate one another!" I declare from the bottom of my heart, that I am more and more convinced that the principles I have preached are the word of God. Pray what do you do at Change; is there such a thing as a Presbyterian, or Independent, or Church-walk there? Are there any chambers there for the Presbyterians, and Independents, and Churchmen to deal in? People may boast of their wildfire-zeal for God, till they can't bear the sight of a person that differs from them. The apostle commends Gaius for his catholic love, for his love to strangers. That was a glorious saying of a good woman in Scotland, "Come in," says she, "ye blessed of the Lord"; I have a house that will hold a hundred, and a heart that will hold ten thousand. God give us such a heart; "he that dwelleth in love, dwelleth in God." I could mention twenty marks, and so go on wire-drawing till nine or ten o'clock; but it is best to deal with our souls as with our bodies, to eat but little at a time. It is so with preaching; though I don't proceed any farther in my discourse, God bless what has been said.

But is there a child of God here that can go away without a drooping heart? I don't speak that you may think me humble; I love sincerity, inward, and outward, and hate guile. When I think what God has done for me, how often he has pruned me, and dug and dung'd about me, and when I think how little I have done for God, it makes me weep if possible tears of blood; it makes me cry, "O my leanness, my leanness," as I expressed myself with my friend today. This makes me long if my strength of body would permit, to begin to be in earnest for my Lord. What say you, my dear friends, have all of you got the same temper? have you made the progress you ought to have done!

O London! London! highly favoured London! what would some people give for thy privileges? what would the people I was called to preach to but this day se'ennight? A good, a right honourable lady, about three-and-twenty miles off, has brought the gospel there. The people that I preached to longed and thirsted after the same message; they said, they thought they never heard the truth before. You have the manna poured out round the camp, and I am afraid you are calling it "light bread"; at least, I am afraid you have had a bad digestion. Consider of it, and for Jesus Christ's sake tremble for fear "God should remove his candlestick from among you."

Labourers are sick; those that did once labour are almost worn out, and others they only bring themselves into a narrow sphere, and so confine their usefulness. There are few that like to go out into the fields; broken heads and dead cats are no more the ornaments of a Methodist, but silk scarves. Those honourable badges are now no more: the languor has got from the ministers to the people, and if you don't take care, we shall all fall dead together. The Lord Jesus rouse us, the Son of God rouse us all. Ye should show the world the way, and ye that have been Methodists of many years standing, show the young ones that have not the cross to bear as we once had, what ancient Methodism was.

As for you who are quite negligent about the prosperity of your souls, who only mind your bodies, who are more afraid of a pimple in your faces, than of the rottenness of your hearts; that will say, O give me a good bottle and a fowl, and keep the prosperity of your souls to yourselves. You had better take care what you say, for fear God should take you at your word. I knew some tradesmen and farmers, and one had got a wife perhaps with a fortune too, who prayed they might be excused, they never came to the supper, and God sent them to hell for it too; this may be your case.

I was told today of a young woman, that was very well on Sunday when she left her friends, when she came home was racked with pain, had an inflammation in her bowels, and is now a breathless corpse. Another that I heard of, a Christless preacher, that always minded his body, when he was near death, he said to his wife, I see hell opened for me, I see the damned tormented, I see such a one in hell that I debauched; in the midst of his agony he said, I am coming to thee, I am coming, I must be damned, God will damn my soul, and died. Take care of jesting with God; there is room enough in hell, and if you neglect the prosperity of your souls what will become of you? what will you give for a grain of hope when God requires your souls? "awake thou that sleepest"; hark! hark! hark! hear the word of the Lord, the living God.

Help me, O ye children of God: I am come with a warrant from Jesus of Nazareth tonight. Ye ministers of Christ that are here, help me with your prayers: ye servants of the living God, help me with your prayers. O with what success did I preach in Moorfields when I had ten thousand of God's people praying for me; pray to God to strengthen my body: don't be afraid I shall hurt myself tonight: I don't care what hurt I do myself if God may bless it; I can preach but little, but may God bless that little. I weep and cry and humble myself before God daily for being laid aside; I would not give others the trouble if I could preach myself. You have had the first of me, and you will have the last of me: the angels of God awaited for your conversion, and are now ready to take care of the soul when it leaves the rotten carcass.

The worst creature under heaven, that has not a penny in the world, may be welcome unto God. However it has been with us in times past, may our souls prosper in time to come; which God grant of his infinite mercy, Amen.

FOR ADDITIONAL INFORMATION ABOUT GEORGE WHITEFIELD:

Hardy, Edwin N. *George Whitefield, The Matchless Soul Winner.* New York: American Tract Society, 1938.

Henry, Stuart Clark. *George Whitefield: Wayfaring Witness.* New York: Abingdon Press, 1957.

Kirton, John W. and Andrews, J. R. *Wesley and Whitefield: The Two Great Evangelists of the Last Century; Their Lives, Their Work and Their Times.* London: Morgan & Scott, n.d.

Macartney, Clarence. "George Whitefield." *Six Kings of the American Pulpit.* Philadelphia: The Westminster Press, 1942.

McConnell, Francis John. "George Whitefield." *Evangelicals, Revolutionists and Idealists: Six English Contributors to American Thought and Action.* New York: Abingdon-Cokesbury Press, 1942.

McGraw, James. "George Whitefield." *Great Evangelical Preachers of Yesterday.* New York: Abingdon Press, 1961.

Pattison, Thomas Harwood. "George Whitefield." *The History of Christian Preaching.* Philadelphia: American Baptist Publication Society, 1903.

Whitefield, George. *Journals.* London: Banner of Truth Trust, 1960.

FOR OTHER SERMONS BY GEORGE WHITEFIELD:

Eighteen Sermons Preached by the Late Rev. George Whitefield. Edited by Andrew Gifford. Boston: n.p., 1820.

Select Sermons of George Whitefield. Edited by J. C. Ryle. London: Banner of Truth Trust, 1958.

TIMOTHY DWIGHT

1752 - 1817

TIMOTHY DWIGHT, an engraving by J. B. Forrest after
Trumbull. The Mansell Collection.

TIMOTHY DWIGHT

1752	Born in Northampton, Massachusetts
1769	Graduated from Yale; became headmaster of Hopkins Grammar School
1771	Became tutor at Yale
1774	Joined the church
1776	Delivered valedictory address
1777	Licensed to preach; began to preach; married Mary Woolsey; joined the Continental Army
1778	Returned home upon death of father
1783	Became pastor of the Congregational church at Greenfield; started a school
1795	Elected president of Yale; served also as professor of divinity
1817	Died January 11 while president of Yale

TIMOTHY DWIGHT—grandson of Jonathan Edwards, president of Yale University, and author of the famous hymn "I Love Thy Kingdom, Lord"—did more than any one man in the newborn United States of America to stem the tide of atheism and advance the cause of the Christian faith. His preaching deserves more attention than it has received.

LIFE AND TIMES

If ancestry equips a man for greatness, Timothy Dwight came into the world well-prepared. His grandfather, Colonel Timothy Dwight, served as a distinguished military officer and judge in the colonies. Active in political life, he was a distinguished lawyer. He lived in Northampton, Massachusetts, and was a member of Jonathan Edwards' church. In the controversy which led to the dismissal of Edwards, Colonel Dwight stood by the famous theologian. He even offered to divide his income with Edwards if he would stay and minister to the families in Northampton who remained loyal to him. Edwards, of course, refused.

Timothy Dwight's father followed in the footsteps of Colonel Dwight. He was known as a Christian gentleman of great integrity. He served in the military, then succeeded his father as judge of the Court of Common Pleas in Northampton. Six feet, four inches tall, perfectly proportioned, muscular, he attracted attention wherever he went.

Timothy Dwight's other grandfather, Jonathan Edwards, won fame as a pastor, theologian, and leader of the Great Awakening. Mary Edwards displayed much of her father's brilliance and temperament. In Timothy Dwight's life there converged the best of the Dwight and Edwards families.

Born in 1752, he spent his early years in the house next door to the one in which his mother had grown up. His early education was carefully guided by his mother. A brilliant child, Dwight was reading rapidly by the time he was four, and he was teaching local Indians the catechism by the time he was five. When he was six, he began to study English grammar seriously.

In 1769 he graduated from Yale, although his career there had a shaky beginning. At first he found himself more interested in playing cards than in studying; but a helpful tutor guided him back into the academic way, and Dwight compiled a brilliant academic career. He graduated at the top of his class.

He continued graduate studies at Yale; and in order to finance his schoolwork, he became headmaster of Hopkins Grammar School. This work gave him superb training for the teaching which was to occupy so much of his life. He was appointed a tutor at Yale in 1771 and excelled at the task.

While studying and teaching at Yale, he threw himself into his work with such zeal that he ruined his health. He studied twenty hours out of every twenty-four. He refused to allow himself more than four hours of sleep a day or twelve good bites of food at any meal. He begrudged any time away from his studies. He took no exercise. The combination of lack of sleep, lack of exercise, and lack of proper diet broke his health. He suffered a total collapse and almost lost his eyesight.

His father came to Yale and carried him home. For several months Timothy rested, exercised, and ate nourishing food. He also took medicine prescribed by a doctor which included healthy portions of wine and a mixture prepared by brewing tree bark. At least the medicine did him no harm, and with the exercise and good food he recovered sufficiently to return to his duties at Yale.

The experience left permanent marks on his life: he never fully recovered his eyesight; for the rest of his life he was hampered by an inability to read for long periods of time or in dim light. His body as a whole, however, regained total health. In fact, because of the experience he resolved never to neglect exercise and good food, and he remained robust and healthy throughout his life.

While recuperating from his lengthy illness, he pondered religious matters and gave himself fully to Christ in faith. In 1774 he joined the church; for him, this was a solemn and meaningful occasion.

Upon his return to Yale, he discovered the students in the grips of war fever. On Friday, April 21, 1775, a sophomore at the college scribbled this revealing entry in his daily diary:

> Today tidings of the battle of Lexington, which is the first engagement with the British troops, arrived at New Haven. This filled the country with alarm, and rendered it impossible for us to pursue our studies to any profit.[1]

Dwight contributed to the war spirit. A convinced patriot, he advocated total declaration of independence from the English crown. In a valedictory address delivered in 1776 he proclaimed that America would become an independent nation; and further, that she would become the greatest empire in the history of the world.

In 1777 Dwight entered the Christian ministry. Licensed to preach, he began to preach in surrounding churches whenever a pulpit was vacant. He studied theology — often on his own, sometimes under the direction of ministers. In this same year, he married Mary Woolsey. But he remained with his bride only a short time before joining the Continental Army as a chaplain.

---

1. Diary of Ebenezer Fitch quoted in C. Durfee, *Sketch of the Late Reverend Ebenezer Fitch*, p. 24, as cited in Charles E. Cuningham, *Timothy Dwight: A Biography* (New York: The Macmillan Co., 1942), p. 50.

Dwight spent a year as a chaplain. In many ways the year affected his life more than any other single experience. He saw firsthand the horrors of war. The brutality and suffering convinced him that war was a horror to be condemned by all sensitive Christians. In the army he ministered to a cross section of American life, which helped to release him from his provincial background. As a chaplain he learned more about human nature than his books had ever taught him. During the war he preached, wrote poetry, and made numerous friends. Among those who noticed the brilliance of the young chaplain was General George Washington.

Meanwhile, Dwight's own family experienced severe hardship. His father, Major Dwight, a man of unbending integrity, refused to break his oath of allegiance to the British crown. He sympathized with his neighbors and did not join actively in the Tory cause nor fight in the British ranks. But in the emotional climate of the day, anyone who was not for the patriots was counted as against them. The Dwights, harassed and persecuted by their neighbors, determined to move to a new location. Major Dwight purchased land on the Mississippi River. On a trip to defend the land from Spanish intruders, he died. The family, left without a father, drifted toward bankruptcy.

Timothy Dwight resigned from the army, returned home, and assumed the leadership of his family. Since everyone in Northampton knew of his patriotic sentiments, persecution against the family lessened. He worked on the family farms, taught school in order to earn extra income, and preached on the weekends. Through incessant toil he held the family estate together, provided a living for all of his family, and managed to continue his preaching.

When the war came to an end, conditions in Northampton returned to a more normal state. Dwight left affairs in the hands of others and assumed the pastorate of the Congregational church at Greenfield. With a growing family, the pastor found his salary insufficient. In order to supplement his income, he started a school. In many ways, it was a revolutionary school: he admitted women as well as men and allowed them to mingle together. In the New England of Dwight's day this was nearly scandalous.

His abilities gained wide recognition. When the presidency of Yale became vacant, his name came up for consideration.

Earlier, when he was only twenty-five, some had pushed him forward as a candidate for the presidency. He wisely had declined. But now when the offer was given him at the age of forty-three, he accepted.

When Dwight became president in 1795, Yale was a center of atheism. The students openly scorned the Christian faith. They ridiculed anyone who held Christian convictions. Everyone wondered what course the preacher from Greenfield would take in this tense situation. The former president had squelched discussion about Christian issues. As a result, such discussion had gone underground. Dwight determined not to follow this course. Instead, when the students wanted to discuss such issues as whether or not the Bible was the word of God, he agreed.

He allowed the unbelieving students to state their case against the Bible. After he had heard all of their arguments, he tore their position to shreds; then in brilliant fashion he constructed his arguments for the Christian faith. The student leaders for athesim were routed. By no means did they all become Christians, but at least they came to respect the ability of the new president.

Dwight believed in direct frontal assault upon the enemies of the faith. He believed that pretending evils did not exist accomplished nothing. He once remarked to the seniors of Yale:

> A gentleman once asked me whether I allowed my children to read the books of infidels. I told him yes: for they must become acquainted with them sooner or later, and while I am living I can confute the arguments they use. I should be unwilling to have them find these arguments unawares, with nobody to meet them.[2]

Dwight served also as professor of divinity. In his classes and in his chapel sermons, he constantly held up the validity of the Scripture and the worthiness of the Christian faith. He preached earnestly and prayed fervently for his students.

But Dwight faced formidable obstacles in bringing religious revival to Yale. When the class entered in the fall of 1796, only one freshman was a professing Christian. The sophomore class contained none; the junior class, one; and the senior class,

2. Cuningham., p. 304.

only eight or ten. The college church had dwindled to only two members. Professing Christian students suffered ridicule and abuse by the other students. During the third winter of Dwight's presidency, things were little better; the very Bible he used for college services disappeared one night from the chapel.

Dwight's patient work bore fruit in the spring of 1802. A momentous revival occurred – the first of a series. One-third of Yale's 230 students became professing Christians; over thirty of these entered the ministry. The revival spread beyond Yale to other centers of higher learning.

These revivals of religion were no flash-in-the-pan affairs. Dwight carefully nurtured them, and they burned for years and years under his wise leadership. Soon many ministers of the Christian faith were coming from Yale. Instead of a center of infidelity, it became a center of religious revival.

In many ways Timothy Dwight could be compared to his grandfather, Jonathan Edwards. Both studied at Yale. Both became tutors. Both entered the Congregational ministry. Both pastored in Massachusetts. Both became presidents of universities. Both were leaders in religious revivals.

Although Jonathan Edwards's brilliance may have excelled his grandson's, in many ways Dwight was the superior. Edwards apparently had difficulty relating to people. Though a devout Christian, he did not clearly understand the art of leadership. Timothy Dwight, on the other hand, excelled in leading men. As a result, his efforts were less fraught with storm and were more enduring than those of his famous grandfather. Edwards dipped here and there into Christian theology; whatever issues he touched, he dealt with in great depth. Dwight did not deal in depth, but he did develop a system of theology which at that time was sorely needed in New England. The revivals of Edwards were short-lived; Edwards himself did not do as much as others – such as George Whitefield – to keep the revival fires burning in New England. On the other hand, Timothy Dwight nurtured and kept alive the revival which broke out under his leadership. When he died in 1817, the revival was still in progress.

Dwight truly was an amazing man. Though he reflected the influence of his era in many ways, particularly in regard to his Calvinistic theology, in other ways he transcended his times. In education he was a revolutionary pioneer: he advocated that women had as much right as men to attend schools of higher education; he insisted that women not only be taught the rudiments of reading and math but also be instructed in subjects such as the classics, philosophy, and theology.

In social concerns, he demonstrated compassion for people and the zeal to do something about it. He served his community in civil government and argued for prison reform, relief for the poor, and anything that seemed to be for the improvement of human life.

Slavery and prejudice drew condemnation from him. As early as 1792, the Connecticut Society for the Abolition of Slavery listed Dwight among its members. He backed a school which was established in New Haven to teach Negro children how to read. When civil authorities objected to the project, he threw his influence behind it—and the school was established. In addition he raised money for the venture and contributed to it himself.

When people argued that the colored races of the world were inferior to the white, he soundly refuted them. He insisted that all men had a common origin and that differences in skin color were due to differences in climate. He concluded that "men, therefore, are not black, white, nor red necessarily; but merely as incidental circumstances direct."[3]

Dwight's concern for the poor and the enslaved was not merely an academic one; he frequently went out of his way to minister to the illiterate, the servants, and the poor. In his own home, a retarded Negro cook received special attention from him. He carefully and patiently instructed her. According to his standard of values, every human being—whether a white senator or a black cook—had the same ultimate importance.

Timothy Dwight remained active until the very end of his life. He continued his writing, his teaching, and his administrative affairs. One evening he finished his *Essays on the Evidences of Divine Revelation*, stitched the cover on the manuscript, and said, "There, I have done."[4] Three days later, he died.

Preaching and Sermons

As pastor of Greenfield, Dwight acquired a national reputation. His church was in a small country village; but as his fame spread, travelers between New York and Boston often interrupted their journey to visit his church and listen to him

---

3. Ibid., p. 312.
4. Ibid., p. 352.

preach. The visitors were invariably impressed. The Reverend Heman Humphrey, a competent critic, heard many of his sermons; he called Dwight one of the most elegant preachers he had ever heard or that the country had ever produced. One who heard his sermon on "Harvest is Past"—a sermon credited with starting two revivals—called Dwight's delivery "earnest and impassioned," his language "pungent and emphatic," and the whole sermon "solemn and impressive."

Because Dwight suffered from poor eyesight, he found it virtually impossible to write his sermons in full. As a result he had to deliver most of them extemporaneously. In the long run this proved to be a great advantage to him—not to be tied to a manuscript, as were most preachers of that era, improved his fluency. Once during a revival Dwight preached a sermon which he had written out fully, but he became so excited toward the end of his sermon that he added an extemporaneous conclusion. One gentleman in the congregation later asked permission to see the manuscript, explaining that he wanted to read the conclusion because he considered it the most elegant he had ever heard. To his surprise he discovered that the conclusion was the only part of the sermon not carefully composed in advance. It had been created under the inspiration of the moment.

Before going to Greenfield as pastor, Dwight had written very few of his sermons; in his twelve years at Greenfield he probably wrote fewer than twenty manuscripts. During that time he preached twice on Sundays, lectured on Wednesdays, and delivered numerous discourses on special occasions. He must have preached well over a thousand sermons during his pastorate at Greenfield.

His method of sermon preparation was simple. During the week he went over each sermon in his mind during "free moments"—such as hoeing his garden, riding his horse to call on parishioners, or visiting the sick. By the end of the week he had written nothing, but he had the material for his sermon completely planned and organized. By Sunday his two sermons were ready. An hour before the service he jotted down a brief outline of the principal points he wished to make. Even this step required only a few moments because he wrote quickly and in an abbreviated shorthand. The entire sermon could be contained on a quarter sheet of paper which he held in his hand. Occasionally Dwight referred to his outline, but he usually relied on the inspiration of the moment for the development of the sermon. Those who heard him reported that he never hesitated, was never at a loss for words, and usually preached for an hour.

Dwight spoke rapidly but with excellent enunciation and word stress. He rarely used gestures — never theatrics — and his manner was dignified and impressive. He radiated an air of complete command of his subject; his confidence impressed all who heard him.

During his later years Dwight dictated his more important sermons, sometimes too rapidly for his secretary to write. He seldom revised what he had dictated. His sentences flowed with an even smoothness. His material was organized in a logical fashion and he was exact in his language. Dwight displayed excellent choice of words in his composition.

He appealed with equal success to the logic and to the emotion of his hearers. Dwight once preached at Bridgeport on honesty, and he provoked so many consciences that the next day "borrowed" axes, hoes, pitchforks, and other tools found their way back to their rightful owners.

The Reverend Ashbel Green of Philadelphia described Dwight:

> [He] is, in my estimation, a man of real genius; his imagination is lively and brilliant; his perceptions are quick and strong; his taste is rather acute than delicate and distinguishing; his knowledge various and extensive; and he has great confidence in himself. . . .
>
> I like him much and whoever is capable of being influenced by benevolence . . . will not, I think, fail to like him.[5]

Dwight was an effective revival preacher; a single sermon of his was credited for starting nearly a half-dozen distinct revivals. Many others were equally inspiring. Although he disapproved of "enthusiasm," Dwight defended revivals of the quiet kind. He called these outpourings of the Holy Spirit "the springtime of salvation."[6]

So strong were Dwight's feelings that he usually abandoned his notes during the seasons of revival at Yale and made his ap-

---

5. Ibid., p. 117.
6. Ibid., p. 328.

peal to the students extemporaneously. He was always ready to counsel those who fell under the conviction of sin and to urge upon them the acceptance of grace. Unlike many revivals, this movement had lasting effect upon many of those who were involved in it—due largely to the sympathetic concern and helpful preaching of Dwight.

The existing sermons of Timothy Dwight do not reveal much of the spontaneity and fervor that accompanied their free delivery. Nevertheless, they remain as worthy monuments to a great preacher who turned the religious tide in the early days of this country toward an evangelical Christian faith.

Sermons

EACH MAN'S LIFE A PLAN OF GOD

"Verily, verily, I say unto thee, When thou wast young, thou girdedst thyself and walkedst whither thou wouldest: but when thou shalt be old, thou shalt stretch forth thy hands, and another shall gird thee, and carry thee whither thou wouldest not. This spake he, signifying by what death he should glorify God. And when he had spoken this, he saith unto him, Follow me. Then Peter, turning about, seeth the disciple whom Jesus loved following; which also leaned on his breast at supper, and said, Lord, which is he that betrayeth thee? Peter seeing him saith to Jesus, Lord, and what shall this man do? Jesus saith unto him, If I will that he tarry till I come, what is that to thee? follow thou me. Then went this saying abroad among the brethren, that that disciple should not die: yet Jesus said not unto him, He shall not die; but, If I will that he tarry till I come, what is that to thee?" (John 21:18–23).

THESE VERSES of the closing chapter of John's Gospel present before us some of the last words of Jesus, which were addressed to two of His most prominent disciples. With reference to both of them the words apparently foretell something of their future career, and especially somewhat as to the manner of their dying. I propose to consider them as they may offer directly or indirectly certain thoughts and teachings.

The characters and work of the two men were very different. Peter, as he is presented before us in the New Testament, and according to the picture which we form of him, was full of energy, ardent, impulsive, ready for every new and worthy undertaking, practical, a leader for other men of action to follow. John, at least as we know him in his later years, was quiet, calm, thoughtful, dwelling more in the internal than the external, a lover of the truth and meditating upon it, rather than one who found his chief joy and satisfaction in the activi-

Reprinted from Timothy Dwight, *Thoughts of and for the Inner Life* (Dodd, Mead & Co., 1899), pp. 19–31.

ties of the world. It is certainly suggestive to thought, if we notice what Jesus said to them, as connected with these differences — especially if we bear also in mind what the future in each case proved to be, so far as the tradition of the Church has made it known to us.

In the first place, the manner of living and dying which is predicted for each of the two men is in accordance with the character of each. The man of fiery energy, and eager for action and conflict, had begun his career by the carrying out of his own impulses. He was the impersonation, as we may say, of youth, in his younger years — pushing his way forward according to his personal will; a firm believer in himself and his own powers; arrested by no difficulties or opposition; determined to conquer and to succeed. The future for him, according to the ordinary laws of life, was to open toward greater conflicts and harder struggles. His very method of working would bring him into the midst of dangers and enmities. He would rouse the evil passions of men, and excite them to throw every possible hindrance in his path, or even to contend against him with their deadliest weapons. In an age like that in which he lived and a work such as the one in which he was engaged, a man of his character would be peculiarly exposed to violent opposition. He would be as a single man contending against a thousand. The truth for which he strove was disbelieved. It was rejected by men of every class. It was hated by all who saw in it danger to their own systems of faith, or to their personal success or power. The career of such a man must be filled with fightings. In any period of the world's history, it must be liable to end in defeat for himself, if not for the cause which he advocates. But, in such an epoch as that in which Peter was living, defeat meant death, and that by violence. Jesus predicted only what might, not unnaturally, be expected — that the time was coming when, having grown old in the conflict and in the years, the ardent and active disciple, who had in his earlier life girded himself and moved whithersoever he would, would be overcome and led forth at the will of others, even to execution. He would glorify God by a martyr's death.

But equally in the case of the other disciple was the prophecy of Jesus in accordance with the natural movement and ending of a life like his. The calm spirit, which thinks and loves — which tells its thoughts and shows its love — awakens violent opposition. It dwells apart from strifes, even if it dwells near the world's active life. It moves serenely forward, and the years go by. If the life chances to be lengthened out to extreme old age, and the mind is in its full power at the latest season, the passing on and the passing away may be but as the change of the daylight hour to the beautiful evening time.

The suggestion of the text, in this view of it, I think may be this: that as, in the ordering of Providence, we are born with varying characters and gifts, and are assigned to different works for God in the world, so we may believe that there is a plan for every one, formed, and watched over, and carried to its completion by the Divine Friend who calls us into His service. How often we find, in our individual experience, that we never escape the besetment of peculiar difficulties or trials, which other men around us either do not have, or grow out of as the years move onward. We hope to escape them – we wonder that we do not, it may be – but we find them always with us. Is it not the Lord's appointment – not as an arbitrary or outward thing, but as a part and outgrowth of our peculiar nature? Is not the true way of looking at it this: that we – in our individuality of nature – were made for the accomplishment of a special Divine purpose; for the showing forth of a Divinely-formed character and life in one particular light; and that all allotments of experience are wisely fitted to realise the end? The work of Peter as a disciple of Jesus was intended to be different from that of John. He was to show the development of true life in a different way. The career followed the line of the native endowments. The trials and successes, the defeats and victories, as they were seen in the progress of his living and foreseeen by the Master, were in accordance with what was foreshadowed in that manifestation of the Divine purpose which was seen in the making of the man.

We do not penetrate the heavenly wisdom, indeed, and we cannot say that this is a full account of what we call the Providential dealing with us. But may we not say that it is a partial one? And if it is so, surely it takes up all our living, and every part of our experience, into God's plan and purpose – and brings us the lesson of trust and confidence that the natural movement of our life, as we call it, is under a supernatural guidance, and that, in our allotment of every sort, and in the dying at the end, we are guarded and guided by a Father's love.

In the second place, we may notice what Jesus says to Peter in answer to his inquiry respecting the appointed destiny of his friend and associate. The manner of his own dying had been foretold to him; and now, as he sees this friend approaching, his mind naturally turns to the thought of *his* future. What of this man – what shall be his experience? The Lord answers, If I will that he tarry till I come, what is that to thee? There is in this answer nothing of definiteness – at the most, only a suggestion that John's life would be longer and quieter than that of Peter himself. But the main word for the latter disciple is the pointed question, What is that to thee? with the bidding, Follow thou me.

What is the lesson given here? Evidently, as a first part of it, that curious inquiry into what may lie before our friends, or even ourselves, is not the thing to occupy our minds. The appointed work for us is, to follow the Lord, each one for himself. Peter had, indeed, been told, as most men are not, and even the other disciples were not, that a death of violence was before him, and would come when he should have passed within the limits of old age. But the language used in giving him this assurance was figurative in its character, and might naturally suggest a career of trial and defeat, rather than its ending only. Indeed the form of expression used by the evangelist is such as to intimate that the understanding of the words with reference alone to Peter's death came to the minds of the disciples only at a later period. As to the time and particular mode of dying, they were certainly indefinite. But when the inquiry was turned to John's fate, the answer was only with an *if*, and it revealed nothing beyond the possibility of the Divine will. The *if* did not gain its interpretation till the fact was realised – nor, indeed, even then, for, if we may believe in any measure the story which has come down to us, many thought, after John had made the correction which he gives, and after he had passed away, that he was not dead, but was to live until the Lord's second coming. Not questioning, but working, is the Christian's duty; – this is the first part of the lesson.

And a second part seems to be this – that, in the working, duty lies in the pathway of individual capacities and powers. Peter was called to follow the Lord in the line where, with his natural characteristics, he could best serve Him; the line which would end, indeed, in martyrdom. But he was not to be planning for martyrdom, or thinking of it. The prophecy which foretold it was, at the most, to be an inspiration to him in his career – for the reason that the career was to end in a glorifying of God after the manner in which Jesus Himself was about to glorify Him. The following of the Master was to be the object of his thought – a daily following, according as the way of service should become manifest, and the way in which the Master would have walked, had He been in his place, should be made known. Think not of tomorrow, or the end, is the teaching – think of today, and its work. How simple the bidding was: Follow me. How peaceful it was – The future belongs to God; it is the object of His care and thought; it will be one thing for one of his children, and another for another; and for both alike it will be but the following out of that plan which He undertook to carry on at the beginning. If each shall follow – today as it comes, and tomorrow as it comes – the call of the Lord, the ending will be provided for, and, whatever it be, it will be a glorifying of God.

It is significant that this same bidding follows the prophecy of Peter's death and the answer respecting John's future. As if Jesus had said: When the vision is given for a moment, and in a figure as it were, of what is before thyself, let it only move thee to a more earnest devotion to the duty which offers itself at the same moment – and when the sight of another's destiny is absolutely denied thee, still have the same earnestness. And so His last words to these two most intimate and beloved friends are the words which He uttered at the beginning

of His public ministry: Live the right life today, and be not anxious
for tomorrow.

What a wonderful peace there must have been in the inmost souls of
these two disciples if they guided their lives by these words in the
years which came afterward – the one moving on to his martyrdom,
and the other to his quiet death and the falling asleep that seemed to
those about him to be another thing than death, but both hearing the
Lord's voice daily, saying, "Follow me," for the present; and, "What
is it to thee?" of the future.

A third suggestion of the text is as to the true estimate which is to be
placed upon different kinds of life. The praise of mankind is always
prone to go towards those whose lives are passed, as we say, on the
scene of action – the leaders of men in the struggle and warfare. But
it is a striking fact, worthy of serious reflection, that it was not Peter,
but John, to whom in the Divine plan the longest life was assigned.
And this longest life was not mere living, but the accomplishing of a
great work. Peter followed the Master, and did an honourable service,
and glorified God, at its ending, by a death which corresponded with
his life. But we may not forget that it was the meditative and thoughtful disciple – the one whom Jesus loved, and who leaned on His breast
at the supper – to whom the last work of the Apostolic age was appointed. After Peter and Paul had fulfilled their mission, he came to
finish what they had begun. And the message which he sent down the
ages is the most precious inheritance of the Church. Peter is an
interesting character, but we know little of what He taught or thought,
in its distinctive peculiarities, and comparatively little of what he did.
But the thoughts of John give us the setting forth of the deepest
mysteries of the Christian truth, and let us into the innermost secret of
Christian living, and open before us the heart of God, and read us lessons for which the thoughts of the other greatest Apostles are only
preparatory. Our vision of the future places, as all Christian thinkers
hold, the Johannean age as the final one in Christian development,
and the disciple of love as greater than those of faith and of hope.

The world is governed more by men of thought than by men of action – when we take the great progress of the ages into account – and it
is so peculiarly in Christian history, and above all in Christian experience.

But the teaching of the text, in this line of thought, is also that,
according to the true Christian estimate, what seems the quiet, calm
life, away from the stir and strife of the world – withdrawn, perhaps
by necessity, from the great activities of mankind – is a life as near,
or even nearer it may be, to the heart of Christ, than the one which is
most conspicuous in its Christian labours seen of men. It was the
meditative, loving disciple, whose work came after the struggles and
conflicts were over – the one whose life was longest, partly no doubt

because he was outside of the tumult, and whose death was so like a sleep—it was this disciple, whom the Lord loved, and to whom He committed the task of writing the story of His own Divine life among men,which should bear witness most fully of the Divinity and the humanity in their marvellous union. The believer who thinks and loves stands on an equality with the one who works and wars; Peter and John were together in that final interview recorded in this Gospel. He may even have a higher standing; as John was living after Peter and Paul had passed away.

We may also observe, in connection with the thought of the future of these two men as that future is hinted at in these verses, the importance to the Christian work in the world of the union of the two characters within the Church. The work of Christianity is to bring the world towards the perfectness of God. But the work is to be accomplished by human agencies and in human lives. The perfectness is therefore to be realised, not in any one individual, but rather in the combining together of the full developments in all. Each man is to manifest what the Divine power in Christianity can do for him. Were the more active virtues alone to be seen, the end would be but half secured. Were they not seen at all, the aggressive force upon the world would be mainly lost. But God has joined the man of energy and the man of quiet and thoughtful spirit, and given to each his own sphere of working for Him; and if they follow along the line of His appointment, with no misunderstanding of each other, the result is reached— all combining for the common end, even as the writings of Peter and Paul, on the one hand, and John on the other, have made their way together into human souls everywhere, and transformed them from the earthly into the heavenly mode of living. And so the teaching of these words is that those who believe are to grow and work together, but not after precisely the same pattern, or in the same way.

I think we may fitly notice, once more, what I may call the incidental character of the words. The meeting of Jesus with the disciples on this occasion seems to have taken place almost by an accident. They had come together for an ordinary occupation, and apparently they were not thinking of Him, or of His possible presence with them. In the early morning, as they were in the disappointment of a failure of their work, He stands upon the shore, and gradually, and in a peculiar way, He makes Himself known. He teaches them of their office and their dependence upon Himself, and perhaps of the confidence which they may have in His aid whenever they put forth their efforts in His cause. This is what comes first and foremost. Then he seems to take this opportunity—because it chances to present itself—to call Peter's attention to his three denials, his threefold failure in love, and to ask him to look into his own character. But the object is not self-examination, but forgiveness; and so He restores him fully to his office, committing to him once more the care of the flock, and bidding him feed and tend and shepherd all the sheep. Directing his thought in this way to his work and duty, He easily and naturally speaks of what was awaiting him in the future, and of the death which should terminate his career. The allusion to the future and the death of John was even more accidental, as it were – occasioned simply by the fact of his happening to move along the path by which Jesus was walking with Peter, and then by the chance question suggested to Peter's mind by what he had heard respecting himself. How prominent the thought of the ending is as we look at the *close* of the chapter. How secondary and subordinate, as we move towards it from the *beginning*.

Is it not so with the ending of every life? In our ordinary thinking of this ending, it seems like the one great event, which gathers about itself all solemnity, and seems to include within itself the sum of all the past and all the future. But when we move forward in our thought from the beginning and through the life, it becomes an incidental thing, the natural ending of the life whatever it may be; the subordinate, not the principal event – subordinate to duty and service and character, which are the principal things; the passage-way from a living in one sphere of activity to a living in another. And, in this view of it, does not the question which was addressed to Peter respecting his fellow-apostle come with a Divine emphasis, and a Divine tenderness, to each one of us with reference to himself: What is it to thee? We enter upon the duties and struggles of our coming life – and the call from the Master is, Follow me. We know not the end, but it will be the end of service to Him here, and the opening of something higher and better than earth.

The writer of the Gospel closes the chapter in which this story of the two disciples is found with the words: And there are also many other things which Jesus did, the which if they should be written every one, I suppose that even the world itself would not contain the books that should be written. We may often wish that the words which He said might have been all preserved to us. But those which we have received are full of suggestion, and the thoughts of Jesus grow in their greatness and power within our hearts until they more than fill all the sphere of our living. The one word: Follow me, fills all the sphere of duty; and the one word: What is it to thee? commits the future to His keeping, and thus may give to us, each and every one, a perfect peace.

DEPRAVITY OF MAN — ITS DEGREE

"Because sentence against an evil work is not executed speedily, therefore the heart of the sons of men is fully set in them
to do evil" (Ecclesiastes 8:11).

IN THE TWO LAST DISCOURSES, I proposed for consideration the following doctrine: *That in consequence of the Apostacy of Adam all
men have sinned;* and endeavored to prove the Universality of sin in
the former of these discourses;

First: From Revelation: and,

Secondly: From Facts:

And in the latter *from the great fact, that mankind have rejected
the Word of the Lord.*

It is now my design to examine, in several particulars, *the Degree,
in which the sinfulness of man exists.* On this subject I observe,

*First: That the human character is not depraved to the full ex-
tent of the human powers.*

It has been said, neither unfrequently, nor by men void of understanding, *that man is as depraved a being, as his faculties will permit him to be;* but it has been said without consideration, and without
truth. Neither the Scriptures, nor Experience, warrant this assertion.
"Wicked men and seducers," it is declared, "will wax worse and worse;
deceiving and being deceived." During the first half of human life
this may, perhaps, be explained by the growth of the faculties; but during a considerable period, preceding its termination, it cannot be thus
explained: for the faculties decay, while the depravity still increases.
Nations, also, are declared, to be at some periods of time, far worse
than at others; although it cannot be pretended, that during the period specified their faculties were superior. *Saul* appears to have been
a man of more talents than *Jeroboam; Jeroboam* than *Ahab;* and
Uzziah than either; yet *Ahab* was a worse man than *Jeroboam; Jeroboam* than *Saul;* and *Saul* than *Uzziah.* The *Young Man,* who came to
Christ, to know *what good thing he should do, to have eternal life,*
was certainly less depraved, than his talents would have permitted
him to be.

Like him, we see, daily, many men, who neither are, nor profess to
be, Christians, and who, instead of being wicked to a degree commensurate to the extent of their faculties, go through life in the exercise of dispositions so sincere, just, and amiable, and in the performance of actions so upright and beneficent, as to secure a high degree
of respect and affection from ourselves, and from all with whom they

Reprinted from Timothy Dwight, *Theology: Explained and Defended* (New
Haven: S. Converse, 1823), pp. 461–76.

are connected. It certainly cannot be said, that such men are as sinful as many others possessed of powers far inferior; much less that they are as sinful as they can be. We also see individuals, at times, assume, without any visible enlargement of their faculties, a new and surprising degree of depravity at once; and become suddenly far more fraudulent, false, lewd, cruel, revengeful, impious, and universally abandoned, than at a period not long preceding. In the families, of which we are members, we have abundant opportunity to learn, from so intimate a connexion, the true characters of all who compose them; and are furnished daily with decisive evidence, that they are far less profligate than, with their faculties, they might become. Those, who make the assertion, against which I am contending, will find themselves, if they will examine, rarely believing, that their wives and children, though not Christians, are Fiends.

Secondly: There are certain characteristics of human nature, which, considered by themselves, are innocent.

Such are hunger, thirst, the fear of suffering, and the desire of happiness; together with several others. All these are inseparable, not only from the rational, but also from the animal, nature, as existing in this world; and accompany the Christian through every degree of holiness, which he attains, as truly as the sinner. The two last; the desire of happiness, and the fear of suffering; are inseparable from the rational, and even from the percipient, nature.

Thirdly: Some of the natural human characteristics are amiable.

Such are natural affection: the simplicity and sweetness of disposition in children, often found also in persons of adult years; compassion; generosity; modesty; and what is sometimes called natural conscientiousness; that is, a fixed and strong sense of the importance of doing that, which is right. These characteristics appear to have adorned *the Young Man*, whom I have already mentioned. We know that they are amiable, because we are informed that *Jesus, beholding him, loved him.* In the same manner we, and all others, who are not abandoned, love them always, and irresistibly, whenever they are presented to our view. They all, also, are required, and exist, in every Christian; enhancing his holiness, and rendering him a better man. Without them it is not easy to perceive how the Christian character could exist. Accordingly, *St. Paul* exhibits those, who are destitute of these attributes, as being literally profligates.

Fourthly: These and all other qualities of the mind are, however, means either of virtue, or sin, according to the nature of that controlling Disposition, or Energy, which constitutes the moral character.

By this disposition, or energy, I intend *that unknown cause, whence it arises, that the actions of the mind are either sinful or virtuous.* On this energy depends the moral nature of all actions, and the moral character of every mind. This character, and these actions, are variously, and extensively, modified by the attributes above mentioned. But the moral nature is not changed. So far as they have a prevailing influence, a sinful disposition is checked, and prevented from operating in the worst manner, and degree. Under the prevalence of a sinful disposition, these attributes are partly extinguished, and partly converted into instruments of sin. In a virtuous mind they all become means of virtue, and increase the energy of such a mind.

Fifthly: There is not in the Mind, by nature, or in an unregenerated state, any real moral excellence, or Evangelical virtue.

"For I know," says *St. Paul,* "that in me, (that is, in my flesh) dwelleth no good thing. The carnal mind," says the same Apostle, "is enmity against God, not subject to his law, neither indeed can be." And again; "The natural man receiveth not the things of the Spirit of God; for they are foolishness unto him; neither can he know them, for they are spiritually discerned. That which is born," saith our Saviour, "of the flesh, is flesh. Without faith," says *St. Paul,* "it is impossible to please God."

Sixthly: The heart of Man, after all the abatements are made, which can be made, is set to do evil, in a most affecting and dreadful manner.

Of this truth, the Text is a direct and very forcible assertion. The word, which is rendered, *fully set,* in our translation, is used by *Ahasuerus* (Esther 7:5), to express *the daring presumption, with which Haman had risen up to destroy Esther and her nation.* It is also said to denote *being filled with a violent propensity, as the sails of a ship are filled, when borne along by a powerful blast.* A strong tendency to evil in the heart of the sons of men, therefore, is here asserted in very forcible terms.

In considering the degree of iniquity, indicated in this and similar passages, it is not my design, nor within my power or wish, to settle this point with mathematical exactness. In the Scriptures, God has exhibited this subject in an indefinite, and yet in a more impressive and affecting manner, than any, which mankind have substituted. No views of human corruption are so affecting, or so awful, as those, which are presented to us in the Word of God. This example may be confidently followed; and no man is required to limit this subject more exactly, than it has been done by his Maker.

With these observations premised, I shall proceed to adduce several proofs of the doctrine, expressed in the text.

I. *The Scriptures directly assert this doctrine in the fullest manner.*

"Every imagination of Man's heart," saith God, "is only evil, continually." Of the Gentiles, the Apostle declares, that "they are without excuse; because that, when they knew God, they glorified him not as

God, neither were thankful; but became vain in their imaginations; and their foolish heart was darkened. Professing themselves to be wise, they became fools. Who changed the truth of God into a lie, and worshipped, and served the creature, more than the Creator, who is blessed for ever. Amen. For this cause God gave them up to vile affections. And as they did not like to retain God in their knowledge, God gave them up to a reprobate mind. Being filled with all unrighteousness, fornication, wickedness, covetousness, maliciousness; full of envy, murder, debate, deceit, malignity, Whisperers, backbiters, haters of God, despiteful, proud, boasters, inventers of evil things, disobedient to parents, Without understanding, covenant-breakers, without natural affection, implacable, unmerciful: Who knowing the judgment of God (that they, which commit such things, are worthy of death) not only do the same, but have pleasure in them that do them."

Of the *Jews*, the same Apostle says (Rom. 3:9–20), "What then, are we better than they? No, in no wise; for we have before proved both Jews and Gentiles, that they are all under sin. As it is written, There is none righteous, no, not one. There is none that understandeth; there is none that seeketh after God. They are all gone out of the way; they are together become unprofitable; there is none that doeth good, no, not one. Their mouth is an open sepulchre; with their tongues they have used deceit; the poison of asps is under their lips. Whose mouth is full of cursing and bitterness; their feet are swift to shed blood. There is no fear of God before their eyes. — Now we know, that what things soever the Law saith, it saith to them, who are under the Law; that every mouth might be stopped, and all the world become guilty before God. — Therefore, by deeds of Law, shall no flesh living be justified."

Such is the character of men, given in form, and in the course of the most important logical discussion contained in the Scriptures, by the Apostle *Paul*. Consonant with this representation are all the exhibitions, made in the Old and New Testament, of this subject. The depravity, represented, is not only declared to be universal, but also to be of this high and dreadful malignity. Mankind are not exhibited as prone to one sin only, but to all these, and all other sins; and not *prone* to these sins merely, but filled with them as attributes, and executing them swiftly and dreadfully as practices.

II. *The same truth is evident to every man, if he examines the subject faithfully, from the state of his own heart and life.*

This very extensive field of evidence can now be explored only in a very imperfect manner: but a little attention to it will in no small degree illustrate and prove the doctrine.

First: Every Man, who scrutinizes his own heart at all, knows, that, naturally, he in no sense obeys the first and great command of the Law of God: Thou shalt love the Lord, thy God, with all thy heart.

This is the first, and altogether the most important, duty of Intelligent creatures; and is plainly that duty, separated from which, no other can be performed. All possible motives in the highest possible degrees conspire to induce a rational being to perform it. If, then, these motives do not influence the heart; if we love not our Creator, Preserver, and Benefactor, and Author of all good, and himself the Infinite Good; we cannot be imagined to love with right principles any other being. If we perform not our plain duty to him, we cannot be supposed to perform our duty to any other.

Secondly: All men are daily reproached by their own Consciences, as being greatly and continually guilty of Sin.

The fear of the anger of God, and of future punishment, and the pride, which every man feels in thinking himself of a good and honourable character, are biases, which strongly influence us to reject, as much as possible, so humiliating a doctrine as this. But, in spite of both, our Consciences, irresistibly impelled by the truth, declare the greatness of our depravity every day; and we cannot hide our eyes from the humiliating declaration. Were it possible to avoid the acknowledgment, we should certainly avoid it: but the truth is so obvious, and so undeniable, that we cannot escape.

The only exception to this remark proves the truth of the doctrine still more strongly. The man, whose Conscience does not thus testify, is plainly of a *peculiarly* depraved character; not merely because his Conscience does not thus testify, but because he is always guilty of gross sin in various other respects. So common, or rather so universal, is this fact, as to become the subject of proverbial remark. He therefore, who is thus situated, is still more depraved than mankind in general.

Thirdly: The Stupidity of mankind, and their Hardness of Heart, are strong exhibitions of the same doctrine.

That Men should be thus guilty, and yet be insensible to the nature and degree of their depravity, is an event, certainly not to have been expected from the Reason, of which we so continually boast. Our sins are committed against the Infinite God, the eternal and unchangeable Enemy of Sin; and are, therefore, the means of exposing us in an awful manner to his wrath and vengeance. At the same time, the character is in itself debased, deformed, and hateful, beyond expression. Who, then, can be supposed to possess any share of Reason, and not be humbled beyond measure at the latter of these considerations, and equally alarmed by the former? Yet Mankind by nature are universally, not only not humbled, but haughty; not only not alarmed, but stupid, as to their danger; and cheerful, gay, exulting, and insolent, in the career of their iniquity.

In the meantime, no warnings are sufficient to awaken them to a sense of guilt, danger, or duty; no counsels, to persuade them to return to obedience; no motives, to deter them from sin. The heart is, like the nether millstone, incapable of any useful, serious, divine, impression; daily becoming more and more guilty, stupid, and hardened; and wandering farther and farther from duty and from God, from hope and from Heaven.

Eternal Life is offered, and has been offered, to those, now before me, ten thousand times. Who has accepted the offer? Their sins have been ten thousand times reproved and condemned. Who has repented, and forsaken them? Their duty has in countless instances been pressed upon them. Who has obeyed? God has called, Christ has entreated, the Spirit of Grace has striven. Who has listened, complied, and yielded? To continue in sin is to be exposed to endless misery. To repent, and turn to God, is to secure endless life. Every hardened, impenitent sinner declares, therefore, that, in his view, sin, with endless misery for its reward, is more to be chosen than holiness, or obedience, with endless life. What greater proof of dreadful depravity can be given, or demanded?

III. *The same doctrine is most affectingly evinced by the whole course of human conduct.*

This evidence will advantageously appear,

First: From the Private Conduct of mankind, as individuals.

I shall not here insist at large on the most private and retired scenes of life, where we see, in multitudes of instances, notwithstanding all the concealment and disguise, with which Vice hides itself from the observation of the world, innumerable forms and degrees of corruption acted out in a very painful and humiliating manner. In spite of the veil, which night and solitude cast over the innumerable perpetrations of the human race, how many kinds of deformity rise up daily to our view! How many early, bitter, and unnatural contentions, even of little children! What affecting tokens even of infantine selfishness, wrath, revenge, and cruelty! How many proofs of filial impiety, ingratitude, and rebellion, in the morning of Life! What unbrotherly and unsisterly coldness and alienation, what unkind and unforgiving hearts, appear in those, *who are bone of the same bone, and flesh of the same flesh!* How many jealous, hard-hearted, little, base sentiments and actions afflict the bosom of parental tenderness in those, whom nature makes inexpressibly beloved, in spite of every fault, as well as of every folly!

What a task is it to rear a single family, without leaving such faults unextirpated, as are open and infamous! How vast a labour to train up even one child to virtue and to duty; or even to prevent one from becoming grossly sinful, and finally lost! What toils and pains; what cares and watchings; how many reproofs, restraints, and corrections; how many prayers, and sighs, and tears, are employed and suffered, before this hard task can be accomplished! How rarely is it accomplished at all! What then must be the corruption of that heart, which makes all these efforts necessary; and which can resist and overcome them all?

From this summary view let us turn our thoughts to the *obvious* conduct of men; as it exists in our own and every other country. What *amazing selfishness* visibly appears in the general conduct of mankind; and how little are they, amidst all the culture of education and humanity, all the restraints of Law, and all the illuminations, injunctions, and threatenings, of Religion, disposed to act agreeably to the dictates of truth, righteousness, and benevolence towards each other? A little property, a little power, a very humble office, or some other trifling object of ambition, will, at any time, make those, who have been for life bosom friends, vehement and irreconcileable enemies. A furious and long continued lawsuit is resorted to, in order to decide the unsettled property; a lawsuit, carried on with bitterness, fraud, and perjury; and terminated in insolent victory and sullen defeat, in riveted hatred and gloomy retaliation. The place of honour and power is sought for with electioneering, caballing, slander, fraud, and falsehood; and is enjoyed with insolence, or lost with envy, malice, and secret resolutions of future revenge.

In the common bargains between Men, how rarely is it the design to exchange an equivalent for that which is received; although the only possible rule of honesty; and how generally, to make what is called a *good* and what is in reality a *fraudulent*, bargain! How perpetual are the efforts to impose on our neighbours commodities of less than the professed value; commodities imperfect, corrupted, and decayed! How many persons obtain their whole living, and spend their whole lives, in this kind of fraud! What pains are also taken to conceal, or belie, the state of the markets; of our own circumstances; our real intentions; or our ability to fulfil the engagements, into which we enter! What base deceptions are practised in cases of bankruptcy; and what frauds perpetrated, in order to attain legally the character, and immunities, of a bankrupt! How difficult has it been even to make a Law, which can at all secure to creditors an equitable share in the actual remains of a bankrupt's property! How strange would the observations, which I am now making, appear in a world of honest, virtuous beings!

Friendship is plainly one of the things, most to be looked for among rational beings; as it is one of the most profitable, and most pleasing, of all those, which are in our power. To this union of affections, this perpetual correspondence of hearts, this delightful harmony of life, all our interests strongly lead us, with motives highly noble and affectingly persuasive. Yet *Solomon* could say, and with plain propriety could say, "*A faithful man who can find?*" Not a small part of our conversation, or of our writings, is filled with bitter complaints of frail, alloyed, treacherous, broken friendship; and of unworthy, false, and perfidious friends. Why are we not friends? Can Virtue furnish any part of the reason?

The pleasures of Men, their darling and customary pleasures, have ever seemed to me an affecting proof of extreme depravity in our nature.

St. James directs, "*Is any man afflicted, let him pray. Is any merry*, (that is, cheerful) *let him sing psalms.*" In other words, let the hours of cheerfulness be spent innocently, (for such is the employment recommended) gratefully to God, and profitably to ourselves. Such are the amusements, such the pleasures, recommended by an Apostle.

In examining the pleasures, actually sought by mankind, I shall, without any particular notice, pass by the brutal entertainments, so greedily sought, so highly enjoyed, and so firmly established, under the sanctions of law, in *Greece, Rome*, and other Heathen countries: the public games, in which naked men contended for superiority in feats of agility and strength; the gladiatorial shows, in which men, trained for the purpose, butchered each other for the amusement of their fellow-men; and the exposures of human beings to the fury of wild beasts, while thousands enjoyed the sport of seeing them torn asunder, as a mere entertainment. I will not dwell upon the fact, that, beside the vulgar and the savage, men of high rank, of enlightened minds, and of polished manners, and, what is still more humiliating and disgusting, women of the first birth, education, and character, were regularly present. I will pass by the *Saturnalia*, in which *Rome* sunk, for a week every year, into the coarsest and most vulgar brutism, and all distinction and decency were abolished. Useful as the investigation might be, it must, for the want of time, be omitted on the present occasion.

Let me then ask, What are the actual pleasures, usually sought with eager favouritism in countries, claiming the title of Christian? Go to *the table*, where *provision is* professedly *made for the flesh, to fulfil the lusts thereof;* and you will find one answer to the question. What a circle is very frequently seated around it! Or rather, what does that circle in many instances become, before the table is deserted? To pass the enormous expense, care, and anxiety, with which nature and art are employed and ransacked, to gratify the demands of a sickly and fastidious palate; in how many instances, throughout even the civilized and Christian world, is a feast the mere resort of gluttony and drunkenness! How swinishly are the overflowing bounties of the Infinite God abused to the prostitution of Man; to the destruction of his health, the waste of his time, the perversion of his talents, the neglect of his duty, the corruption of his heart, the stupefaction of his reason, the loss of his usefulness, and the ruin of his Soul! How many drunkards, think you, My Brethern, have been found in a single century, the most enlightened and improved, since the beginning

of the world, and in the countries inhabited by Christians, around
the festive boards of the well-informed and polished members of
society? How many more gluttons? What a scene of low and vulgar
brutism, at the same time, is daily presented by taverns, ale-houses,
and dram-shops; and on days of public rejoicing and festivity!

Turn we hence to *the Horse-race;* another darling diversion of
mankind; and not of the ignorant and clownish only, but of the enlightened and polished; nay, even of the noble and dignified, ranks of
men. What has gathered the concourse? The professed object is to
see two or more horses run a race, and one outstrip the other in his
speed. Without calling in question the lawfulness of setting these
animals upon the stretch of their powers for our amusement: what
a picture is presented to our view by the bets which are laid, the fraud
and falsehood practised; the perjuries, oaths, curses, and blasphemies,
uttered; the drunkenness and sloth, which are indulged; the battles,
which are fought; and the universal prostitution of morals, which is
accomplished.

At *a Cockpit,* another darling scene of amusement to vast multitudes of mankind, all these gross and dreadful iniquities abound;
together with a cruelty causeless, shameless, and horrid; a cruelty
impossible to that *righteous man, who is merciful to his beast,* and
of course to every harmless creature in his power.

Of the same deplorable nature is the amusement of *Bull-baiting:*
an amusement warranted by the voice of law, and the deliberate
decisions of senatorial wisdom and royal dignity. The strength and
courage of this animal are here made the very means of torturing him
with the most exquisite agonies, which can easily be devised: all not
only quietly suffered, but established, for the sake of guarding the
palate of the epicure from offence and disappointment, on the one
hand; and on the other, for the purpose of slaking the thirst for pleasure in minds, which can find delight in ferocity, anguish, and death.

From these humiliating scenes, direct your steps to *the Gaming
table.* I need not tell you how chosen a diversion, or set of diversions,
is found here; or to what an incomprehensible extent sought in every
country, civilized and savage. Here, fraud in every form begins, carries
on, and closes, the business. Here, is the chamber of moroseness,
gloom, discontent, animosity, profaneness, contention, drunkenness,
and universal depravity. Here, property is wickedly lost, and wickedly
won. Here, time is most shamefully and sinfully wasted. Here, all
duties are most dreadfully neglected; and here, the estate, the health,
the character, the family, and the soul, are consigned to perdition.

From the gaming table turn your researches next to *the Theatre.*
Think, first, of *the almost uniform character* of the miserable wretches,
who are trained to create the diversion. How low are they, almost
without an exception, fallen; and how low do they fall, of course, by
the deplorable employment, to which they are most wickedly tempted

to devote themselves! If you are at a loss, read a history, or even a professed panegyric, of this class of mankind. You will find it filled up with crimes, which disgrace the name even of sinful Man, and with characters, which are a blot even on this guilty world. Consider, next, *the Performances*, which these unhappy men and women are employed to exhibit. How few can be read without a blush, or without a sigh, by a person, not seduced by habit, or not lost to virtue, and even to sobriety! How great a part are mere means of pollution! What art, labour, and genius, are engaged in them to garnish gross and dreadful vice; to disguise its nature and effects; to robe it in the princely attire of virtue; and to crown it with the rewards of well-doing! How often is even common decency insulted, ridiculed, and put to flight! In how many ways, and with how much art, is corruption softly and secretly instilled into the soul! In how many instances is Virtue defaced, dishonoured, and, like the Saviour of Mankind, crowned with thorns, sceptered with a reed, and mocked with pretended and insolent homage!

Turn your eyes, next, to *the Audience*, whose wishes and property give birth to the whole establishment. Of whom is this audience composed? Of how few persons, whom Virtue ever knew, or with whom she would not blush to confess her acquaintance! Of how many, who are strangers to all good! Of how many, who are ignorant even of decency; to whom vice is pleasing, and grossness an entertainment!

Accordingly, all the course of exhibition, except a little part thrust in as a sacrifice to decency and reputation, is formed of polluted sentiments, and polluted characters; in which whatever is not directly and openly abominable is meant merely as the white covering intended to shroud from the eye the death and rottenness within. Our own copious language, employed in thousands of dramatic performances, probably cannot boast of a sufficient number of such plays, as an Apostle would have pronounced innocent, to furnish a single stage for a single season.

From the Stage, men are directly prepared to go to *the Brothel*. The corruption of the one fits the mind with no common preparation to direct its course to the other.

One of the first facts, which here strikes, and afflicts, the thinking mind, is, that these houses of pestilence and ruin, of sin and perdition, are tolerated in countries, inhabited, and ruled by such as profess themselves to be Christians, by those who have been *baptized into the name of the Father, of the Son, and of the Holy Ghost*. Another is, that they are frequented by vast multitudes: and another, that these are not composed of the low, ignorant, and despised only; but, in great numbers, of the wealthy, the enlightened, the polite, and even the noble and the princely. To this we must add, because truth adds, that Seduction has in all instances begun the ruin of the miserable wretches, who inhabit these walls of *Sodom*. This seduction, also, has been accomplished by art, falsehood, serpentine insidiousness, and outrageous perjury. The endless ruin of a soul has been the price of a momentary and debased gratification; and the poor and pitiable victim has been solicited, and induced, to sacrifice eternal Life, to the fiend-like persuasion of her betrayer.

In the meantime, all, or nearly all, those, who are authors of the deception, or haunters of these tenements of prositution, accompany to the same perdition the miserable victims of their treachery. Of *the strange* or polluted *woman*, God saith, "None, that go in unto her, turn again; neither take they hold of the paths of life."

Another fact, to which your attention is called in these dreadful scenes, is, that here all sin springs up as in a hot-bed; that, beside the horrid debasement, which is here the characteristical guilt, all possible sin is rank, luxuriant, and prosperous. Profaneness, drunkenness, treachery, fraud, and murder, haunt these baleful walls, as a collection of infernal beings in a second Hell. Like that dreadful world, also, its doors are barred against all return and repentance, against life and hope. Scarcely an example is found, in which those, who have once entered, ever make their escape. *Sin* and *Perdition* are marked on the gateway; and over the door is read, in letters of fire, *This house is the way to Hell, going down to the chambers of Death.*

The last subject, which, in this complicated mass of iniquity, demands your investigation, *is the immense extent of the pollution, and the incomprehensible numbers of mankind which it involves, and has ever involved.* A prophet has recorded *Sodom*, as a monument of eternal infamy. Were prophets to exist in every land, *Sodoms* would not improbably be portrayed on many pages of every historical record. The great Capitals of most *European* and *Asiatic* countries are, in many respects, perhaps, not a whit behind the impurity, found in those monuments of the divine vengeance, *the Cities of the plain.* I wish I could say our own had a less share in this charge. Modern lewdness, although usually concealed with care from the eye of the world, has yet publicly proceeded to lengths, which amaze the mind even of cool contemplation, sicken the heart of delicacy, and turn back the eye of virtue with horror. The world has become complaisant to it; and changed its very language, to give soft and imposing names to the wretches, who have robbed the swine of their sty, or wallowed at their side in the mire. The prostitute is misnamed with softening appellations, intended to veil her odious character, and her enormous crimes. The lewd man is styled a man of gayety, spirit, and life; a man of the world; a liberal man; a man unshackled by fanaticism or superstition.

At the same time, means innumerable, tolerated by law, and pursued with impunity, are employed to cherish this worst, this most fatal, of all evils. Houses of pollution in immense numbers are erected, allowed, and frequented. Abandoned women are brought forward to places of public and honourable resort; admitted without opposition to assemblies for amusement, made up of those, who fill the upper spheres of life; seated at tables of distinction; and rolled on the wheels of splendour. Genius prostitutes its elevated powers to seduce the miserable victim, to varnish the guilt of pollution, to sooth to torpor the wounded conscience, and to make the way to Hell smooth, pleasant, and unsuspected; forms and tunes the enchanting song, to imbrute the heedless mind; fashions and animates the marble into every form of temptation: traces on the canvass its lines of symmetry and beauty, and sheds the splendour of its colouring, only to corrupt and to ruin. The shop, to complete the havoc, publicly holds out the infamous book, the alluring image, and the fascinating picture, to every passenger; and, in defiance of laws and magistrates, eagerly helps forward the work of destruction.

All these are chosen, and customary pursuits of mankind. Those, who follow them, are immortal beings, who have souls to be saved, sins to be forgiven, and endless life to be secured. All of them have heard the Gospel of Salvation; have been exhorted to yield themselves to the Redeemer; and have been earnestly invited to enter into heaven.

The life of all is a vapour; the day of grace and of pardon, is bounded by that momentary life; and each feels his time to be so short, that he cannot find even an hour to employ on the great work of Repentance, and the Salvation of his soul.

Such, then, are *the pleasures* of mankind. What, it may now be asked, are those employments of men, which wear a more serious aspect?

Among these, the first, which strikes the mind of a serious investigator, is *their general and wonderful profanation of the name of God.* To this sin, it is generally acknowledged, there is hardly any temptation. Wickedness here assumes, therefore, the character of disinterestedness; and the sin is committed from the pure love of sinning. Yet how immensely extensive is this evil practice! The Heathen and the Mohammedan, the Jewish and the Christian nations, professing widely different views, in other respects, concerning the Ruler of all things, quietly unite in profaning his awful name. Men of all ages and characters, however discordant otherwise, harmonize here. The sage and the blockhead, the gentleman and the clown, the nobleman and the peasant, join their voices in unison; and form one great chorus, not for the praise, but for the dishonour, of God. The Prince swears on his throne, and the beggar on his dunghill; the child lisps out the imperfect curse, and the tongue of the man of grey hairs trembles beneath the faltering blasphemy. From *California* to *Japan* the general voice of mankind rises up to Heaven, not *as the odour of sweet incense,* but as one vast exhalation of impiety, infinitely disgraceful to our reason, immensely ungrateful, and immensely wicked.

The next dreadful effusion of this evil spirit is the *multiform falsehood,* which in such an astonishing manner clouds and disgraces this miserable world. Truth is the foundation of all virtue, and consequently of all happiness. Without it, society, in the proper sense, cannot exist. Even the dreadful bands of thieves and ruffians are proverbially acknowledged to be indebted to it for their own horrid union. But cast your eyes over this wide world, and mark how extensively *truth has fallen in the streets* of cities, the solitary habitations of the country, and the wild retreats of the savage and barbarian. Mark how soon falsehood begins to blacken the tongue of the child, and how greatly to deepen its hue with the increase of years. Trace, if you can, without intense mortification, the secret windings of the private slanderer; and behold, if you can, without amazement, in endless multitudes, the impudent, unblushing lies of public newspapers. Survey with horror, for without horror you cannot survey, the perjuries of testimony, the perjuries of elections, the perjuries of the custom-house, and the perjuries of public office. Look with still more amazement and regret, on the falsehoods of the great and powerful. "Truth," said *King John of France,* "if banished from the rest of the world, ought still to find a mansion in the bosoms of princes." Yet how regularly from year to year, and from century to century, courts and legislatures assert, and deny, successively, the same facts, without a retraction, and without a blush. Cast your eyes, and tell me, if they do not sicken while you cast them, on the mountainous mass of falsehood heaped up by insidious Learning, and infidel philosophy, against the Word of God, and against all the interests, virtue, and happiness, of Man. When you have done these things; finish the humiliating investigation by gazing at the whole nation of the *French,* swearing eternal hatred to royalty and eternal fealty to six successive constitutions of Government, adopted within little more than six sucessive years, and then bowing down quietly at the foot of a despot!

From falsehood the transition is almost necessary to *fraud.* On this subject, however, as on all the remaining ones, I can dwell but a moment. The laws of all civilized nations have been chiefly employed in repressing this sin, and in repressing it with every suffering, which ingenuity could devise, or human nature sustain. Yet in spite of the whip, the brand, the prison, and the galley, in spite of the gibbet and the cross, the rack and the faggot, what commodity, what kind of dealing, is not the subject of fraud; and what child of *Adam* is not its mortified object? All kinds of money are counterfeited; all kinds of instruments for conveyance, or security, are forged. Vast multitudes of mankind gain their livelihood from cheating. The beggar cheats you in his tale of suffering; the man of business in his commodity; the statesman plunders the public; the prince defrauds his subjects by false representations of his wants, and false representations of his expenditures. In *London* only, a very corrupt, but far from being the most corrupt, city in *Europe*, 115,000 human beings, among whom are 50,000 abandoned females, live, according to the sagacious and upright Colquhoun, either partly or wholly, by customary fraud; and annually plunder their fellow-men of Two millions Sterling; while on the River *Thames* a more systematized robbery has yearly wrested from individuals no less than 500,000 pounds of the same currency; and from the Crown, during a century, ten millions.

Duelling and Suicide present to our view two other kindred testimonies of enormous corruption. On these, however, I cannot, and need not, dwell. Instead of expatiating on them, I will exhibit to you two official accounts of the moral state of the Capital of *France*. By a public return to the Government, of births, deaths, &c. in *Paris*, in the year 1801, it appears, that there were,

Legitimate births	14,829	
Illegitimate	4,841 }	About one-quarter of the whole.
Marriages	3,826	
Divorces	720 }	About one-sixth of the whole.
Died in their own houses . .	12,510	
In poor houses and hospitals .	8,257 }	About two-fifths of
Found dead in the streets . .	201 }	the whole.

In the Republican year, ending Sept. 23, 1803, by the report of *the Prefect of Police* to *the Grand Judge for the District of Paris,* the number of

Suicide was	{Men, .	490}	657
	{Women,	167}	
Murdered persons . . .	{Men, .	81}	150
	{Women,	69}	
Divorces			644
Murderers executed			155
Condemned to the galleys			1,210
Condemned to hard labour and imprisonment			1,626
Branded with hot irons			64

Among the criminals executed were *Seven Fathers,* who had poisoned their children: *Ten Husbands,* who had murdered their wives: *Six wives,* who poisoned their husbands: and *Fifteen children,* who destroyed their parents.

During that year also 12,076 lewd women had been registered, and paid for the protection of the Police; 1552 kept mistresses were noted; and 308 public brothels licensed, by the Prefect of Police at Paris.

This tremendous recital admits no comment. The spectator shrinks from it with horror; and, forced to acknowledge those, comprised in the story, to be *human beings*, wishes to deny, that himself is *a man.*

Secondly: The doctrine is dreadfully evinced in the Public Conduct of mankind.

On this part of the subject, copious and important as it is, I shall make a very few observations only, under the following heads.

First: Their government.

Under a righteous administration of Government, the intense corruption of the human character is gloomily manifested *by Subjects,* in the violation of their allegiance, and their evasions or their transgressions of Law. God has made it our duty to *render tribute to whom tribute is due; custom to whom custom; and honour to whom honour.* Nor has He permitted us to perform these duties with less scrupulous exactness than any other. Compare with this precept the reluctant payment of reasonable taxes; the unceasing, and immense, smuggling; the innumerable frauds, practised on the Custom-house; the murmurings, the seditions, the revolts, the malignant factions, and the furious civil discords, which have blackened the annals even of the freest and happiest nations; and you cannot want evidence of the depravity of that spirit, which has given birth to these enormities.

On the other hand, how often is the *Government* itself no other than an administration of iniquity! The endless train of evils, however, which have flowed in upon mankind from this source, have been, here, so long the ruling theme both of conversation and writings; the oppression, fraud, plunder, baleful example, and deplorable corruption, of despotic princes, have been so thoroughly learned by heart; as to render a particular discussion of them, at the present time, unnecessary. But however frequently they have been repeated, they are not on that account less real, or dreadful, manifestations of human turpitude. I know, that it is a common refuge of the objectors to this doctrine to attribute both these kinds of evidence of human corruption to the form of the government, and not to the nature of Man. But this complaisance to human nature is out of place. Kings and princes are mere men; and differ from other men, only because they are surrounded by greater temptations. Their nature and propensities are precisely the same with yours and mine. Their opportunities of doing good are, at the same time, immensely greater; and were they originally virtuous, would be seized, and employed, with an avidity, proportioned to their extent, for this great purpose only. Were human nature pure, as is professed; were it not dreadfully corrupted; kings would be the best of men; as possessing the greatest power, and the widest means of beneficence. How unlike this has been the fact, not with respect to kings only, but almost all men invested with high authority. Republican Legislatures have been at least as oppressive to mankind as Monarchs; particularly to the dependencies of their empire. *Rome and Sparta* ground their provinces with a harder hand than the *Persian Despot;* and no human tyranny was ever marked with such horrors as the Republican tyranny of *France.*

Secondly: The Wars of Mankind are a still more dreadful exhibition of wickedness than their Government.

Here, as if the momentary life of Man was too long, and his sufferings too few, and too small, men have professedly embarked in the design of cutting off life, and enhancing the number and degree of sufferings. War has prevailed through every age, and in every country; and in all has waded through human blood, trampled on human corpses, and laid waste the fields and the dwellings, the happiness and the hopes, of mankind. It has been employed to empty Earth, and people Hell; to make Angels weep, and Fiends triumph, over the deplorable guilt and debasement of the human character.

Thirdly: The doctrine is not less strongly evidenced by the Religion of Mankind.

With this subject I shall wind up the melancholy detail. JEHOVAH created this world, stored it with the means of good, and filled it with rational and immortal beings. Instead of loving, serving, and adoring Him, they have worshipped Devils, the vilest of all beings, and alike his enemies and their own. They have worshipped each other; they have worshipped brutes; they have worshipped vegetables. The Smith has molten a god of gold; the Carpenter has hewn a god of wood; and millions have prostrated themselves to both in praise and prayer. To appease the anger of these gods, they have attempted to wash their sins away by ablutions, and to make atonement for them by penance. To these gods they have offered up countless hecatombs; and butchered, and tortured, and burnt, their own children. Before these gods their religion has enjoined, and sanctioned, the unlimited prostitution of matrons and virgins to casual lust and systematized pollution. The same religion has also sanctioned war and slaughter, plunder and devastation, fraud and perjury, seduction and violation, without bounds. Its persecutions have reddened the world with blood, and changed its countries into catacombs. On *the pale horse*, seen in the Apocalyptic vision, *Death* has gone before it; *and Hell following after,* has exulted in its deplorable follies, its crimes without number, and the miseries, which it has occasioned without end.

FOR ADDITIONAL INFORMATION ABOUT TIMOTHY DWIGHT:

Calkins, Harold L. "Timothy Dwight." *Master Preachers.* Washington,
   D. C.: Review and Herald Publishing Association, 1960.
Cuningham, Charles E. *Timothy Dwight.* New York: Macmillan
   Co., 1942.
Smyth, Egbert. *A Sketch of the Life and Ministry of William T.
   Dwight, D.D.* Boston: Nichols and Noyes, 1869.
Thompson, Joseph P. *A Memoir of the Late Timothy Dwight: With
   the Sermon Delivered on the Occasion of His Death.* New Haven:
   J. H. Benham, 1844.

FOR OTHER SERMONS BY TIMOTHY DWIGHT:

Sermons. 2 vols. New Haven: Yale Press, 1828.
Theology. 5 vols. London: Houlston & Son, 1831.

LYMAN BEECHER

1775-1863

LYMAN BEECHER, from the original portrait by F. B. Carpenter at Lane Theological Seminary, courtesy of the Trustees of Lane Seminary.

LYMAN BEECHER

1775	*Born October 2, in New Haven, Connecticut*
1797	*Graduated from Yale*
1799	*Pastor in East Hampton, Long Island*
1809	*Received M. A. from Yale*
1810	*Pastor in Litchfield, Connecticut*
1813	*Son, Henry Ward Beecher, born*
1826	*Pastor, Hanover Street Congregational Church, Boston*
1832	*President of Lane Theological Seminary, Walnut Hills, Ohio*
1852	*Retired*
1863	*Died in Brooklyn, New York*

LYMAN BEECHER deserves a permanent place in American history for at least two reasons: Harriet Beecher Stowe and Henry Ward Beecher. Both of these famous Americans were his children. But Lyman Beecher should be noted for more than his offspring. He was himself a famous and effective preacher: his contemporaries felt that he was the greatest pulpiteer of his day.

LIFE AND TIMES

With his birth on October 2, 1775, in New Haven, Connecticut, and his death in 1863 in New York, the life of Lyman Beecher bracketed the beginning of America's two most important wars — the war which gave birth to the nation and the war which preserved the unity of the nation.

While a student at Yale, Beecher came under the influence of Timothy Dwight, president of Yale. In his autobiography Lyman Beecher described his experience under the preaching of Timothy Dwight: "When I heard him preach on 'The harvest

209

is past, the summer is ended, and we are not saved,' a whole
avalanche rolled down on my mind. I went home weeping every
step."[1] President Dwight's arguments made a deep impression
on young Beecher. He took notes on his sermons and lectures
and later gave testimony to all that Dwight had meant to him.

As a preacher he was deeply evangelistic. When asked, "Dr.
Beecher, you know a great deal—tell us what is the greatest of
all things," he answered, "It is not theology; it is not controversy; but it is to save souls."[2] Like most great preachers, his
evangelistic zeal was balanced by deep social concern; each was
incomplete without the other.

The key issues of his day drew Beecher's attention. The
churches were torn with theological struggles. Unitarianism
was making great inroads, particularly in New England.
Beecher felt that one of his main tasks was to counter the teachings of Unitarianism. There were many reasons for the rise of
Unitarianism. Unbelief and skepticism had swept across the
Atlantic from the turbulence of the French Revolution. The
popular stance of the day was to be either an unbeliever or a
Unitarian. Many of the churches of more orthodox persuasion
were cold and lifeless.

Many careful scholars of this period feel that Lyman Beecher
was the chief human factor that turned the tide in New England
for an evangelical faith. His fiercest battles with Unitarianism
took place in Boston, the heart of the Unitarian movement. In
1826 he became pastor of the Hanover Street Congregational
Church in Boston; he came with the determination to drive
Unitarianism into the sea. Many of his sermons during this
period were directed toward what he felt to be the errors of
Unitarianism. He thundered forth with great earnestness and
turned many people back to an evangelical Christian faith.

But theological issues were not all that claimed his attention;
he was also concerned about social issues. The young pastor
was still in his first parish, East Hampton, Long Island, when
Alexander Hamilton fell in a duel with Aaron Burr. Lyman
Beecher preached a sermon on dueling which attracted wide
attention and had much to do with putting an end to dueling
in the United States.

---

1. Charles Beecher, ed. *Autobiography,* 2 vols. (New York: Harper & Bros.,
1864), 1:46.
2. Arthur S. Hoyt, *The Pulpit and American Life* (New York: Macmillan Co.,
1921), p. 57. Used by permission.

Drunkenness was another of Beecher's deep concerns. He was among the first preachers in this nation to protest the evil done by alcohol. He consistently fought the practice of drinking, but he met with resistance both in the church and out. Clergymen were as guilty of excessive drinking as almost any others in this period of New England history. As Beecher's sermons[3] began to have an effect, a series of resolutions was approved in the church boards against the use of alcohol at church meetings. Lyman Beecher passed on his torrid disdain for alcohol to his son, Henry Ward Beecher. His stand for total abstinence was an extension of his father's own concern for the social application of the gospel.

Beecher was no Don Quixote dueling with windmills; he was an effective combatant against significant issues. That which he attacked fell before the force of his preaching. When he attacked Unitarianism and liberalism, many of his hearers turned to orthodoxy; when he delivered his appeals for temperance, hard liquor disappeared from church meetings; when he preached against the evil of dueling, laws were passed to make dueling illegal.

Lyman Beecher was a courageous man who never hesitated to stand firm whenever he felt truth was at stake. Some historians regard Beecher's position in the slavery controversy as an exception. There is no doubt that he was firmly opposed to slavery. But as president of Lane Theological Seminary he approved trustee action to abolish the antislavery movement on campus. He favored the gradualist approach to the slavery question rather than the more radical abolitionist position advocated by many of the students. On the other hand, his stand at Lane may be an example of his uncompromising approach. He refused to back down, even though practically the entire student body left in protest.

He had a strength of character which won widespread admiration. Beecher, however, was the kind of person who drew criticism as well as respect. He was regarded with suspicion by some because of his religious beliefs and was charged with heresy on more than one occasion, but he was acquitted each time.

Nevertheless, it takes more than courage to be successful in

---

3. For his notable sermon series on temperance see *Works of Lyman Beecher*, vol. 1 (Boston: John P. Jewett and Co., 1852), pp. 347–425.

handling controversial issues, and Beecher had other talents. He was earnest, possessed of strong powers of observation, discipline, eloquence, and armed with a ready wit.

Beecher also had remarkable physical vitality; he was exuberant and thoroughly alive. He had to be at the center of things. He was not a big man, but he had boundless energy; he did the work of two or three men all of his life. In one place he wrote, "I was made for action. . . . The Lord drove me, but I was ready. I've always been going at full speed."[4]

Beecher loved to work in the fields or spend long hours hunting and fishing. He always had the spirit of play about him, and his house full of active boys kept him busy. He kept an entire gymnasium in his back yard: parallel bars, a single bar, a ladder, and other simple gymnastic equipment. Sometimes he startled his sedate visitors by climbing ropes hand over hand, lifting weights, and performing other athletic exercises. Near the end of his life he astonished a guest by vaulting over a hedge to greet him. He disliked morbid introspection and believed in good mental health.

The intellectual vitality of Lyman Beecher was as noticeable as his physical vitality. His mind was open to impression. He was quick to catch new ideas. He had few books, but he knew the New England theologians – particularly Edwards and Dwight – and he knew his Bible. He was a lover of literature – as scarce as it was to come by in New England homes – and he particularly loved Milton and Scott. His boys tested his strength in intellectual arguments as well as physical contests. He kept a running debate going in his home among his boys, often taking the wrong side or playing "devil's advocate" to test their minds. When they failed, as they usually did, he would carefully instruct them in what they ought to have said.

Lyman Beecher made great contributions to American life through his pastoral work, but during the last part of his life he went from a pastoral role to an academic one. In 1832 he assumed the presidency of Lane Theological Seminary, Walnut Hills, Ohio. He served both as president of the school and as a professor; his own son, Henry Ward Beecher, studied under him. Lyman Beecher served as president of this school for twenty years and retired in 1852. Thirteen years later he died in Brooklyn where his son, Henry Ward Beecher, was a pastor.

---

4. Hoyt, p. 57.

Lyman Beecher's sons and daughters were living testimony to the fact that he was not only an effective pastor, an eloquent preacher, a courageous combatant for righteousness, but a superb Christian father as well. He seemingly never once set a poor example before his children. Henry Ward Beecher had nothing but praise for his father. He said of him, "I never heard from him a word of uncharitableness, nor saw a symptom of envy or jealousy."[5]

Henry Ward Beecher also recognized the greatness of his father as a preacher. He established a lectureship on preaching at Yale University in memory of his father. For decades, the Lyman Beecher lectures have done what Lyman Beecher himself did during his own lifetime—influence the direction of American preaching and the lives of those who proclaim the gospel.

The life of Lyman Beecher is worthy of note for anyone, but especially for preachers. He demonstrated that a pastor can have an effective Christian home life. His life clearly reveals that when one enters the ministry he must not be afraid to deal with controversy; rather, if one takes the gospel seriously, he will enter courageously those fights which call for Christian action. Yet in the midst of it all he maintained dignity, sympathy for others, good will, and a sense of humor.

Preaching and Sermons

The one word most frequently used to describe Lyman Beecher is "vitality"; "electricity" runs a close second. If we only had his written sermons by which to judge his preaching, it would be hard to find two words that *less* describe his work; Beecher's printed sermons are anything but "electric." There is a certain vitality about them, but "heavy," "wooden," or at least "overworked" might be more fitting.

Some of his sermons do contain vigorous passages such as this excerpt from his notable sermon against dueling:

> What has torn yonder wretches from the embraces of their wives and their children, and driven them to the field of blood—to the confines of hell? What nerves those

5. William C. Beecher, *A Biography of Reverend Henry Ward Beecher* (New York: C. L. Webster Co., 1888), p. 17.

arms, rising to sport with life and heaven? It is honor; the pledge of patriotism, the evidence of rectitude! Ah, it is done! The blood streams, and the victim welters on the ground.

And, see the victor coward running from the field, and, for a few days, like Cain, a fugitive and vagabond, until the first burst of indignation has passed, and the hand of time has soothed the outraged sensibility of the community; then, publicly, and as if to add insult to injustice, returning to *offer his services*, and *to pledge his honor*, that *your* lives and *your* rights shall be safe in his hand.

For knowledge of the power of Beecher's preaching we have to rely almost solely upon the testimony of those who knew him. His sermons apparently depended upon an audience for their passionate expression. Lyman Beecher was an exciting personality whose vigorous delivery and impetuous manner could not be captured on the printed page. Harwood Pattison described him: "Gifted with the orator's ardent temperament, the same impetuosity that made him when a boy spring into the water after the first fish that dropped from his hook, characterized all his attempts as a fisher of men."[6] Beecher's own statement of his philosophy of preaching suggests the vitality which characterized his life:

Whether I am qualified to do it or not, I am well convinced that the peace and power of the Church demands nothing so imperiously as a ministry inspired with zeal, enlarged by comprehensive views, blessed with a discriminating intellect, and an acute but animated and popular argumentation, untrammeled by reading polished sermons, and able, with a clear mind and full heart, to look saint and sinner in the face with an eye that speaks, and the hand that energizes, and a heart that overflows, and words that burn; competent and disposed, under the guidance of the wisdom that is from above, to convince gainsayers, allay fears, soothe prejudice, inspire confidence and cooperation in revivals and public charities, and all good things on the part of all . . . who substantially hold fast the truth, and love our Lord Jesus Christ in sincerity.[7]

---

6. T. Harwood Pattison, *The History of Christian Preaching* (Philadelphia: American Baptist Publication Society, 1903), pp. 366–67.
7. Hoyt, pp 62–63.

It is a shame that the remarkable humanness and healthy spirit of Beecher is not more evident in his sermons which still exist. Imagine him rushing into the pulpit, beginning his sermon with great enthusiasm, then drawing his glasses over his head in the excitement of speech, borrowing another pair — which wound up on the same resting place on his head — and going on until the top of his head was crowned with borrowed glasses. His enthusiasm was perennial. He spoke extemporaneously, but he never trusted himself to his natural gifts. He continually prepared himself for his work; his mind was full of invention. He believed in hard work and once wrote to one of his sons:

> You will not forget every week to make your sermons as good as you can, not depending on extemporaneous readiness without careful and discriminating thought. Have one sermon every week that will tax your intellect and the intellect of your hearers.[8]

Beecher had a practical spirit in his preaching. Whether he was preaching on temperance, on charity, or on doctrine, he sought to make a practical application of the theory to human practice. He was a fervent evangelist as well and preached an evangelical revival theology. Beecher never allowed Christian doctrine to remain in the stratosphere of mere possibility but applied its principles vigorously to the specific sins of men in need of redemption.

He appealed to the imagination: Beecher used more illustrations than other speakers of his time. His hearers were never disappointed by his sermons. Beecher's sentences were so vivid and epigrammatic that he was quoted more than any other man of his time except Benjamin Franklin. Unfortunately much of that genius for illustrating is not apparent in his sermons which were printed; only in a few places does his illustrative genius shine through.

Apparently such free-wheeling preaching was regarded as more of an embarrassment or an eccentricity than anything else, since virtually all of the preachers of his time suffered terribly in editing. In fact, many preachers in various centuries have suffered from the same problem: we know for a fact that Spurgeon, Whitefield, Phillips Brooks, and George Truett — as well as others — suffered all sorts of stilted revision and prudish

---

8. Ibid., p. 63.

pruning in a mistaken attempt to bring their vigorous style into the dreary prose that was regarded as proper.

But no amount of bad editing can silence the testimony of history. Beecher's own comment summarizes the life he poured into his sermons:

> The feeling which I now have, and have from the beginning breathed out in all my sermons, is the same, if I can judge, which Jesus himself experienced, who was moved with compassion when he saw the multitude, because they fainted and were scattered abroad as sheep having no shepherd.
>
> Now in addressing such an audience I have not felt once the spirit of rebuke; have not uttered an ironical or sarcastic expression; have not struck one stroke at an antagonist, or spoke as if I was aware that there were any hearing who thought differently from myself.
>
> I have taken the course of luminous exposition calculated to prevent objections, and applied closely, as to its experimental bearings, on conscience and heart, and held up in various forms the experience of renewed and unrenewed men, enabling Christians to feel that they have religion, and compelling sinners to concede that they have not.[9]

Perhaps Beecher's contemporary, Dr. John Dodd, was right after all when he said of Beecher, "A thunderbolt . . . You never knew where it would strike, but you never saw him rise to speak without feeling that so much electricity must strike."[10]

9. Ibid., pp. 66–67.
10. Pattison, p. 367.

Sermons

NATURE AND OCCASIONS OF INTEMPERANCE

"Who hath woe? who hath sorrow? who hath contentions? who hath babbling? who hath wounds without cause? who hath redness of eyes? They that tarry long at the wine; they that go to seek mixed wine. Look not thou upon the wine when it is red, when it giveth his colour in the cup, when it moveth itself aright. At the last it biteth like a serpent, and stingeth like an adder. Thine eyes shall behold strange women, and thine heart shall utter perverse things. Yea, thou shalt be as he that lieth down in the midst of the sea, or as he that lieth upon the top of a mast. They have stricken me, shalt thou say, and I was not sick; they have beaten me, and I felt it not: when shall I awake? I will seek it yet again" (Proverbs 23:29–35).

THIS IS A GLOWING DESCRIPTION of the sin of intemperance. No pencil but that of inspiration could have thrown upon the canvas so many and such vivid traits of this complicated evil, in so short a compass. It exhibits its woes and sorrows, contentions and babblings, and wounds and redness of eyes; its smiling deceptions in the beginning, and serpent-bite in the end; the helplessness of its victims, like one cast out upon the deep; the danger of destruction, like that of one who sleeps upon the top of a mast; the unavailing lamentations of the captive, and the giving up of hope and effort. "They have stricken me, and I was not sick; they have beaten me, and I felt it not; when shall I awake? I will seek it yet again" — again be stricken and beaten, again float upon the deep, and sleep upon the mast.

No sin has fewer apologies than intemperance. The suffrage of the world is against it; and yet there is no sin so naked in its character, and whose commencement and progress is indicated by so many signs, concerning which there is among mankind such profound ignorance.

Reprinted from Lyman Beecher, *Lectures on Political Atheism*, Beecher's Works, vol. 1 (Boston; John P. Jewett & Co., 1852), pp. 347–61.

All reprobate drunkenness; and yet, not one of the thousands who fall into it dreams of danger when he enters the way that leads to it.

The soldier approaching the deadly breach, and seeing rank after rank of those who preceded him swept away, hesitates sometimes, and recoils from certain death. But men behold the effects upon others of going in given courses — they see them begin, advance, and end in confirmed intemperance — and unappalled rush heedlessly upon the same ruin.

A part of this heedlessness arises from the undefined nature of the crime in its early stages, and the ignorance of men concerning what may be termed the experimental indications of its approach. Theft and falsehood are definite actions. But the first effect of intemperance is a state of internal sensation, and the indications may exist long, and multiply, and the subject of them not be aware that they are the signs of intemperance. It is not unfrequent that men become irreclaimable in their habits, without suspicion of danger. Nothing, therefore, seems to be more important than a description of this broad way, thronged by so many travellers; that the temperate, when they come in sight of it, may know their danger, and pass by it and turn away.

What I shall deliver on this subject has been projected for several years, has been delayed by indisposition and the pressure of other labors, and is advanced now without personal or local reference.

Intemperance is the sin of our land, and, with our boundless prosperity, is coming in upon us like a flood; and if anything shall defeat the hopes of the world, which hang upon our experiment of civil liberty, it is that river of fire which is rolling through the land, destroying the vital air, and extending around an atmosphere of death.

It is proposed, in this and the subsequent discourses, to consider the nature, the occasions, the signs, the evils, and the remedy of intemperance. In this discourse, we shall consider *the Nature and Occasions of Intemperance.*

The more common apprehension is, that nothing is intemperance which does not prevent the regular operation of the mental faculties and the bodily organs. However much a man may consume of ardent spirits, if he can command his mind, his utterance, and his bodily members, he is not reputed intemperate. And yet, drinking within these limits, he may be intemperate in respect to inordinate desire, the quantity consumed, the expense incurred, the present effect on his health and temper and moral sensibilities, and, what is more, in respect to the ultimate and inevitable results of bodily and mental imbecility, or sottish drunkenness.

God has made the human body to be sustained by food and sleep, and the mind to be invigorated by effort, and the regular healthfulness of the moral system, and the cheering influence of his moral government. And whoever, to sustain the body, or invigorate the mind, or cheer the heart, applies habitually the stimulus of ardent spirits, does violence to the laws of his nature, puts the whole system into disorder, and is intemperate long before the intellect falters, or a muscle is unstrung.

The effect of ardent spirits on the brain and the members of the body is among the least effects of intemperance, and the least destructive part of the sin. It is the moral ruin which it works in the soul, that gives it the denomination of giant wickedness. If all who are intemperate drank to insensibility, and, on awaking, could arise from the debauch with intellect and heart uninjured, it would strip the crime of its most appalling evils. But among the woes which the Scriptures denounce against crime, one is, "Woe unto them that are mighty to drink wine, and men of strength to consume strong drink." These are captains in the bands of intemperance, and will drink two generations of youths into the grave, before they go to lie down by their side. The Lord deliver us from strong-headed men, who can move the tongue when all are mute around them, and keep the eye open when all around them sleep, and can walk from the scene of riot, while their companions must be aided, or wait until the morning.

It is a matter of undoubted certainty, that habitual tippling is worse than periodical drunkenness. The poor Indian, who, once a month, drinks himself *dead* all but simple breathing, will outlive, for years, the man who drinks little and often, and is not, perhaps, suspected of intemperance. The use of ardent spirits daily, as ministering to cheerfulness or bodily vigor, ought to be regarded as intemperance. No person probably ever did, or ever will, receive ardent spirits into his system once a day, and fortify his constitution against its deleterious effects, or exercise such discretion and self-government, as that the quantity will not be increased, and bodily infirmities and mental imbecility be the result, and, in more than half the instances, inebriation. Nature may hold out long against this sapping and mining of the constitution which daily tippling is carrying on; but, first or last, this foe of life will bring to the assault enemies of its own formation, before whose power the feeble and the mighty will be alike unable to stand.

All such occasional exhilaration of the spirits by intoxicating liquors as produces levity, and foolish jesting, and the loud laugh, is intemperance, whether we regard those precepts which require us to be sober-minded, or the effect which such exhilaration and lightness have upon the cause of Christ, when witnessed in professors of religion. The cheerfulness of health, and the excitement of industry and social intercourse, is all which nature demands, or health or purity permits.

A resort to ardent spirits as a means of invigorating the intellect, or of pleasurable sensation, is also intemperance. It is a distraint upon nature, to extort, in a short time, those results of mind and feeling which, in her own unimpelled course, would flow with less impetuosity, but in a more equable and healthful current. The mind has its limits of intellectual application, and the heart its limits of feeling, and the nervous system of healthful exhilaration; and whatever you gain through stimulus, by way of anticipation, is only so much intellectual and vital power cut off at the latter end of life. It is this occult intemperance, of daily drinking, which generates a host of bodily infirmities and diseases: loss of appetite, nausea at the stomach, disordered bile, obstructions of the liver, jaundice, dropsy, hoarseness of voice, coughs, consumption, rheumatic pains, epilepsy, gout, colic, palsy, apoplexy, insanity, are the body-guards which attend intemperance in the form of tippling, and where the odious name of drunkenness may perhaps be never applied.

A multitude of persons who are not accounted drunkards create disease and shorten their days by what they denominate a "prudent use of ardent spirits." Let it, therefore, be engraven upon the heart of every man, *that the daily use of ardent spirits, in any form or in any degree, is intemperance.* Its effects are certain and deeply injurious, though its results may be slow, and never be ascribed to the real cause. It is a war upon the human constitution, carried on ostensibly by an auxiliary, but which never fails to subtract more vital power than it imparts. Like the letting out of waters, by little and little, it widens the breach, till life itself is poured out. If all diseases which terminate in death could speak out at the grave, or tell their origin upon the coffin-lid, we should witness the most appalling and unexpected disclosures. Happy the man who so avoids the appearance of evil as not to shorten his days by what he may call the prudent use of ardent spirits.

But we approach now a state of experience in which it is supposed generally that there is some criminal intemperance. I mean when the empire of reason is invaded, and weakness and folly bear rule; prompting to garrulity or sullen silence; inspiring petulance or anger, or insipid good-humor and silly conversation; pouring out oaths and curses, or opening the store-house of secrets – their own and others'. And yet, by some, all these have been thought insufficient evidence to support the charge of intemperate drinking, and to justify a process of discipline before the church. The tongue must falter, and the feet must trip, before, in the estimation of some, professors of religion can be convicted of the crime of intemperance.

To a just and comprehensive knowledge, however, of the crime of intemperance, not only a definition is required, but a philosophical analysis of its mechanical effects upon the animal system.

To those who look only to the outward appearance, the triumphs of intemperance over conscience, and talents, and learning, and character, and interest, and family endearments, have appeared wonderful. But the wonder will cease when we consider the raging desire which it enkindles, and the hand of torment which it lays on every fibre of the body and faculty of the soul.

The stomach is the great organ of accelerated circulation to the blood, of elasticity to the animal spirits, of pleasurable or painful vibration to the nerves, of vigor to the mind, and of fulness to the cheerful affections of the soul. Here is the silver cord of life, and the golden bowl at the fountain, and the wheel at the cistern; and as these fulfil their duty, the muscular and mental and moral powers act in unison, and fill the system with vigor and delight. But, as these central energies are enfeebled, the strength of mind and body declines, and lassitude, and depression, and melancholy, and sighing, succeed to the high beatings of health, and the light of life becomes as darkness.

Experience has decided that any stimulus applied statedly to the stomach, which raises its muscular tone above the point at which it can be sustained by food and sleep, produces, when it has passed away, debility—a relaxation of the overworked organ proportioned to its preternatural excitement. The life-giving power of the stomach falls, of course, as much below the tone of cheerfulness and health, as it was injudiciously raised above it. If the experiment be repeated often, it produces an artificial tone of stomach, essential to cheerfulness and muscular vigor, entirely above the power of the regular sustenance of nature to afford, and creates a vacuum which nothing can fill but the destructive power which made it; and when protracted use has made the difference great between the natural and this artificial tone, and habit has made it a second nature, the man is a drunkard, and in ninety-nine instances in a hundred is irretrievably undone. Whether his tongue falter and his feet fail him or not, he will die of intemperance. By whatever name his disease may be called, it will be one of the legion which lie in wait about the path of intemperance, and which abused Heaven employs to execute wrath upon the guilty.

But, of all the ways to hell which the feet of deluded mortals tread, that of the intemperate is the most dreary and terrific. The demand for artificial stimulus to supply the deficiencies of healthful aliment is like the rage of thirst, and the ravenous demand of famine. It is famine; for the artificial excitement has become as essential now to strength and cheerfulness as simple nutrition once was. But nature, taught by habit to require what once she did not need, demands gratification now with a decision inexorable as death, and to most men as irresistible. The denial is a living death. The stomach, the head, the heart and arteries and veins, and every muscle and every nerve, feel the exhaustion, and the restless, unutterable wretchedness which puts out the light of life, and curtains the heavens, and carpets the earth with sackcloth. All these varieties of sinking nature call upon the wretched man, with trumpet-tongue, to dispel this darkness, and raise the ebbing tide of life, by the application of the cause which produced these woes, and after a momentary alleviation will produce them again, with deeper terrors and more urgent importunity; for the repetition at each time renders the darkness deeper, and the torments of self-denial more irresistible and intolerable.

At length, the excitability of nature flags, and stimulants of higher power, and in greater quantities, are required to rouse the impaired energies of life; until, at length, the whole process of dilatory murder and worse than purgatorial suffering having been passed over, the silver cord is loosed, the golden bowl is broken, the wheel at the cistern stops, and the dust returns to the earth as it was, and the spirit to God who gave it.

These sufferings, however, of animal nature, are not to be compared with the moral agonies which convulse the soul. It is an immortal being who sins, and suffers; and as his earthly house dissolves, he is approaching the judgment-seat, in anticipation of a miserable eternity. He feels his captivity, and in anguish of spirit clanks his chains, and cries for help. Conscience thunders, remorse goads, and, as the gulf opens before him, he recoils and trembles, and weeps and prays and resolves and promises, and reforms, and "seeks it yet again"; again resolves and weeps and prays, and "seeks it yet again." Wretched man! he has placed himself in the hands of a giant who never pities, and never relaxes his iron gripe. He may struggle, but he is in chains. He may cry for release, but it comes not; and Lost! Lost! may be inscribed upon the door-posts of his dwelling.

In the meantime, these paroxysms of his dying moral nature decline, and a fearful apathy, the harbinger of spiritual death, comes on. His resolution, his mental energy, and his vigorous enterprise, fail; and nervous irritation and depression ensue. The social affections lose their fulness and tenderness, conscience loses its power, and the heart its sensibility, until all that was once lovely and of good report retires, and leaves the wretch abandoned to the appetites of a ruined animal. In this deplorable condition, reputation expires, business falters and becomes perplexed, and temptations to drink multiply as inclination to do so increases, and the power of resistance declines. And now the vortex roars, and the struggling victim buffets the fiery wave with feebler stroke and warning supplication, until despair flashes upon his soul, and, with an outcry that pierces the heavens, he ceases to strive, and disappears.

A sin so terrific should be detected in its origin, and strangled in the cradle; but ordinarily, instead of this, the habit is fixed, and the hope of reformation is gone, before the subject has the least suspicion of danger. It is of vast importance, therefore, that the various occasions of intemperance should be clearly described, that those whose condition is not irretrievable may perceive their danger and escape, and that all who are free may be warned off from these places of temptation and ruin. For the benefit of the young, especially, I propose to lay down a map of the way to destruction, and to rear a monument of warning upon every spot where a wayfaring man has been ensnared and destroyed.

The first occasion of intemperance which I shall mention is found in the free and frequent use of ardent spirits in the family, as an incentive to appetite, an alleviation of lassitude, or an excitement of cheerfulness. In these reiterated indulgences children are allowed to partake, and their tender organs of digestion are early perverted, and predisposed to habits of intemperance. No family, it is believed, accustomed to the daily use of ardent spirits, ever failed to plant the seeds of that dreadful disease which sooner or later produced a harvest of woe. The material of so much temptation and mischief ought not to be allowed a place in the family, except only as a medicine; and even then it would be safer in the hands of the apothecary, to be sent for like other medicine, when prescribed.

Ardent spirits, given as a matter of hospitality, are not unfrequently the occasion of intemperance. In this case the temptation is a stated inmate of the family. The utensils are present, and the occasions for their use are not unfrequent. And when there is no guest, the sight of the liquor, the state of the health, or even lassitude of spirits, may indicate the propriety of the "prudent use"; until the "prudent use" becomes, by repetition, habitual use, and habitual use becomes irreclaimable intemperance. In this manner, doubtless, has many a father and mother, and son and daughter, been ruined forever.

Of the guests, also, who partake of this family hospitality, the number is not small who become ensnared; especially among those whose profession calls them to visit families often, and many on the same day. Instead of being regarded, therefore, as an act of hospitality, and a token of friendship, to invite our friends to drink, it ought to be regarded as an act of incivility to place ourselves and them in circumstances of such high temptation.

Days of public convocation are extensively the occasions of excess which eventuates in intemperance. The means and temptations are ostentatiously multiplied, and multitudes go forth prepared and resolved to yield to temptation, while example and exhilarated feeling secure the ample fulfilment of their purpose. But when the habit is once acquired of drinking ever *"prudently,"* as it will be called, on all the days of public convocation which occur in a year, a desire will be soon formed of drinking at other times, until the healthful appetite of nature is superseded by the artificial thirst produced by ardent spirits.

Evening resorts for conversation, enlivened by the cheering bowl, have proved fatal to thousands. Though nothing should be boisterous, and all should seem only the "feast of reason and the flow of soul," yet, at the latter end, "it biteth like a serpent, and stingeth like an adder." Many a wretched man has shaken his chains, and cried out, in the anguish of his spirit, O, that accursed resort of social drinking!

there my hands were bound and my feet put in fetters; there I went a freeman, and became a slave – a temperate man, and became a drunkard.

In the same class of high temptation are to be ranked all convivial associations for the purpose of drinking, with or without gambling and late hours. There is nothing which young men of spirit fear less than the exhilaration of drinking on such occasions, nor anything which they are less able to resist than the charge of cowardice when challenged to drink. But there is no one form of temptation before which more young men of promise have fallen into irretrievable ruin. The connection between such beginnings and a fatal end is so manifest, and the presumptuous daring of Heaven is so great, that God, in his righteous displeasure, is accustomed to withdraw his protection, and abandon the sinner to his own way.

Feeble health and mental depression are to be numbered among the occasions of intemperance. The vital sinking, and muscular debility, and mental darkness, are for a short time alleviated by the application of stimulants. But the cause of this momentary alleviation is applied and repeated, until the habit of excessive drinking is formed, and has become irresistible.

Medical prescriptions have no doubt contributed to increase the number of the intemperate. Ardent spirits, administered in the form of bitters, or as the medium of other medicine, have let in the destroyer; and while the patient was seeking health at the hand of the physician, *he* was dealing out debility and death.

The distillation of ardent spirits fails not to raise up around the establishment a generation of drunkards. The cheapness of the article, and the ease with which families can provide themselves with large quantities, the product of their own labor, eventuate in frequent drinking and wide-spread intemperance.

The vending of ardent spirits, in places licensed or unlicensed, is a tremendous evil. Here those who have no stated employment loiter away the day for a few potations of rum, and here those who have finished the toils of the day meet to spend a vacant hour – none content to be lookers-on; all drink, and none for any length of time drink temperately. Here, too, the children of a neighborhood, drawn in by enticements, associate for social drinking, and the exhibition of courage and premature manhood. And here the iron hand of the monster is fastened upon them, at a period when they ought not to have been beyond the reach of maternal observation.

The continued habit of dealing out ardent spirits, in various forms and mixtures, leads also to frequent tasting, and tasting to drinking, and drinking to tippling, and tippling to drunkenness.

A resort to ardent spirits as an alleviation of trouble results often in habits of confirmed intemperance. The loss of friends, perplexities of business, or the wreck of property, bring upon the spirits the distractions of care and the pressure of sorrow; and instead of casting their cares upon the Lord, they resort to the exhilarating draught; but, before the occasion for it has ceased, the remedy itself has become a calamity more intolerable than the disease. Before, the woes were temporary; now, they have multiplied, and have become eternal.

The use of ardent spirits to invigorate the intellect, or restore exhausted nature under severe study, is often a fatal experiment. Mighty men have been cast down in this manner, never to rise. The quickened circulation does, for a time, invigorate intellect, and restore exhausted nature. But, for the adventitious energy imparted, it exhausts the native energy of the soul, and induces that faintness of heart and flagging of the spirits which cry incessantly, "Give, give," and never, but with expiring breath, say "It is enough."

The use of ardent spirits, employed as an auxiliary to labor, is among the most fatal, because the most common and least suspected, causes of intemperance. It is justified as innocent—it is insisted on as necessary; but no fact is more completely established by experience than that it is utterly useless, and ultimately injurious, besides all the fearful evils of habitual intemperance to which it so often leads. *There is no nutrition in ardent spirit. All that it does is, to concentrate the strength of the system, for the time, beyond its capacity for regular exertion.* It is borrowing strength for an *occasion* which will be needed for futurity, without any provision for payment, and with the certainty of ultimate bankruptcy.

The early settlers of New England endured more hardship, and performed more labor, and carried through life more health and vigor, than appertains to the existing generation of laboring men. And they did it without the use of ardent spirits.

Let two men of equal age and firmness of constitution labor together through the summer, the one with and the other without the excitement of ardent spirits, and the latter will come out at the end with unimpaired vigor, while the other will be comparatively exhausted. Ships navigated as some now are, without the habitual use of ardent spirits, and manufacturing establishments carried on without, and extended agricultural operations, all move on with better industry, more peace, more health, and better income to the employers and the employed. The workmen are cheerful and vigorous, friendly and industrious, and their families are thrifty, well fed, well clothed, and instructed; and instead of distress and poverty, and disappointment and contention, they are cheered with the full flow of social affection, and often by the sustaining power of religion.

But where ardent spirit is received as a daily auxiliary to labor, it is commonly taken at stated times; the habit soon creates a vacancy in the stomach, which indicates, at length, the hour of the day, with as much accuracy as a clock. It will be taken, besides, frequently at other times, which will accelerate the destruction of nature's healthful tone, create artificial debility, and the necessity of artificial excitement to remove it; and when so much has been consumed as the economy of the employer can allow, the growing demand will be supplied by the evening and morning dram from the wages of labor, until the appetite has become insatiable, and the habit of intemperance nearly universal; until the nervous excitability has obliterated the social sensibilities, and turned the family into a scene of babbling and woe; until voracious appetite has eaten up the children's bread, and abandoned them to ignorance and crime; until conscience has become callous, and fidelity and industry have disappeared, except as the result of eye-service; and wanton wastefulness and contention, and reckless wretchedness, characterize the establishment.

THE NATIVE CHARACTER OF MAN

"Every one that loveth is born of God" (1 John 4:7).

THE LOVE here spoken of is holy love, which assimilates the subject to God. It is that love which is styled the fulfilling of the law, and which is the principle of evangelical obedience. It is religion; for every one that loveth knoweth God. But to know God is life eternal—is religion. This love does not belong to man by nature. It is never a quality of his heart as a consequence of his birth, but is the result, in all cases, of a special divine interposition. "Which were born, not of blood, nor of the will of the flesh, nor of the will of man, but of God."

It will be the object of this discourse to show that man is not religious by nature. By religion I mean supreme love to God. By man I mean the entire race. And by the proposition that man is not religious by nature, I mean that there is nothing in him which is religion, and nothing of which religion is the natural effect or consequence, without a special divine interposition. When natural objects produce certain

Reprinted from Lyman Beecher, *View of Theology*, Beecher's Works, vol. 3 (Boston: John P. Jewett & Co., 1853), pp. 53–71.

effects uniformly, we suppose there is in them some cause for such results, which we call their nature; and if there be certain effects which they never produce, we say that it is not in their nature to produce them.

When it is affirmed, therefore, of man, that he is not religious by nature, we mean that there is nothing in his constitution of mind or body of which religion is the result without a special divine interposition, and that the *first accountable character* which he sustains is not a religious character. It will not be denied, that if religion exists at all in man it must exist in his heart, and must consist primarily in the state of his will and affections towards God — must include a predominant benevolence for God, and complacency in his character, and delight in his law, and obedience to his Gospel, and resignation to his will.

In view of these explanations, therefore, I observe,

I. *That the consciousness of every man in view of the requirements of the law and the Gospel, is evidence to himself that he possesses no religion.*

I appeal to the experience of every one in this assembly that has not been born again, whether religious affections have found a place in your heart, from your earliest recollection. Do you believe that you are truly pious? Can you lay your hand upon your heart, and look up to heaven and say, Thou knowest that I love thee more than all things beside? Do you love his word, his worship, his people? Do you maintain, with pleasure, secret prayer? Are you meek under provocation, and self-denying in temptation, and resigned in affliction? This is religion. But is this the experience of any one in this assembly who has no reason to believe that he is born of God? And if not, certainly you are not religious by nature. And if you present this outline of religious experience to your neighbor, you will find that he has nothing that answers to it. And if you extend the inquiry through the world, you will not find one whose first development of character is that of religion.

II. *The uniform experience of awakened sinners corroborates the same doctrine.* From the day of Pentecost to the present hour, multitudes have experienced deep anxiety for their souls, but universally the cause of it has been that they had no religion. They have perceived, always, that the law of God required of them a love which they did not feel, and Christian graces to which they were strangers. And nothing has been found more to aggravate their distress than the simple direction to love supremely the Lord their God, and Jesus Christ. Uniformly the reply has been, We cannot love; we cannot repent; we cannot believe. I am sensible that there are many who are not thus awakened; but does their stupidity discredit the consciousness of those who are awakened in respect to their own character? This consciousness, then, of all who are awakened, that they have no religion, is strong presumptive evidence that the same is the fact with respect to those who are not awakened.

III. *To this may be added the testimony of those who furnish evidence of piety.* Their uniform testimony is that their religious experience is a state of the will and affections wholly unknown before.

It is not to be denied that some persons profess religion who disclaim the existence of any great change in the state of their will and affections towards God, and claim that they have always, from their earliest years, loved God. But it must be remembered that the religion which they claim is not such religion as has been described. To this they make no pretension, but ridicule it as visionary, enthusiastic and fanatical. Doubtless men may have such religion as these persons profess, without a change of heart. But I insist that the outline of religious experience which has been given is the religion of the Bible; and that all who are conscious of possessing it do testify that it is a state of the affections entirely new; and this testimony of the pious strengthens the presumption that religion is never the first character of man, but always the result of a divine interposition.

IV. *The history of the world is utterly inconsistent with the supposition of native piety in man.*

If a man is religious by nature, we should expect to witness the effects of early and universal piety in the history of the world. A world whose inhabitants all begin their accountable course religiously, could not surely furnish the same materials for history as a world whose early character is that of alienation from God. But does the history of the world confirm the supposition that man is religious by nature? Of those who, in adult age, afford credible evidence of piety, three-fourths at least continue to do so; and the reasons would be stronger in favor of perseverance, if religion were the first character of all men. But do three-fourths of the human race, or one-fourth, afford evidence of piety from childhood upward? Has it not been, till lately, a rare event to find it at all among children? Among real Christians religion is a predominant principle of action. But does the history of the world show that religion has been the predominant principle of action in the human race? What is the origin of governments, but necessity? Families cannot dwell in safety in this world without protection, and therefore associate in tribes; and tribes, wearied with the action and reaction of violence, coalesce for safety, and form the more extended communities of nations. Until these great associations were formed, the world had no rest, and the arts of civilized life were scarcely known. But nations have displayed the same principles of ambition and violence towards each other which marked the conduct of individuals, and families, and tribes. The history of nations is the history of crime and blood, and not of peace and good-will to men. If men were religious by nature, we might expect that the knowledge and worship of the true God would be in every age universal. Instead of this, two-thirds of the human family have been idolaters. Notwithstanding the invisible things of God are clearly seen by the things that are made, even his eternal power and God-head—and notwithstanding all that God has done by revelation, and by miracle, and by his Spirit—two-thirds of the human family have changed the glory of the incorruptible God into an image made like to corruptible man, and to four-footed beasts and creeping things. Why is this? The evidence of His being is not obscure, and the divinity of idols is not supported by even specious evidence. The service of God is reasonable, pure, and benign; while that of idols is obscene, expensive, and bloody. Could a race, of which every individual commenced his accountable course under the influence of religion, have done thus?

V. *It is the uniform testimony of the Bible, that men are not religious by nature.*

This is strongly implied in the utter silence of the Scriptures in respect to the piety of man by nature. If the first character which man sustains is a religious character, the Scriptures could not have failed to recognize it. It would be a commanding fact, which would extend its implications through every page, and modify every doctrine. Surely the descriptions of a religious, and of an alienated world, could not be the same. But let one examine, one by one, all the passages which speak of the heart of man, and he will find there is not *one* which declares, or implies, that it is the subject of religion by nature. Whence this silence? It is one great object of the Bible to make man acquainted with his own heart; and much is disclosed concerning its wickedness. Why is nothing said of its excellence, if religion be one of its native attributes? This silence, though only negative testimony, corroborates greatly the preceding evidence, that man is not religious by nature.

VI. *The Bible ascribes to the natural heart of man a character utterly incompatible with the existence of religion.* Before the flood, every imagination of *man's heart* is described as being *evil only, continually;* and after that event, as *evil still,* from his youth. This last declaration is made also as a reason why God in all future ages will no more curse the ground for man's sake—affording testimony, not only that the heart of man was evil then from his youth, but that it would continue to be so through all ages future; unreclaimed by judgments, however numerous or severe. Thirteen hundred years later the hearts of the sons of men are described as "full of evil." And later still as "deceitful above all things, and desperately wicked." The account which is given of the heart by our Saviour is as explicit and forcible as any of the preceding—"Out of the heart proceed evil thoughts, murders, adulteries, fornications, blasphemies."

Upon this testimony of the Bible I remark, that the heart of man is never described as becoming thus wicked by any change *from native goodness to evil, since the fall of Adam;* but, when described as evangelically good, it is always done in terms which imply a change from *evil* to *goodness.*

Whenever men conduct wickedly, they are regarded as illustrating their own natural character—as obeying the dictates of their own hearts. But when they manifest religious affections, these are described as the fruits of the Spirit; and when they are given up to irreclaimable wickedness, they are given up to their own hearts' lust—to their foolish and darkened hearts—to vile affections through the lust of their own hearts, after their hard and impenitent hearts, treasuring up wrath. How, then, stands the testimony of the Bible concerning the heart of man? It is silent as to the existence in it of religion. That heart is described in terms which preclude its existence. That heart is never represented as becoming bad by the loss of religion, or as being good except as the effect of a divine interposition; and when abandoned to itself, it is always represented as being desperately wicked. Will it be alleged that this testimony is ancient, and that the heart of man may have changed for the better? To break the force of the testimony, it must not only be *possible* that a change *may* have taken place, but it must be proved that it *actually has taken place.* Can such proof be found in the Bible? Is there a passage which asserts or implies that a universal change has taken place in the heart of man since the preceding descriptions of it were placed upon record?

Will it be alleged that Enoch, and Noah, and Moses, and Abraham, and others, are spoken of as righteous, without any *mention* that they had experienced a change of heart? If it were so, it would not prove that no change had been experienced. The omission, in the record, to recognize the change, does not prove that it never happened. But it is implied of all these that they did experience a change of character. Faith implies a change of character, and is the gift of God. But by faith Abel offered a more excellent sacrifice than Cain, and this was a faith that works by love. By faith, Enoch walked with God. By faith, Abraham offered his son. By faith, Moses refused to be called the son of Pharaoh's daughter. Will it be said that the preceding proof is contained in a few detached texts of Scripture? These texts are the testimony of God. They relate to the subject in question, and are direct and explicit. They are not detached from the context, and made to speak a meaning which they would not be authorized to speak in their connection. And as to their being detached in any other sense, what if they were all contained on one page—would that increase their perspicuity? Or what if they were multiplied an hundred-fold—would that increase the evidence of divine testimony? How near together must the declarations of God be placed, and how often must they be repeated, to be entitled to credit? And what is the character of those to whom the Lord speaketh once, yea, twice, and they regard it not?

VII. *The Scriptural account of childhood and youth implies that mankind are not religious by nature.* "The imagination of man's heart is evil from his youth." "Childhood and youth are vanity." "Foolishness is bound in the heart of a child." "The wicked are estranged from the womb."

Could all this be said of childhood and youth, if the first accountable character they sustain were a religious character? Is every imagination of the pious, evil? Is religion vanity, or folly, or estrangment from God? It must be remembered also that the preceding are not specific descriptions of *some* children and youth, but descriptions of the entire race of man in the early periods of life.

VIII. *The generic descriptions of man, contained in the Bible, are such as preclude the supposition that he is religious by nature.*

The term *man* includes all men of all nations. One nation is not man. All nations but one, are not man. Every individual of the race is included; and whatever is declared of the *genus* is declared concerning every individual. Is the lion ferocious? It is the character of all his race. Is the asp venomous? It is true of every asp. Is man born unto trouble as the sparks fly upward? None, then, escape trouble. Does he die and waste away? There is no discharge, then, in that war.

When it is demanded, then, what is man, that he should be clean, or he that is born of a woman, that he should be righteous, it is a positive declaration that man is not clean, is not righteous—as a natural consequence of his birth. He possesses strength, and intelligence, and memory, and will, and affections, and appetites and passions, as the result of the constitution with which he is born. But moral purity—righteousness—it is expressly declared, is not, like these, the consequence of natural birth.

The *world* is another generic term by which the human race is characterized; and always in a manner which excludes the supposition of religion as being the first or natural character of man. We know that we (Christians) are of God—that is, are born of God—and the whole world lieth in wickedness. "He (Christ) was in the world, and the world knew him not." "O, righteous Father, the world hath not known thee." "Know ye not that the friendship of the world is enmity with God?" "If the world hate you, ye know that it hated me before it hated you." "I have given them thy word, and the world hath hated them." "If ye (my disciples) were of the world, the world would love his own; but because ye are not of the world, but I have chosen you out of the world, therefore the world hateth you." In these passages the world is contrasted with the pious; and both together, like the ancient terms Jew and Gentile, include all men. There is no middle class, which belongs neither to the pious nor to the world. But the world is described as ignorant of God; as alienated from God; as opposed to Jesus Christ, and his cause and people; as lying in wickedness; as dead in trespasses and sins. Is this the description of a race whose first accountable character is that of loyalty to God?

The term *flesh* is also a generic term, descriptive of man in his native state. "My Spirit shall not always strive with man, for that (or because) he also is *flesh.*" His being an animal furnished no reason, surely, why the Spirit of God should not strive with him. It is his moral nature, therefore, which is called flesh; and which is described in other places as alienated from God, and as lusting against the Spirit; furnishing an obvious reason why the Spirit might abandon man. In his discourse with Nicodemus, our Saviour speaks of the *flesh* as being that *moral* nature of man which is the consequence of his natural birth. "That which is born of the flesh is flesh, and that which is born of the Spirit is spirit." Our Saviour would not surely undertake to convince Nicodemus that the animal body is flesh. Flesh and spirit are therefore moral qualities contrasted: the one, forming the first character of man; the other, the result of a special interposition of the divine Spirit. The one disqualifying, and the other fitting, a man for the kingdom of heaven. The one intending that moral nature of man which renders regeneration indispensable; the other that holy nature which is produced by the Spirit of God, when he renews the heart.

The flesh is in other places described as the comprehensive principle of moral evil in man; as the Spirit is described as being the efficient cause of all good. The works of the flesh are adultery, fornication, idolatry, hatred, seditions, heresies, envyings, murders, drunkenness, revellings, and such like: but the fruits of the Spirit are love, joy, peace, long-suffering, gentleness, goodness, faith, meekness, and temperance. The flesh comprehends the depravity which remains in the Christian after he is renewed. "I know that in me, that is, in my flesh, dwelleth no good thing." All my goodness is the result of regeneration; all my sin, the remains of my corrupt nature, called the flesh. "The flesh lusteth against the spirit, and the spirit against the flesh; and these are contrary the one to the other, so that ye cannot do the things that ye would." The flesh, then, being the first character of man, and the comprehensive principle of evil in him, is so described as to preclude the possibility of religion as the characteristic of his first moral nature. For the carnal or fleshly mind is "enmity against God." To be carnally minded is death; and they that are in the flesh cannot please God; and they that live after the flesh shall die.

IX. *All those terms which divide the race of man into two great moral divisions, imply that not a religious, but a depraved character, is first sustained.* Such are the righteous and the wicked, the holy and the unholy, the godly and the ungodly, the just and the unjust. That these terms of contrast include all men is certain. From the nature of free agency, and from the declaration of God, we know that neutrality cannot exist among accountable beings. Where men are qualified to obey, and love is required, neutrality would be disobe-

dience. To regard God, as compared with the creature, with indifference, would be adding insult to rebellion. But such a state of mind is
impossible. No man can serve two masters, nor be indifferent towards
them. He will love or hate, obey or despise. All men, then, are holy or
unholy, righteous or wicked. But which is the first character sustained
by man? Not the holy, but the unholy. There is not intimation in the
Bible that men become unholy by any change from good to bad; but
Christians are continually described as becoming holy by a change
from bad to good. They are begotten again. They are born of God.
They are created anew. They are raised from the dead. The old man is
put off, and the new man is put on. By all this variety of language it
is implied that the sinful nature of man is first, and that his holy nature
is the result of a special divine interposition.

X. *The avowed object of the death of Christ decides that mankind
are not religious by nature.* His death was rendered necessary by a
character sustained by all men. And what was the character sustained,
which awakened the compassion of God, and called from heaven his
only-begotten son to die for man? It was that of alienation from God.
Herein is the love of Christ commended, in that while we were yet
enemies he died for us. He suffered, the just for the unjust. "He died
for all"; but it was because they "were all dead." In accordance with
these representations, men are addressed by the Gospel as *dead;* and
are commanded to arise from the dead — as blind; and are commanded
to see — as wicked; and are commanded to forsake their wicked way,
and turn to God. They are addressed as impenitent; and are called upon
to repent — as in unbelief; and are commanded to believe. Every
condition of pardon proposed to men in the Gospel, implies that they
do not by nature possess it. The apostles, in their great commission,
were directed to address every creature as impenitent; and Paul, in
particular, was sent to the heathen, to open their eyes, and to turn
them from darkness to light, and from the power of Satan to the living
God.

When men obey the Gospel, they are described as renewed — as
reconciled — as sustaining new affections. Old things are passed away;
behold all things are become new. The entire Christian character is
described in the Bible as the work of the Spirit. The fruit of the Spirit
is love, joy, peace, faith, &c. But the Spirit operates only in the application of the redemption purchased by Christ, in carrying into effect
the objects of his death. Before he renews the hearts of the men for
whom Christ died, they are therefore enemies, unjust, and dead in sin.

Those who reject the Gospel, and perish, are represented as sustaining their own original character; as despising the riches of the
goodness of God, and, after their hard and impenitent heart, treasuring
up wrath; as refusing when the Saviour called, and disregarding when
he stretched out his hand. In short, men are described as becoming
wicked as a consequence of the fall of Adam, and religious as the

consequence, and only as the consequence, of the interposition of Jesus Christ, and the renewing of the Holy Ghost.

XI. *It is declared in direct terms, expressly and unequivocally, that mankind are not religious in their first character.*

"The Lord looked down from heaven upon the children of men, to see if there were any that did understand and seek God." To know and to seek God, implies religion. This investigation, therefore, was instituted to decide the question whether there was an individual of the human race who was religious by nature. Not whether any had returned, of those who had gone astray—for of such we read in the context, and throughout the Bible—but to ascertain whether there were any of the race of man who had never turned away from God, but remained, like Abdiel, "faithful among the faithless." The result of this omniscient scrutiny is, "They are all gone aside; they are all together become filthy; there is none that doeth good; no, not one." This is the declaration of God concerning the children of men: the result of an omniscient investigation, made expressly to decide whether the effects of the fall were universal, or whether any religious affection remained. The apostle Paul quotes this declaration of the Most High to prove, and he says that it does prove, "both Jews and Gentiles" (terms which then included all men), "that they are all under sin." But to be under sin is to be under its dominion, and under condemnation; for he proves the fact, that all are under sin, to cut off the hope of justification by the deeds of the law, and to establish the doctrine of justification by faith. But to be under the dominion of sin, and in an *unjustified* condition, is surely inconsistent with the existence of religion. To corroborate his argument, the apostle quotes the following passage from the Old Testament, and he quotes it that every mouth may be stopped, and the whole world become guilty before God. "Their throat is an open sepulchre; with their tongues they have used deceit; the poison of asps is under their lips; whose mouth is full of cursing and bitterness; their feet are swift to shed blood; destruction and misery are in their ways; and the way of peace have they not known; there is no fear of God before their eyes."

Now, abate from this passage as much as is possible on the ground of metaphor, yet, as it is quoted in a regular argument to stop every mouth, and to prove the whole world guilty before God, it does most certainly exclude the supposition of piety in those who are thus characterized. An open sepulchre is not the place of life; the poison of asps is not an emblem of health; and cursing and bitterness are not the fruits of the Spirit; nor are destruction and misery found in the ways of wisdom; nor can it ever be said of the truly pious that they have no fear of God before their eyes. Language is of no use, and inspiration affords no evidence of truth, if these terms, applied to stop every mouth and prove the whole world guilty before God, do not prove that man is not religious by nature.

XII. *There is also in the Scriptures much inferential evidence on this subject.* If man, in his first character, is religious, we should expect that the fact would be implied in all the doctrines of the Bible; and if he is not religious, that such a fact would also be implied. The difference is so great that the same doctrines cannot be alike true on either supposition. But to which of the two suppositions are the doctrines of the Bible accommodated? If man is not religious by nature, we should expect to find the necessity of a great moral change inculcated in the Bible. And do we not find it? "Except a man be born again he cannot see the kingdom of God." We should expect to find Christians described as those who had experienced this great change: and thus they are described as born of God, created anew, and passed from death unto life. As there can be no medium between religion and irreligion, we should expect the change would be sudden. And do not all the terms which describe it imply that it is sudden? It is a creation. Is there a point of time in the process of creation in which a substance is neither in being nor out of being? It is a resurrection from the dead. Is there a moment in which the body is neither dead nor alive? If all men in the beginning withhold from God the homage of the heart, we should expect they would continue to do so, until reclaimed by a divine interposition. And thus we read of those who received Christ, that they were born, not of blood, nor of the will of the flesh, nor of man, *but of God.*

If religion in man is the result of a divine interposition, we should expect to find it described as an act of grace which God might grant, or withhold, according to his good pleasure. And do we not read that he hath mercy on whom he will have mercy? If men are without religion, we should expect that they would be required to give the heart to God, and repent, and believe immediately, and that those who perished would be represented as self-destroyers. And is it not so? "Repent, believe on the Lord Jesus Christ." Today, if ye will hear his voice, harden not your hearts." And do not all who perish under the light of the Gospel perish by neglecting the great salvation? "Turn ye, for why will ye die?" "I have called, and ye have refused." "This is the condemnation, that light is come into the world, and men loved darkness rather than light."

If men are not religious in their first character, we should expect to find all their actions charged with sinful defect. And in accordance with this expectation we read, "The sacrifice of the wicked is an abomination to the Lord." "The ploughing of the wicked is sin." "So then they that are in the flesh cannot please God." And "without faith it is impossible to please him."

In conclusion of the argument, I have only to add, that if the first accountable character of man is a religious character, this entire body of evidence must be reversed. All men must be conscious of supreme love to God in early life; and conviction of sin and a moral renovation must be confined to those who have lost their religion; while the great body of Christians must be supposed to be such without the consciousness of any change. At the same time, the history of the world must be held to be a history of the fruits of piety – idolatry itself being only an aberration of religious affection in children emulous to please their heavenly Father! It should, moreover, be found written upon the unerring page, "Every imagination of man's heart is *good* from his youth. The children of men have *not* gone out of the way. There is none who *doth not* understand and seek God, and do good; no, not one. The heart of the sons of men is full of *goodness,* out of which proceed *holy* thoughts, benevolent deeds, chastity, truth, and reverence for God. What, therefore, is man, that he should be *wicked*? or he that is born of a woman, that he should *not* be religious? How *lovely* and pure is man, who drinketh in *righteousness* like water! This is the *approbation,* that *darkness* is come into the world, and men have loved *light* more than darkness, because their deeds are *good*. The whole world lieth in *righteousness*. He [Christ] was in the world, and the world *knew* him. O, righteous Father, the world hath *known* thee. The friendship of the world is *friendship with God*. If the world hath loved you, ye know that it loved *me* before it loved you. Be, ye, therefore, *conformed* to the world, and be ye *not transformed* by any renewing of your mind. My Spirit shall *always* strive with man, because *he* is spirit. For that which is born of the *flesh* is *spirit*. Marvel not that I say unto you ye *must not* be born again. For the works of the *flesh* are *love, joy, peace, faith;* and the fruits of the Spirit are love, joy, peace, faith. In me – that is, in my flesh – dwelleth *every* good thing. Jesus Christ came to seek and to save those who were *not* lost, and he died *not* for his enemies – *not* the just for the unjust." The Gospel demands of men *no new character;* and all the doctrines of the Bible imply the early and universal piety of the human family.

And now who is prepared thus to reverse the whole testimony of experience, of history, and of the holy Scriptures? In view of such overwhelming evidence to the contrary, will any man pretend to believe that mankind are religious by nature?

If you had as much evidence that your water was poisoned as you have that the heart of man by nature is not holy, would you drink it? Were the proof as clear that an assassin would meet you on turning a corner, would you go thither? Were it proved by as various and conclusive evidence that the fire was kindling on your dwelling, would you compose yourself to sleep? Will you, then, in opposition to such evidence, still endeavor to persuade yourself of the native goodness of the human heart? If it were merely the body whose life was threatened by the deception, I might still cry earnestly to you to beware; but it is your *soul,* and your future and eternal well-being, which you put in jeopardy by setting at naught such evidence. Without religion you cannot be admitted to heaven, and would not enjoy heaven if you were admitted. Without religion you can neither keep the law nor obey the Gospel, and cannot escape the condemnation which rests upon transgression and unbelief.

Will you, then, shut your eyes against light, and stop your ears against admonition? It is but for a moment, compared with eternity, that you can thus deceive yourself, and cry Peace. The overwhelming consciousness must soon press upon your amazed heart, that you are without holiness and cannot see the Lord, and that the harvest is past, the summer ended, and you not saved. There is no hope in your case while you think your heart is good, and feel no need of a divine renovation. They that are whole need not the physician, but they that are sick; and Jesus Christ came to call, not the righteous, but sinners, to repentance. While the delusion prevails that you are rich, and stand in need of nothing, you will reject the counsel of Christ, to apply to him for eye-salve that you may see, and for white raiment to cover the shame of your nakedness. You will do nothing to save your own soul, and God will do nothing to save it, while, under the concentrated light of evidence, you remain wilfully ignorant of your malady, and wilfully negligent of your only remedy. Admit, then, the painful, alarming fact, that you have no religion, and without delay commence the inquiry what you must do to be saved, and thus escape the coming wrath, and lay hold on eternal life. All men who are now in heaven were once, like you, without God, and without Christ, and without hope; and all who are now on earth, strangers and pilgrims seeking a better country, were once, like you, without religion. But He who commanded the light to shine out of darkness has shined in their hearts, and the same blessed Spirit is able and willing to enlighten you; but you must confess, and not cover your sin; you must come to the light, and not shun it; you must be convinced of sin, of righteousness, and of a judgment to come; you must be born again, or you cannot see the kingdom of God.

THE REMEDY FOR DUELLING

"And judgment is turned away backward, and justice standeth afar off: for truth is fallen in the street, and equity cannot
enter" (Isaiah 59:14–15).

THE PEOPLE OF ISRAEL, when this passage was written, had become
exceedingly corrupt, and were sinking under the pressure of fearful judgments.

But although they are hardened in sin, they are not insensible to
misery; and though regardless of God as their benefactor, they mur-
mur and tremble before him as the author of their calamities.

They admit, indeed, their sinfulness, but suppose that they have
made already a sufficient atonement for it. It is not for sending judgments, therefore, that they impeach the Almighty, but for continuing
them; not because he is just, but because he has no mercy. "Wherefore
have we fasted (say they), and thou seest not—have we afflicted our
soul, and thou takest no knowledge?"

The Majesty of Heaven condescends to reply. He declares their sin to
be the cause of his judgments, and their hypocrisy and impenitence
the ground of their continuance.

The sins which brought down the judgments of Heaven were, it
appears, national sins. As individuals, they were guilty, and each had
contributed to augment the national stock; but, of all classes, their
rulers, and men of wealth and eminence, had been the most liberal
contributors. Their private character was abominable, and their public character was no better. They perverted justice, their feet ran to
evil, their hands were defiled with blood. Their thoughts were thoughts
of iniquity; wasting and destruction were in their paths. . . .

Doubtless, in the humble walks of life, there were some who had es-
caped this contagion of bad example, and who, had they been united
and courageous, might have set bounds to these evils; but they neglected to make exertion—they were dismayed, and gave up the cause
of God without an effort.

I have no conception that this state of the Jewish nation is, in general, a correct portrait of our own. But are there no points of resemblance? I allude now only to the conduct of such of our rulers and men
of eminence as denominate themselves men of honor; and who, despising the laws of their country and their God, adjust with weapons of
death their private quarrels. To such, the character ascribed to the

Reprinted with a few omissions from Lyman Beecher, *Sermons Delivered on
Various Occasions*, Beecher's Works, vol. 2 (Boston: John P. Jewett & Co.,
1852), pp. 34–74.

Jewish rulers is affectingly applicable. Their hands are full of blood; and wasting and destruction are in their paths.

I allude also to the impunity with which, in a community nominally Christian, and under the eye of the law, these deeds of violence are committed in a duel, "judgment is turned away backward, and justice standeth afar off: truth is fallen in the street and equity cannot enter."

It may be added, that, as among the Jews, the *people,* who by the influence of public sentiment might have limited the evils of their day, remained inactive; so the great body of this nation, although they abhor the crime of duelling, remain inactive spectators of the wide-wasting evil.

"But," it will be demanded, "how can the people prevent duelling? Already laws are enacted, with severe penalties. Besides this, what can we do?" You can rescue these laws from contempt, by securing their prompt execution. Do you demand how? By withholding your suffrage from every man whose hands are stained with blood, or who has been directly or indirectly concerned in a duel; and by intrusting to men of fair moral character, and moral principle, the making and execution of your laws.

It will, therefore, be the object of this discourse, to suggest and illustrate the reasons which should induce every man to withhold his vote from any person who has fought, or aided in fighting, a duel.

1. The elevation of duellists to power is a practice in direct opposition to the precepts of the Christian religion.

Civil government is a divine ordinance. The particular form is left to the discretion of men; but the character of rulers God has himself prescribed. They must be *just men:* such as *fear God; a terror to evil doers, and a praise to them that do well.* Do duellists answer to this description? Are they just men? Do they fear God? Look at their law of honor. It constitutes the party judge in his own cause, and executer of his own sentence. Its precepts, like those of Draco, are written in blood. Death, or exposure to it, is its lightest penalty; and this, with unrelenting severity, is inflicted for the most trifling offence, as well as for the most enormous crime; and as often, perhaps, upon the innocent, as upon the guilty.

When arrested by the fatal challenge, no plea of reverence for God, of respect for human law, of conscience, of innocency, absence of anger, actual friendship, affection to parents, wife, or children, the hope of heaven or fear of hell, is for one moment admitted. All obligations are cancelled; all ties are burst asunder; all consequences are disregarded. "Nor justice nor mercy may interpose, to mitigate the rigors of the controversy. The peaceable must fight the quarrelsome; the rich man, the bankrupt; the father of a family, the libertine; the son of many hopes, the worthless prodigal." It is a law which inculcates no virtue, and which prohibits no crime, if it be *honorably committed.* It tolerates adultery, blasphemy, intemperance, revenge, and murder. "Thou shalt kill" is its first and great command, and too much conscience to obey it is the only unpardonable sin. The obedient subjects of a law so impious, so unmerciful and unjust, God has denounced as unfit to govern men. They are disfranchised by Heaven. But,

2. The duellist is a murderer; and, were there no sentence of exclusion from civil power contained in the Word of God, the abhorrence of murder should exclude from confidence these men of blood. . . .

What has torn yonder wretches from the embraces of their wives and their children, and driven them to the field of blood – to the confines of hell? What nerves those arms, rising to sport with life and heaven? It is honor; the pledge of patriotism, the evidence of rectitude!

Ah, it is done! The blood streams, and the victim welters on the ground. And, see the victor coward running from the field, and, for a few days, like Cain, a fugitive and vagabond, until the first burst of indignation has passed, and the hand of time has soothed the outraged sensibility of the community; then, publicly, and as if to add insult to injustice, returning to *offer his services,* and to *pledge his honor,* that *your* lives and *your* rights shall be safe in his hand. Nor is this the only case where honor becomes the temptation to crime; it operates in all cases where the maxims of this infernal combination have attached disgrace to the performance of duty, and honor to the perpetration of iniquity. And, beside the crimes which honor tolerates, and the scarcely inferior number which it enjoins, there are a variety of cases where it will not restrain from treacheries confessedly dishonorable. . . .

I know it is said that a man's principles and his private character are nothing to us. If his ability be adequate, and his politics correct and his public conduct as yet irreproachable, this is sufficient. But are you prepared to be the dupes of such wild absurdity? According to this sentiment, a man may set his mouth against the heavens – he may be a drunkard in the intervals of official duty, a prodigal, a tyrant, a mere savage in his family – and still be trumpeted, by unprincipled politicians and electioneering hand-bills, as the great champion of liberty, the very Atlas on whose shoulders rests the destiny of his country. But what is a man's political creed, what is his past conformity to your wishes, when his profligate private life demonstrates that he is prepared to betray you the first moment he shall find it for his interest? Dispense with moral principle and private virtue, and all is gone. You can find no substitute; honor is a cobweb, and patriotism an empty name, in the hour of trial. The single circumstance that neither the interest nor the reputation of the duellist will come in competition with your interest, is your only security that, if able, he will not sport with your liberties as wantonly as he has sported with, or is prepared to sport with, the life of his neighbor. Admit that there are instances in which men, destitute of principle, have acted with integrity in public stations; can you tell me *how many thousands have betrayed their trust for want of it?* There are exempt cases – the persons did not happen to be tempted. But do you desire no better pledge of rectitude than the mere absence of temptation? Will you confide in thieves and swindlers to legislate, because two in a thousand, though utterly unprincipled, may have found it for their interest not to cheat you? It is in trying emergencies, when the price of perfidy is high, and temptation imperious, that unprincipled men are weighed in the balance and found wanting. And will you appoint cowards and traitors to command your armies, because they might answer in time of peace; or intrust your lives to quacks in medicine, because, under slight indispositions, they might suffice to administer herb-drink? Why does this lingering confidence in the duellist still survive the extinction of moral principle? One crime of equal magnitude, in any other case, would decide his fate forever. The failing merchant, convicted of dishonesty, is *recorded* a knave; the receipt of a bribe by a judge is irrevocable infamy; perjury cancels forever all confidence; the thief solicits in vain the public suffrage; the highway robber can find none to exercise charity, none to palliate his crime; and the common murderer, might he live, would be doomed to linger out a life of disgusting infamy. But the duellist, who, in cold blood, or with bitter malice and burning rage, murders his neighbor, can find enough to exercise charity, and palliate his crime: a whole state, a whole nation, to testify, by their votes, that they consider it nothing.

But, alas! the duellist, *frail man*, is overcome by temptation. *He* has peculiar sensibilities, habits of education, and modes of thinking, which, in this *one case*, led him astray, without inferring at all a general deficiency of principle, religious or moral.

In plain language, because the duellist is *educated* a duellist, the crime of wilful murder in him is very small, and is consistent with religious and moral principle. If men, then, are only *educated* to thieving, assassination, and robbery – if, by habit and false reasoning, they are so familiarized to crime as to rob, and steal, and destroy life, without much consciousness of guilt – *then*, indeed, they are *very honest men*, and are fit to superintend the affairs of the nation! . . .

But, waiving all moral considerations, what security have we that the duellist will not, if intrusted with our liberties, desert us in the hour of danger? What security can we have, when it is in the power of every factious rival who can shoot straight to compel him to the field; and, by destroying his life, to derange, perhaps to annihilate, the government? What if Washington, in the crisis of our fate, had fallen in a duel? What if the *governors*, the *senators*, the *judges* of the States, were so infatuated with the madness of honor, that, in the moment of peril, we could have no other security of their constancy than that no person should tempt them to hazard their lives, and put in jeopardy their country?

4. The system of duelling is a system of despotism, tending directly and powerfully to the destruction of civil liberty.

A free government is a government of laws, made by the people for the protection of life, reputation, and property. A despotic government is where life and all its blessings are subject to the caprice of an individual. Those maxims and practices, therefore, which remove life, reputation, and property, from under the protection of law, and subject them to the caprice of an individual, are the essence of despotism. Nor is it material whether this is done by open violence, or by the application of unlawful motives, which as effectually answer the purpose. Every man conforming to the laws of his country has a right to the peaceable enjoyment of life, and all its immunities. Nor has any individual a right, directly or indirectly, to interrupt this enjoyment. No man has a right to tempt his neighbor to renounce the protection of law, and much less to punish him with heavy penalties for refusing to do it. But this is precisely the despotic privilege which duellists have arrogated to themselves. The man who refuses a challenge, so far as their accursed influence extends, is outlawed – is branded with infamy, and exposed to perpetual insult. But what has he done? He has feared to offend his God; and, under trying temptations to the contrary, has bowed submissive to the laws of his country; and for this he is punished – substantially punished, in a free country, without trial, without law, nay, even in opposition to law! . . .

5. The inconsistency of voting for duellists is glaring. To profess attachment to liberty, and vote for men whose principles and whose practices are alike hostile to liberty – to contend for equal laws, and clothe with power those who despise them – to enact laws, and intrust their execution to men who are the first to break them – is a farce too ridiculous to be acted by freemen. In voting for the duellist, we patronize a criminal whom, in our law, we have doomed to die. With one hand we erect the gallows, and with the other rescue the victim; at one breath, declare him unfit to live, and the next, constitute him the guardian of our rights. Cancel, I beseech you, the laws against duelling, annihilate your criminal code, level to the ground your prisons, and restore to the sweets of society, and embraces of charity, their more innocent victims. Be consistent. If you tolerate one set of villains, tolerate them all; if murder does not stagger your confidence, let it not waver at inferior crimes.

In our prayers, we request that God would bestow upon us good rulers, *just men, ruling in the fear of God*. But, by voting for duellists, we demonstrate the insincerity of such prayers; for when by the providence of God, it is left to our choice whom we will have, we vote for

murderers. Unless, therefore, we would continue to mock God by hypocritical prayers, we must cease praying for good men, or we must cease
to patronize men of blood. Do we not pray also for the preservation of
liberty, and the continuance of national prosperity? And do we not
know that good rulers are the chosen instruments of the divine blessing; and that, when God would chastise a people, unprincipled rulers
are the rod of his anger? When, therefore, the selection of rulers is
left to ourselves, shall we disregard his chosen instruments of mercy,
and expect his blessing? Shall we put into his hand the rod of his
anger, and expect to escape chastisement?

6. To vote for the duellist is to assist in the prostration of justice,
and indirectly to encourage the crime of duelling.

Laws in republics depend for their prompt execution upon a correct
and efficient public sentiment. The highway robber need not publish
his daring exploits in a newspaper, to attract notice. A common indignation glows in the public mind: in all directions the son of violence is
pursued, and when arrested and convicted, is sure to die. In several
districts of the United States, a murder committed in a duel would
excite equal exertion to detect the murderer, who, on detection, would
be equally sure to die. The great officers of government, and other
influential characters, dare not, if disposed, connive at the crime. The
public indignation, like a high swollen river, would sweep away any
one who should presume to turn aside or obstruct its course. But, in
other parts of the land, the frequency of the crime, and its immemo-
rial impunity, had deadened the public feeling. Many disapprove, but
do not sufficiently abhor, the crime; they are *sorry*, but are not indignant. They *wish* the officers of government would execute the law, but
do not *compel* them to do it. Duellists are apprized of this debilitated
state of public feeling, and are, therefore, not afraid to contravene the
feeble public will. It is not a torrent, unmanageable and dreadful, but
a puny stream, which they dare to oppose, and which they have
learned to manage.

When, therefore, a murder is committed in a duel, immediately a
great bustle is made. The culprit is arrested, *or is to be arrested*—but,
alas! he cannot be found; or if found, alas! there are no witnesses; or if
there are witnesses, alas! the indictment is defective, and this is the
last we hear of it. The first effect of public indignation is a little
feared. Justice may not as yet be "turned backward" without some
little manoeuvring; and this blustering is made just to amuse until
the first emotion subsides; and when the danger is over, the sword of
justice, drawn only to deceive, is returned to its scabbard. The criminal creeps from his hiding-place, triumphs in his guilt, and, if insulted,
fights again. We blame our rulers; but by whom are such men made
rulers, and by whose negligence are they emboldened to wink at this
most accursed sin? Were the officers of justice men of moral principle,

who really abhorred duelling, and desired to put a stop to it, would the laws be thus inefficacious? Would it be so difficult to make a law that should fasten upon the culprit—so difficult to arrest, convict and execute? Is there any such difficulty in bringing to justice the thief, the robber, and the common murderer?

I tell you, Nay; the traitor is in the citadel; we have ourselves put him there, knowing also that he would let the criminal go; of course, we are accessory to his escape, and to the prostration of justice, as really as if with our own hands we unbarred and threw open the gates of his prison. Indeed, by removing the only restraints which duellists can feel, we indirectly encourage the crime. . . .

7. The contempt with which duellists treat the opinions and feelings of the community is a reason why we should cease to confide in them.

The people, whatever men of honor may think of them, constitute the strength, the virtue and glory, of the nation; and their opinions and wishes demand respect from those who legislate for them. The feelings of the great body of the people are decidedly opposed to duelling. This is manifest from the laws on this subject, and from the fact that the mass of the people discard those notions of Gothic honor, and rest satisfied with that protection and redress which the laws afford. It is but a handful of men only, compared with the whole, that uphold this bloody system. That which by duellists is denominated public opinion, and which constitutes the dire necessity of spilling each other's blood, is the opinion of duellists only—the opinion of not more than one in a thousand of the inhabitants of the nation. But the opinion of this handful is, by those who compose it, deemed of far greater consequence than the opinion and feelings of the great mass of the people. Duellists well know our aversion to their crimes, our grief at their conduct, and our desires to wipe off this disgrace of a Christian land. But little do they care for our opinions or our feelings. They move in a sphere too much above us, to let themselves down to the standard of our conceptions, or to give themselves concern about our desires or aversions. When an election is pending, when they need our votes to gratify their ambition, or satiate their avarice, then, indeed, they sympathize most tenderly with the people. The people are everything; their wishes are sacred, and their voice is the voice of God.

But let this end be accomplished, and a challenge or an insult be given, and neither liberty, nor patriotism, nor the voice of the people, nor the voice of God, can avail to deter them from deeds the most barbarous and despotic. Shall we, then, vote for men who treat with contempt our opinions and our feelings, who basely prostrate our laws, when we have nothing to bestow; and who again creep through all the dirty windings of hypocrisy, when their promotion depends on our will? What are all their professions of patriotism, contradicted by their conduct? And shall they deceive us still? Let them plead for liberty with the tongue of men and angels, and adore her cause with the fervor of seraphs—they are hypocrites, mere sounding brass and tinkling cymbals.

8. Withhold the public suffrage from the duellist, and the practice of fighting duels will speedily cease. . . .

9. Withholding the public suffrage from duellists is the only method in which there is the least prospect of arresting the practice of duelling.

We may reason, and ridicule, and lament, and remonstrate, and threaten, and legislate, and multiply penalties—and the evil will still progress. Environed by the subtilties of law, and shielded by the perverted patronage of men in office, regardless of our grief, and fearless of our indignation, they will laugh at our zeal, and defy our efforts. *There is no way to deal with these men, but to make them feel their dependence on the people; and no way to effect this, but to take the punishment of their crimes into our own hands. Our conscience must be the judge, and we must ourselves convict, and fine, and disgrace them at the polls. Here, and nowhere beside, will our voice be heard, and our will become law.*

10. The evils justly to be apprehended from the continuance of duelling call loudly upon us to awake in earnest to this subject, and apply with vigor the proposed remedy.

It every year robs our country of men qualified (this epidemic madness expected) for extensive usefulness. It cuts down our young men, and fills the land with widows and with orphans. The tax is too heavy; the victims offered to Moloch are too numerous. Might the evil, however, be confined to its present limits, it would be less intolerable; but we have no ground to indulge such a hope. In Europe, where duelling originated, the great inequality of rank has usually prevented the practice from descending to the common walks of life. It is there the unenvied privilege of great men to kill one another. But in our own country there is no such barrier. The genius of our government has inspired every man with a spirit of independence and self-importance —a spirit desirable when duly regulated, but dreadful when perverted, and, in young men especially, very liable to be perverted. We are all honorable men; and if the laws of the land are insufficient to protect the reputation of one man, they are equally defective to all. If the military officer, the civil officer, and the lawyer, must take the protection of their reputation into their own hands, so may the merchant, the merchant's clerk, the gentleman, and the gentleman's son; so may the mechanic, the farmer, and the planter. And they not only may, but they will do it, if an end be not put to this lawless practice. The horrid evil will not be confined to cities; it will break out in the country. It will stalk through our towns, and desolate our villages. Let not these anticipations be deemed chimerical; they are legitimate inferences from the known principles of the human mind and the peculiar situation of our country; and they are justified also by experience.

The mad example of Charles V and Francis I, King of France, descended like a mighty torrent, from the highest elevations of rank, down to the humble vale of private life. Through all Europe the pulse of honor began to throb, and all orders of men caught the fever. The nobleman and the nobleman's servant, the general and the common soldier, the lawyer, the merchant, the tailor, and the hair-dresser, became suddenly inflated with the inspirations of honor. The forms of law were disregarded; every man became his own protector and avenger, until, in this crusade of honor, the earth smoked with the blood of its miserable inhabitants. "Much of the best blood in Christendom was shed, many useful lives sacrificed, and at some periods war itself hath hardly been more destructive than these private contests of honor."

In our own country, and by a similar infatuation, duelling is steadily progressing; the example of great men and rulers is sweeping all before it, and is bending its destroying course to the vale of common life. Instances have come to my knowledge of challenges given, by those whom our grandfathers would have called boys, to adjust by weapons of death their hasty disputes. Already, and far remote from cities, does the vapor of honor begin to swell with fancied importance many a stripling, leading him to threaten what, as yet, he has not courage to perform. This shows what effect the frequency of the crime, and the impunity attending it, is beginning to have upon youthful minds. The leaven has begun to operate; and if no stop be put to it, the time is not distant when every petty quarrel of hot-headed young men must be adjusted by powder and ball. In the southern and western States, such events are already frequent. The youth extensively are enrolled on the lists of honor, and are bound to attack and defend according to its rules. Expertness in firing the pistol is a qualification of indispensable attainment: and the Sabbath is often devoted to the most Christian employment of learning to shoot expertly.

The genius of our government favors, also, not only the descent of the practice, but multiplies to an unlimited extent the occasions of duelling. Political disputes are the usual provocation. These display their influence through every class of society. As our country increases in wealth, luxury and vice—as parties multiply and become ardent— these controversies will naturally become more keen and vindictive, until duelling will become a common alternative; until elections shall turn, not on the merits of the candidate, but on superior skill in aiming the pistol to destroy his competitor. I have been assured, that already, in certain parts of our Union, duelling is not an unknown expedient to secure an election, by removing out of the way a rival candidate. Indeed, in the city of New York, and in a public paper, it has been declared, that at a certain period there was a systematic scheme formed to take off by duelling certain leading characters of one political party, by some of the leading characters of another political party. The fact asserted is, in itself, by no means incredible; it is a natural consequence of duelling—just what might be expected; and the duels which took place about that time, and the characters engaged, clothe the subject with an air of high probability. . . .

11. The present may be the only time in which it shall be practicable to suppress this great evil.

The practice of duelling is rapidly progressing, disseminating its infection, and deadening the public sensibility. The effect already is great and alarming. If not so, why does the crime shrink before the stern justice of New England, and rear its guilty head in New York, and stalk with bolder front as you pass onward to the south? If the effect is not great, why this distinction in crimes of the same class—why so alive to the guilt of robbery, assassination, and murder of one kind, so dead to the guilt of duelling? If the effect of duelling upon the public mind is not great, why is it that murder can be committed in open day—the crime be made notorious, nay, proclaimed in the newspaper—and the murderer remain unmolested in his dwelling? Why does he not flee? Why are not rewards offered by those authorized by the laws, and expresses hastened in all directions to arrest and bring to justice the guilty fugitive? Because no one is enough shocked at his crime to make these exertions. Because, if such measures were taken, the public mind would awake from its torpor—duelling would become a disgraceful crime, and the criminal would be lost to himself and to his country.

He could neither be *governor,* nor *senator,* nor *judge.* He would be exiled from public favor, immured in a dungeon, transported to the gallows, and launched into eternity. If the prevalence of duelling has not, and to an awful degree, affected the public mind, why such a number of half-apologists for the crime; and how can we so patiently hear, and candidly weigh, and almost admit, their arguments? Could you hear with equal patience assassination justified, though (as it well might be) by arguments equally conclusive? Why is it, if this deadly evil had not already palsied the feelings of the community, that even the members of our churches have heretofore, with so little hesitation, voted for men of blood? Is Christianity compatible with murder? Can you patronize the murderer by granting him your suffrage, and not become a partaker in his sin? Admit as the mildest, and as in general the true construction, that this has been done by Christians ignorantly, not knowing often that those for whom they voted were duellists—or inconsiderately, not realizing the enormity of the crime—why do they not know? why do they not consider? The reason is obvious:

> Vice is a monster of so frightful mien,
> As, to be hated, needs but to be seen;
> Yet, seen too oft, familiar with her face,
> We first endure, then pity, then embrace.

This is precisely our alarming state. We have sunk through all these grades of moral degradation. We endure, we pity, we embrace murderers. And what will be next? A total apathy to crime.

What is done, therefore, must be done quickly. Let the maxims of duelling once break out, and spread in the country, and infect the rising generation—let the just abhorrence of the community be a little more effaced by the growing frequency of the crime—and we are undone. There will be no place to make a stand. Our liberties will be lost, our bands will become brass, and our fetters iron; no man's life will be safe; the laws of the land will be a nullity; every man must tremble, and walk softly, and speak softly, lest he implicate his neighbor's honor, and put in jeopardy his own life; and duelling will become as common, as irremediable, and as little thought of, as assassination is in Spain, in Italy, and South America.

Then, indeed, will the descriptions of the prophet be horribly realized. "Judgment will be turned away backward. Justice will stand afar off, truth will fall in the street, and equity be unable to enter. Yea, truth will fail, and he that departeth from evil will make himself a prey." None will call for justice; revenge and murder will be the order of the day. "We shall grope for the wall as the blind; we shall stumble at noon-day as in the night; we shall be in desolate places as dead men."

Shall we sit and calmly await the approach of these evils? Shall we bow our neck to the yoke? Shall we thrust our hands into the manacles preparing for them? What if these evils may not be realized in our day —have we no regard to posterity? What if every man, woman and child, may not fall in a duel—is there nothing to be dreaded from the sword, or pestilence, or famine, because they do not extirpate our race?

12. The facility with which, in the way proposed, this evil may be suppressed, will render us forever inexcusable, will constitute us partakers in the sin, if we do not make the attempt.

There are, indeed, many duellists in our land, and many half-apologists for the crime, from whom no aid is to be expected. There are many too unprincipled, and others too indolent, to be engaged by considerations of duty; and there are some, and even professors of religion, whose strong party prejudices, and political attachments to duellists, will be liable to steel them against conviction, or impel them to make shipwreck of faith and a good conscience. But, after all these deductions, there are yet remaining multitudes, thousands and thousands, whose abhorrence of duelling, though diminished by the frequency of the crime, is still sufficient to overwhelm its abettors with infamy. Nothing is necessary to awaken and embody in one formidable phalanx of opposition the great mass of our plain and honest people but to place the crime, in its horrid aspect and fearful connections, full before them. Only let them see, and they will feel; let them feel, and they will act—will hurl indignant every duellist whom they have elevated from his eminence, and consign to merited infamy every one who shall solicit their favor. Nor is it impracticable thus to exhibit the subject. Ministers of different denominations, all united, would be able to effect it perfectly. Let each, in his appointed sphere, make due exertion to enlighten his flock, and the fire of indignation would soon begin to blaze through all the nation. And if, beside such exertions, further efforts should be needful, the newspaper, the magazine, and tract, may be enlisted as auxiliaries.

Nor can any reasonably object to such conduct on the part of ministers; nor will any one probably attempt it, who does not, for himself or some favorite, fear the consequences. Our obligations are most solemn to lift up our voice, and to put forth our exertions, against this sin. Our God calls to us from heaven; the damned call to us from hell; the blood of murdered victims from the ground lifts up its voice, and mingles with the cry of the widow and the fatherless; the example of our Saviour, of the prophets, of the apostles, forbids us to be silent or inactive.

It is in vain to cry out "priestcraft," or "political preaching"; these watch-words will not answer here. The crime we oppose is peculiar to no party; it is common to all. It is a crime too horrid to be palliated, too threatening to be longer endured in officers of government. Any political effect would be the consequence merely, not the object, of our exertions. It would also be small and momentary; but, should it be great, such effect ought not to bring censure upon us, or alter the course of our duty. If we may not denounce duelling, because men of political eminence are guilty of the crime—because the enlightening of the consciences of our people would affect an election—every crime would soon find a sanctuary in the example of some great politician. Our mouths would be shut; we might not whisper the guilt of crimes, lest, by awakening your consciences, it should produce some political effect.

It is practicable, then, and it is the duty of ministers to direct the attention of their people, and arouse their just indignation towards criminals of this description. Nor will it be difficult for the people, once awake and engaged, to effect their purpose.

If only the members of Christian churches become decided in their opposition to duelling, it will produce a sensation through the land.

The votes of professed Christians of different denominations are too numerous and important to be thrown away. And will not the churches awake? Will professors of religion, a religion commanding "love to enemies," and breathing "peace on earth and good will to men," uphold deliberately, and encourage by their suffrage, the practice of duelling? On this ground only, a formidable stand may be made.

But the churches will not be left to stand alone. In every part of the nation there are multitudes, conscientious and patriotic, whose zealous cooperation may be expected. Voluntary associations may be formed, correspondences may be established, and a concert of action secured. And even should the contest be more arduous — if, in the tempest of an election, all these exertions should seem to be swept away, and religion, and conscience, and patriotism, to be lost in the delirium of passion — are there not, in every church, and in every congregation, a chosen few who would brave the storm; whom no sophistry could deceive, no influence bend, and no passion move from their purpose? Are there not, in every parish, at least ten righteous persons, to avert the curse of Heaven, and commence a reformation? But ten persons in every congregation in the land would constitute a weight of influence ultimately decisive. In a government like ours, where a State is often almost equally divided, a few thousand votes are too precious to be lost. When, therefore, it comes once to be known that the fighting of a duel is a serious blot upon the character of a candidate, and that, in every district and in every town, there are considerate and conscientious people who will not vote for him, parties will not risk their cause upon the shoulders of such men; duellists will become unpopular candidates; and those will be selected who shall merit and insure your suffrage. . . .

Duelling is a great national sin; with the exception of a small section of the Union, the whole land is defiled with blood. From the lakes of the north to the plains of Georgia, is heard the voice of lamentation and woe — the cries of the widow and the fatherless. This work of desolation is performed often by men in office, by the appointed guardians of life and liberty. On the floor of Congress, challenges have been threatened, if not given; and thus powder and ball have been introduced as the auxiliaries of deliberation and argument. Oh, tell it not in Gath, publish it not in the streets of Askelon! Alas! it is too late to conceal our infamy; the sun hath shined on our guilt, and the eye of God with brighter beams surveys the whole. He beholds and he will punish. His quiver is full of arrows, his sword is impatient of confinement; ten thousand plagues stand ready to execute his wrath; conflagration, tempest, earthquake, war, famine, and pestilence, wait his command only, to cleanse the land from blood — to involve in one common ruin both the murderer and those who tolerate his crimes. Atheists may scoff, but there is a God — a God who governs the earth in righteousness — an avenger of crimes, the supporter and destroyer of nations. And as clay is in the hand of the potter, so are the nations of the earth in the hand of God. At what instant he speaks concerning a nation, to pluck up, to pull down, and destroy it, if that nation repent, God will avert the impending judgment. And at what instant he shall speak concerning a nation, to build and to plant it, if it do evil in his sight, he will arrest the intended blessing, and send forth judgments in its stead. Be not deceived: the greater our present mercies and seeming security, the greater is the guilt of our rebellion, and the more certain, swift, and awful, will be our calamity. We are murderers, a nation of murderers, while we tolerate and reward the perpetrators of the crime. And shall I not visit for these things, saith the Lord? Shall not my soul be avenged on such a nation as this?

But, it will be said, especially in cases of contested elections, if you refuse to vote for this man because he is a duellist, his opponent, a worse man, will come in.

A worse man cannot come in. The duellist is a murderer; and is a man's difference from you in political opinion more criminal than murder? And will you vote for a murderer, a despot, proud, haughty and revengeful, to keep out another man, perhaps equally qualified and of a fair fame, merely because he thinks not in politics exactly as you do? To what will such bigotry lead? There will soon be no crime too gross to be overlooked by party men, and no criminal too loathsome and desperate to float into office on the tide of party. When the violence of competition rises so high in our country as to lead parties, in their struggles for victory, to tread down the laws of God, disregarding entirely the moral characters of candidates for office; if their being on our side will sanctify their crimes, and push them reeking with blood into office; the time is not distant when we shall have no liberties to protect. Such a people are too wicked to be free; and God will curse them, by leaving them to eat of the fruit of their way. . . .

But perhaps the liberties of our country are at stake; might we not for once, and on such an emergency, vote for a duellist? The same song has been sung at every election these twenty years, and by each party. It is an electioneering trick to excite your fears, to awaken your prejudices, to inflame your passions, to overpower your consciences, and to get your vote, whether right or wrong.

But suppose your liberties are in danger; if they are so far gone as to depend on the election of one man, and that man a tyrant, a murderer, they are gone irretrievably. Beside the absurdity of appointing a *murderer* to protect life, and a *despot* to protect liberty, it is to be remembered that God is our only efficient protector. Men are merely instruments; but will God bless such instruments, selected in contempt of his authority, and rescued from the sword of his justice? All attempts to avert perdition by means at war with precepts of Heaven will prove abortive; you hatch the cockatrice egg, and weave the web of the spider. If your liberties are in danger, reform — pray —

and call to your aid men of rectitude, men of clean hands, whose counsels God may be expected to bless.

"But it is difficult to know in all cases who are good men." True; and will you therefore vote for those whom you know to be bad men? Rather discard those whom you know to be bad, and scrutinize critically the characters of those who profess to be good, and, after your utmost care, you will be sufficiently exposed to deception.

But the reply is ever at hand, "If they will fight, let them fight and kill each other; the sooner we get rid of them, the better." And are you prepared to intrust your lives, and all dear to you, to such men; to men whom you confess to be a nuisance, and whose death would be a public blessing? Beside, there is no such thing as killing all; the example of the duellist is a wide-spreading contagion. Every duel that is fought inspires twenty, perhaps a hundred, with the same accursed frenzy; and the blood of duellists is the seed of duelling, as really as the blood of the martyrs was the seed of the church.

"But why so vehement against duelling in particular?" Because, at present, it is a great and alarming national sin; because no other crime with such shameless effrontery bids defiance to the laws of God and man; because no other crime is so palliated, justified, and with such impunity sanctioned by the example of the great; and, of course, no other crime has so alarming an aspect upon the principles of our young men, and the moral sensibilities of our country. I may add, that no other description of criminals, if they escape with impunity, may publish their crimes, glory in their shame, and still be rewarded with the confidence and honors of their country. The crisis is an awful one; and this apathy to a crime of the deepest dye, is a prelude of approaching death. But, though there is a peculiar reason for attempting to arouse the listless attention of the public to this sin, there are *decisive objections* to the appointment to office of any immoral man. The prodigal, the drunkard, the profane, the Sabbath-breaker, the adulterer, the gambler, are all disqualified to act as legislators; and no man with an enlightened conscience can vote for them.

"But if we are so critical in our scrutiny of character, we shall never be able to find men duly qualified to manage our affairs." Most humiliating confession! But how has it come to pass (if true) that so many public characters are immoral men? It is because we, the people, have not even requested them to behave better. We have never made it necessary for them to be moral. We have told them, and we have told our youth who are rising to active life, that private character is a useless thing, as it respects the attainment of our suffrage. We have told them that, if they pleased, they might associate for drunkenness and midnight revelry, pour contempt upon the institutions of religion, neglect the worship of God, and spend the Sabbath in gambling and intemperance, and still be esteemed hallowed patriots. If it be true that a strict scrutiny of character would exile from office many who now fill public stations, it is our *criminal negligence* that has brought this to pass. But the inference, that setting up moral character as a test would leave us destitute of proper candidates, is groundless; it is the very way to multiply them. Let it once be made known that a fair private character is indispensable to the attainment of public suffrage, and reformations will take place. And, besides this, our young men will be growing up to habits of virtue, under the guardian influence of this restraint. At first, you may encounter a little self-denial, by dismissing men of irregular lives, in whom you have been accustomed to confide. But their places will soon be supplied by a host of men of fair fame, and better qualified to serve their country.

But, allowing that a proper exercise of suffrage would restrain from the practice of fighting duels all actually concerned, or expecting to be concerned, in civil life, how should this reclaim those who have no such expectation, and are no way affected by the votes of the people? How would it restrain military and naval officers, men usually the most addicted to the crime?

1. The prospect of success, though an encouragement, is not the chief ground of obligation to withhold our votes from duellists. It is sinful to vote for them, even though withholding our votes would not reclaim an individual.

2. If the method proposed would reclaim even men immediately concerned, or expecting to be concerned, in government, the good effected would be great. Laws do much good, although they do not entirely extinguish crimes.

3. The example of men in civil life subtracted from the support of this crime, and arrayed against it, would render the practice dishonorable among gentlemen of every description. Military officers are citizens, as well as officers; and that conduct which is deemed disgraceful by gentlemen in civil life will soon be felt to be such, and will be abandoned, by military and naval officers. And were such an effect less certain, it might be made certain by the exercise of that discretion which the civil ruler possesses in the appointment of officers. Let our legislators cease to fight duels, and desire to extinguish the practice of duelling, and they would soon fill the army and the navy with commanders who would be disposed and able to second their views.

And now let me ask you solemnly, with these considerations in view, will you persist in your attachment to these guilty men? Will you any longer either deliberately or thoughtlessly vote for them? Will you renounce allegiance to your Maker, and cast the Bible behind your back? Will you confide in men void of the fear of God, and destitute of moral principle? Will you intrust *life* to *murderers,* and *liberty* to *despots?* Are you patriots, and will you constitute those legislators who despise you, and despise equal laws, and wage war with the eternal principles of justice? Are you Christians, and, by upholding duellists, will you deluge the land with blood, and fill it with widows and with orphans? Will you aid in the prostration of justice, in the escape of criminals, in the extinction of liberty? Will you place in the chair of State, in the senate, or on the bench of justice, men who, if able, would murder you for speaking truth? Shall your elections turn on expert shooting, and your deliberative bodies become a host of armed men? Will you destroy public morality, by tolerating, yea, by rewarding, the most infamous crimes? Will you teach your children that there is no guilt in murder? Will you instruct them to think lightly of duelling, and train them up to destroy or be destroyed in the bloody field? Will you bestow your suffrage, when you know that, by withholding it, you may arrest this deadly evil—when this, too, is the only way in which it can be done, and when the present is perhaps the only period in which resistance can avail—when the remedy is so easy, so entirely in your power—and when God, if you do not punish these guilty men, will most inevitably punish you?

If the widows and the orphans which this wasting evil has created, and is yearly multiplying, might all stand before you, could you witness their tears, or listen to their details of anguish? Should they point to the murderers of their fathers, their husbands, and their children, and lift up their voice and implore your aid to arrest an evil which had made them desolate, could you disregard their cry? Before their eyes could you approach the poll, and patronize, by your vote, the destroyers of their peace? Had you beheld a dying father conveyed, bleeding and agonizing, to his distracted family, had you heard their piercing shrieks and witnessed their frantic agony, would you reward the savage man who had plunged them in distress? Had the duellist destroyed your neighbor, had your own father been killed by the man who solicits your suffrage, had your son, laid low by his hand, been brought to your door pale in death and weltering in blood, would you then think the crime a small one? Would you honor with your confidence, and elevate to power by your vote, the guilty monster? And what would you think of your neighbors, if, regardless of your agony, they should reward him? And yet, such scenes of unutterable anguish are multiplied every year. Every year the duellist is cutting down the neighbor of somebody. Every year, and many times in the year, a father is brought dead or dying to his family, or a son laid breathless at the feet of his parents; and every year you are patronizing by your votes the men who commit these crimes, and looking with cold indifference upon, and even mocking, the sorrows of your neighbor. Beware—I admonish you to beware, and especially such of you as have promising sons preparing for active life—lest, having no feeling for the sorrows of another, you be called to weep for your own sorrow; lest your sons fall by the hand of the very murderer for whom you vote, or by the hand of some one whom his example has trained to the work of blood!

With such considerations before you, why do you wish to vote for such men? What have they done for you, what can they do, that better men cannot as happily accomplish? And will you incur all this guilt, and hazard all these consequences, for nothing? Have you no religion, no conscience, no love to your country, no attachment to liberty, no humanity, no sympathy, no regard to your own welfare in this life, and no fear of consequences in the life to come? O, my countrymen, awake! Awake to crimes which are your disgrace – to miseries which know not a limit – to judgments which will make you desolate!

For additional information about Lyman Beecher:

Beecher, Charles, ed. *Autobiography.* 2 vols. New York: Harper & Bro., 1864–65.
Beecher, Lyman. *Beecher's Works.* 3 vols. Boston: John P. Jewett & Co., 1852.
Hoyt, Arthur S. "Lyman Beecher." *The Pulpit and American Life.* New York: Macmillan Co., 1921.
Macartney, Clarence Edward. "Lyman Beecher." *Sons of Thunder.* New York: Fleming H. Revell Co., 1929.
Rourke, Constance Mayfield. *Trumpets of Jubilee.* New York: Harcourt, Brace & Co., 1927.

For other sermons by Lyman Beecher:

Sermons; Beecher's Works, vol. 2. Boston: John P. Jewett & Co., 1852.
Views of Theology; Beecher's Works, vol. 3. Boston: John P. Jewett & Co., 1853.
Also: *Six Sermons on the Nature, Occasions, Signs, Evils and Remedy of Intemperance* (1827).

THOMAS CHALMERS

1780 - 1847

THOMAS CHALMERS, from a portrait by Thomas Duncan, from *Thomas Chalmers* by Mrs. Oliphant (Boston: Houghton, Mifflin & Co., 1893), frontispiece.

THOMAS CHALMERS

1780   *Born in East Anstruther, Scotland, March 17*
1791   *Entered college in St. Andrews*
1799   *Licensed to preach, July 31*
1803   *Ordained as a minister in the Church of Scotland, called to parish of Kilmany; also served as assistant professor of mathematics, St. Andrews University*
1811   *Experienced meaningful spiritual conversion*
1815   *Began ministry in parish of Tron in Glasgow*
1818   *Began ministry in parish of St. John's in Glasgow*
1823   *Elected to chair of moral philosophy, St. Andrews University*
1828   *Elected to the chair of theology, University of Edinburgh*
1831   *Served as moderator of the Established Church of Scotland*
1843   *Led revolt from Established Church to establish the Free Church of Scotland, became moderator of the Free Church and professor and principal of the newly founded Free Church College in Edinburgh*
1847   *Died May 30 in Edinburgh*

WILBERFORCE WROTE IN HIS DIARY, "All the world is wild about Dr. Chalmers."[1] He had good reason to make such a statement. When Chalmers preached, churches were always crowded. In many instances twice as many people packed into a church as it was built to contain. At one place the crowd was so thick that Chalmers had to climb in a window to reach the pulpit. Often on Sundays he would preach to 3,000 people in each of several preaching services. On some occasions people

---

1. Harry C. Howard, *Princes of the Christian Pulpit and Pastorate*, 2d ser. (Nashville: Cokesbury Press, 1928), p. 155.

broke down closed doors in order to try to get into the crowded churches. At his first lecture on theology at the University of Edinburgh, police were required to restrain the people who tried to pack into the classroom. His most strenuous spiritual exercise was fighting against the pride and vanity that tempted him because of his popularity.

LIFE AND TIMES

Thomas Chalmers was born into a respectable and relatively wealthy family in East Anstruther, Scotland, on March 17, 1780. His childhood was not pleasant. His father was too busy in business affairs to have much time with his children. Thomas was the sixth of fourteen children; with such a large family, his mother had little opportunity to devote individual attention to her children. At two years of age, Thomas was placed in the care of a nurse; cruel and deceitful, she haunted his memories throughout life.

When he went away to boys' school, his experience was no better; the instructor was an unreasonable tyrant. Nevertheless, Chalmers was a genius: when he was only eleven years old, he enrolled as a student in the United College of St. Andrews. Because of his age he was not mature enough to function well as a college student, and he stumbled through his first two years in a haphazard and lazy way. During his third year he became intensely interested in mathematics and began to give most of his attention to this subject.

As a little child he had expressed interest in becoming a minister. During college he pursued this vocational interest. As a fourth-year college student, he enrolled in the divinity program at St. Andrews. The study of theology, however, had little interest for him; his main academic concern was still mathematics. Yet his gifts for expression were already evident. As a divinity student, when his turn for prayers came, people gathered from the surrounding area to listen to him pray.

Licensed to preach in 1799, Chalmers was ordained as a minister in the Church of Scotland in 1803 and called to the parish of Kilmany. This was a small church which required little of his time, so he accepted also a position as assistant professor of mathematics at St. Andrews. After a year he was relieved of his teaching position, but his interest in teaching was so great that he began a private instruction program.

During his first few years in the church at Kilmany he was an unpopular and ineffective minister. His sermons all but emptied the church. He failed to carry out pastoral duties. In fact, he had little interest in the Christian faith at all; his main concern was teaching.

All of this changed in 1811. In that year he experienced a deep spiritual awakening which completely altered his life. Several factors led to this transforming event. He was assigned the task of writing an article on Christianity for an encyclopedia. As he studied the Christian faith carefully, he became more and more convinced of its truth. A second event — the death of a sister — brought him face to face with life's ultimate questions. Next, a serious illness of his own, resulting in confinement for four months, gave him the opportunity and stimulation to evaluate his own life. Finally, the reading of Wilberforce's book, *Practical View of Christianity*, led to his conversion. What had been only an intellectual knowledge of the Christian faith became a practical, personal experience. From this time forward his whole life was caught up in his relationship to God through Christ.

As a result of these experiences, his entire ministry was dramatically transformed. He immediately began to visit the persons in his parish and to share with them the good news of Christ. His sermons took on new urgency. He ceased giving attention to mathematics and began careful study of the Bible. A neighbor noted this new interest in the Bible and said, "I never come in now sir, but I find you aye at your Bible." "All too little, John, all too little," was the answer.[2] The effects of this change in his life and ministry were revolutionary: people began to flock to hear him preach; lives were changed; many persons confessed faith in Jesus Christ and began to follow a new way of life.

He remained in Kilmany four years after his conversion experience. In 1815, he was called to the parish of Tron in Glasgow, Scotland. He went to this church reluctantly: it was a large and demanding parish, and he had a very pleasant and stressless ministry in Kilmany. Glasgow was a huge city filled with problems common to the cities in the midst of the Industrial Revolution. Teeming masses, packed into multi-story apartment houses, lived in horrible slums. To reach and minis-

---

2. Harold L. Calkins, *Master Preachers* (Washington, D.C.: Review and Herald Pub. Assoc., 1960), p. 25.

ter to the poor seemed an impossible task. The city was also divided along religious lines: some of the church leaders were advocates of the evangelical position, held by Chalmers; while others were committed to the more staid, high church position.

In spite of these difficulties, Chalmers' ministry in Glasgow was an instant success. People from all classes of society crowded to hear him preach. He was among the first churchmen to see the significance of the Industrial Revolution for the life of the church. He began an extensive church program to reach and minister to all elements of society. The poor particularly attracted his attention, and he began work to improve their conditions. He started schools and provided special education for their children. He insisted that the poor should be cared for by the church through freewill offerings rather than by the state through enforced taxation.

For eight years he labored under the strenuous demands of a metropolitan parish. Finally the hard work began to take its toll: he became fatigued and discouraged about his ability to keep up the pace necessary for an adequate ministry. When he was offered the chair of moral philosophy at St. Andrews University in 1823, he accepted. He believed that this teaching position would afford him more of an opportunity to do what he felt he must do within the Christian movement.

Even then, he was not merely a teacher; Chalmers began immediately to be active in various ministries in St. Andrews, and again his attention turned primarily to the poor. He also had a significant influence over the university students. There was a noticeable shift toward upright living and a concern for Christian faith among the academic community.

Five years later, in 1828, Chalmers was elected to the chair of theology in the University of Edinburgh. His fame as a preacher continued to increase, but he was also becoming a noted professor. Huge throngs of students attended his classes, and he held special classes for the poor of the city apart from his regular routine of teaching.

He remained active in the life of his church. In 1831 he was elected to serve as moderator of the Established Church in Scotland. He became involved in significant debates concerning the life of the church, and increasingly he felt that reform was needed in the Established Church. Evangelistic and missionary zeal were lacking and standards of discipline were low. The state also exercised more influence over the church than

Chalmers thought was permissible: court rulings had declared that a local congregation must accept any minister assigned to it, and Chalmers regarded this as undue interference from the state.

By 1843 the conflict within the Church of Scotland had reached revolutionary pitch. In that year Chalmers led the revolt from the Established Church to establish the Free Church of Scotland. Over four hundred persons walked out of the General Assembly with him and moved to another hall to establish the Free Church. He was elected moderator of the new church group and became professor and principal of the newly-founded Free Church College in Edinburgh.

He continued his duties as professor, principal, preacher, and leader of the new movement until his death in 1847. On the evening of May 30, he left the family circle in a cheerful mood and retired to his room. That night he died in his sleep. But the powerful quality of his life could not be stilled by death. Many aspects of his character which made him such a great man continued to exercise their influence.

One obvious quality of his life was his concern for people; he cared for them in the name of Christ because as a Christian it was his nature to care. Nowhere was his concern and compassion more evident than in his relation to the poor. In every situation, he sought them out and ministered to them. Chalmers spoke of the preaching of the Bible, the teaching of the young, and the care of the poor as the three essential activities of a parish church. He was not just interested in giving handouts; he tried desperately to give a helping hand. He wanted the poor to maintain their dignity.

Though he could have preached in the most magnificent churches of Scotland, he frequently preferred the churches of the poor. In Edinburgh, as a distinguished professor of theology, he spent much of his time in a ministry in Westport, a district of the city in which poverty abounded. There he established Christian agencies for the uplift of the impoverished population. A tanner's loft was his preaching place: he poured forth a flood of Christian eloquence on a mass of poor, harrassed, and illiterate people.

Not only did he minister personally to the poor, he urged others to do likewise. For example, Thomas Guthrie came from a beautiful parish to St. John's in Edinburgh. He stood one day on George IV Bridge surveying with discouragement the slums which made up his new field of work. He felt a heavy hand on his shoulder and heard a gruff voice say, "A magnificent field of operations, sir—a magnificent field of operations!"[3] The voice was that of Chalmers.

Courage was another attribute of Chalmers' life. He had the courage to leave the tranquillity of a rural pastorate and tackle the chaos of Glasgow. He had the courage to leave a successful pastorate and enter a new career in teaching after he was forty years of age. He had the courage to buck the established church and to follow the course dictated by his convictions. It was no easy thing to establish the Free Church of Scotland; he and his fellow revolutionaries forsook their salaries, positions, and state support. Yet Chalmers felt that it was right to leave, and he did.

Involvement with the issues of his day was another significant characteristic of Chalmers. His sermons dealt with the real problems of real people. He was not given to flights of theological fancy. People were concerned about the conflict of science and religion; he spoke eloquently to the issue. The threats of Napoleon were of deep concern during the days of his pastoral ministry; he spoke words of comfort and words of encouragement. The relation of church and state was an issue that plagued his time; he spoke on the subject with forthright conviction and courage. The blight of poverty created by the ups and downs of the economic life of Europe left many in despair; Chalmers saw it as an opportunity to relate the gospel to life.

Evangelistic and ethical preaching were both important for him. In his day some preachers rejected one or the other as improper. Chalmers refuted such tactics; he wrote, "There is a most unfortunate distinction kept up in the country between moral and evangelical preaching. It has the effect of instituting an opposition where no opposition should be supposed to exist; and a preference for the one is in this way made to carry along with it a hostility or indifference to the other."[4]

Whatever the issues, Chalmers grappled with them and struggled to find a solution in keeping with the spirit of Christ: it is no wonder that all the world was "wild about Dr. Chalmers."

---

3. Howard, p. 155.
4. Andrew J. Campbell, *Two Centuries of the Church of Scotland, 1707–1929* (Paisley, Scotland: Alexander Gardner, 1930), p. 186.

PREACHING AND SERMONS

Thomas Chalmers didn't take long to attract attention. At the age of sixteen the people of St. Andrews flocked to the prayer hall when he was to pray. His flow of eloquent and vivid descriptions of the character of God, along with a brilliant portrayal of the miseries of people in need of God, astounded the hearers.

Throughout his ministry he would be noted for his descriptive abilities. He excelled as a pastor who knew the needs of his people and had the ability to describe those needs with clarity. His imagination was endless; his diction and imagery were colorful. His sermons might frequently contain only one or two vital points, but Chalmers always depicted these points brilliantly by a series of apt and vivid illustrations.

He was likewise noted for his repetitions. Chalmers' gifted preaching contemporary, Robert Hall, once said, "Did you ever know any man who had that singular faculty of repetition possessed by Dr. Chalmers? Why, sir, he often reiterates the same thing ten or twelve times in the course of a few pages."[5] Dargan made a similar observation: "The most marked [peculiarity] in Chalmers' preaching was his method of repeating the same idea with great variety of expression."[6]

In 1845, Daniel Sharpe, pastor of Charles Street Baptist Church in Boston, said of Chalmers' preaching:

> It was not ornate or so diffuse as I had expected. It was far better. It was simple, clear, forcible and fervid. Every sentence was delivered with an earnestness of one who believed what he said, and considered it to be of present and eternal importance.[7]

In addition to the qualities of eloquent description and earnest repetition must be added one other: clarity. There was never any doubt about what Chalmers was trying to say. His themes were understandable and his texts were plain. Repetition and illustration aided this clarity. His sermons became models of directness and simplicity.

---

5. Edwin Charles Dargan, *A History of Preaching*, vol. 2 (Grand Rapids: Baker Book House, 1954), p. 492.
6. Ibid.
7. Daniel Sharp, "Elements of Useful Eloquence," *The American Pulpit* 3 (August 1847): 112.

Nevertheless, some criticized his preaching. He was regarded as coarse. No doubt this criticism in part came from his physique itself. Chalmers was a burly person of robust form and powerful build. He was neither handsome nor delicate. His vigorous gestures emphasized his power; his hands continually sawed the air. He read all of his sermons from a manuscript, yet the manuscript never interfered with his constant, powerful gesturing. Amazingly enough, he was able to sustain concentrated beauty of expression while reading a manuscript written in shorthand.

Some of the criticisms of Chalmers — like the criticisms of many in his day — were due to the affected elegance of the age in which he lived. His direct, blunt, highly illustrative style was far too modern for his own generation. Chalmers was great in his own day; but unlike most of his contemporaries, he could step a century ahead and be equally as great.

Nonetheless, some criticisms of Chalmers seem valid. His sentences are entirely too long — some contained over 400 words! He was known for this weakness. One contemporary wrote:

> He swells out his sentences almost interminably, linking on clause after clause, adding illustration to illustration, with many a strange word, and colloquial peculiarity, and sometimes an uncouth expression, and superfluous "why" and "now," breaks them up with dashes, and obscures them with parentheses, and cumbers them with ornament.[8]

Again, however, these criticisms are far more valid for written, literary products than for spoken products. The very elements to which his critics objected are those elements most characteristic of contemporary speech. Thomas Chalmers was speaking in oral style. The abruptness, the breaks in thought, the colloquialisms, the "uncouth expressions" — all are the marks of vigorous, oral speech. Chalmers had learned to write as he spoke: his manuscripts were written in a fluid, oral style. This fact both accounts for the criticisms of his written sermons and the praise of his spoken sermons — even though delivered from a lengthy manuscript.

---

8. Samuel Brown, "The Works of Thomas Chalmers," *The American Biblical Repository* 10 (October 1837): 385.

On the other hand, some of his sermons do seem unnecessarily loose, rambling, and discursive. His explanations are frequently diffuse. Occasionally he wastes too much time on preliminary matters. Nor can there be any doubt that he was anything but a graceful speaker: his voice was neither easy nor pleasant; his pronunciation was both national and provincial. He was indeed "a storm amid the hills of his native land."

What of the content of his sermons? His texts came two-thirds from the New Testament and one-third from the Old Testament. Virtually every sermon has strong biblical authority; they are marked with traditional themes. He preached on the depravity of man, the divinity of Christ, and the personal needs of the common man. He centered his preaching on Jesus as the Savior of mankind.

His sermons also ring with the zeal of social reform. He sought to awaken the merchants of Glasgow to a sense of guilt for their indifference to the needs of the poor. He was deeply disturbed by the crushing effects of industrialism and his sermons mirrored that concern. He believed that the gospel must lie at the heart of all personal and social reform. He earnestly believed that the evils which afflict mankind are rooted in sin. It would be difficult to find a preacher more balanced in his piety and social zeal than Thomas Chalmers. His sermons are proof that personal piety and public reform need not be strangers to one another.

His most famous sermon was preached in St. John's Church: "The Expulsive Power of a New Affection." It is remembered among the dozen so-called "great" sermons of the Christian church. Among many others, it stands as an eloquent testimony to the superb preaching of Thomas Chalmers.

Sermons

IMMORTALITY BROUGHT TO LIGHT
BY THE GOSPEL

"Who hath abolished death, and brought life and immortality to light by the gospel" (2 Timothy 1:10).

THE MEN OF THE EARTH carry on their designs and their doings, just as if on earth they were to live for ever. Each is so intent upon his own earthly object—every mind is so occupied with its own earthly scheme—every countenance speaks such deep and eager anxiety after some favourite yet earthly ambition—each individual is so decidedly embarked, with all his powers of attention and perseverance, on some earthly undertaking—That surely one might think, it can be nought of a trifling or temporary nature, which either creates or keeps up so mighty a stir among our species. And yet it is not the less true, that all the busy activities of all these people have their upshot in forgetfulness. It is not the greatness or the durability of the objects, which has called forth the effort and the strenuousness of men. It is the folly of men, which urges them to the pursuit of paltry and evanescent objects—a folly which overlooks the arithmetic of our few little years, and has invested time with the characters of eternity—a folly which all the demonstrations of experience have been unable to rectify; and which, after the mighty sweep of countless generations from the face of our world, reigns with unabated strength over the human heart, and finds the men of the present day as unwise and as infatuated as ever.

Death is a theme of mighty import; and every variety of eloquence has been exhausted, upon the magnitude of its desolations. There is not a place where human beings congregate together, that does not, in the fleeting history of its inmates, give forth the lesson of their mortality. Is it a house? Death enters unceremoniously there, and with rude hand tears asunder the dearest of our sympathies. Is it a town?

Reprinted from Thomas Chalmers, *Sermons and Discourses* (New York: Robert Carter & Bros., 1863), pp. 174–82.

Every year death breaks up its families; and the society of our early days is fast melting away from us. Is it a market place? Death works among the people at short and rapid intervals; and though at the end of twenty years, I see a crowd as busy and as numerous as before — these are new faces which meet my eye, and new names which fall upon my ear. Is it a church? The aspect of the congregation is changing perpetually; and in a little time another people will enter these walls, and another minister will speak to them. Is it the country at large? On every side we see a shifting population — another set of occupiers to the farms, and other names or other men annexed to the properties.

But this is viewing the subject at a distance. Every assemblage of objects is composed of individuals; and think of the numbers that must have suffered, to accomplish the changes which we have now set before you. Think that each of these individuals carried in his bosom a living principle, and that that principle is now to all appearance extinguished — that each felt as warm and as alive to the world as perhaps any who now hears me, and that this world the stern severity of death forced him to abandon for ever — that each was as feelingly open to pain and to terror, and that the forebodings and the reluctance and the agonies of death came upon all of them — that each had hopes and plans and wishes to accomplish, but that death carried him away; and they are all buried in forgetfulness along with him.

All is vanity, says the preacher; and it is death which stamps this character on the affairs of the world. It throws a mockery on all that is human. It frustrates the wisest plans and absolutely converts them into nothingness. All the ecstasies of pleasure, all the splendours of fame, all the triumphs of ambition, all the joys of domestic tenderness, all the eye can look for or the heart aspire after — this, this is their affecting termination. Death absorbs all — it annihilates all. Our fathers who strutted their little hour on this very theatre, were as active and as noisy as we. The loud laugh of festivity was heard in their dwellings; and in the busy occupation of their callings, they had their days of labour, and their nights of thoughtful anxiety. The world carried on it then the same face of activity as now; and where are the men who kept it up in their allotted generation? They are where we shall soon follow them. They have gone to sleep; but it is the sleep of death. Their bed is a coffin in which they are mouldering. The garment which they have thrown aside is their body, which served them through life; but is now lying in loose and scattered fragments, among the earth of their grave.

And it does aggravate our hopelessness of escape from death, when we look to the wide extent and universality of its ravages. We see no exception. It scatters its desolations with unsparing cruelty among all the sons and daughters of Adam. It perhaps adds to our despair, when we see it extending to the other animals. Everything that has life dies; and even the lovely forms of the vegetable creation dissolve into nothing. It appears to be the condition of every organic being; and so looks as if it were some tremendous necessity, under which we have nothing for it but helplessly to acquiesce. It carries to our observation all the immutability of a general law. Man can look for no mitigation to the big and incurable distress. He cannot reverse the processes of Nature, nor bid her mighty elements obey him.

Is there no power then superior to Nature, and which can control her? To us a law of the universe carries the idea of some fixed and in-alienable necessity along with it; and none more certain, more unvary-ing and more widely extended in its operation, than the law of death. In the wide circuit of things, does there exist no high authority which can abolish this law? – no power which can overthrow death, and spoil him of his principality? – no being travelling in the greatness of his strength, who can grapple this mighty monarch and break his tyranny to pieces? We never saw that Being. But the records of past ages have come down to us; and we there read of an extraordinary visitor who lighted on these realms, where death has reigned so long in all the triumphs of undivided empire. Wonderful enterprise, He came to destroy death. Vast undertaking, He came to depose Nature from her conceived immutability. He came to shift her processes – and a law that embraced in its wide grasp all which lives and moves on the face of the world, he came to overturn it. And He soon gave tokens of a power commensurate to the mighty undertaking. That Nature, to whose operations we are so apt to ascribe some stubborn and invin-cible necessity, gave way at His coming. She felt His authority through all her elements, and she obeyed it. Wonderful period, when the con-stancy of Nature was broke in upon by Him who established it – when the Deity vindicated His honours; and the miracles of a single age, committed to authentic history, gave evidence to all futurity that there is a Power above Nature and beyond it. What more unchanging than the aspect of the starry Heavens; in what quarter of her domin-ions does Nature maintain a more silent and solemn inflexibility, than in the orbs which roll around us?

Yet at the coming of the mighty Saviour, these Heavens broke si-lence. Music was heard from their canopy, and it came from a concord of living voices, which sung the praises of God, and made them fall in articulate language upon human ears. After this, who can call Nature unalterable? Jesus Christ while He tarried on earth made per-petual invasions upon her constancy; and she never in a single in-stance, resisted the word of His power. What manner of man is this, said His disciples, who can make the wind and the seas obey Him? Philosophers love to expatiate; and they tell us of the laws of the ani-mal and the vegetable kingdom. These laws may prove an impassable barrier to us, but in the hand of the omnipotent Saviour they were nothing. He reversed or suspended them at pleasure. He blasted the fig tree by a single word; and, what to us was the dawn of some high anticipation, He made man the subject of His miracles. He restored sight to the blind. He restored speech to the dumb. He restored motion to the palsied. And to crown His triumph over Nature and her processes, He restored life to the dead. He laid down His own life, and He took it up again. The disciples gave up all for lost, when they saw the champion of their hopes made the victim of that very mortality, which He promised to destroy. It was like the revenge and the victory of Nature, over Him who had so often prevailed against her. But it was only to make His triumph more illustrious. He died and was buried; but He rose again. He re-entered that mysterious bourne, from which it has been said that no traveller ever returns; but He did. He burst asunder the mighty barriers of the grave. He re-entered and reanimated that body which expired on the cross; and by that most striking of all testimonies, His own unaltered form emerging from the tomb, He has given us to know, that He fought against the law of death and He carried it.

But man not only wants power to achieve his own immortality, he also wants light to discover it. If such, in spite of every appalling exhibition to the contrary, is really to be the ultimate state of man, this doctrine is not brought to light by reason. The text indeed says as much, in saying that it is brought to light by the gospel. It represents this great truth as dark by Nature, and only made clear by Revelation. It seems to cast discredit on all the arguments of science in behalf of a future state; and, just for want of a sufficient basis in the evidence of Philosophy on which to rear this noble anticipation, it would rest and establish it chiefly on the evidence of faith.

In the further prosecution of this discourse, let us first advert to what may be called the physical state, and then to the moral state of the mind; and under each head, let us endeavour to contrast the insufficiency of the light of nature, with the sufficiency and fulness of the light of the gospel.

I. An argument for its immortality has been drawn from the consideration of what we should term the physics of the mind—that is, from the consideration of its properties, when it is regarded as having a separate or substantive being of its own. For example it has been said that spirit is not matter, and therefore must be imperishable. We confess that we see not the force of this reasoning. We are not sure by nature of the premises; and neither do we apprehend how the conclusion flows from it. We think ourselves familiar with the subtleties and the scholastics that have been uttered upon the subject. To us they are far from satisfactory; nor can we perceive aught of that evidence, on which we rest our belief in any coming event or coming state of the futurity which lies before us—we can perceive no such force of practical evidence in those abstract or metaphysic generalities, which are employed to demonstrate the endurance or rather the indestructibleness of the thinking principle—so as to be persuaded, that it shall indeed survive the dissolution of the body, and shall separately maintain its consciousness and its powers on the other side of the grave.

Now, in the recorded fact of our Saviour's resurrection, we see what many would call a more popular; but what we should deem a far more substantial and satisfactory argument for the soul's immortality, than any that is furnished by the speculation which we have now alluded to. To us the one appears as much superior to the other, as History is more solid than Hypothesis, or as Experience is of a texture more firm than Imagination, or as the Philosophy of our modern Bacon, is of a surer and sounder character than the Philosophy of the old schoolmen. Now it is upon the fact of His own resurrection that Christ rests the hope and the promise of resurrection to all of us. If He be not risen from the dead, says one of His apostles, we are of all men the most miserable. It is to this fact, that he appeals as the foundation and the hope of immortality. To every cavil and to every difficulty he opposes the emphatic argument, that Christ has risen. This was Paul's argument; and it has descended by inheritance to us. We have received the testimony. We have access to the documents. We can take a view of the unexampled evidence, which has been carried down to us upon the vehicles of history; and in opposition to all which fancy or speculation can muster against us, we can appeal to the fact. It is not a doctrine excogitated by the ingenuities of human reasoning. It is a doctrine submitted to the observation of the human senses. It is not an untried experiment. While Jesus Christ lived, He made it repeatedly, and with unvaried success, upon others; and, in giving up His body to the cross, He made it upon Himself. One who could carry an experiment such as this to a successful termination, has a claim to be listened to; and He tells by the mouth of an apostle, that the fact of Himself having risen, bears most decisively upon the doctrine that we shall rise also. "For if we believe that Jesus died and rose again, even so them also which sleep in Jesus will God bring with him."

Let it be remarked, before we conclude this head of discourse, that the word which we render "abolished," signifies also, "made of no effect." The latter interpretation of the word is certainly more applicable to our first or our temporal death. He has not abolished temporal death. It still reigns with unmitigated violence, and sweeps off its successive generations with as great sureness and rapidity as ever. This part of the sentence is not abolished, but it is rendered ineffectual. Death still lays us in the grave; but it cannot chain us there to everlasting forgetfulness. It puts its cold hand upon every one of us; but a power mightier than death will lift it off, and these frames be again reanimated with all the warmth of life and of sentiment. The church-yard has been called the land of silence; and silent it is indeed to those who occupy it. The Sabbath bell is no longer heard; nor yet the tread of the living population above them. But though removed from the hearing of every earthly sound, yet shall they hear the sound of the last trumpet. It shall enter the loneliness of their dwellings, and be heard through Death's remotest caverns. When we open the sepulchres of the men of other times, the fragments of skeletons and the moulder-ing of bones form indeed a humiliating spectacle. But the working of the same power which raised Jesus from the dead, shall raise cor-ruption to a comelier form, and invest it in all the bloom and vigour of immortality. So is the resurrection of the dead. It is sown in corrup-tion. It is raised in incorruption. It is sown in dishonour. It is raised in glory. It is sown in weakness. It is raised in power. It is sown a natural body. It is raised a spiritual body. This corruptible must put on incor-ruption; and this mortal must put on immortality. So when this cor-ruption shall have put on incorruption, and this mortal shall have put on immortality, then shall be brought to pass the saying that is written, Death is swallowed up in victory.

II. But another argument for the immortality of man, has been drawn by philosophers from the moral state of his mind; and more especially from that progressive expansion, which they affirm it to have undergone, in respect of its virtues as well as of its powers. Still we fear, that, in respect of this argument too, the flowery description of the moralists has no proof, and more particularly no experience to support it. There is a beauty we do confess in many of their represen-tations; but beauty is only for them who sit at ease. It is a cruel mock-ery to the man who is surrounded by the agonies of a death-bed; and has in his immediate view, the dread images of annihilation or ven-geance. Yes! we have heard them talk, and with eloquence too, of the good man and of his prospects – of his progress in life being a splendid career of virtue, and of his death being a gentle transition to another and a better world – of its being the goal where he reaps the honour-able reward that is due to his accomplishments, or being little more than a step in his proud march to eternity. This is all very fine, but it is the fineness of poetry. Where is the evidence of its being any better than a deceitful imagination?

We might believe that there was something real in this stately pro-gression to eternity, if we saw it; but we see it not. Why so cruel an interruption to the progress? What means this awful and mysterious death? Why is the good man not suffered to carry on in his triumphant progress; and how comes this dark and inexplicable event, to be inter-posed between him and the full accomplishment of his destiny? You may choose to call it a step; but there is no virtue in a name to quell our suspicion. It bears in every circumstance all the marks of a termination. We see the gradual decay of those faculties, which you tell us, but tell us falsely, are ripening and expanding. We see those virtues which you have represented as in a state of constant perseverance — we see them giving way to the power of disease — we see them withering into feebleness; and, instead of that which confers grace or dignity on man, we see the peevishness, the discontent, the fretfulness of age. We see the body bending to the dust. We see it extended in all the agony of helplessness and pain. To call this a triumphant procession to eternity — or to disguise those actual horrors which the ear hears and the eye witnesses, by the gildings of a flimsy imagination! We observe the emission of the last breath; and, whether the spirit is extinguished or fled to another residence, Nature tells us not — but when the academic declaimer talks of his fancied career of perfection, we should lift the honest front of experience against him, and call upon him to reveal to us the mystery of death. How comes an event so unseemly to meet the hero of immortality, on the path he was treading with such security and triumph? What the purpose of such an interruption at all? Why has the being, whom they would proudly assimilate to angels, such an ordeal to undergo? Why like them does he not flourish in perpetual vigour? And how shall we explain that mighty change, with all its affecting accompaniments of reluctance and agony and despair?

Death gives the lie to all the speculations of all the moralists; but it only gives evidence and consistency to the statements of the gospel. The doctrines of the New Testament will bear to be confronted with the rough and vigorous lessons of experience. They attempt no ornament and no palliation. They give the truth in all its severity — nor do they attempt to strew flowers around the sepulchre, or pour a deceitful perfume into the rottenness of the grave. Were a physician to take up my case, and speak lightly of my ailments, while I knew that a consuming disease was working and making progress within me, I should have no confidence in him, or in his remedies. I should like him to see the mischief in its full extent, that the medicine applied may be such as to meet and to combat with it. Now Christ the Physician of souls has taken up their disease in all its malignity. There is no softening, no disguise, in the representation of His messengers. Their account of death accords with our experience of it. What they tell us of death, is what we feel it to be — not that thing of triumph, which out of Christianity and beyond the circle of its influence it never is; but a thing of distress, and horror, and unnatural violence. He who is weak enough to be carried along by the false and the flimsy eloquence of sentimental moralists, might be led to believe that the man who dies is only sinking gently to repose, or winging his way to a triumphant eternity. But the Bible tells us differently — that out of Christ there is no triumph and no gentleness about it. It talks of the sting, and of the pains, and of the fear of death; and what we feel and know of the shrinkings of nature, proves that it has experience on its side. And the book which characterizes so truly death in itself, is worthy at least of our attention, when it treats of death in its moral or spiritual bearings.

Death then, as it appears to the eye of the senses, is but the extinction of that life which we now live in the world; but death, as revealed to us in Scripture, is the effect and the sentence of sin. Sin is the root of the mischief; and it is a mischief which Scripture represents as stretching in malignity and duration, far beyond the ken of the senses. Had we no other guide than our senses, we might conceive death to be a mere annihilation; and the utter destruction of their being, to be the whole amount of the calamity inflicted upon sinners. But distinct from this death of the body, there is what may be termed the death of the soul—not a death which consists in the extinction of its consciousness, for the conscience of guilt will keep by it forever—not a death which implies the cessation of feeling, for to feeling it will continue to be all alive, though the feeling of intense suffering—not a death by which all sense of God will be expunged, for the sense of God's offended countenance will abide by it and agonize it through all eternity. He who undergoes this second, this spiritual death, does not thereby cease to have life; but he ceases to have that favor of God which is better than life. He lives it is true, but it is the life of an exile from hope and from happiness. He lives, but it is in a state of hopeless distance from the fountain of living water. God is at enmity towards him; and in his own heart there is enmity towards God. This at least is the death of enjoyment. It is the death of all those pleasures, and of all those perceptions, which belong to a right moral state of existence. In this sense truly the soul is dead, though alive and most pungently alive to the corrosions of that worm which dieth not. In this sense there has been a quenching of its life, though all awake to the pain and the anguish of the fire that is not quenched. The temporal death is only the portal to sorer calamities. All who sin shall die; but this is not the conclusion of the sentence. All who die in sin shall live in torment.

Now it promises well for our Saviour's treatment of this sore malady—that He hath as it were placed Himself at the source of the mischief, and there made head against it. He has combated the radical force and virulence of the disease. He has probed it to the bottom. He has grappled with sin in its origin and its principle. He has taken it away—for by the sacrifice of Himself on the accursed tree, He has expiated its guilt; and, by the operation of the Spirit in the heart of the believer, He is rooting out its existence. Had He only put together the fragments of my body, and recalled my soul to its former tenement—He would have done nothing. Sin, both in its power and in its condemnation, would have claimed me as its own—and, in dreary banishment from God, it would have recalled me to life, but a life of misery; and stamped on me immortality, but an immortality of despair. But the Author of the gospel has swept off the whole burden of the calamity. He has made a decisive thrust into the very heart and principle of the disease. He has destroyed sin, for He has both cancelled the sentence and washed away the pollution; and, by the accomplishment of a mystery which angels desire to look into, He brings sinners unto God, where they shall ever rejoice in the purest light and the happiest immortality.

To estimate aright the new moral existence into which Christ ushers every sinner who receives Him – we have only to reflect how it is that every sinner, apart from Christ, stands towards God. He is either immersed in deep oblivion and unconcern, and so may well be accounted dead to the Being who made and who upholds him; or if his conscience be at all awake to a true sense of his delinquencies from the law, he must view the lawgiver with a feeling of dread and discomfort and jealousy. There is a wide gulf of alienation between him and his Maker; and the habitual, the haunting apprehension of God's displeasure towards him, engenders in him back again a habitual dislike towards God. There is no community of affection or confidence betwixt them; and pursued as he is by a conviction of guilt, which he cannot resist and cannot escape from, he imagines a scowl on the aspect of the Divinity – an awful barrier of separation, by which he is hopelessly and irrecoverably exiled from the sacred throne of the Eternal. His spirit is not at ease. It is glad to find relief, in the day-dreams of a passing world, from those solemn realities, the thought of which so agitates and disquiets it. It seeks an opiate in the things of sense and time, against the disturbance which it finds in the things of eternity; and so, cradled in profoundest lethargy, it, while alive unto the world, is dead unto God.

We cannot imagine a greater revolution in the heart, than that which would ensue on the burden of this distrust or of this apathy being done away – when, instead of viewing God with terror, or shrinking from the thought of Him, the sinner would steadfastly gaze upon His reconciled countenance, and be assured of the complacency and the good-will that were graven thereupon. Now a simple faith in the glad tidings of the gospel is competent to achieve this. It would loosen the spirit's bondage, by merely transforming the aspect of the Divinity from that of an enemy to that of a friend. It would change our indifference or our hatred into love; and this affection, from the central the presiding place which it occupies, would subordinate the whole man, and so utterly change his moral system as to make a new creature of him. The faith of the gospel is something more than the germ of a new hope. It is the germ of a new heart, and so of a new character. The believer's taste and sensibilities are now awake to objects, to which before he was utterly dead; or from which he wont to recoil with strong and sensitive aversion. In other words, he has become alive to these objects. He expatiates on another theatre of contemplation; and he rejoices in other scenes and other prospects than before. He has lost his relish for that in which he formerly delighted. He delights in that for which formerly he had no relish. It is just as if old senses had been extinguished, and as if new ones had been substituted in their place. If he is not ushered into life for the first time he is at least ushered into a new mode of life for the first time. He undergoes preferment from the animal to the spiritual life; and this life, with the immortality annexed to it, is not only made clear by the gospel – but faith in the gospel may be said to have created it.

Now all this is the doing of the Saviour. I cannot trust the physician who plays upon the surface of my disease, and throws over it the disguise of false colouring. I have more confidence to put in him, who, like Christ the Physician of my soul, has looked the malady fairly in the face – has taken it up in all its extent, and in all its soreness – has resolved it into its original principles – has probed it to the very bottom; and has set himself forward to combat with the radical elements of the disease. This is what the Saviour has done with death. He has plucked it of its sting. He has taken a full survey of the corruption, and met it in every one quarter where its malignity operates. It was sin which constituted the virulence in the disease, and he hath extracted it. He hath put it away. He hath expiated the sentence; and the believer, rejoicing in the assurance that all is clear with God, serves Him without fear in righteousness and in holiness all the days of his life. The sentence is no longer in force, against us who believe. The Saviour took the sentence upon Himself. He bore our iniquity. He became sin for us, though He knew no sin, that we might become the righteousness of God in Him. The sentence is no longer in force against us. The Saviour has cancelled it; and he has done more than this. He has not only cancelled the guilt of sin, he has extinguished its power. He reigns in the heart of the believer. He sweeps it of all its corruptions. He takes it such as it is – He makes it such as it should be. He brings the whole man under a thorough process of sanctification – so that while he lives he adds one degree of grace unto another – when he dies he rejoices in hope of the coming glory – when he stands at the bar of judgment, he is presented holy and unreprovable in the sight of God and of His Saviour. In the whole of this treatment, I see the skill and intelligence and superior management of a physician who is up to the disease; and knows where the main force of its malignity lies – who has a thorough insight into the principle of the mischief, and has reached forward an appropriate remedy to confront it – who, to abolish death, has directed the strength of His attack against sin which is its origin – who has averted the condemnation of sin, by an expiatory sacrifice—and who is destroying its power and its existence, by the operation of that mighty spirit, whereby He can break down the corruption of the human heart and subdue it unto all righteousness.

Believe this done; and the veil is thrown aside which separates you from the glories of heaven—the way lies clear and open before you; and light, pure and satisfying light, gives the highest evidence and splendour to the great doctrine of life and immortality. The grand mystery is resolved. The barrier which kept the sinner at a distance from God is levelled and put away. That barrier was sin; and Christ, by the mighty instruments of His sacrifice and His spirit, has overthrown it. But a victory over sin is a victory over death. Where sin hath no longer any dominion, death hath no longer any claim; and that mighty Being who spoiled principalities and powers hath abolished death, because He conquered sin. True, it still reigns in these mortal bodies; and till the new system of things be established, it will scatter its desolation over the surface of the world. But the new system is preparing. A place is fitting up in Heaven, for those to whom our Saviour hath given the assurance, that, in His Father's house there are many mansions; and on earth, the Spirit is now working in the hearts of the destined occupiers, and making them meet for the inheritance. These vile bodies must be put off; and others put on, over which death shall have no power. They will persist in bloom and in vigour to eternity. Mighty change in the constitution of the species—mighty change in the material system around us—mighty change in the souls of men, as well as in the bodies which they animate. The bodies we now wear shall moulder into dust—the earth we now tread upon shall be burnt up—the heavens we now gaze at shall pass away as a scroll—But we look for new heavens and a new earth, wherein dwelleth righteousness; and the beings who live in it shall never die.

Before we conclude, let us refer your attention to the grand agent in this wonderful restoration of a fallen world. The work is His, and it is His only. We must take Him not as a fellow-helper in the cause, but as the Captain of our salvation. It was He who trode the wine press alone. His was all the contest, and to Him be all the triumph. Let no man offer to usurp or to share it with Him. To Him belongs the work of our redemption, in all its extent and in all its particulars. It was His sacrifice which redeemed us from the punishment of sin; and it is His spirit which redeems us from its pollution. And we contend that man is not in the right attitude for receiving the mighty benefit, till he has cast down all his lofty imaginations, and resigned himself with gratitude and quietness into the Saviour's hands. "Here I am under the twofold misery, of having been a sinner in time past, and being a sinner still—of having incurred a sentence which I cannot expiate, and of persevering in a path of destruction which I cannot turn from. The case in all its helplessness, and in all its difficulties, I make over wholly to the Saviour. I may as well try to level yonder mountain, as try to master it by my own independent exertions. I obey the invitation of the Saviour – 'Come unto me' – I put the case into His hand; and, if I do it in the assured hope that His redemption will provide for it, I shall not be disappointed. If I offer Him the case, He will not refuse to take it up. 'Him that cometh unto me, I will in no wise cast out.' He takes up the case which I have submitted to Him. He examines it in its two leading particulars. I cannot expiate the sentence; but the blood of His atonement can do it for me. I cannot turn from the paths of sin; but He can turn me by His grace – He can reign in me by His spirit – so that though without Him I can do nothing – yet with Him for my strengthener and my friend I can do all things." This then is the finished work, the complete salvation of Jesus Christ. "Whosoever believeth in Him hath everlasting life." Believe, and you will come forth with alacrity at His call. From the contemplation of your own nothingness, you will cast yourself upon the Saviour and upon His sufficiency. You will make an entire and unconditional surrender of yourselves to Him; and be assured, that, from the first moment of your doing so, there will emerge the new hope of the redeemed, and the new life of the sanctified disciple.

And you Christians, who have sat at His table – who have eaten of that bread which is the symbol of His body, and drunk of that wine which is the symbol of His blood – be assured, that, if you have done so, with all the spirituality of a firm and believing dependence on Him as your Saviour, upon you shall the whole of this great redemption be accomplished. You have brought your bodies into contact with the elements of the ordinance; and if you have brought your minds into contact with the things represented by these elements, we can state to you in decisive language what will be the fruit of such fellowship. God is not unfaithful who hath called you unto the fellowship of His Son, Jesus Christ our Lord; and we can assert, upon the fidelity of God, upon the unfailing promises of Heaven, upon the strength of a high and unchangeable attribute, upon that truth of the Deity which is printed on all His works, and shines through all His revelations – In a word, we can assert upon the solemn asseveration, nay, upon the oath of the Divinity Himself, that all who believe in His Son shall have their fruit unto holiness, and the end everlasting life.

Such is the hope of your calling. Hold it firm and fast even unto the end; and the bed of death will be to you a scene of triumph – the last messenger will be a messenger of joy; and those bright images of peace and rapture and elevation, which, out of Christ, are the mere fabrication of the fancy, will, in Christ, be found to have a reality and a fulfilment, which shall bear you up in the midst of your dying agonies, with a joy unspeakable and full of glory. It is no longer an idle declamation now. There is many a minister of Christ who could give you experience for it. He can take you to the house of mourning – to the mansion of pain and of sickness – to the chamber of the dying man. He can draw aside the curtain which covers the last hours of the good man's existence, and show you how a Christian can die. He can ask you to bend your ear, and to catch the faltering accents of praise and of piety. What meaneth that joy in the midst of suffering – that hope in the midst of breathlessness and pain – that elevation in the midst of cruellest agonies? It is not his own merit which sustains him. – It is the merit of a benevolent Saviour. It is not a sense of his own righteousness which gives intrepidity to his expiring bosom. It is the righteousness of Christ. It is the hope of being found in Him, and a sense of the grace and forgiveness which he has received through His hands. In a word it is Christ who resolves the mystery. It is His presence which throws tranquillity and joy around the scene of distress. It is He who administers vigour to the dying man; and, while despair sits on every countenance, and relatives are weeping around him, He enables him to leave them all with this exulting testimony – O death where is thy sting – O grave where is thy victory!

FAST-DAY DISCOURSE

"The king's heart is in the hand of the Lord, as the rivers of water: he turneth it whithersoever he will" (Proverbs 21:1).

IT IS CONSOLATORY to think that this earthly scene, in spite of the misery and apparent confusion which prevail in it, is under the absolute control of infinite wisdom – that the God who sitteth above and reigns in heaven, also presides over the destinies of this lower world – that every event in history is of His appointment – that every occurrence in the course of human affairs is in the order of His providence – that He reigns in the heart of man, and can control all its purposes – that the violence of human ambition is only an instrument which He employs, to carry on His government and accomplish the purposes of His wisdom.

Reprinted from Thomas Chalmers, *Sermons and Discourses* (New York: Robert Carter & Bros., 1863), pp. 415–19.

When we see combined in the same person the genius of an angel and the malignity of a tyrant—when we see a power that no human energy can resist, and this power directed to the slavery and degradation of the species—when we see strewed around his throne the mangled liberties of a generous and intrepid people—when we follow him in the brilliant career of his victories, and in the history of his guilty triumphs anticipate the new miseries which his ambition is to bring upon the world, it certainly brightens up the dreariness that lies before us when we think that he is only an instrument in the hand of the Almighty—that it is God that worketh in him to will and to do—that the heart of man is in the Lord's hand as the rivers of water, and that He turneth it wheresoever He will.

It is the sublimest exercise of piety to refer everything around us to the wisdom of God—to acknowledge Him in all the events of His providence—to place our refuge in His wisdom in the evil days of darkness and disorder, and to rest our confidence on the Almighty Being who sitteth above, and presides in high authority over the theatre of human affairs. Such are the consolations of piety—such the elevation of heart which religion confers—an elevation which the world knoweth not, and which the tyrant of this world cannot take away. Life is short, and its anxieties are soon over. The glories even of the conqueror will soon find their hiding-place in the grave. In a few years, and that power which appals the world will feel all the weakness of mortality—the sentence of all must pursue him—the fate of all must overtake him; he must divest himself of his glories, and lie down with the meanest of his slaves—that ambition which aspires to the dominion of the whole earth, will at last have but a spot of dust to repose on—it will be cut short in the midst of its triumphs—it will sleep from all its anxieties, and be fast locked in the insensibility of death. There the wicked cease from troubling, and the weary are at rest.

We live in a busy and interesting period. Every year gives a new turn to the history of the world, and throws a new complexion over the aspect of political affairs. The wars of other times shrink into insignificance when compared with the grand contest which now embroils the whole of civilized society. They were paltry in their origin—they were trifling in their object—they were humble and insignificant in their consequences. A war of the last generation left the nations of Europe in the same relative situation in which it found them; but war now is on a scale of magnitude that is quite unexampled in the history of modern times. Not to decide some point of jealousy or to secure some trifling possessions, it embraces a grander interest—it involves the great questions of Existence and Liberty. Every war is signalized with the wreck of some old empire and the establishment of a new one —all the visions of romance are authenticated in the realities which pass before us—the emigration of one royal family, the flight and the imprisonment of another, the degradation of a third to all the obscurity of private life—these are events which have ceased to astonish us because their novelty is over, and they are of a piece with those wonderful changes which the crowded history of these few years presents to our remembrance.

Such a period as this, then, gives full scope for the exercise of piety. Let everything be referred to God; in this diversity of operations, let us remember that it is He who worketh all in all—let us recognize Him as the author of all these wonders—and amid this bewildering variety of objects, let us never lose sight of that mighty Being who sustains all and directs all. It is His judgments that are abroad in the world—it is His magnificent plans that are verging to their accomplishment—it is His system of beauty and order and wisdom, that is to proceed from this wild uproar of human passions. He can restrain the remainder of human wrath—He can allay the fury and the turbulence of human ambition—He can make order spring out of confusion, and attune every heart and every will to His purposes.

Let it not be disguised. There is ground for apprehension in the character and talents of the enemy. There is a wisdom in his politics, there is a power and a rapidity in his decisions, there is a mysterious energy in his character, there is a wealth and a population in his empire that are sufficient to account for the tide of success which has accompanied him in all his efforts against the imbecility of the old governments. The governments he had to contend with were old, and they had all the infirmities of age. They wanted that vigour and impulse and purity which a revolution communicates to every department of the State. With the one party we see an energy pervading every department of the public service—with the other we see the most important administrations intrusted to the minions of a court, to the puny lordlings of hereditary grandeur—a set of beings who had nothing to sustain them but the smile of a minister, or nothing to protect them from insignificance but the blazoned heraldry of their ancestors.

There is no denying that in France the military appointments are decided by the questions of merit and fitness and character. In the other countries of Europe—and I blush to say that even in this vaunted abode of purity and of patriotism, almost everything connected with the interest of the public comes under the putrifying touch of money or of politics—that corruption has insinuated itself into every department of the State—that men are summoned up into offices of distinction who are only calculated to cover a nation with disgrace, and expose it to the derision of its enemies—that the public voice has lost its energy, and the united indignation of a whole people is often unable to drag to punishment those delinquents whom patronage has exalted and the smiles of a court have sheltered from infamy.

This surely affords a heartless and a mortifying spectacle, and is calculated to alarm any lover of his country when he compares it with that dreadful energy which its enemies can muster up to overwhelm it. We see no imbecility there—no corruption in the military appointments of Bonaparte—no submissive accommodation to the interest of great families—the truth is, that his power renders him independent of it. In him we see vested in one person the simple energy of a despotism. He is so far exalted above the greatest of his subjects that to his eye all are equal. He needs not to temporize or accommodate or allure the friendship of a great family with the bribery of corruption—he throws open the career of preferment to the whole of his immense population—he calls upon all to enter into this generous and aspiring competition of talent, and it is a competition that has often exalted the veriest child of raggedness and obscurity to the proudest offices of the empire.

I do not speak in the tone of disaffection—I speak in the tone of patriotism. I do not mean to pursue the errors of my Government in the spirit of hostility—it is in that spirit of regret that proceeds from the sincerity of my attachment—from my conviction that the Government of England is worth the contending for—that every lover of his country should stand by it to maintain its purity, as well as to defend its existence—that he should not only risk his life in fighting the battles of his country against the enemies of its independence, but that he should risk all the advantages of patronage and preferment in fighting the battles of the Constitution against the enemies of its purity and its vigour.

Let us hope that the present state of affairs will operate as an effectual lesson to the rulers of the country—that the sense of danger will animate the public mind to all the enthusiasm of virtue—that the ardour of patriotism will chase away all the obliquities of a selfish and interested politics—that our legislation will turn with shame from the low game of party dissension, and lend their unanimity to that noble struggle that is to decide the liberty of the future age, and give a lasting complexion to the history of future times.

But let us not forget our dependence upon God—that mighty Being who reigns supreme over the will of man, and exerts an absolute control over all hearts and all purposes. He who hardened the heart of Pharaoh against the calamities of his country can exert the same influence over the minds of the rulers of the present day. He can infatuate the mind of the country against the feeling of its dangers—He can throw a slumbering indifference over the land—He can lay us asleep on the brink of destruction, and send that torpor, that security into the hearts of our rulers which is the melancholy symptom of a falling empire.

But we hope better things; that the same God who can turn the heart of man wheresoever he will, will send a wise and a righteous spirit over the government of public affairs – that the country will awaken to its dangers – and that purity and patriotism will at length preside over the administration of its interests.

In this day set apart for the expression of public sentiments, you should rise in gratitude to the Ruler of nations, that mighty Being who has turned the battle from your gates; who has singled you out among the countries of Europe, and given you the exclusive privilege of living in peace while the world around you is involved in all the cruelty and turbulence of war. I fear that none of us have a lively enough conception of the gratitude that we ought to feel for so inestimable a blessing – that we live in the bosom of domestic tranquillity – that we have no midnight alarm to disturb us – no sound of horror to strike upon our ear, and keep us awake and trembling in the agony of apprehension – no moaning of wounded acquaintances – no shrieks of the dying to rend the heart of sensibility – no hostile footsteps to warn us of the nearness of a brutal and enraged soldiery – no loud and stormy reproaches, to send anguish into the mother's heart, and make her weep in the wildness of despair over the members of her shrinking and devoted family.

What a picture of horror – the seat of war – when the marauding army of the conqueror is let loose upon the country – when they separate into parties, and each singles out its own house or its own neighbourhood as the object of its brutality and its vengeance – when every nerve is strained to deeds of barbarity – when pity is laughed at as a weakness, or its gentle whispers are drowned in the wild uproar of rapacity and desolation and murder. What a contrast to the country in which we live! – what a spectacle of peace in the midst of a wild and troubled theatre! What would not the houseless victims of Spain give for the warmth and security of our dwellings? – where every man lives under his own vine and his own fig-tree – where he steps forth in the morning and prosecutes in safety the labours of the day – where he returns in the evening, and has his peaceful fireside enlivened by the smiling aspect of his family around him – where the Sabbath morn still continues to bless the humble abode of the poor man and of the labourer – where the church-bell is still heard to waft its delightful music along our valleys, and to call an assembled people to the exercise of piety. Let the piety of this day be gratitude to that mighty Being who takes up the hills in His hands, and weighs the nations in a balance. He has thrown around our happy country the shelter of a protecting ocean – He has mustered his own elements to defend us. The green island of the north sits in the bosom of security – it hears the sound of the battle from afar, but quietness dwells there, and peace and joy are among its children.

Look at the extent of Britain, and it is a speck on the surface of the world. Look at the map, and it appears like an humble appendage to that immense continent that is in arms against it. Yet how high it stands in the proud lists of glory—how great in the independence of its empire—how awful in the thunder of its power that is heard on the remotest corners of the world—how firm in the patriotism and intrepidity of its people, who rally round the standard of their liberties, and maintain the name and dignity of their nation against the fury of a devouring ambition!

We have to thank the God of battles that Britain, though deceived perhaps in her aspiring wishes for the liberties of Europe—yet that Britain herself stands as secure and as independent as ever. In the very last event of her history there may have been disaster, but there has been no disgrace—there may have been loss, but there has been no infamy—there may have been retreat from the power of numbers, but even this retreat has been emblazoned in the splendours of victory, and the annals of our country's renown are crowded with the names of dead and of living heroes.

Grant that we abandon the liberty of Europe—yet the question of Britain's liberty is entire. We are no worse than before. The enemy does not stand in a more menacing attitude—nor does invasion lower more frightfully than at first upon our beloved island. The country has witnessed the talent and the prowess of our commanders—its confidence is exalted. Our late campaigns have furnished a most useful accession to military skill and military experience. That alarm which seized our politicians at the bug-bear of our commercial embarrassments, has subsided. It is not above a year since it was anticipated, from the suspension of all intercourse with other nations, that something in the shape of a convulsion was to come upon the country.

The convulsion has never made its appearance—it has spared us for one year, and it will spare us for twenty, if circumstances impose upon us the necessity of prolonging the experiment to such an extent. The public interest is as flourishing as ever. We witness the same animation and extent and prosperity in all the departments both of the public service and of private industry. The experience of every day is vindicating to the eyes of the world the independence of our resources, and that we have a vigour within which is native and inherent and imperishable.

Do not think that I am turning your attention from religion to politics. I am enumerating the circumstances on which your prosperity is founded; but I give God the glory and praise for being the author of these circumstances. The explanation of any event or of any appearance upon natural principles should have no effect whatever in extinguishing piety. I am correct in saying, that we enjoy light in the daytime, because then the sun is above the horizon; but it does not therefore follow that I stop short at this explanation—that I forget that mighty Being who gave the sun its existence, who fixed this astonishing mass of luminous matter in the centre of our system, and bade it give light and cheerfulness and joy to the worlds that roll around it.

I am correct in saying that the future security and independence of our empire is founded on the patriotism of our people, on the attachment which the country feels to its government, and on the extent of those resources which it is the province of an enlightened economy to unfold and to establish; but it does not follow that I overlook God – that I withdraw your attention from Him who is the author of all facts and of all principles – that I withhold the homage of my gratitude and my piety from that great comprehensive power that presides in high authority over the moral as well as over the material universe – or that I offer an idolatry to second causes, which I would take away from that supreme and animating mind that formed all things and sustains all things.

A dark and tremendous uncertainty hangs over the future history of the world. Events succeed each other with a rapidity that absolutely benumbs the faculties and annihilates the sensation of wonder. As much happens in the space of a single year, as would formerly have been enough to signalize a whole century. During the wars of Frederick of Prussia all Europe hung upon his enterprises – every eye was turned as to a splendid theatre where the genius and intrepidity of a great man commanded the homage of an admiring world, and the report of his victories filled all people with terror and astonishment. This same Prussia is annihilated in the space of a few days – and mark the difference of the public mind: it has ceased to be spoken of. All the interest and wonder and novelty of this great occurrence evaporates in the course of a single month. The attention of the public is hurried away to other objects – new scenery is presented to engross every eye and eclipse the memory of the old. The mind is fatigued with the rapidity of the succession – it seeks for repose in indifference – and the same public that was once so feelingly alive to the fate of a ruined kingdom or the interests of a trifling principality, would now slumber in apathy though all Europe were in commotion and its oldest empires fell in this wild war of turbulence and disorder.

Let us rise in gratitude to Heaven that we stand aloof from this theatre of convulsions. Our security depends upon ourselves. No wisdom, no energy can save us, if we flinch from the cause of patriotism and virtue. The strength of a country lies in the heart of its inhabitants. This is a day of fasting; but we should remember that to fast is to repent, and to repent is to reform. It is not the visionary reform of political enthusiasts that I speak of – it is a reform in the lives and hearts of individuals – that reform which would settle the reign of integrity in the councils of our nation, and would settle the influence of piety among our families and cottages – that reform which would descend to your children, and secure the character of yet future ages – that reform of which every great man should give the example that every poor man should be proud to imitate – that reform which would reconcile all the orders of the community, and make them feel that they had but one cause and one interest – that reform which would banish prejudice and disaffection from the land, and bind to the throne of a beloved sovereign the homage of a virtuous and affectionate people.

FURY NOT IN GOD

"Fury is not in me: who would set the briers and thorns against me in battle? I would go through them, I would burn them together. Or let him take hold of my strength, that he may make peace with me; and he shall make peace with me" (Isaiah 7:3–5).

THERE ARE THREE DISTINCT LESSONS in this text. The first, that fury is not in God: the second, that He does not want to glorify Himself by the death of sinners – "Who would set the thorns and briers against me in battle?" the third, the invitation – "Take hold of my strength, that you may make peace with me; and you shall make peace with me."

I. First, then, Fury is not in God. But how can this be? is not fury one manifestation of His essential attributes? do we not repeatedly read of His fury – of Jerusalem being full of the fury of the Lord – of God casting the fury of His wrath upon the world – of Him rendering His anger upon His enemies with fury – of him accomplishing His fury upon Zion – of Him causing His fury to rest on the bloody and devoted city? We are not therefore to think that fury is banished altogether from God's administration. There are times and occasions when this fury is discharged upon the objects of it; and there must be other times and other occasions when there is no fury in Him.

Reprinted from Thomas Chalmers, *Sermons and Discourses* (New York: Robert Carter & Bros., 1863), pp. 599–608.

Now, what is the occasion upon which He disclaims all fury in our text? He is inviting men to reconciliation; He is calling upon them to make peace; and He is assuring them, that if they will only take hold of His strength, they shall make peace with Him. In the preceding verses He speaks of a vineyard; and in the act of inviting people to lay hold of His strength, He is in fact inviting those who are without the limits of the vineyard to enter in. Fury will be discharged on those who reject the invitation. But we cannot say that there is any exercise of fury in God at the time of giving the invitation. There is the most visible and direct contrary. There is a longing desire after you. There is a wish to save you from that day in which the fury of a rejected Saviour will be spread abroad over all who have despised Him. The tone of invitation is not a tone of anger – it is a tone of tenderness. The look which accompanies the invitation is not a look of wrath – it is a look of affection.

There may be a time, there may be an occasion when the fury of God will be put forth on the men who have held out against Him and turned them away in infidelity and contempt from His beseeching voice; but at the time that he is lifting this voice – at the time that He is sending messengers over the face of the earth to circulate it among the habitations of men – at the time particularly among ourselves, when in our own place and our own day Bibles are within the reach of every family, and ministers in every pulpit are sounding forth the overtures of the gospel throughout the land – surely at such a time and upon such an occasion, it may well be said of God to all who are now seeking His face and favour, that there is no fury in Him.

It is just as in the parable of the marriage feast: many rejected the invitation which the king gave to it – for which he was wroth with them, and sent forth his armies and destroyed them, and burned up their city. On that occasion there was fury in the king, and on the like occasion will there be fury in God. But well can He say at the time when He is now giving the invitation – there is no fury in me. There is kindness – a desire for peace and friendship – a longing earnestness to make up the quarrel which now subsists between the Lawgiver in heaven, and His yet impenitent and unreconciled creatures.

This very process was all gone through at and before the destruction of Jerusalem. It rejected the warnings and invitations of the Saviour, and at length experienced His fury. But there was no fury at the time of His giving the invitations. The tone of our Saviour's voice when He uttered – "O Jerusalem, Jerusalem," was not the tone of a vindictive and irritated fury. There was compassion in it – a warning and pleading earnestness that they would mind the things which belong to their peace; and at that time when He would willingly have gathered them as a hen gathereth her chickens under her wings – then may it well be said that there was no fury in the Son of God, no fury in God.

Let us make the application to ourselves in the present day. On the last day there will be a tremendous discharge of fury. That wrath which sinners are now doing so much to treasure up will all be poured forth on them. The season of God's mercy will then have come to an end; and after the sound of the last trumpet, there will never more be heard the sounding call of reconciliation. Oh, my brethren, that God who is grieved and who is angry with sinners every day, will in the last day pour it all forth in one mighty torrent on the heads of the impenitent. It is now gathering and accumulating in a store-house of vengeance; and at the awful point in the successive history of nature and providence, when time shall be no more, will the door of this store-house be opened, that the fury of the Lord may break loose upon the guilty, and accomplish upon them the weight and the terror of all his threatenings.

You misunderstand the text, then, my brethren, if you infer from it that fury has no place in the history or methods of God's administration. It has its time and its occasion—and the very greatest display of it is yet to come, when the earth shall be burned up and the heavens shall be dissolved, and the elements shall melt with fervent heat, and the Lord Jesus shall be revealed from heaven with His mighty angels in flaming fire, taking vengeance on those who know not God, and obey not the gospel of our Lord Jesus Christ; and they shall be punished with everlasting destruction from the presence of the Lord and from the glory of His power. It makes one shudder seriously to think that there may be some here present whom this devouring torrent of wrath shall sweep away; some here present who will be drawn into the whirl of destruction and forced to take their descending way through the mouth of that pit where the worm dieth not, and the fire is not quenched; some here present who so far from experiencing in their own persons that there is no fury in God, will find that throughout the dreary extent of one hopeless and endless and unmitigated eternity, it is the only attribute of His they have to do with.

But hear me, hear me ere you have taken your bed in hell; hear me, ere that prison door be shut upon you which is never, never again to be opened! hear me, hear me ere the great day of the revelation of God's wrath comes round, and there shall be total breaking up of that system of things which looks at present so stable and so unalterable! On that awful day I might not be able to take up the text and say— that there is no fury in God. But, oh! hear me, for your lives hear me— on this day I can say it. From the place where I now stand I can throw abroad amongst you the wide announcement—that there is no fury in God; and there is not one of you into whose heart this announcement may not enter, and welcome will you be to strike with your beseeching God a league of peace and of friendship that shall never be broken asunder.

Surely when I am busy at my delegated employment of holding out the language of entreaty, and of sounding in your ears the tidings of gladness and of inviting you to enter into the vineyard of God—surely at the time when the messenger of the gospel is thus executing the commission wherewith he is charged and warranted, he may well say—that there is no fury in God. Surely at the time when the Son of God is inviting you to kiss Him and to enter into reconciliation, there is neither the feeling nor the exercise of fury. It is only if you refuse, and if you persist in refusing, and if you suffer all these calls and entreaties to be lost upon you—it is only then that God will execute His fury, and put forth the power of His anger. And therefore He says to us, "Kiss the Son, lest He be angry, and ye perish from the way, when His wrath is kindled but a little." Such, then, is the interesting point of time at which you stand.

There is no fury in God at the very time that He is inviting you to flee from it. He is sending forth no blasting influence upon the fig-tree, even though hitherto it had borne no fruit, and been a mere cumberer of the ground, when He says, we shall let it alone for another year, and dig it, and dress it, and if it bear fruit, well; and if not, then let it be afterwards cut down. Now my brethren, you are all in the situation of this fig-tree; you are for the present let alone; God has purposes of kindness towards every one of you; and as one of His ministers I can now say to you all—that there is no fury in Him. Now when the spiritual husbandman is trying to soften your hearts he is warranted to make a full use of the argument of my text—that there is no fury in God. Now that the ambassador of Christ is plying you with the offers of grace and of strength to renew and to make you fruitful, he is surely charged with matter of far different import from wrath and threatening and vengeance.

Oh! let not all this spiritual husbandry turn out to be unavailing; let not the offer be made now, and no fruit appear afterwards; let not yours be the fate of the barren and unfruitful fig-tree. The day of the fury of the Lord is approaching. The burning up of this earth and the passing away of these heavens is an event in the history of God's administration to which we are continually drawing nearer; and on that day when the whole of universal nature shall be turned into a heap of ruins and we shall see the gleam of a mighty conflagration, and shall hear the noise of the frame-work of creation rending into fragments, and a cry shall be raised from a despairing multitude out of the men of all generations, who have just awoke from their resting-places—and amid all the bustle and consternation that is going on below, such a sight shall be witnessed from the canopy of heaven as will spread silence over the face of the world, and fix and solemnize every individual of its incumbent population.

Oh, my brethren, let us not think that on that day when the Judge is to appear charged with the mighty object of vindicating before men and angels the truth and the majesty of God—that the fury of God will not then appear in bright and burning manifestation. But what I have to tell you on this day, is, that fury is not in God—that now is the time of those things which belong to the peace of our eternity; and that if you will only hear on this the day of your merciful visitation, you will be borne off in safety from all those horrors of dissolving nature, and amid the wild war and frenzy of its reeling elements, will be carried by the arms of love to a place of security and everlasting triumph.

II. This brings us to the second head of discourse—God is not wanting to glorify Himself by the death of sinners—"Who would set the thorns and the briers against me in battle?" The wicked and the righteous are often represented in Scripture by figures taken from the vegetable world. The saved and sanctified are called trees of righteousness, the planting of the Lord that He might be glorified. The godly man is said to be like a tree planted by the rivers of water, which bringeth forth its fruit in its season. The judgment which cometh upon a man is compared to an ax laid to the root of a tree. A tree is said to be known by its fruits; and as a proof that the kind of character of men is specified by the kind of tree in the woods, we read that of thorns men do not gather figs, nor of the bramble bush gather they grapes. You will observe that the thorn is one of the kinds instanced in the text, and when God says, I would go through them, I would burn them together, He speaks of the destruction which cometh on all who remain in the state of thorns and briers; and this agrees with what we read in the epistle to the Hebrews, "That which beareth thorns and briers is rejected, and is nigh unto cursing, whose end is to be burned."

Thorns and briers are in other places still more directly employed to signify the enemies of God. "And the light of Israel shall be for a fire," says one of the prophets, "and his Holy One for a flame, and it shall burn and devour His thorns and His briers in one day." Therefore, when God says in the text, "Who would set the thorns and the briers against me in battle? I would go through them, I would burn them together," He speaks of the ease wherewith He could accomplish His wrath upon His enemies. They would perish before Him like the moth. They could not stand the lifting up of the red right arm of the displeasure of Almighty God. Why set up, then, a contest so unequal as this? Why put the wicked in battle array against Him who could go through them and devour them in an instant by the breath of His fury?

God is saying in the text that this is not what He is wanting. He does not want to set Himself forth as an enemy, or as a strong man armed against them for the battle—it is a battle He is not at all disposed to enter into. The glory He would achieve by a victory over a host so feeble, is not a glory that His heart is at all set upon. Oh, no! ye children of men, He has no pleasure in your death; He is not seeking to magnify Himself by the destruction of so paltry a foe; He could devour you in a moment; He could burn you up like stubble; and you mistake it if you think that renown on so poor a field of contest is a renown that He is at all aspiring after. Who would set the grasshoppers in battle array against the giants? Who would set thorns and briers in battle array against God? This is not what He wants: He would rather something else. Be assured, He would rather you were to turn, and to live, and to come into His vineyard, and submit to the regenerating power of His spiritual husbandry, and be changed from the nature of an accursed plant to a tree of righteousness. In the language of the next verse, He would rather that this enemy of His, not yet at peace with Him and who may therefore be likened to a brier or a thorn – He would rather that he remained so that he should take hold of God's strength, that he may make peace with Him – and as the fruit of his so doing, he shall make peace with Him.

Now tell me if this do not open up a most wonderful and a most inviting view of God? It is the real attitude in which He puts Himself forth to us in the gospel of His Son. He there says, in the hearing of all to whom the word of this salvation is sent, "Why will ye die?" It is true that by your death He could manifest the dignity of His Godhead; He could make known the power of His wrath; He could spread the awe of His truth and His majesty over the whole territory of His government and send forth to its uttermost limits the glories of His strength and His immutable sovereignty. But He does not want to magnify Himself over you in this way; He has no ambition whatever after the renown of such a victory, over such weak and insignificant enemies. Their resistance were no trial whatever to His strength or to His greatness. There is nothing in the destruction of creatures so weak that can at all bring Him any distinction, or throw any aggrandizement around Him. And so in Scripture everywhere do we see Him pleading and protesting with you that He does not want to signalize Himself upon the ruin of any, but would rather that they should turn and be saved.

And now, my brethren, what remains for you to do? God is willing to save you: are you willing to be saved? The way is set before you most patiently and clearly in the Bible – nay, the very text, brief as it is, points out to you the way, as I shall endeavour to explain and set before you in the third head of discourse. But meanwhile, and all the better to secure a hearing from you, let me ask you to lay it upon your consciences whether you are in a state that will do for you to die in. If not, then I beseech you to think how certainly death will, and how speedily it may, come upon the likeliest of you all. The very youngest among you know very well, that if not cut off previously—which is a very possible thing—then manhood will come, and old age will come and the dying bed will come and the very last look you shall ever cast on your acquaintances will come and the agony of the parting breath will come, and the time when you are stretched a lifeless corpse before the eyes of weeping relatives will come, and the coffin that is to inclose you will come, and that hour when the company assemble to carry you to the churchyard will come, and that minute when you are put into the grave will come, and the throwing in of the loose earth into the narrow house where you are laid, and the spreading of the green sod over it—all, all will come on every living creature who now hears me; and in a few little years the minister who now speaks, and the people who now listen, will be carried to their long homes, and make room for another generation.

Now, all this, you know, must and will happen—your common sense and common experience serve to convince you of it. Perhaps it may have been little thought of in the days of careless and thoughtless and thankless unconcern which you have spent hitherto; but I call upon you to think of it now, to lay it seriously to heart and no longer to trifle and delay when the high matters of death and judgment and eternity are thus set so evidently before you. And the tidings wherewith I am charged—and the blood lieth upon your own head and not upon mine, if you will not listen to them—the object of my coming amongst you, is to let you know what more things are to come; it is to carry you beyond the regions of sight and of sense to the regions of faith, and to assure you, in the name of Him who cannot lie, that as sure as the hour of laying the body in the grave comes, so surely will also come the hour of the spirit returning to the God who gave it.

Yes, and the day of final reckoning will come, and the appearance of the Son of God in heaven, and His mighty angels around Him, will come, and the opening of the books will come, and the standing of the men of all generations before the judgment-seat will come, and the solemn passing of that sentence which is to fix you for eternity will come. Yes, and if you refuse to be reconciled in the name of Christ, now that He is beseeching you to be so and if you refuse to turn from the evil of your ways, and to do and to be what your Saviour would have you, I must tell you what that sentence is to be—"Depart from me, ye cursed, into everlasting fire, prepared for the devil and his angels."

There is a way of escape from the fury of this tremendous storm. There is a pathway of egress from the state of condemnation to the state of acceptance. There is a method pointed out in Scripture by which we, who by nature are the children of wrath, may come to be at peace with God. Let all ears be open then to our explanation of this way, as we bid you in the language of our text take hold of God's strength, that you may make peace with Him, and which if you do, you shall make peace with Him.

III. Read now the fifth verse: – "Or let him take hold of my strength, that he may make peace with me; and he shall make peace with me." *Or* here is the same with *rather*. Rather than that what is spoken of in the fourth verse should fall upon you – rather than that I should engage in battle with mine enemies – rather than that a result so melancholy to them should take place, as my going through them and burning them together – rather than that all this should happen, I would greatly prefer that they took hold of my strength in order to make peace with me; and I promise, as the sure effect of this proceeding, that they shall make peace with me.

We have not far to seek for what is meant by this strength, for Isaiah himself speaks (ch. 33:6) of the strength of salvation. It is not your destruction but your salvation that God wants to put forth His strength in. There has strength been already put forth in the deliverance of a guilty world – the very strength which He wants you to lay hold of. He will be glorified in the destruction of the sinner, but He would like better to be glorified by his salvation. To destroy you is to do no more than to set fire to briers and thorns, and to consume them; but to save you – this is indeed the power of God and the wisdom of God – this is the mighty achievement which angels desire to look into – this is the enterprise upon which a mighty Captain embarked all the energy that belonged to Him, and travelled in the greatness of His strength until that He accomplished it; and now that it is accomplished, God would much rather be glorified in the salvation of His saints than glorified in the destruction of sinners (2 Thess. 1:7–10).

God will show His wrath, and make His power known in the destruction of the sinner. But it is a more glorious work of power to redeem that sinner, and this He engages to do for you if you will take hold of His strength. He would greatly prefer this way of making His power known. He does not want to enter into battle with you, or to consume you like stubble by the breath of His indignation. No; He wants to transform sinners into saints: He wants to transform vessels of wrath into vessels of mercy, and to make known the riches of His glory on those whom He had afore prepared unto glory. There is a strength put forth in the destruction of the sinner, but there is also a strength put forth in the salvation of a sinner, and this is the strength which He wants you to lay hold of in my text – this is the strength by the display of which He would prefer being glorified. He would rather decline entering into a contest with you sinners; for to gain a victory over you would be no more to Him than to fight with the briers and the thorns, and to consume them. But from enemies to make friends of you; from the children of wrath to transform you into the children of adoption; from the state of guilt to accomplish such a mighty and a wonderful change upon you, as to put you into the state of justification; from the servants of sin to make you in the day of His power the willing servants of God; to chase away from your faculties the darkness of nature, and to make all light and comfort around you; to turn you from a slave of sense, and to invest with all their rightful ascendency over your affections the things of eternity; to pull down the strongholds of corruption within you, and raise him who was spiritually dead to a life of new obedience; — this is the victory over you which God aspires after. It is not your destruction or your death that He delights in or that He wants to be glorified by—it is your thorough and complete salvation from the punishment of sin, and the power of sin, on which He is desirous of exalting the glory of His strength, and this is the strength which he calls you to take hold upon.

Let me now, in what remains, first say a few things more upon this strength–the strength of salvation which is spoken of in the text—and then state very briefly what it is to lay hold of it.

And first we read of a mighty strength that had to be put forth in the work of a sinner's justification. You know that all men are sinners, and so all are under the righteous condemnation of God. How, in the name of all that is difficult and wonderful, can these sinners ever get this condemnation removed from them? By what new and unheard of process can the guilty before God ever again become justified in His sight? How from that throne, of which it is said that judgment and justice are the habitation, can the sentence of acquittal ever be heard on the children of iniquity? How can God's honour be kept entire in the sight of angels, if we men who have repeatedly mocked Him and insulted Him, and made our own wish and our own way take the precedency of His high and solemn requirements—if we, with all this contempt of the Lawgiver expressed in our lives, and all this character of rebellion against Him written upon our foreheads, shall be admitted to a place of distinction in heaven—and that too after God has committed Himself in the hearing of angels—after He had given us a law by the disposition of angels, and we had not kept it— and after He had said how the wicked shall not go unpunished, but that cursed is every one who continueth not in all the words of the book of God's law to do them? But what is more, it was not merely the good and the obedient angels who knew our rebellion—the malignant and fallen angels not only knew it, but they devised and they prompted it. And how, I would ask, can God keep the awful majesty of His truth and justice entire in the sight of His adversaries, if Satan and the angels of wickedness along with him shall have it in their power to say—we prevailed on man to insult Him by sin, and have compelled God to put up with the affront, and to connive at it?

Now, just in proportion to the weight and magnitude of the obstacle was the greatness of that strength which the Saviour put forth in the mighty work of moving it away. We have no adequate conception upon this matter, and must just take our lesson from revelation about it – and whether we take the prophecies which foretold the work of our Redeemer, or the history which relates it, or the doctrine which expatiates on its worth and its efficacy – all go to establish that there was the operation of a power – that there was the severity of a conflict – that there was the high emprise of an arduous and mighty warfare – that there were all the throes and all the exertions of a struggling, and at length a prevailing energy in the execution of that work which our Saviour had to do – that He had a barrier to surmount, and that, too, with the cries and the pains and the sorrows of heavy suffering and labour – that a mighty obstacle lay before Him, and He, in the business of removing it, had to travel in all the greatness of the faculties which belonged to Him – that there was a burden laid upon His shoulders, which by no one else but the Prince of Peace could have been borne – that there was a task put into His hand which none but he could fulfil.

And had the question ever been reasoned throughout the hosts of paradise, Who can so bend the unchangeable attributes of God, who can give them a shift so wonderful, that the sinners who have insulted Him may be taken into forgiveness, and His honour be kept untainted and entire? – there is not one of the mighty throng who would not have shrunk from an enterprise so lofty. There is not one of them who could at once magnify the law and release man from its violated sanctions. There is not one of them who could turn its threatening away from us, and at the same time give to the truth and the justice of God their brightest manifestation. There is not one of them who could unravel the mystery of our redemption through all the difficulties which beset and which surround it. There is not one of them who, by the strength of his arm, could have obtained the conquest over these difficulties. And however little we may enter into the elements of this weighty speculation, let us forget not that the question was not merely between God and man – it was between God and all the creatures He had formed. They saw the dilemma; they felt how deeply it involved the character of the Deity; they perceived its every bearing on the majesty of His attributes, and on the stability of the government that was upheld by Him. With them it was a matter of deep and most substantial interest; and when the Eternal Son stepped forward to carry the undertaking to its end, the feeling amongst them all was that a battle behooved to be fought, and that the strength of this mighty Captain of our salvation was alone equal to the achievement of the victory.

"Who is this that cometh from Edom, with dyed garments from Bozrah? this that is glorious in His apparel, traveling in the greatness of His strength? I that speak in righteousness, mighty to save. Wherefore art thou red in thine apparel, and thy garments like him that tread-eth in the wine-fat? I have trodden the wine-press alone; and of the people there was none with me: for I will tread them in mine anger, and trample them in my fury; and their blood shall be sprinkled upon my garments, and I will stain all my raiment. For the day of vengeance is in mine heart, and the year of my redeemed is come. And I looked, and there was none to help; and I wondered that there was none to uphold; therefore mine own arm brought salvation unto me; and my fury, it upheld me."

The way of redemption has been found out in the unsearchable riches of divine wisdom, and Christ is called the wisdom of God. But the same Christ is also called the power of God. In the mighty work of redemption He put forth a strength, and it is that strength that we are called to take hold upon. There was a wonderful strength in bearing the wrath which would have fallen on the millions and millions more of a guilty world. There was a strength which bore Him up under the agonies of the garden. There was a strength which supported Him under the hidings of His Father's countenance. There was a strength which upheld Him in the dark hour of the travail of His soul, and which one might think had well-nigh given way when He called out, "My God, my God, why hast Thou forsaken me?" There was a strength which carried Him in triumph through the contest over Satan when he buffeted Him with his temptations; and a strength far greater than we know of in that mysterious struggle which He held with the powers of darkness, when Satan fell like lightning from heaven, and the Captain of our salvation spoiled principalities and powers, and made a show of them openly, and triumphed over them. There was a strength in over-coming all the mighty difficulties which lay in the way between the sinner and God, in unbarring the gates of acceptance to a guilty world, in bringing truth and mercy to meet, and righteousness and peace to enter into fellowship—so that God might be just, while He is the justifier of him who believeth in Jesus.

So much for the strength which is put forth in the work of man's redemption. But there is also a strength put forth in the work of man's regeneration. Christ hath not only done a great work for us in making good our reconciliation with God—He further does a great work in us when He makes us like unto God. But I have not time to dwell upon this last topic, and must content myself with referring you to the following Scriptures—Ephesians 1:19, 2:10; Philippians 4:13; 2 Corinthians 12:9-10; John 15:5. The power which raised Jesus from the dead is the power which raises us from our death in trespasses and sins. The power that was put forth on creation is the power that makes us new creatures in Jesus Christ our Lord.

Neither have I time to make out a full demonstration of what is meant by laying hold of that strength. When you apply to a friend for some service, some relief from distress or difficulty, you may be said to lay hold of him; and when you place firm reliance both on his ability and willingness to do the service, you may well say that your hold is upon your friend — an expression which becomes all the more appropriate should he promise to do the needful good office, in which case your hold is not upon his power only, but upon his faithfulness. And it is even so with the promises of God in Christ Jesus — you have both a power and a promise to take hold of. If you believe that Christ is able to save to the uttermost all who come unto God through Him, and if you believe the honesty of His invitation to all who are weary and heavy-laden, that they might come unto Him and have rest unto their souls, thus judging Him to be faithful who has promised, then indeed will you lay hold of Christ as the power of God unto salvation, and according to the faith which has thus led you to fix upon the Saviour so will it be done unto you. To continue in this faith is in the language of Scripture to hold fast your confidence and the rejoicing of your hope firm unto the end. Cast not away this confidence which hath great recompense of reward; or if you have not yet begun to place this confidence in the assurances of the gospel, lay hold of them now — they are addressed to each and to all of you. It is not a vague generality of which I am speaking. Let every man amongst you take up with Christ, and trust in Him for yourself.

I am well aware that unless the Spirit reveal to you, all I have said about Him will fall fruitless upon your ears, and your hearts will remain as cold and as heavy and as alienated as ever. Faith is His gift, and it is not of ourselves. But the minister is at his post when he puts the truth before you; and you are at your post when you hearken diligently, and have a prayerful spirit of dependence on the Giver of all wisdom — that He will bless the word spoken, and make it reach your souls in the form of a salutary and convincing application. And it is indeed wonderful — it is passing wonderful, that there should be about us such an ungenerous suspicion of our Father who is in heaven. It cannot be sufficiently wondered at that all the ways in which He sets Himself forth to us should have so feeble an influence in the way of cheering us on to a more delighted confidence. How shall we account for it — that the barrier of unbelief should stand so obstinately firm in spite of every attempt and every remonstrance — that the straitening should still continue — not the straitening of God toward us, for He has said everything to woo us to put our trust in Him — but the straitening of us towards God, whereby, in the face of His every kind and exhilarating declaration, we persist in being cold and distant and afraid of Him.

I know not, my brethren, in how far I may have succeeded, as an humble and unworthy instrument, in drawing aside the veil which darkens the face of Him who sitteth on the throne. But oh, how imposing is the attitude, and how altogether affecting is the argument with which He comes forward to us in the text of this day! It is not so much His saying that there is no fury in Him—this He often tells us in other passages of Scripture; but the striking peculiarity of the words now submitted to us is the way in which He would convince us how little interest He can have in our destruction, and how far it is from His thoughts to aspire after the glory of such an achievement, as if He had said—it would be nothing to me to consume you all by the breath of my indignation—it would throw no illustration over me to sweep away the whole strength of that rebellion which you have mustered up against me—it would make no more to my glory than if I went through the thorns and briers and burned them before me.

This is not the battle I want to engage in—this is not the victory by which I seek to signalize myself; and you mistake me—you mistake me, ye feeble children of men, if you think that I aspire after anything else with any one of you than that you should be prevailed on to come into my vineyard, and lay hold of my strength, and seek to make peace with me, and you shall make peace with me. The victory that my heart is set upon is not a victory over your persons—that is a victory that will easily be gotten in the great day of final reckoning over all who have refused my overtures, and would none of my reproof, and have turned them away from my beseeching offers of reconciliation.

In that great day of the power of mine anger it will be seen how easy it is to accomplish such a victory as this—how rapidly the fire of my conflagration will involve the rebels who have opposed me in that devouring flame from which they never, never can be extricated—how speedily the execution of the condemning sentence will run through the multitude who stand at the left hand of the avenging judge; and rest assured, ye men who are now hearing me, and whom I freely invite all to enter into the vineyard of God, that this is not the triumph that God is longing after. It is not a victory over your persons then of which He is at all ambitious—it is a victory over your wills now—it is that you do honour to His testimony by placing your reliance on it—it is that you accept of His kind and free assurances that He has no ill-will to you—it is that you cast the whole burden of sullen fear and suspicion away from your hearts, and that now, even now, you enter into a fellowship of peace with the God whom you have offended.

Oh! be prevailed upon. I know that terror will not subdue you; I know that all the threatenings of the law will not reclaim you; I know that no direct process of pressing home the claims of God upon your obedience will ever compel you to the only obedience that is of any value in His estimation—even the willing obedience of the affections to a father whom you love. But surely when He puts on in your sight the countenance of a Father—when He speaks to you with the tenderness of a Father—when He tries to woo you back to that house of His from which you have wandered, and to persuade you of His good-will descends so far as to reason the matter, and to tell you that He is no more seeking any glory from your destruction than He would seek glory from lighting into a blaze the thorns and the briers, and burning them together—ah! my brethren, should it not look plain to the eye of faith how honest and sincere the God of your redemption is, who is thus bowing Himself down to the mention of such an argument! Do lay hold of it, and be impressed by it, and cherish no longer any doubt of the good-will of the Lord God, merciful and gracious; and let your faith work by love to Him who hath done so much and said so much to engage it, and let this love evince all the power of a commanding principle within you, by urging your every footstep to the new obedience of new creatures in Christ Jesus your Lord.

Thus the two-fold benefit of the gospel will be realized by all who believe and obey that gospel. Reconciled to God by the death of His Son, regenerated by the power of that mighty and all-subduing Spirit who is at the giving of the Son, your salvation will be complete—washed, and sanctified, and justified in the name of the Lord Jesus, and by the Spirit of our God.

THE EXPULSIVE POWER
OF A NEW AFFECTION

"Love not the world, neither the things that are in the world.
If any man love the world, the love of the Father is not in him"
(1 John 2:15).

THERE ARE TWO WAYS in which a practical moralist may attempt to displace from the human heart its love of the world—either by a demonstration of the world's vanity, so as that the heart shall be prevailed upon simply to withdraw its regards from an object that is not worthy of it; or, by setting forth another object, even God, as more

Reprinted from Thomas Chalmers, *The Select Works of Thomas Chalmers,* vol. 4 (New York: Robert Carter & Bros., n. d.), pp. 271–390.

worthy of its attachment, so as that the heart shall be prevailed upon not to resign an old affection, which shall have nothing to succeed it, but to exchange an old affection for a new one. My purpose is to show, that from the constitution of our nature, the former method is altogether incompetent and ineffectual—and that the latter method will alone suffice for the rescue and recovery of the heart from the wrong affection that domineers over it. After having accomplished this purpose, I shall attempt a few practical observations.

Love may be regarded in two different conditions. The first is, when its object is at a distance, and then it becomes love in a state of desire. The second is, when its object is in possession, and then it becomes love in a state of indulgence. Under the impulse of desire, man feels himself urged onward in some path or pursuit of activity for its gratification. The faculties of his mind are put into busy exercise. In the steady direction of one great and engrossing interest, his attention is recalled from the many reveries into which it might otherwise have wandered; and the powers of his body are forced away from an indolence in which it else might have languished; and that time is crowded with occupation, which but for some object of keen and devoted ambition, might have drivelled along in successive hours of weariness and distaste—and though hope does not always enliven, and success does not always crown this career of exertion, yet in the midst of this very variety, and with the alternations of occasional disappointment, is the machinery of the whole man kept in a sort of congenial play, and upholden in that tone and temper which are most agreeable to it. Insomuch, that if through the extirpation of that desire which forms the originating principle of all this movement, the machinery were to stop, and to receive no impulse from another desire substituted in its place, the man would be left with all his propensities to action in a state of most painful and unnatural abandonment.

A sensitive being suffers, and is in violence, if, after having thoroughly rested from his fatigue, or been relieved from his pain, he continue in possession of powers without any excitement to these powers; if he possess a capacity of desire without having an object of desire; or if he have a spare energy upon his person, without a counterpart, and without a stimulus to call it into operation. The misery of such a condition is often realized by him who is retired from business, or who is retired from law, or who is even retired from the occupations of the chase, and of the gaming table. Such is the demand of our nature for an object in pursuit, that no accumulation of previous success can extinguish it—and thus it is, that the most prosperous merchant, and the most victorious general, and the most fortunate gamester, when the labour of their respective vocations has come to a close, are often found to languish in the midst of all their acquisitions, as if out of their kindred and rejoicing ele-

ment. It is quite in vain with such a constitutional appetite for employment in man, to attempt cutting away from him the spring or the principle of one employment, without providing him with another. The
whole heart and habit will rise in resistance against such an undertaking. The else unoccupied female, who spends the hours of every
evening at some play of hazard, knows as well as you, that the pecu-
niary gain, or the honourable triumph of a successful contest, are
altogether paltry. It is not such a demonstration of vanity as this that
will force her away from her dear and delightful occupation. The habit
cannot so be displaced, as to leave nothing but a negative and cheerless vacancy behind it – though it may so be supplanted as to be followed up by another habit of employment, to which the power of some
new affection has constrained her. It is willingly suspended, for example, on any single evening, should the time that wont to be allotted
to gaming, require to be spent on the preparations of an approaching
assembly.

The ascendant power of a second affection will do, what no exposition, however forcible, of the folly and worthlessness of the first,
ever could effectuate. And it is the same in the great world. You never
will be able to arrest any of its leading pursuits, by a naked demonstration of their vanity. It is quite in vain to think of stopping one of these
pursuits in any way else, but by stimulating to another. In attempting
to bring a worldly man, intent and busied with the prosecution of his
objects, to a dead stand, you have not merely to encounter the charm
which he annexes to these objects – but you have to encounter the
pleasure which he feels in the very prosecution of them. It is not
enough, then, that you dissipate the charm, by your moral, and eloquent, and affecting exposure of its illusiveness. You must address to
the eye of his mind another object, with a charm powerful enough to
dispossess the first of its influence, and to engage him in some other
prosecution as full of interest, and hope, and congenial activity, as the
former. It is this which stamps an impotency on all moral and pathetic
declamation about the insignificance of the world. A man will no more
consent to the misery of being without an object, because that object is
a trifle, or of being without a pursuit, because that pursuit terminates
in some frivolous or fugitive acquirement, than he will voluntarily submit himself to the torture, because that torture is to be of short duration. If to be without desire and without exertion altogether, is a state
of violence and discomfort, then the present desire, with its correspond-
ent train of exertion, is not to be got rid of simply be destroying it. It
must be by substituting another desire, and another line or habit of
exertion in its place – and the most effectual way of withdrawing the
mind from one object, is not by turning it away upon desolate and unpeopled vacancy – but by presenting to its regards another object still
more alluring.

These remarks apply not merely to love considered in its state of desire for an object not yet obtained. They apply also to love considered in its state of indulgence, or placid gratification, with an object already in possession. It is seldom that any of our tastes are made to disappear by a mere process of natural extinction. At least, it is very seldom that this is done through the instrumentality of reasoning. It may be done by excessive pampering—but it is almost never done by the mere force of mental determination. But what cannot be thus destroyed, may be dispossessed—and one taste may be made to give way to another, and to lose its power entirely as the reigning affection of the mind. It is thus, that the boy ceases, at length, to be the slave of his appetite, but it is because a manlier taste has now brought it into subordination—and that the youth ceases to idolize pleasure, but it is because the idol of wealth has become the stronger and gotten the ascendency—and that even the love of money ceases to have the mastery over the heart of many a thriving citizen, but it is because drawn into the whirl of city politics, another affection has been wrought into his moral system, and he is now lorded over by the love of power.

There is not one of these transformations in which the heart is left without an object. Its desire for one particular object may be conquered; but as to its desire for having some one object or other, this is unconquerable. Its adhesion to that on which it has fastened the preference of its regards, cannot willingly be overcome by the rending away of a simple separation. It can be done only by the application of something else, to which it may feel the adhesion of a still stronger and more powerful preference. Such is the grasping tendency of the human heart, that it must have a something to lay hold of—and which, if wrested away without the substitution of another something in its place, would leave a void and a vacancy as painful to the mind, as hunger is to the natural system. It may be dispossessed of one object, or of any, but it cannot be desolated of all. Let there be a breathing and a sensitive heart, but without a liking and without affinity to any of the things that are around it, and in a state of cheerless abandonment, it would be alive to nothing but the burden of its own consciousness, and feel it to be intolerable. It would make no difference to its owner, whether he dwelt in the midst of a gay and goodly world, or placed afar beyond the outskirts of creation, he dwelt a solitary unit in dark and unpeopled nothingness. The heart must have something to cling to—and never, by its own voluntary consent, will it so denude itself of all its attachments that there shall not be one remaining object that can draw or solicit it.

The misery of a heart thus bereft of all relish for that which wont to minister enjoyment, is strikingly exemplified in those, who, satiated with indulgence, have been so belaboured, as it were, with the variety and the poignancy of the pleasurable sensations that they have experienced, that they are at length fatigued out of all capacity for sensation whatever. The disease of ennui is more frequent in the French metropolis, where amusement is more exclusively the occupation of higher classes, than it is in the British metropolis, where the longings of the heart are more diversified by the resources of business and politics. There are the votaries of fashion, who, in this way, have at length become the victims of fashionable excess – in whom the very multitude of their enjoyments, has at last extinguished their power of enjoyment – who, with the gratifications of art and nature at command, now look upon all that is around them with an eye of tastelessness – who, plied with the delights of sense and of splendour even to weariness, and incapable of higher delights, have come to the end of all their perfection, and like Solomon of old, found it to be vanity and vexation. The man whose heart has thus been turned into a desert, can vouch for the insupportable languor which must ensue, when one affection is thus plucked away from the bosom, without another to replace it.

It is not necessary that a man receive pain from anything, in order to become miserable. It is barely enough that he looks with distaste to everything – and in that asylum which is the repository of minds out of joint, and where the organ of feeling as well as the organ of intellect, has been impaired, it is not in the cell of loud and frantic outcries where you will meet with the acme of mental suffering. But that is the individual who outpeers in wretchedness all his fellows, who throughout the whole expanse of nature and society, meets not an object that has at all the power to detain or to interest him; who neither in earth beneath, nor in heaven above, knows of a single charm to which his heart can send forth one desirous or responding movement; to whom the world, in his eye a vast and empty desolation, has left him nothing but his own consciousness to feed upon – dead to all that is without him, and alive to nothing but to the load of his own torpid and useless existence.

It will now be seen, perhaps, why it is that the heart keeps by its present affections with so much tenacity – when the attempt is, to do them away by a mere process of extirpation. It will not consent to be so desolated. The strong man, whose dwelling-place is there, may be compelled to give way to another occupier – but unless another stronger than he, has power to dispossess and to succeed him, he will keep his present lodgment inviolable. The heart would revolt against its own emptiness. It could not bear to be so left in a state of waste and cheerless insipidity. The moralist who tries such a process of dispossession at this upon the heart, is thwarted at every step by the recoil of its own mechanism. You have all heard that Nature abhors a vacuum. Such at least is the nature of the heart, that though the room which is in it may change one inmate for another, it cannot be left void without the pain of most intolerable suffering.

It is not enough then to argue the folly of an existing affection. It is not enough, in the terms of a forcible or an affecting demonstration, to make good the evanescence of its object. It may not even be enough to associate the threats and terrors of some coming vengeance, with the indulgence of it. The heart may still resist the every application, by obedience to which it would finally be conducted to a state so much at war with all its appetites as that of downright inanition. So to tear away an affection from the heart, as to leave it bare of all its regards, and of all its preferences, were a hard and hopeless undertaking – and it would appear as if the alone powerful engine of dispossession, were to bring the mastery of another affection to bear upon it.

We know not a more sweeping interdict upon the affections of Nature, than that which is delivered by the Apostle in the verse before us. To bid a man into whom there is not yet entered the great and ascendant influence of the principle of regeneration, to bid him withdraw his love from all the things that are in the world, is to bid him give up all the affections that are in his heart. The world is the all of a natural man. He has not a taste, nor a desire, that points not to a something placed within the confines of its visible horizon. He loves nothing above it, and he cares for nothing beyond it; and to bid him love not the world, is to pass a sentence of expulsion on all the inmates of his bosom.

To estimate the magnitude and the difficulty of such a surrender, let us only think that it were just as arduous to prevail on him not to love wealth, which is but one of the things in the world, as to prevail on him to set wilful fire to his own property. This he might do with sore and painful reluctance, if he saw that the salvation of his life hung upon it. But this he would do willingly, if he saw that a new property of tenfold value was instantly to emerge from the wreck of the old one. In this case there is something more than the mere displacement of an affection. There is the overbearing of one affection by another. But to desolate his heart of all love for the things of the world, without the substitution of any love in its place, were to him a process of as unnatural violence, as to destroy all the things he has in the world, and give him nothing in their room. So that, if to love not the world be indispensable to one's Christianity, then the crucifixion of the old man is not too strong a term to mark that transition in his history, when all old things are done away, and all things are become new.

We hope that by this time, you understand the impotency of a mere demonstration of this world's insignificance. Its sole practical effect, if it had any, would be to leave the heart in a state which to every heart is insupportable, and that is a mere state of nakedness and negation. You may remember the fond and unbroken tenacity with which your heart has often recurred to pursuits, over the utter frivolity of which it sighed and wept but yesterday. The arithmetic of your short-lived days, may on Sabbath make the clearest impression upon your under-standing—and from his fancied bed of death, may the preacher cause a voice to descend in rebuke and mockery on all the pursuits of earth-liness—and as he pictures before you the fleeting generations of men, with the absorbing grave, whither all the joys and interests of the world hasten to their sure and speedy oblivion, may you, touched and solemnized by his argument, feel for a moment as if on the eve of a practical and permanent emancipation from a scene of so much vanity.

But the morrow comes, and the business of the world, and the ob-jects of the world, and the moving forces of the world come along with it—and the machinery of the heart, in virtue of which it must have something to grasp, or something to adhere to, brings it under a kind of moral necessity to be actuated just as before—and in utter repulsion towards a state so unkindly as that of being frozen out both of delight and of desire, does it feel all the warmth and the urgency of its wonted solicitations—nor in the habit and history of the whole man, can we detect so much as one symptom of the new creature—so that the church, instead of being to him a school of obedience, has been a mere sauntering place for the luxury of a passing and theatrical emotion; and the preaching which is mighty to compel the attendance of multi-tudes, which is mighty to still and to solemnize the hearers into a kind of tragic sensibility, which is mighty in the play of variety and vigour that it can keep up around the imagination, is not mighty to the pulling down of strong-holds.

The love of the world cannot be expunged by a mere demonstration of the world's worthlessness. But may it not be supplanted by the love of that which is more worthy than itself? The heart cannot be pre-vailed upon to part with the world, by a simple act of resignation. But may not the heart be prevailed upon to admit into its preference an-other, who shall subordinate the world, and bring it down from its wonted ascendency? If the throne which is placed there, must have an occupier, and the tyrant that now reigns has occupied it wrongfully, he may not leave a bosom which would rather detain him, than be left in desolation. But may he not give way to the lawful sovereign, appear-ing with every charm that can secure his willing admittance, and tak-ing unto himself his great power to subdue the moral nature of man, and to reign over it? In a word, if the way to disengage the heart from the positive love of one great and ascendent object, is to fasten it in positive love to another, then it is not by exposing the worthlessness of the former, but by addressing to the mental eye the worth and ex-cellence of the latter, that all old things are to be done away, and all things are to become new.

To obliterate all our present affections, by simply expunging them, and so as to leave the seat of them unoccupied, would be to destroy the old character, and to substitute no new character in its place. But when they take their departure upon the ingress of other visitors; when they resign their sway to the power and the predominance of new affections; when, abandoning the heart to solitude, they merely give place to a successor who turns it into as busy a residence of desire, and interest, and expectation as before—there is nothing in all this to thwart or to overbear any of the laws of our sentient nature—and we see how, in fullest accordance with the mechanism of the heart, a great moral revolution may be made to take place upon it.

This, we trust, will explain the operation of that charm which accompanies the effectual preaching of the gospel. The love of God, and the love of the world, are two affections, not merely in a state of rivalship, but in a state of enmity—and that so irreconcilable, that they cannot dwell together in the same bosom. We have already affirmed how impossible it were for the heart, by any innate elasticity of its own, to cast the world away from it, and thus reduce itself to a wilderness. The heart is not so constituted, and the only way to dispossess it of an old affection, is by the expulsive power of a new one. Nothing can exceed the magnitude of the required change in a man's character —when bidden as he is in the New Testament, to love not the world; no, nor any of the things that are in the world—for this so comprehends all that is dear to him in existence, as to be equivalent to a command of self-annihilation.

But the same revelation which dictates so mighty an obedience, places within our reach as mighty an instrument of obedience. It brings for admittance, to the very door of our heart, an affection which, once seated upon its throne, will either subordinate every previous inmate, or bid it away. Beside the world, it places before the eye of the mind, him who made the world, and with this peculiarity, which is all its own—that in the Gospel do we so behold God, as that we may love God. It is there, and there only, where God stands revealed as an object of confidence to sinners—and where our desire after him is not chilled into apathy, by that barrier of human guilt which intercepts every approach that is not made to him through the appointed Mediator. It is the bringing in of this better hope, whereby we draw nigh unto God—and to live without hope, is to live without God, and if the heart be without God, the world will then have all the ascendency. It is God apprehended by the believer as God in Christ, who alone can dispost it from this ascendency. It is when he stands dismantled of the terrors which belong to him as an offended lawgiver, and when we are enabled by faith, which is his own gift, to see his glory in the face of Jesus Christ, and to hear his beseeching voice, as it protests good will to men, and entreats the return of all who will to a full pardon, and a gracious acceptance—it is then, that a love paramount to the love of the world, and at length expulsive of it, first arises in the regenerating bosom. It is when released from the spirit of bondage, with which love cannot dwell, and when admitted into the number of God's children, through the faith that is in Christ Jesus, the spirit of adoption is poured upon us—it is then that the heart, brought under the mastery of one great and predominant affection, is delivered from the tyranny of its former desires, and in the only way in which deliverance is possible. And that faith which is revealed to us from heaven, as indispensable to a sinner's justification in the sight of God, is also the instrument of the greatest of all moral and spiritual achievements on a nature dead to the influence, and beyond the reach of every other application.

Thus may we come to perceive what it is that makes the most effective kind of preaching. It is not enough to hold out to the world's eye the mirror of its own imperfections. It is not enough to come forth with a demonstration, however pathetic, of the evanescent character of all its enjoyments. It is not enough to travel the walk of experience along with you, and speak to your own conscience, and your own recollection of the deceitfulness of the heart, and the deceitfulness of all that the heart is set upon. There is many a bearer of the Gospel message, who has not shrewdness of natural discernment enough, and who has not power of characteristic description enough, and who has not the talent of moral delineation enough, to present you with a vivid and faithful sketch of the existing follies of society. But that very corruption which he has not the faculty of representing in its visible details, he may practically be the instrument of eradicating in its principle. Let him be but a faithful expounder of the gospel testimony.— Unable as he may be to apply a descriptive hand to the character of the present world, let him but report with accuracy the matter which revelation has brought to him from a distant world—unskilled as he is in the work of so anatomizing the heart, as with the power of a novelist to create a graphical or impressive exhibition of the worthlessness of its many affections—let him only deal in those mysteries of peculiar doctrine, on which the best of novelists have thrown the wantonness of their derision. He may not be able, with the eye of shrewd and satirical observation, to expose to the ready recognition of his hearers the desires of worldliness—but with the tidings of the gospel in commission, he may wield the only engine that can extirpate them. He cannot do what some have done, when, as if by the hand of a magician, they have brought out to view, from the hidden recesses of our nature, the foibles and lurking appetites which belong to it.—But he has a truth in his possession, which into whatever heart it enters, will, like the rod of Aaron, swallow up them all—and unqualified as he may be, to describe the old man in all the nicer shading of his natural and constitutional varieties, with him is deposited that ascendent influence under which the leading tastes and tendencies of the old man are destroyed, and he becomes a new creature in Jesus Christ our Lord.

Let us not cease, then, to ply the only instrument of powerful and positive operation, to do away from you the love of the world. Let us try every legitimate method of finding access to your hearts for the love of him who is greater than the world. For this purpose, let us, if possible, clear away that shroud of unbelief which so hides and darkens the face of the Deity. Let us insist on his claims to your affection — and whether in the shape of gratitude, or in the shape of esteem, let us never cease to affirm, that in the whole of that wondrous economy, the purpose of which is to reclaim a sinful world unto himself — he, the God of love, so sets himself forth in characters of endearment, that nought but faith, and nought but understanding, are wanting, on your part, to call forth the love of your hearts back again.

And here let me advert to the incredulity of a worldly man; when he brings his own sound and secular experience to bear upon the high doctrines of Christianity — when he looks on regeneration as a thing impossible — when feeling as he does, the obstinacies of his own heart on the side of things present, and casting an intelligent eye, much exercised perhaps in the observation of human life, on the equal obstinacies of all who are around him, he pronounces this whole matter about the crucifixion of the old man, and the resurrection of a new man in his place, to be in downright opposition to all that is known and witnessed of the real nature of humanity.

We think that we have seen such men, who, firmly trenched in their own vigorous and homebred sagacity, and shrewdly regardful of all that passes before them through the week, and upon the scenes of ordinary business, look on that transition of the heart by which it gradually dies unto time, and awakens in all the life of a new-felt and ever-growing desire towards God, as a mere Sabbath speculation; and who thus, with all their attention engrossed upon the concerns of earthliness, continue unmoved, to the end of their days, amongst the feelings, and the appetites, and the pursuits of earthliness. If the thought of death, and another state of being after it, comes across them at all, it is not with a change so radical as that of being born again, that they ever connect the idea of preparation. They have some vague conception of its being quite enough that they acquit themselves in some decent and tolerable way of their relative obligations; and that, upon the strength of some such social and domestic moralities as are often realized by him in whose heart the love of God has never entered, they will be transplanted in safety from this world, where God is the Being with whom it may almost be said, that they have had nothing to do, to that world where God is the Being with whom they will have mainly and immediately to do throughout all eternity. They admit all that is said of the utter vanity of time, when taken up with as a resting place. But they resist every application made upon the heart of man, with the view of so shifting its tendencies, that it shall not henceforth find in the interests of time, all its rest and all its refreshment. They, in fact, regard such an attempt as an enterprise that is altogether aerial – and with a tone of secular wisdom, caught from the familiarities of every-day experience, do they see a visionary character in all that is said of setting our affections on the things that are above; and of walking by faith; and of keeping our hearts in such a love of God as shall shut out from them the love of the world; and of having no confidence in the flesh; and of so renouncing earthly things as to have our conversation in heaven.

Now, it is altogether worthy of being remarked of those men who thus disrelish spiritual Christianity, and, in fact, deem it an impracticable acquirement, how much of a piece their incredulity about the demands of Christianity, and their incredulity about the doctrines of Christianity, are with one another. No wonder that they feel the work of the New Testament to be beyond their strength, so long as they hold the words of the New Testament to be beneath their attention. Neither they nor any one else can dispossess the heart of an old affection, but by the impulsive power of a new one – and, if that new affection be the love of God, neither they nor any one else can be made to entertain it, but on such a representation of the Deity, as shall draw the heart of the sinner towards him. Now it is just their unbelief which screens from the discernment of their minds this representation. They do not see the love of God in sending his Son into the world. They do not see the expression of his tenderness to men, in sparing him not, but giving him up unto the death for us all. They do not see the sufficiency of the atonement, or of the sufferings that were endured by him who bore the burden that sinners should have borne. They do not see the blended holiness and compassion of the Godhead, in that he passed by the transgressions of his creatures, yet could not pass them by without an expiation. It is a mystery to them, how a man should pass to the state of godliness from a state of nature – but had they only a believing view of God manifest in the flesh, this would resolve for them the whole mystery of godliness. As it is, they cannot get quit of their old affections, because they are out of sight from all those truths which have influence to raise a new one. They are like the children of Israel in the land of Egypt, when required to make bricks without straw – they cannot love God, while they want the only food which can aliment this affection in a sinner's bosom – and however great their errors may be both in resisting the demands of the Gospel as impracticable, and in rejecting the doctrines of the Gospel as inadmissible, yet there is not a spiritual man (and it is the prerogative of him who is spiritual to judge all men) who will not perceive that there is a consistency in these errors.

But if there be a consistency in the errors, in like manner is there a consistency in the truths which are opposite to them. The man who believes in the peculiar doctrines, will readily bow to the peculiar demands of Christianity. When he is told to love God supremely, this may startle another, but it will not startle him to whom God has been revealed in peace, and in pardon, and in all the freeness of an offered reconciliation. When told to shut out the world from his heart, this may be impossible with him who has nothing to replace it – but not impossible with him, who has found in God a sure and a satisfying portion. When told to withdraw his affections from the things that are beneath, this were laying an order of self-extinction upon the man, who knows not another quarter in the whole sphere of his contemplation, to which he could transfer them – but it were not grievous to him whose view has been opened up to the loveliness and glory of the things that are above, and can there find, for every feeling of his soul, a most ample and delighted occupation. When told to look not to the things that are seen and temporal, this were blotting out the light of all that is visible from the prospect of him in whose eye there is a wall of partition between guilty nature and the joys of eternity – but he who believes that Christ hath broken down this wall, finds a gathering radiance upon his soul, as he looks onwards in faith to the things that are unseen and eternal.

Tell a man to be holy – and how can he compass such a performance, when his alone fellowship with holiness is a fellowship of despair? It is the atonement of the cross reconciling the holiness of the lawgiver with the safety of the offender, that hath opened the way for a sanctifying influence into the sinner's heart, and he can take a kindred impression from the character of God now brought nigh, and now at peace with him. Separate the demand from the doctrine, and you have either a system of righteousness that is impracticable, or a barren orthodoxy. Bring the demand and the doctrine together – and the true disciple of Christ is able to do the one, through the other strengthening him. The motive is adequate to the movement; and the bidden obedience of the Gospel is not beyond the measure of his strength, just because the doctrine of the Gospel is not beyond the measure of his acceptance. The shield of faith, and the hope of salvation, and the Word of God, and the girdle of truth – these are the armour that he has put on; and with these the battle is won, and the eminence is reached, and the man stands on the vantage ground of a new field and a new prospect. The effect is great, but the cause is equal to it – and stupendous as this moral resurrection to the precepts of Christianity, undoubtedly is, there is an element of strength enough to give it being and continuance in the principles of Christianity.

The object of the Gospel is both to pacify the sinner's conscience, and to purify his heart; and it is of importance to observe, that what mars the one of these objects, mars the other also. The best way of casting out an impure affection is to admit a pure one; and by the love of what is good, to expel the love of what is evil. Thus it is, that the freer the Gospel, the more sanctifying is the Gospel; and the more it is received as a doctrine of grace, the more will it be felt as a doctrine according to godliness. This is one of the secrets of the Christian life, that the more a man holds of God as a pensioner, the greater is the payment of service that he renders back again. On the tenure of "Do this and live," a spirit of fearfulness is sure to enter; and the jealousies of a legal bargain chase away all confidence from the intercourse between God and man; and the creature striving to be square and even with his Creator, is, in fact, pursuing all the while his own selfishness instead of God's glory; and with all the conformities which he labours to accomplish, the soul of obedience is not there, the mind is not subject to the law of God, nor indeed under such an economy ever can be.

It is only when, as in the Gospel, acceptance is bestowed as a present, without money and without price, that the security which man feels in God is placed beyond the reach of disturbance – or, that he can repose in him, as one friend reposes in another – or, that any liberal and generous understanding can be established betwixt them – the one party rejoicing over the other to do him good – the other finding that the truest gladness of his heart lies in the impulse of a gratitude, by which it is awakened to the charms of a new moral existence. Salvation by grace – salvation by free grace – salvation not of works, but according to the mercy of God – salvation on such a footing is not more indispensable to the deliverance of our persons from the hand of justice, than it is to the deliverance of our hearts from the chill and the weight of ungodliness. Retain a single shred or fragment of legality with the Gospel, and you raise a topic of distrust between man and God. You take away from the power of the Gospel to melt and to conciliate. For this purpose, the freer it is, the better it is. That very peculiarity which so many dread as the germ of Antinomianism, is, in fact, the germ of a new spirit, and a new inclination against it. Along with the light of a free Gospel, does there enter the love of the Gospel, which in proportion as you impair the freeness, you are sure to chase away. And never does the sinner find within himself so mighty a moral transformation, as when under the belief that he is saved by grace, he feels constrained thereby to offer his heart a devoted thing, and to deny ungodliness.

To do any work in the best manner, you would make use of the fittest tools for it. And we trust, that what has been said may serve in some degree, for the practical guidance of those who would like to reach the great moral achievement of our text – but feel that the tendencies and desires of Nature are too strong for them. We know of no other way by which to keep the love of the world out of our heart, than to keep in our hearts the love of God – and no other way by which to keep our hearts in the love of God, than building ourselves up on our most holy faith. That denial of the world which is not possible to him that dissents from the Gospel testimony, is possible, even as all things are possible to him that believeth. To try this without faith, is to work without the right tool or the right instrument. But faith worketh by love; and the way of expelling from the heart the love that transgresseth the law, is to admit into its receptacles the love which fulfilleth the law.

Conceive a man to be standing on the margin of this green world; and that, when he looked towards it, he saw abundance smiling upon every field, and all the blessings which earth can afford, scattered in profusion throughout every family, and the light of the sun sweetly resting upon all the pleasant habitations, and the joys of human companionship brightening many a happy circle of society—conceive this to be the general character of the scene upon one side of his contemplation; and that on the other, beyond the verge of the goodly planet on which he was situated, he could descry nothing but a dark and fathomless unknown. Think you that he would bid a voluntary adieu to all the brightness and all the beauty that were before him upon earth, and commit himself to the frightful solitude away from it? Would he leave its peopled dwelling places, and become a solitary wanderer through the fields of non-entity? If space offered him nothing but a wilderness, would he for it abandon the homebred scenes of life and of cheerfulness that lay so near, and exerted such a power of urgency to detain him? Would not he cling to the regions of sense, and of life, and of society?—and shrinking away from the desolation that was beyond it, would not he be glad to keep his firm footing on the territory of this world, and to take shelter under the silver canopy that was stretched over it?

But if, during the time of his contemplation, some happy island of the blest had floated by; and there had burst upon his senses the light of its surpassing glories, and its sounds of sweeter melody; and he clearly saw, that there, a purer beauty rested upon every field, and a more heart-felt joy spread itself among all the families; and he could discern there a peace, and a piety, and a benevolence, which put a moral gladness into every bosom, and united the whole society in one rejoicing sympathy with each other, and with the beneficent Father of them all.—Could he further see, that pain and mortality were there unknown; and above all, that signals of welcome were hung out, and an avenue of communication was made for him—perceive you not, that what was before the wilderness, would become the land of invitation; and that now the world would be the wilderness? What unpeopled space could not do, can be done by space teeming with beatific scenes, and beatific society. And let the existing tendencies of the heart be what they may to the scene that is near and visible around us, still if another stood revealed to the prospect of man, either through the channel of faith, or through the channel of his senses—then, without violence done to the constitution of his moral nature, may he die unto the present world, and live to the lovelier world that stands in the distance away from it.

FOR ADDITIONAL INFORMATION ABOUT THOMAS CHALMERS:

Dodds, James. *Thomas Chalmers. A Biographical Study.* New York: Nelson, 1870.

Hanna, William. *Memoirs of the Life and Writings of Thomas Chalmers,* 4 vols. New York: Harper & Bros., 1853–55.

Howard, Harry C. "Thomas Chalmers." *Princes of the Christian Pulpit and Pastorate.* Nashville: Cokesbury Press, 1928.

Macartney, Clarence Edward. "Thomas Chalmers." *Sons of Thunder.* New York: Fleming H. Revell Co., 1929.

White, Paul A. "Thomas Chalmers, Preacher." Unpublished S.T.M. thesis, Temple University School of Theology, 1958.

FOR OTHER SERMONS BY THOMAS CHALMERS:

Congregational Sermons. Vols. 8–10 of *The Works of Thomas Chalmers.* Glasgow: William Collins, n.d.

Sermons Preached on Public Occasions. Vol. 11 of *The Works of Thomas Chalmers.* Glasgow: William Collins, n.d.

Also: *Select Works,* vol. 3, *Sermons* (1848); *Select Works,* vol. 4, *Sermons* (1848); *Sermons and Discourses,* vol. 1 (1844); *Sermons and Discourses and Posthumous Sermons* (1863).

CHARLES G. FINNEY

1792 - 1875

CHARLES FINNEY, photograph, courtesy of the Oberlin
College Archives, Oberlin, Ohio.

CHARLES GRANDISON FINNEY

1792	*Born August 29 in Warren, Connecticut*
1794	*Moved with parents to Oneida County, New York*
1818	*Entered law office in Adams, New York*
1821	*Converted to Christian faith*
1823	*Licensed to preach in Presbyterian church*
1824	*Married Lydia Andrews (died 1847)*
1832	*Assumed pastorate of Second Free Church in New York City*
1834	*Became pastor of Congregational Broadway Tabernacle*
1835	*Went to Oberlin College as professor of theology*
1852	*Became president of Oberlin College*
1875	*Died August 16 in Oberlin, Ohio*

DURING A SERVICE in which Charles Grandison Finney was preaching, a man who had brought a pistol to church with him to kill Finney tumbled from his seat crying, "I am sinking into hell!"[1] In Rochester, New York, nearly the entire bar of the city was converted; forty lawyers went into the ministry following Finney's efforts in that city. After hearing Finney a young and prosperous distiller in Auburn went to his warehouses, broke open the casks, and let the liquor flow into the streets. Throughout his life his preaching caused controversy. When Finney was called to Oberlin College as professor of theology, he agreed to come only if the school would be open to white and black students alike.

Charles Finney had an amazingly varied career: during his long and active life he served as a teacher, lawyer, revivalist, pastor, theology professor, and college president. All of this is

---

1. Frank G. Beardsley, *A Mighty Winner of Souls* (New York: American Tract Society, 1937), p. 49.

even more impressive when it is understood that Finney had no earned degrees and was largely self-educated.

LIFE AND TIMES

Finney was born in Connecticut on August 29, 1792. His parents were non-religious. When he was two, they moved to Oneida County, New York, where it was virtually impossible for him to receive any formal schooling. Nevertheless he learned to read and write and became an avid reader.

He worked hard in farming, in timber cutting, and in doing what chores and work were available. He developed a rugged constitution which was to aid him for the rest of his life.

In 1808 his family moved to Henderson, New York. There Finney taught school. In 1812 he journeyed back to Warren, Connecticut, where he gained some formal education and earned a reputation as a scholar, a leader of men, an orator, and a writer. He intended to enroll in Yale, but a teacher persuaded him not to attend, insisting that Finney could learn in two years privately what he would learn in four years at Yale. Finney spent the next two years teaching school in New Jersey and studying on his own. He learned Greek, Hebrew, and Latin before going on to Adams, New York, to study law under Judge Benjamin Wright. He was admitted to the bar and began practicing law in Adams.

As he read law cases Finney noted how frequently the Bible was cited, so he began to read the Bible. He also began to attend public worship. Finney was a musician and his services were needed to help with the choir. The pastor, George W. Gale, was a hyper-Calvinist in his theology. Finney disagreed with him and they argued frequently. Nevertheless, he became restless and deeply concerned about his spiritual condition. On October 8 and 9, 1821, his work load was light, and so he decided to devote special time to spiritual matters. He read the Bible and prayed earnestly for two days, but nothing significant happened. On Wednesday morning as he was going to his office he heard an inward voice saying, "What are you waiting for?"[2]

According to Finney's own testimony, he then went into the woods and began to pray. For quite some time he continued to pray, weep, and recall those Scriptures which he had read. One

2. Ibid., p. 22.

Scripture he recalled was, "And ye shall seek me, and find me, when ye shall search for me with all your heart." That night, in his room, he experienced a significant religious conversion. He felt that wave after wave of "liquid love" filled his heart as the Holy Spirit came upon him.[3] His feeling of guilt for his sin lifted and he sensed that he had been justified by faith. He called the choir members together and told them what had happened to him. He urged them to accept Christ at once. A revival broke out in the church, then in the city of Adams, and finally in the entire county. Finney lost interest in law and began to devote himself more and more to preaching in revivals with sensational results.[4]

Ministers in the area urged him to attend seminary; he refused, and instead he entered into private study under the guidance of his pastor, George W. Gale. He disagreed with Gale's Calvinism but found discussions with the minister helpful. Finally he was licensed to preach by the Presbyterian Church in Evans Mills, New York, on December 30, 1823.

In 1824 the Female Missionary Society of the Western District of New York commissioned him to become home missionary in the northern part of Jefferson County, New York. When Finney began his work a great revival broke out in the area. Thereafter he went to many villages preaching and stimulating revival. After serving for a time in the villages, he moved on to the larger cities, where significant revivals also occurred.

Finney's marriages were marred by repeated tragedy: he married his first wife, Lydia Andrews, in 1824; she died in 1847. He married again, Mrs. Elizabeth F. Atkinson, of Rochester; she died in 1863. He married a third time, Miss Rebecca Rayl; she outlived him, dying in 1907.

Finney was called as pastor of the Second Free Presbyterian Church in New York City in 1832. He felt a need to settle down. His revival tours had taken him away from his wife and children and his health was beginning to fail, so he accepted the call of the church. The church bought the Chatham Street Theater. At the first service—a prayer meeting held at 5:30 in the morning—800 persons attended. For seventy nights, Finney

---

3. Richard Ellsworth Day, *Man of Like Passions* (Grand Rapids: Zondervan Pub. House, 1952), p. 45; also see Charles G. Finney, *Memoirs* (New York: A. S. Barnes & Co., 1876).
4. Ibid., p. 53 records "that the 'slain of the Lord' fell as if machine-gunned on the village streets."

preached to crowds ranging from 1,500 to 2,500 persons. After this series of meetings Finney was installed as pastor and the church was named Chatham Street Chapel. A number of other Free Presbyterian churches were formed throughout the city as a result of the labor of Finney's church.

Finney came under harsh criticism from many Presbyterians for his theology; he felt increasingly ill at ease in the Presbyterian fellowship. He came to the conclusion that the Congregational type of church administration was the best and decided to change his denomination. Previously he had been affiliated with Congregational churches when he had served as a missionary in Jefferson County, New York. He left the Chatham Street Chapel and organized Broadway Tabernacle in 1834. Finney designed the church building so that every listener would be within 80 feet of the speaker. He served as pastor of the church only a short time before taking up a new work— professor of theology.

Oberlin College in Ohio asked Finney to come as professor of theology. Finney accepted the invitation only on the condition that the school would be open to Negroes on the same basis as it was open to whites. Anti-slavery sentiment was high at Oberlin: many students had transferred to Oberlin from Lane Theological Seminary in Cincinnati, where they had been refused the right to discuss their anti-slavery views. Lyman Beecher, the president at Lane, was not pro-slavery, but he feared that radical anti-slavery views would undercut support for the school. Finney, on the other hand, was an outspoken abolitionist. The students expected to find in him an enthusiastic supporter for their radical views, but they were wrong. Even though Finney was strongly against slavery, he was not radical in his position. Due to Finney's responsible attitude, Oberlin soon won the reputation of being the chief center of anti-slavery sentiment in the West. Graduates from the school spread the cause of abolition throughout the nation, especially the Midwest. In many ways this region became stronger in anti-slavery commitment than New England.

During these days as professor of systematic theology, he developed much of his own theology and put it in writing. Among his writings are: *Lectures on Systematic Theology, Lectures on Revivals,* and *Lectures to Professing Christians.* In 1836 Finney took temporary charge of the Congregational Church at Oberlin; later he became permanent pastor and remained at the post until 1872. In 1851 Finney became president of Oberlin, and the school prospered under his leadership. The year after he became president, the enrollment jumped from 571 to 1070.

Finney was also involved in the famous Great Revival of 1858–59. Some historians credit the beginning of the revival to his preaching; a more conservative evaluation is that he played a significant part in the revival through his preaching. It is estimated that 600,000 persons were brought to Christ during this religious outbreaking. He set a pattern for evangelism which in many ways endured into the twentieth century. His ministry was not limited to the United States. He traveled to both England and Scotland and there led great revivals.

After an exceedingly eventful life, Charles G. Finney died on August 16, 1875. On Sunday, August 15, he attended church with his wife. At 2:00 o'clock on Monday morning he was stricken with a heart attack and died before sunrise.

Those who knew Finney best, and those who have written most completely about his life, stress several outstanding facts about him. Above all, he was deeply dedicated to God and zealous to serve. He was a man of pietistic tendencies who practiced fasting and held long prayer vigils. He believed intently in baptism by the Holy Spirit and thought this experience essential for a ministry of power.

Though almost devoid of formal education, Finney was a highly intelligent man. He was trained in law, and his sermons often displayed brilliant logic. Professionals and intellectuals were awed by his sermons.

He was a compassionate man. His concern for people was evident in his preaching and in his personal relations. Much of his compassion was apparently a natural endowment. Once before becoming a Christian he was in a harbor town, considering enlistment in the navy. A pretty young prostitute approached him and propositioned him. Finney broke into tears of compassion and the prostitute also began to weep; they turned and walked away from one another. This native compassion was stimulated by his relation to Christ and became a significant factor of his life.

Finney was physically strong and vigorous. He had a certain boldness born of his self-confidence. He feared no situation and believed that he could take care of himself in the face of any hostility. His boldness was expressed in many ways. Immediately upon his conversion, for example, he went to see his parents. His father greeted him and Finney replied politely to the welcome. Then the son declared that he had never heard his father pray and that he was concerned about his salvation. Finney soon led both of his parents to trust in Christ. There is no witness more difficult than to one's own family, but Finney did not hesitate to talk to those closest to him.

His courage likewise extended to his attitudes in theology. The prescribed theology of Presbyterianism was Calvinism. Finney rejected many tenets of Calvinism, boldly developed his own theology, and held to it in spite of severe criticism.

He was also bold enough to try new methods in his revivals. Regardless of the source, if a technique or method seemed to be helpful Finney would incorporate it into his meetings. He frequently used the "anxious bench" in his services, a place near the front where persons could come to be counseled personally when they were concerned about salvation. He also freely called for public decisions, an uncommon practice in his day.

Nowhere is his boldness more evident than in his expressed anti-slavery sentiments. Again and again he spoke out against the evils of slavery. He warned that widespread destruction and war would come unless the evil were rooted out of American life. He proved to be a prophet.

Finney declared that evangelistic concern and social concern go hand in hand. It was inconceivable to him that a minister of Jesus Christ could remain silent either in the face of social wrong or in the presence of an unbeliever. Finney showed also that spirituality and education are to be looked upon as comrades, not enemies. His life demonstrated that a balance of evangelism and ethics, education and spiritual discipline, innovations and maturity makes for the best possible ministry.

PREACHING AND SERMONS

The contrasts among famous preachers, even those who served the same congregation, are always fascinating. Who could imagine a greater contrast, for example, than between two of the pastors who served Broadway Tabernacle in New York—Charles Jefferson and Charles Finney? On a closer examination, however, they prove to be alike in their vigorous application of Christian principles to the personal and public problems of their times – in spite of the vast differences in their methods.

Finney was a man of contradictions and surprises. He was an ardent revivalist: blunt, sometimes crude, extravagant and abusive in his language; impassioned, hounding sinners as a lawyer might badger a jury. He could get lost in denouncing the pettiest issues: when he began to catalog and number human faults, his work was so tedious and meticulous that even the apprentice demons must have thought it a waste of time. On the other hand, the only other preachers in America who spoke so forcefully and specifically against slavery were such opposite personalities as Henry Ward Beecher and Theodore Parker. Anti-slavery views seem quite at home with the personality of Beecher, even more so with Parker, but with Charles Finney? – we might expect him to be too preoccupied with revivalism, or lost in pietistic devotions, or entirely devoted to a defense of the Holy Scriptures. Instead we find a man so convinced on the issue of slavery that he refused communion to slaveholders in his congregation! Two pieces, then, must be fitted together to understand this complex man: ardent evangelist and zealous social reformer.

That is the correct order. Finney is primarily remembered, and properly so, as an ardent revivalist. His labors were principally devoted to mass evangelism and lecturing on revivals. The "protracted meetings," which were to become a part of the American religious scene for more than a century after him, were very much his children.

His early training as a lawyer gave Finney both inclination and direction for his revival work.[5] As an attorney, Finney was taught to win a verdict for his client; he decided that he would become God's advocate and plead with men to come to a decision about Christ. He urged men to repent immediately – nothing was to be gained by delay, and all might be lost. His method of calling for public decision offended many; some would stand up and walk out of his services at that point. Yet Finney never relented. He denounced as the worst of evils that theology which insisted that men should wait to become a Christian until some nebulous feeling swept over them. He

---

5. Arthur S. Hoyt, *The Pulpit and American Life* (New York: Macmillan Co., 1921), pp. 156–57.

argued that the Bible insisted upon a decision for which man was personally responsible, and for which no one could answer but the individual himself. Therefore in every service he gave people an opportunity to declare themselves for the Christian faith.

His enemies sent reports to the press that his meetings were too loud and boisterous and were too long. (Finney frequently preached for two hours.) He was accused of being irreverent and offensive in his prayers—during which he called people by name—and of being too personal in his religion. He was also accused of holding revivals in churches when not invited by the pastors. These charges, for the most part, were either greatly exaggerated or untrue altogether.

It is true that he was intensely personal. He did pray for people by name. He utilized the anxious bench. He always applied his truths specifically to his congregation. At times he was blunt almost to the point of rudeness. In all of these things he displayed a zealous interest in the personal conversion of his hearers. Whether he was offensive or not is a matter of personal opinion.[6]

His preparation in oratory and his training in law combined to make Finney an effective speaker. He spoke in simple language; his illustrations were taken from common experiences. His preaching was conversational. He disliked speaking from a manuscript and urged his students at Oberlin to follow the extemporaneous method of delivery. Nevertheless, in reading his sermons today, it is impossible to believe that Finney spoke entirely extemporaneously. Such intricate outlines must have required at least some notes taken into the pulpit. A careful reading of these sermons would suggest that the numbered items were read from notes while the body of the discussion was delivered freely. There is good evidence that Finney used such notes; in the preface to his *Lectures,* the reporter who took down the sermons which formed these lectures wrote: "It is hardly necessary to mention, that Mr. Finney never writes his sermons; but guides his course of argument by a skeleton, or brief, carefully prepared, and so compact, that it can be written on one side of a card, about half as large as one of these printed pages."[7]

---

6. Beardsley, p. 68.
7. Charles G. Finney, *Lectures on Revivals of Religion,* (New York: Leavitt, Lord & Co., 1835), p. v.

He said of his preaching, "I talk to the people as I would have talked to the jury."[8] This style in itself was one of his greatest failings: his preaching was often repetitive and argumentative, even hostile. But no one could deny the personal, specific, plain nature of his messages.

In Finney's sermon "How to Promote a Revival," his gift of personal application is well illustrated. In numerous places he refers directly to his audience, applying biblical truths to their various needs. The same is true of the sermon "God's Love for a Sinning World." There also his incessant repetition can be seen, which in this case serves to strengthen this sermon rather than weaken it. The form of this particular sermon is a homily, with sub-development under the various phrases of the text. The theme is hammered home by personal application and by repetition of the principal ideas.

Many of these same traits appear in the sermon "The Excuses of Sinners Condemn God." Finney is eminently the lawyer in this sermon. Notice the specific application at one point where Finney directs his printed remarks to those "in this house." This particular sermon also exhibits some of Finney's weaknesses as well as his strengths. His language is extravagant: in several places he uses such expressions as, "Oh, what stupid nonsense"; "It is . . . absurd and utter nonsense!"; "Away with such teaching to the nether pit whence it came!" His court-room training is likewise apparent in this vivid descriptive passage:

> How can you stand before God in the judgment, if your excuses are so mean that you cannot seriously think of bringing one of them before God in this world? O, sinner, that coming day will be far more searching and awful than anything you have seen yet. See that dense mass of sinners drawn up before the great white throne—far as the eye can sweep they come surging up— a countless throng; and now they stand, and the awful trump of God summons them forward to bring forth their excuses for sin.
>
> Ho, sinners—any one of you, all—what have you to say why sentence should not be passed on you? Where are all those excuses you were once so free and bold to make? Where are they all? Why don't you make them now? *Hark!* God waits; He listens; there is silence in

8. Beardsley, p. 42.

heaven—all through the congregated throng—for half an hour—an awful silence—that may be felt; but not a word—not a moving lip among the gathered myriads of sinners there; and now the great and dreadful Judge arises and lets loose His thunders. O, see the waves of dire damnation roll over those ocean-masses of self-condemned sinners.

Did you ever see the judge rise from his bench in court to pass sentence of death on a criminal? There, see, the poor man reels—he falls prostrate—there is no longer any strength in him, for death is on him and his last hope has perished!

O, sinner, when that sentence from the dread throne shall fall on thee! Your excuses are as millstones around your neck as you plunge along down the sides of the pit to the nethermost hell!

This passage is powerful, and would be even more powerful if it had not indulged in a certain amount of oratorical excess. The entire sermon is a prototype of all evangelistic "excuse" sermons which would follow it. Finney lists no less than twenty-two separate excuses, each fully described, with countless subdivisions. The detail of his outline is reminiscent of the preaching which preceded him, particularly that of Jonathan Edwards upon whom Finney depended for justification of his revivalistic concern and from whom he quoted extensively. Some of Finney's passages that describe the fate of the damned sound very much like echos from "Sinners in the Hands of an Angry God." Unlike Edwards, however, Finney called upon his hearers to register their decisions at the close of the service. (For further references to Jonathan Edwards, see Finney's sermon "Hindrances to Revivals," pp. 371–95.)

In the sermon on "Hindrances," Finney defended his revival meetings by saying that "not less than two hundred thousand persons have been converted" during the previous ten years. During that time, he said, many hindrances to his revivals developed. In discussing these hindrances, Finney attacked pride on the part of evangelists and people alike. He also firmly denounced a mechanical approach to revivals. Proselyting among denominations was listed as another of the hindrances that had developed; Finney called upon all participants in the meetings to avoid that un-Christian practice. He urged all who believed in his work to avoid contention with others who were opposed to revivals. There must have been many who were opposed to his work since Finney devoted so much attention to that problem.

In the same sermon it is not surprising to hear Finney attack those who were engaged in the "liquor traffic," since traditionally that has been a favorite target of evangelists; but his hotly worded attack on slavery is more surprising:

> Revivals are hindered when ministers and *churches take wrong ground in regard to any question involving human rights.* Take the subject of *slavery,* for instance. The time was when this subject was not before the public mind. John Newton continued in the slave trade after his conversion. And so had his mind been perverted, and so completely was his conscience seared, in regard to this most nefarious traffic, that the sinfulness of it never occurred to his thoughts until some time after he became a child of God. Had light been poured upon his mind previously to his conversion, he *never could* have been converted without previously abandoning this sin. And after his conversion, when convinced of its iniquity, he could no longer enjoy the presence of God, without abandoning the sin forever.
>
> So, doubtless, many slave dealers and slave holders in our own country have been converted, notwithstanding their participation in this abomination, because the sinfulness of it was not apparent to their minds. So ministers and churches, to a great extent throughout the land, have held their peace, and borne no testimony against this abominable abomination, existing in the church and in the nation.
>
> But recently, the subject has come up for discussion, and the providence of God has brought it distinctly before the eyes of all men. Light is now shed upon this subject, as it has been upon the cause of temperance. Facts are exhibited, and principles established, and light thrown in upon the minds of men, and this monster is dragged from his horrid den, and exhibited before the church, and it is demanded of them, *"Is this sin?"* Their testimony *must* be given on this subject. They are God's witnesses. They are sworn to tell "the truth, the whole truth, and nothing but the truth." It is impossible that their testimony should not be given, on one side or the other. Their silence can no longer be accounted for upon the principle of ignorance, and that

they have never had their attention turned to the subject. Consequently, the silence of Christians upon the subject is virtually saying *that they do not* consider slavery as a sin. The truth is, it is a subject upon which they cannot be silent without guilt.

The time has come, in the providence of God, when every southern breeze is loaded down with the cries of lamentation, mourning and woe. Two millions of degraded heathen in our own land stretch their hands, all shackled and bleeding, and send forth to the church of God the agonizing cry for help. And shall the church, in her efforts to reclaim and save the world, deafen her ears to this voice of agony and despair? God forbid. The church cannot turn away from this question. It is a question for the church and for the nation to decide, and God will push it to a decision.

That is not all that Finney says upon the subject, but it will do for an example. Later in that sermon he insisted that the church take its full responsibility; he declared that the slavery question was primarily a church question, since church people both condoned the practice and owned slaves themselves. Finney said that if the churches would do what they ought to do the problem could be resolved within three years. He reminded the people that the specter of war loomed above their heads; he warned that if the church did not act, the revival movement would suffer as well as the nation itself.

Finney's opposition to slavery cannot be too strongly emphasized: his opinions upon the subject were so decided that he withheld communion from slaveholders within his own church:

We have excluded slaveholders and all concerned in the traffic from our communion. By some out of this church this course has been censured as unwarrantable and uncharitable, and I would by no means make my own judgment, or the example of this church, a rule for the government of other ministers and churches. Still, I conscientiously believe that the time is not far distant when the churches will be united in this expression of abhorrence against this sin.

If I do not baptize slavery by some soft and Christian name, if I call it *sin*, both consistency and conscience conduct to the inevitable conclusion, that while this sin is persevered in, its perpetrators cannot be fit subjects for Christian communion and fellowship.

When some protested to Finney that ministers of the Presbyterian church were themselves slaveholders, Finney replied that he had no authority to do anything about them, but that he would exercise authority in his own church. He insisted that it was his responsibility to belong to the church even if the devil himself belonged to it, and that he would not allow slaveholders to participate in communion in his church as long as they persisted in their sin. He called upon the church at large to abandon its neutrality, proclaim the truth, abandon prejudice, and always avoid a contentious spirit while pursuing the cause of freedom.

In an epilogue to this sermon, written years later when these sermons appeared in a revised edition (1868), Finney reflected upon the course of events that had followed his predictions. He remarked that the revival movement had been justified by the fruits of its labors. He observed that many in the north had had their consciences awakened by his preaching against slavery. He found it necessary, however, to make this general evaluation upon the entire situation: "Upon the question of slavery the church was too late in her testimony to avoid the War."[9] Who would argue? The lawyer had made his point.

---

9. Finney, p. 293.

Sermons

GOD'S LOVE FOR A SINNING WORLD

"For God so loved the world that he gave his only begotten Son, that whosoever believeth in Him should not perish, but have everlasting life" (John 3:16).

SIN IS THE MOST EXPENSIVE THING in the universe. Nothing else can cost so much. Pardoned or unpardoned, its cost is infinitely great. Pardoned, the cost falls chiefly on the great atoning Substitute; unpardoned, it must fall on the head of the guilty sinner.

The existence of sin is a fact everywhere experienced – everywhere observed. There *is* sin in our race everywhere, and in awful aggravation.

Sin is the violation of an infinitely important law – a law designed and adapted to secure the highest good of the universe. Obedience to this law is naturally essential to the good of creatures. Without obedience there could be no blessedness even in heaven.

As sin is a violation of a most important law, it cannot be treated lightly. No government can afford to treat disobedience as a trifle, inasmuch as everything – the entire welfare of the government and of all the governed – turns upon obedience. Just in proportion to the value of the interests at stake is the necessity of guarding law and of punishing disobedience.

The law of God must not be dishonored by anything *He* shall do. It has been dishonored by the disobedience of man; hence, the more need that God should stand by it, to retrieve its honor. The utmost dishonor is done to law by disowning, disobeying, and despising it. All this, sinning man has done. Hence, this law being not only good, but intrinsically necessary to the happiness of the governed, it becomes of all things most necessary that the law-giver should vindicate his law. He must by all means do it.

Hence, sin has involved God's government in a vast expense. Either the law must be executed at the expense of the well-being of the whole

---

Reprinted from Charles G. Finney, *Sermons on Gospel Themes* (Oberlin, Ohio: E. J. Goodrich, n.d.), pp. 1–18.

race, or God must submit to suffer the worst results of disrespect to His law — results which in some form must involve a vast expense.

Take for example any human government. Suppose the righteous and necessary laws which it imposes are disowned and dishonored. In such a case the violated law must be honored by the execution of its penalty, or something else not less expensive, and probably much more so, must be endured. Transgression must cost happiness, somewhere, and in vast amount.

In the case of God's government it has been deemed advisable to provide a substitute — one that should answer the purpose of saving the sinner, and yet of honoring the law. This being determined on, the next great question was — *How shall the expense be met?*

The Bible informs us how the question was in fact decided. By a voluntary conscription — shall I call it — or donation? Call it as we may, it was a voluntary offering. Who shall head the subscription? Who shall begin where so much is to be raised? Who will make the first sacrifice? Who will take the first step in a project so vast? The Bible informs us. It began with the Infinite Father. He made the first great donation. He gave His only begotten Son — this to begin with — and having given Him first, He freely gives all else that the exigencies of the case can require. First, He gave His Son to make the atonement due to law, then gave and sent His Holy Spirit to take charge of this work. The Son on His part consented to stand as the representative of sinners, that He might honor the law, by suffering in their stead. He poured out His blood, made a whole life of suffering a free donation on the altar — withheld not His face from spitting, nor His back from stripes — shrunk not from the utmost contumely that wicked men could heap on Him. So the Holy Ghost also devotes Himself to most self-denying efforts unceasingly, to accomplish the great object.

It would have been a very short method to have turned over His hand upon the wicked of our race, and sent them all down quick to hell, as once He did when certain angels "kept not their first estate." Rebellion broke out in heaven. Not long did God bear it, around His lofty throne. But in the case of man He changed His course — did not send them all to hell, but devised a vast scheme of measures, involving most amazing self-denials and self-sacrifices, to gain men's souls back to obedience and heaven.

For whom was this great donation made? "God so loved the *World*," meaning the whole race of men. By the "world" in this connection cannot be meant any particular part only, but the whole race. Not only the Bible, but the nature of the case shows that the atonement must have been made for the whole world. For plainly if it had not been made for the entire race, no man of the race could ever know that it was made for himself, and therefore not a man could believe on Christ in the sense of receiving by faith the blessings of the atonement.

There being an utter uncertainty as to the persons embraced in the limited provisions which we now *suppose* to be made, the entire donation must fail through the impossibility of rational faith for its reception. Suppose a will is made by a rich man bequeathing certain property to certain unknown persons, described only by the name of "the elect." They are not described otherwise than by this term, and all agree that although the maker of the will had the individuals definitely in his mind, yet that he left no description of them, which either the persons themselves, the courts, nor any living mortal can understand. Now such a will is of necessity altogether null and void. No living man can claim under such a will, and none the better though these elect were described as residents of Oberlin. Since it does not embrace all the residents of Oberlin, and does not define which of them, all is lost. All having an equal claim and none any definite claim, none can inherit. If the atonement were made in this way, no living man would have any valid reason for believing himself one of the elect, prior to his reception of the Gospel. Hence he would have no authority to believe and receive its blessings by faith. In fact, the atonement must be wholly void — on this supposition — unless a special revelation is made to the persons for whom it is intended.

As the case is, however, the very fact that a man belongs to the race of Adam — the fact that he is human, born of woman, is all-sufficient. It brings him within the pale. He is one of the *world* for whom God gave His Son, that whosoever would believe in Him might not perish, but have everlasting life.

The subjective motive in the mind of God for this great gift was *love*, love to the world. God so loved the world that He gave His Son to die for it. God loved the universe also, but this gift of His Son sprang from love to our world. True in this great act He took pains to provide for the interests of the universe. He was careful to do nothing that could in the least let down the sacredness of His law. Most carefully did He intend to guard against misapprehension as to His regard for His law and for the high interests of obedience and happiness in his moral universe. He meant once for all to preclude the danger lest any moral agent should be tempted to undervalue the moral law.

Yet farther, it was not only from love to souls, but from respect to the spirit of the law of His own eternal reason, that He gave up His Son to die. In this the purpose to give up His Son originated. The law of His own reason must be honored and held sacred. He may do nothing inconsistent with its spirit. He must do everything possible to prevent the commission of sin and to secure the confidence and love of His subjects. So sacred did He hold these great objects that He would baptize His Son in His own blood, sooner than peril the good of the universe. Beyond a question it was love and regard for the highest good of the universe that led Him to sacrifice His own beloved Son.

Let us next consider attentively the *nature* of this love. The text lays special stress on this—God *so* loved—His love was of such a nature, so wonderful and so peculiar in its character, that it led Him to give up His only Son to die. More is evidently implied in this expression than simply its greatness. It is most peculiar in its character. Unless we understand this, we shall be in danger of falling into the strange mistake of the Universalists, who are forever talking about God's love for sinners, but whose notions of the nature of this love never lead to repentance or to holiness. They seem to think of this love as simply good nature, and conceive of God only as a very good-natured being, whom nobody need to fear. Such notions have not the least influence towards holiness, but the very opposite. It is only when we come to understand what this love is in its nature that we feel its moral power promoting holiness.

It may be reasonably asked, If God so loved the world with a love characterized by greatness, and by greatness only, why did He not save all the world without sacrificing His Son? This question suffices to show us that there is deep meaning in this word *so,* and should put us upon a careful study of this meaning.

1. This love in its nature is not *complacency*—a delight in the character of the race. This could not be, for there was nothing amiable in their character. For God to have loved such a race *complacently* would have been infinitely disgraceful to Himself.

2. It was not a mere emotion or feeling. It was not a blind impulse, though many seem to suppose it was. It seems to be often supposed that God acted as men do when they are borne away by strong emotion. But there could be no virtue in this. A man might give away all he is worth under such a blind impulse of feeling, and be none the more virtuous. But in saying this we do not exclude all emotion from the love of benevolence, nor from God's love for a lost world. He had emotion, but not emotion *only.* Indeed the Bible everywhere teaches us that God's love for man, lost in his sins, was paternal—the love of a father for his offspring—in this case, for a rebellious, froward, prodigal offspring. In this love there must of course blend the deepest compassion.

3. On the part of Christ, considered as Mediator, this love was *fraternal.* "He is not ashamed to call them *brethren.*" In one point of view He is acting for brethren, and in another for children. The Father gave Him up for this work and of course sympathizes in the love appropriate to its relations.

4. This love must be altogether *disinterested,* for He had nothing to hope or to fear—no profit to make out of His children if they should be saved. Indeed, it is impossible to conceive of God as being selfish, since His love embraces all creatures and all interests according to their real value. No doubt He took delight in saving our race—why should He not? It is a great salvation in every sense, and greatly does it swell the bliss of heaven—greatly will it affect the glory and the

blessedness of the Infinite God. He will eternally respect Himself for love so disinterested. He knows also that all His holy creatures will eternally respect Him for this work and for the love that gave it birth. But let it also be said, He knew they would not respect Him for this great work unless they should see that He did it for the good of sinners.

5. This love was *zealous*—not that cold-hearted state of mind which some suppose—not an abstraction, but a love, deep, zealous, earnest, burning in his soul as a fire that nothing can quench.

6. The sacrifice was a most self-denying one. Did it cost the Father nothing to give up His own beloved Son to suffer, and to die such a death? If this be not self-denial, what can be? Thus to give up His Son to so much suffering—is not this the noblest self-denial? The universe never could have the idea of great self-denial but for such an exemplification.

7. This love was particular because it was universal; and also universal because it was particular. God loved each sinner in particular, and therefore loved all. Because He loved all impartially, with no respect of persons, therefore He loved each in particular.

8. This was a most *patient* love. How rare to find a parent so loving his child as never to be impatient. Let me go round and ask, how many of you, parents, can say that you love all your children so well, and with so much love, and with love so wisely controlling, that you have never felt impatient towards any of them—so that you can take them in your arms under the greatest provocations and love them *down,* love them out of their sins, love them into repentance and into a filial spirit? Of which of your children can you say, Thank God, I never fretted against that child—of which, if you were to meet him in heaven, could you say, I never caused that child to fret? Often have I heard parents say, I love my children, but oh, how my patience fails me! And, after the dear ones are dead, you may hear their bitter moans, Oh, my soul, how could I have caused my child so much stumbling and so much sin!

But God never frets—is never impatient. His love is so deep and so great that He is always patient.

Sometimes, when parents have unfortunate children—poor objects of compassion—they can bear with anything from them; but when they are very wicked, they seem to feel that they are quite excusable for being impatient. In God's case, these are not unfortunate children, but are intensely wicked—intelligently wicked. But oh, His amazing patience—so set upon their good, so desirous of their highest welfare, that however they abuse Him, He sets himself to bless them still, and weep them down, and melt them into penitence and love, by the death of His Son in their stead!

9. This is a *jealous love,* not in a bad sense, but in a good sense—in the sense of being exceedingly careful lest anything should occur to

injure those he loves. Just as husband and wife who truly love each other are jealous with ever wakeful jealousy over each other's welfare, seeking always to do all they can to promote each other's true interests.

This donation is already made—made in good faith—not only *promised,* but actually *made.* The promise, given long before, has been fulfilled. The Son has come, has died, has made the ransom and lives to offer it—a prepared salvation to all who will embrace it.

The Son of God died not to appease vengeance, as some seem to understand it, but under the demands of law. The law had been dishonored by its violation. Hence, Christ undertook to honor it by giving up to its demands His suffering life and atoning death. It was not to appease a vindictive spirit in God, but to secure the highest good of the universe in a dispensation of mercy.

Since this atonement has been made, all men in the race have a right to it. It is open to everyone who will embrace it. Though Jesus still remains the Father's Son, yet by gracious right He belongs in an important sense to the race—to everyone; so that every sinner has an interest in His blood if he will only come humbly forward and claim it. God sent His Son to be the Saviour of the world—of whomsoever would believe and accept this great salvation.

God gives His Spirit to apply this salvation to men. He comes to each man's door and knocks, to gain admittance, if He can, and show each sinner that he may now have salvation. Oh, what a labor of love is this!

This salvation must be received, if at all, *by faith.* This is the only possible way. God's government over sinners is moral not physical, because the sinner is himself a moral and not a physical agent. Therefore, God can influence us in no way unless we will give Him our confidence. He never can save us by merely taking us away to some place called heaven—as if change of place would change the voluntary heart. There can, therefore, be no possible way to be saved but by simple faith.

Now do not mistake and suppose that embracing the Gospel is simply to believe these historical facts without truly receiving Christ as *your* Saviour. If this had been the scheme, then Christ had need only to come down and die; then go back to heaven and quietly wait to see who would believe the facts. But how different is the real case! Now Christ comes down to fill the soul with His own life and love. Penitent sinners hear and believe the truth concerning Jesus, and then receive Christ into the soul to live and reign there supreme and forever. On this point many mistake, saying, If I believe the facts as matters of history it is enough. *No! No!* This is not it by any means. *"With the heart* man believeth unto righteousness." The atonement was indeed made to provide the way so that Jesus could come down to human hearts and draw them into union and sympathy with Himself

— so that God would let down the arms of His love and embrace sinners
— so that law and government should not be dishonored by such tokens
of friendship shown by God toward sinners. But the atonement will
by no means save sinners only as it prepares the way for them to come
into sympathy and fellowship of heart with God.

Now Jesus comes to each sinner's door and knocks. Hark! what's
that? what's that? Why this knocking? Why did He not go away and
stay in heaven if that were the system, till men should simply believe
the historical facts and be baptized, as some suppose, for salvation.
But now, see how He comes down — tells the sinner what He has done
— reveals all His love — tells him how holy and sacred it is, so sacred
that He can by no means act without reference to the holiness of His
law and the purity of His government. Thus impressing on the heart
the most deep and enlarged ideas of His holiness and purity, He enforces the need of deep repentance and the sacred duty of renouncing
all sin.

REMARKS

1. The Bible teaches that sinners may forfeit their birthright and
put themselves beyond the reach of mercy. It is not long since I made
some remarks to you on the manifest necessity that God should guard
Himself against the abuses of His love. The circumstances are such as
create the greatest danger of such abuse, and, therefore, He must
make sinners know that they may not abuse His love, and cannot do it
with impunity.

2. Under the Gospel, sinners are in circumstances of the greatest
possible responsibility. They are in the utmost danger of trampling
down beneath their feet the very Son of God. Come, they say, let us
kill Him and the inheritance shall be ours. When God sends forth,
last of all, His own beloved Son, what do they do? Add to all their other
sins and rebellions the highest insult to this glorious Son! Suppose
something analogous to this were done under a human government.
A case of rebellion occurs in some of the provinces. The king sends
his own son, not with an army, to cut them down quick in their rebellion, but all gently, meekly, patiently, he goes among them, explaining the laws of the kingdom and exhorting them to obedience.
What do they do in the case? With one consent they combine to seize
him and put him to death!

But you deny the application of this, and ask me, Who murdered the
Son of God? Were they not Jews? Aye, and have you, sinners, had no
part in this murder? Has not your treatment of Jesus Christ shown
that you are most fully in sympathy with the ancient Jews in their
murder of the Son of God? If you had been there, would anyone have
shouted louder than you, Away with Him — crucify Him, crucify Him?

Have you not always said, Depart from us—for we desire not the knowledge of Thy ways?

3. It was said of Christ that, Though rich He became poor that we through His poverty might be rich. How strikingly true is this! Our redemption cost Christ His life; it found Him rich, but made Him poor; it found us infinitely poor, but made us rich even to all the wealth of heaven. But of these riches none can partake till they shall each for himself accept them in the legitimate way. They must be received on the terms proposed, or the offer passes utterly away, and you are left poorer even than if no such treasures had ever been laid at your feet.

Many persons seem entirely to misconceive this case. They seem not to believe what God says, but keep saying, *If, if, if* there only were any salvation for me—*if* there were only an atonement provided for the pardon of my sins. This was one of the last things that was cleared up in my mind before I fully committed my soul to trust God. I had been studying the atonement; I saw its philosophical bearings—saw what it demanded of the sinner; but it irritated me, and I said—If I should become a Christian, how could I know what God would do with me? Under this irritation I said foolish and bitter things against Christ— till my own soul was horrified at its own wickedness, and I said—I will make all this up with Christ if the thing is possible.

In this way many advance upon the encouragements of the Gospel as if it were only a peradventure, an *experiment*. They take each forward step most carefully, with fear and trembling, as if there were the utmost doubt whether there could be any mercy for them. So with myself. I was on my way to my office, when the question came before my mind—What are you waiting for? You need not get up such an ado. All is done already. You have only to consent to the proposition—give your heart right up to it at once—this is all. Just so it is. All Christians and sinners ought to understand that the whole plan is complete—that the whole of Christ—His character, His work, His atoning death, and His ever-living intercession—belong to each and every man, and need only to be accepted. There is a full ocean of it. *There* it is. You may just as well take it as not. It is as if you stood on the shore of an ocean of soft, pure water, famishing with thirst; you are welcome to drink, and you need not fear lest you exhaust that ocean, or starve anybody else by drinking yourself. You need not feel that you are not made free to that ocean of waters; you are invited and pressed to drink—yea, to *drink abundantly!* This ocean supplies all your need. You do not need to have in yourself the attributes of Jesus Christ, for His attributes become practically yours for all possible use. As saith the Scripture— He is of God made unto us wisdom, righteousness, sanctification, and redemption. What do you need? Wisdom? Here it is. Righteousness? Here it is. Sanctification? Here you have it. All is in Christ. Can you possibly think of any one thing needful for your moral purity, or your usefulness which is not here in Christ? Nothing. All is provided here. Therefore you need not say, I will go and pray and try, as the hymn —

> I'll go to Jesus tho' my sin
> Hath like a mountain rose,
> *Perhaps* He will admit my plea;
> *Perhaps* will hear my prayer.

There is no need of any *perhaps*. The doors are always open. Like the doors of Broadway Tabernacle in New York, made to swing open and fasten themselves open, so that they could not swing back and shut down upon the crowds of people thronging to pass through. When they were to be made, I went myself to the workmen and told them by all means to fix them so that they must swing open and fasten themselves in that position.

So the door of salvation is open always — fastened open, and no man can shut it — not the Pope, even, nor the devil, nor any angel from heaven or from hell. There it stands, all swung back and the passage wide open for every sinner of our race to enter if he will.

Again, sin is the most expensive thing in the universe. Are you well aware, O sinner, what a price has been paid for you that you may be redeemed and made an heir of God and of heaven? O what an expensive business for you to indulge in sin!

And what an enormous tax the government of God has paid to redeem this province from its ruin! Talk about the poor tax of Great Britain and of all other nations superadded; all is nothing to the sin-tax of Jehovah's government — that awful *sin-tax!* Think how much machinery is kept in motion to save sinners! The Son of God was sent down — angels are sent as ministering spirits to the heirs of salvation; missionaries are sent, Christians labor, and pray, and weep in deep and anxious solicitude — all to seek and save the lost. What a wonderful — enormous tax is levied upon the benevolence of the universe to put away sin and to save the sinner! If the cost could be computed in solid gold, what a world of it — a solid globe of itself! What an array of toil and cost, from angels, Jesus Christ, the Divine Spirit, and living men! Shame on sinners who hold on to sin despite of all these benevolent efforts to save them! who instead of being ashamed out of sin, will say — Let God pay off this tax; who cares! Let the missionaries labor, let pious women work their very fingers off to raise funds to keep all this human machinery in motion; no matter: what is all this to me? I have loved my pleasures and after them I will go! What an unfeeling heart is this!

Sinners can very well afford to make sacrifices to save their fellow sinners. Paul could for his fellow sinners. He felt that he had done his part toward making sinners, and now it became him to do his part also in converting them back to God. But see there – that young man thinks he cannot afford to be a minister, for he is afraid he shall not be well supported. Does he not owe something to the grace that saved his soul from hell? Has he not some sacrifices to make, since Jesus has made so many for him, and Christians too, in Christ before him – did they not pray and suffer and toil for his soul's salvation? As to his danger of lacking bread in the Lord's work, let him trust his Great Master. Yet let me also say that churches may be in great fault for not comfortably supporting their pastors. Let them know God will assuredly starve them if they starve their ministers. Their own souls and the souls of their children shall be barren as death if they avariciously starve those whom God in His providence sends to feed them with the bread of life.

How much it costs to rid society of certain forms of sin, as for example, *slavery*. How much has been expended already, and how much more yet remains to be expended ere this sore evil and curse and sin shall be rooted from our land! This is part of God's great enterprise, and He will press it on to its completion. Yet at what an amazing cost! How many lives and how much agony to get rid of this one sin!

Woe to those who make capital out of the sins of men! Just think of the rumseller – tempting men while God is trying to dissuade them from rushing on in the ways of sin and death! Think of the guilt of those who thus set themselves in array against God! So Christ has to contend with rumsellers who are doing all they can to hinder His work.

Our subject strikingly illustrates the nature of sin as mere selfishness. It cares not how much sin costs Jesus Christ – how much it costs the Church, how much it taxes the benevolent sympathies and the self-sacrificing labors of all the good in earth or heaven – no matter; the sinner loves self-indulgence and will have it while he can. How many of you have cost your friends countless tears and trouble to get you back from your ways of sin? Are you not ashamed when so much has been done for you, that you cannot be persuaded to give up your sins and turn to God and holiness?

The whole effort on the part of God for man is one of suffering and self-denial. Beginning with the sacrifice of His own beloved Son, it is carried on with ever renewed sacrifices and toilsome labors – at great and wonderful expense. Just think how long a *time* these efforts have been protracted already – how many tears, poured out like water, it has cost – how much *pain* in many forms this enterprise has caused and cost – yea, that very sin which you roll as a sweet morsel under your tongue! God may well hate it when He sees how much it costs, and say – O do not that abominable thing that I hate!

Yet God is not unhappy in these self-denials. So great is His joy in the results, that He deems all the suffering but comparatively a trifle, even as earthly parents enjoy the efforts they make to bless their children. See them; they will almost work their very hands off –

mothers sit up at night to ply their needle till they reel with fatigue and blindness; but if you were to see their toil, you would often see also their joy, so intensely do they love their children.

Such is the labor, the joy, and the self-denial of the Father, the Son, and the Holy Ghost, in their great work for human salvation. Often are they grieved that so many will refuse to be saved. Toiling on in a common sympathy, there is nothing, within reasonable limits, which they will not do or suffer to accomplish their great work. It is wonderful to think how all creation sympathizes, too, in this work and its necessary sufferings. Go back to the scene of Christ's sufferings. Could the sun in the heavens look down unmoved on such a scene? O no, he could not even behold it—but veiled his face from the sight! All nature seemed to put on her robes of deepest mourning. The scene was too much for even inanimate nature to bear. The sun turned his back and could not look down on such a spectacle!

The subject illustrates forcibly the worth of the soul. Think you God would have done all this if He had had those low views on this subject which sinners usually have?

Martyrs and saints enjoy their sufferings—filling up in themselves what is lacking of the sufferings of Christ; not in the atonement proper, but in the subordinate parts of the work to be done. It is the nature of true religion to love self-denial.

The results will fully justify all the expense. God had well counted the cost before He began. Long time before He formed a moral universe He knew perfectly what it must cost Him to redeem sinners, and He knew that the result would amply justify all the cost. He knew that a wonder of mercy would be wrought—that the suffering demanded of Christ, great as it was, would be endured; and that results infinitely glorious would accrue therefrom. He looked down the track of time into the distant ages—where, as the cycles rolled along, there might be seen the joys of redeemed saints, who are singing their songs and striking their harps anew with the everlasting song, through the long, long, *long* eternity of their blessedness—and was not this enough for the heart of infinite love to enjoy? And what do you think of it, Christian? Will you say now, I am ashamed to ask to be forgiven? How can I bear to receive such mercy! It is the price of blood, and how can I accept it? How can I make Jesus Christ so much expense?

You are right in saying that you have cost Him great expense—but the expense has been cheerfully met—the pain has all been endured, and will not need to be endured again, and it will cost none the more if you accept than if you decline; and moreover still, let it be considered, Jesus Christ has not acted unwisely; He did not pay too much for the soul's redemption—not a pang more than the interests of God's government demanded and the worth of the soul would justify.

O, when you come to see Him face to face, and tell Him what you think of it — when you are some thousands of years older than you are now, will you not adore that wisdom that manages this scheme, and the infinite love in which it had its birth? O what will you then say of that amazing condescension that brought down Jesus to your rescue! Say, Christian, have you not often poured out your soul before your Saviour in acknowledgment of what you have cost Him, and there seemed to be a kind of lifting up as if the very bottom of your soul were to rise and you would pour out your whole heart. If anybody had seen you they would have wondered what had happened to you that had so melted your soul in gratitude and love.

Say now, sinner, will you sell your birthright? How much will you take for it? How much will you take for your interest in Christ? For how much will you sell your soul? Sell your Christ! Of old they sold Him for thirty pieces of silver; and ever since, the heavens have been raining tears of blood on our guilty world. If you were to be asked by the devil to fix the sum for which you would sell your soul, what would be the price named? Lorenzo Dow once met a man as he was riding along a solitary road to fulfill an appointment, and said to him — Friend, have you ever prayed? No. How much will you take never to pray hereafter? One dollar. Dow paid it over and rode on. The man put the money in his pocket, and passed on, *thinking.* The more he thought the worse he felt. There, said he, I have sold my soul for one dollar! It must be that I have met the *devil!* Nobody else would tempt me so. With all my soul I must repent or be damned forever!

How often have you bargained to sell your Saviour for less than thirty pieces of silver! Nay, for the merest trifle!

Finally, God wants volunteers to help on this great work. God has given Himself, and given His Son, and sent His Spirit, but more laborers still are needed; and what will you give? Paul said, I bear in my body the marks of the Lord Jesus. Do you aspire to such an honor? What will you do — what will you suffer? Say not, I have nothing to give. You can give yourself — your eyes, your ears, your hands, your mind, your heart, all; and surely nothing you have is too sacred and too good to be devoted to such a work upon such a call! How many young men are ready to go? and how many young women? Whose heart leaps up crying — Here am I! send me?

THE EXCUSES OF SINNERS CONDEMN GOD

"Wilt thou also disannul my judgment? Wilt thou condemn me, that thou mayest be righteous?" (Job 40:8).

ALTHOUGH IN THE MAIN, Job had spoken correctly of God, yet in his great anguish and perturbation under his sore trials, he had said some things which were hasty and abusive. For these the Lord rebuked him. This rebuke is contained in our context:

Moreover the Lord answered Job, and said – Shall he that contendeth with the Almighty instruct Him? He that reproveth God, let him answer it.

Then Job answered the Lord, and said – Behold I am vile; what shall I answer thee? I will lay my hand upon my mouth. Once have I spoken, but I will not answer; yea, twice, but I will proceed no further.

Then answered the Lord unto Job out of the whirlwind, and said, – Gird up thy loins now like a man; I will demand of thee, and declare thou unto me. Wilt thou also disannul my judgment? Wilt thou condemn me, that thou mayest be righteous?" (Job 40:1–8).

It is not, however, my object to discuss the original purpose and connection of these words, but rather to consider their present application to the case of sinners. In pursuing this object, I shall

I. Show that every excuse for sin condemns God.

II. Consider some of these excuses in detail.

III. Show that excuse for sin adds insult to injury.

I. *Every excuse for sin condemns God.* This will be apparent if we consider,

1. *That nothing can be sin for which there is a justifiable excuse.* This is entirely self-evident. It therefore needs neither elucidation nor proof.

2. *If God condemns that for which there is a good excuse, He must be wrong.* This also is self-evident. If God condemns what we have good reason for doing, no intelligence in the universe can justify Him.

3. *But God does condemn all sin.* He condemns it utterly, and will not allow the least apology or excuse for it. Hence, either there is no apology for it, or God is wrong.

4. Consequently, *every excuse for sin charges blame upon God,*

Reprinted from Charles G. Finney, *Sermons on Gospel Themes* (Oberlin, Ohio: E. J. Goodrich, n. d.), pp. 72–102.

and virtually accuses Him of tyranny. Whoever pleads an excuse for sin, therefore, charges God with blame.

II. *We will consider some of these excuses, and see whether the principles I have laid down are not just and true.*

1. *Inability.* No excuse is more common. It is echoed and re-echoed over every Christian land, and handed down age after age, never to be forgotten. With unblushing face it is proclaimed that men *cannot* do what God requires of them.

Let us examine this and see what it amounts to. God, it is said, requires what men cannot do. And does He *know* that men cannot do it? Most certainly. Then He has no apology for requiring it, and the requisition is most unreasonable. Human reason can never justify it. It is a natural impossibility.

But again, *upon what penalty* does God require what man cannot do? The threatened penalty is eternal death! Yes, *eternal death*, according to the views of those who plead inability as an excuse. God requires me, on pain of eternal death, to do that which He knows I cannot do. Truly this condemns God in the worst sense. You might just as well charge God outright with being an infinite tyrant.

Moreover, it is not for us to say whether on these conditions we shall or shall not charge God with infinite tyranny, for we cannot help it. The law of our reason demands it.

Hence, those who plant themselves upon these grounds charge God with infinite tyranny. Perhaps, sinner, you little think when you urge the excuse of inability, that you are really arraigning God on the charge of infinite tyranny. And you, Christian, who make this dogma of inability a part of your "orthodox" creed, may have little noticed its blasphemous bearings against the character of God; but your failure to notice it alters not the fact. The black charge is involved in the very doctrine of inability, and cannot be explained out of it. . . .

But you take the ground that no man can obey the law of God. As the Presbyterian Confession of Faith has it, "No man is able, either by himself, or by any grace received in this life, perfectly to keep the commandments of God; but doth daily break them in thought, word, and deed." Observe, this affirms not only that no man is naturally able to keep God's commands, but also that no man is able to do it *"by any grace received in this life,"* thus making this declaration a libel on the Gospel as well as a palpable misrepresentation of the law of its Author, and of man's relations to both. It is only moderate language to call this assertion from the Confession of Faith, *a libel.* If there is a lie either in hell or out of hell, *this is a lie,* or God is an infinite tyrant. If reason be allowed to speak at all, it is impossible for her to say less or otherwise than thus. And has not God constituted the reason of man for the very purpose of taking cognizance of the rectitude of all his ways?

Let God be true though every man be proved a liar! In the present case, the remarkable fact that no man can appease his own conscience and satisfy himself that he is truly unable to keep the law, shows that *man* lies, not God.

2. A second excuse which sinners make is *want of time.*

Suppose I tell one of my sons – "Go, do this or that duty, on pain of being whipped to death." He replies, "Father, I can't possibly do it, for I have not time. I must be doing that other business which you told me to do; and besides, if I had nothing else to do, I could not possibly do this new business in the time you allow." Now if this statement be the truth, and I knew it when I gave him the command, then I am a tyrant. There is no evading this charge. My conduct toward my son is downright tyranny.

So if God really requires of you what you have not time to do, He is infinitely to blame. For He surely knows how little time you have, and it is undeniable that He enforces His requisitions with most terrific penalties. What! is God so reckless of justice, so regardless of the well-being of His creatures, that He can sport with red-hot thunderbolts, and hurl them, despite of justice and right, among His unfortunate creatures? *Never! Never!* This is not true; it is only the false assumption which the sinner makes when he pleads as his excuse, *that he has not time to do what God demands of him.*

Let me ask you, sinner, how much time will it take you to do the first great duty which God requires – namely, *give Him your heart?* How long will this take? How long need you be in making up your mind to serve and love God? Do you not know that this, when done, will be done in one moment of time? And how long need you be in persuading yourself to do it?

Your meaning may be this: Lord, it takes me so long to make up my mind to serve Thee, it seems as if I never should get time enough for this; even the whole of life seems almost too short for me to bring my mind to this unwelcome decision. Is this your meaning, sinner?

But let us look on all sides of the subject. Suppose I say to my son – "Do this now, my son"; and he replies, "I can't, Father, for I must do that other thing you told me to do." Does God do so? No. God only requires the duty of each moment in its time. This is all. He only asks us to use faithfully just all the power He has given us – nothing more. He only requires that we do the best we can. When He prescribes the amount of love which will please Him, He does not say – Thou shalt love the Lord thy God with the powers of an angel – with the burning heart of a seraph – no, but only "with all *thy heart*" – this is all. An infinitely ridiculous plea is this of the sinner's, that he cannot do as well as he can – cannot love God with all his own heart, and soul, and mind, and strength. Thou shalt do the best that thou art able to do, says God to the sinner. Ah, says the sinner, I am not able to do that. Oh, what stupid nonsense!

You charge that God is unreasonable. The truth is, God is the most reasonable of all beings. He asks only that we should use each moment for Him, in labor, or in rest, whichever is most for His glory. He only requires that with the time, talents, and strength which He has given us, we should do all we can to serve Him.

Says that mother—"How can I be religious? I have to take care of all my children." Indeed! and can't you get time to serve God? What does God require of you? That you should forsake and neglect your children? No, indeed; He asks you to take care of your children—good care of them; and *do it all for God.* He says to you—Those are *my* children; and He puts them into your hands, saying—Take care of them for Me, and I will give thee wages. And now will it require more time to take care of your children for God, than to take care of them for yourself? O, but you say, I cannot be religious, for I must be up in the morning and get my breakfast. And how much longer will it take you to get your breakfast ready to please God, than to do the same to please yourself? How much longer time must you have to do your duties religiously, than to do them selfishly?

What, then, do you mean by this plea? The fact is, all these excuses show that the excuser is mad—not insane, but *mad.* For what does God require so great that you should be unable to do it for want of time? Only this, that you should do all *for God.* Persons who make this plea seem to have entirely overlooked the real nature of religion, and of the requisitions that God makes of them. So it is with the plea of inability. The sinner says, "I am unable." Unable to do what? Just what you can do; for God never requires anything beyond this. Unless, therefore, you assume that God requires of you more than you can do, your plea is false, and even ridiculous. If, on the other hand, you do not assume this, then your plea, if true, would not show God to be unjust.

But I was saying that in this plea of having no time to be religious, men entirely overlook or pervert the true idea of religion. The farmer pleads—"I can't be religious; I can't serve God—I must sow my wheat." Well, sow your wheat; but do it *for the Lord.* O but you have *so much* to do! Then do it all for the Lord. Another can't be religious for he must get his lesson. Well, get your lesson, but get it *for the Lord,* and this will be religious. The man who should neglect to sow his wheat or neglect to get his lessons because he wants to be religious, is crazy. He perverts the plainest things in the worst way. If you are to be religious, you must be industrious. The farmer must sow his wheat, and the student must get his lesson. An idle man can no more be religious than the devil can be. This notion that men can't be religious, because they have some business to do, is the merest nonsense. It utterly overlooks the great truth that God never forbids our doing the appropriate business of life, but only requires that we shall do all for Himself. If God did require us to serve Him in such a way as would compel us to neglect the practical duties of life, it would be truly a hard case. But now the whole truth is, that He requires us to do precisely these duties, and do them all honestly and faithfully *for Him,* and in the best possible manner. Let the farmer take care of his farm, and see that he does it well, and above all, do it *for God.* It is God's farm, and the heart of every farmer is God's heart, therefore let the farm be tilled for God, and the heart be devoted to *Him alone.*

3. Men plead *a sinful nature for their excuse.* And pray, what is this sinful nature? Do you mean by it that every faculty and even the very essence of your constitution were poisoned and made sinful in Adam, and came down in this polluted state by inheritance to you? Do you mean that you were so born in sin that the substance of your being is all saturated with it, and so that all the faculties of your constitution are themselves *sin*? Do you believe this?

I admit if this were true, it would make out a hard case. A hard case indeed! Until the laws of my reason are changed, it would compel me to speak out openly and say—Lord, this is a hard case, that Thou shouldst make my nature itself a sinner, and then charge the guilt of its sin upon me! I could not help saying this; the deep echoings of my inner being would proclaim it without ceasing, and the breaking of ten thousand thunderbolts over my head would not deter me from thinking and saying so. The reason God has given me would forever affirm it.

But the dogma is an utter absurdity. For, pray, what *is sin*? God answers—"transgression of law." And now you hold that your nature is itself a breach of the law of God—nay, that it has always been a breach of God's law, from Adam to the day of your birth; you hold that the current of this sin came down in the veins and blood of your race— and *who made it so*? Who created the veins and blood of man? From whose hand sprang this physical constitution and this mental constitution? Was man his own creator? Did sin do a part of the work in creating your physical and your mental constitution? Do you believe any such thing? No; you ascribe your nature and its original faculties to God, and upon Him, therefore, you charge the guilty authorship of your "sinful nature."

But how strange a thing is this! If man is in fault for his sinful nature, why not condemn man for having blue or black eyes? The fact is, sin never can consist in having a nature, nor in what nature *is;* but only and alone in the bad use which we make of our nature. This is all. Our Maker will never find fault with us for what He has Himself done or made; certainly not. He will not condemn us, if we will only make a right use of our powers—of our intellect, our sensibility, and our will. He never holds us responsible for our original nature. If you will observe, you will find that God has given no law prescribing what sort of nature and constitutional powers we should have. He has given no law on these points, the transgression of which, if given,

might somewhat resemble the definition of sin. But now since there is
no law about nature, nature cannot be a transgression. . . .

Now I do not mean to imply that the men who have held this dogma
have intelligently insulted God with it. I do not imply that they have
been aware of the impious and even blasphemous bearings of this
dogma upon Jehovah—I am happy to think that some at least have
done all this mischief ignorantly. But the blunder and the mischief
have been none the less for the honest ignorance in which they were
done.

4. Sinners in self-excuse, say they *are willing to be Christians.*
They are willing, they say, to be sanctified. O yes, they are very willing; but there is some great difficulty lying further back or something
else—perhaps they do not know just where—but it is *somewhere,* and
it will not let them become Christians. . . .

This plea is utterly false, for no sinner is willing to be any better than
he actually is. If the will is right, all is right; and universally the state
of the will is the measure of one's moral character. Those men, therefore, who plead that they are willing to be Christians while yet they
remain in their sins, talk mere nonsense.

5. *Sinners say they are waiting God's time.* A lady in Philadelphia
had been in great distress of mind for many years. On calling to see
her, I asked—"What does God require of you? What is your case?"
"Oh," said she, "God waited on me a long time before I began to seek
Him at all, and now I must wait for Him as long as He did for me. So
my minister tells me. You see, therefore, that I am waiting in great
distress for God to receive me."

Now what is the real meaning of this? It comes to this; God urges
me to duty, but is not ready for me to do it; He tells me to come to the
Gospel feast, and I am ready; but He is not ready to let me in.

Now does not this throw all the blame upon God? Could anything do
so more completely than this does? The sinner says—"I am ready, and
willing, and waiting; but God is not yet ready for me to stop sinning.
His hour has not yet come."

When I first began to preach, I found this notion almost universal.
Often after pressing men to duty, I have been accosted—"What, you
throw all the blame upon the sinner!" "Yes, indeed I do," would be my
reply. An old lady once met me after preaching, and broke out, "What!
you set men to getting religion themselves! You tell them to repent
themselves! You don't mean *so,* do you?" "Indeed, I *do,*" said I. She
had been teaching for many years that the sinner's chief duty is to
await God's time.

6. Sinners plead in excuse, that *their circumstances are very peculiar.* I know my duty well enough, but my circumstances are so
peculiar. And does not God understand your circumstances? Nay, has
not His providence been concerned in making them what they are?

If so, then you are throwing blame upon God. You say—"O Lord, Thou art a hard Master, for Thou hast never made any allowance for my circumstances."

But how much, sinner, do you really mean in making this plea? Do you mean that your circumstances are so peculiar, that God ought to excuse you from becoming religious, at least for the present? If you do not mean as much as this, why do you make your circumstances your excuse at all? If you do mean this, then you are just as much mistaken as you can be. For God requires you, despite of your circumstances, to abandon your sin. If, now, your circumstances are so peculiar that you cannot serve God in them, you must abandon them or lose your soul. If they are such as admit of your serving God in them, then do so at once.

But you say—"I can't get out of my circumstances." I reply, You can—you can get out of the wickedness of them; for if it is necessary in order to serve God, you can change them; and if not, you can repent and serve God in them.

7. The sinner's next excuse is, that *his temperament is peculiar.* "Oh," he says, "I am very nervous; or my temperament is very sluggish; I seem to have no sensibility." Now what does God require? Does He require of you another or a different sensibility from your own? Or does He require only that you should use what you have according to the law of love?

But such is the style of a multitude of excuses. One has too little excitement; another, too much; so neither can possibly repent and serve God! A woman came to me, and pleaded that she was naturally too excitable, and dared not trust herself; and therefore could not repent. Another has the opposite trouble—too sluggish—scarce ever sheds a tear—and therefore could make nothing out of religion if he should try. But does God require you to shed more tears than you are naturally able to shed? Or does He only require that you should serve Him? Certainly this is all. Serve Him with the very powers He has given you. Let your nerves be ever so excitable, come and lay those quivering sensibilities over into the hands of God—pour out that sensibility into the heart of God!—this is all that He requires. I know how to sympathize with that woman, for I know much about a burning sensibility; but does God require feeling and excitement? Or only a perfect consecration of all our powers to Himself?

8. But, says another, my health is so poor that I can't go to meeting, and therefore can't be religious.

Well, what does God require? Does He require that you should go to all the meetings, by evening or by day, whether you have the requisite health for it or not? Infinitely far from it. If you are not able to go to meeting, yet you can give God your heart. If you cannot go in bad weather, be assured that God is infinitely the most reasonable being that ever existed. He makes all due allowance for every circumstance. Does He not know all your weakness? Indeed He does. And do you suppose that He comes into your sickroom and denounces you for not being able to go to meeting, or for not attempting when unable, and for not doing all in your sickness that you might do in health? No, not He; but He comes into your sickroom *as a Father.* He comes to pour out the deepest compassions of His heart in pity and in love; and why should you not respond to His loving-kindness? He comes to you and says — "Give me your heart, my child." And now you reply — "I have no heart." Then He has nothing to ask of you — *He thought you had;* and thought, too, that He had done enough to draw your heart in love and gratitude to Himself. He asks — "What can you find in all my dealings with you that is grievous? If nothing, why do you bring forward pleas in excuse for sin that accuse and condemn God?"

9. Another excuse is in this form — *"My heart is so hard, that I cannot feel."* This is very common, both among professors and non-professors. In reality it is only another form of the plea of inability. In fact, all the sinner's excuses amount only to this — *"I am unable"* — "I can't do what God requires." If the plea of a hard heart is any excuse at all, it must be on the ground of real inability.

But what *is* hardness of heart? Do you mean that you have so great apathy of the sensibility that you cannot get up any emotion? Or, do you mean that you have no power to will or to act right? Now on this point, it should be considered that the emotions are altogether involuntary. They go and come according to circumstances, and therefore are never required by the law of God, and are not, properly speaking, either religion itself, or any part of it. Hence, if by a hard heart you mean a dull sensibility, you mean what has no concern with the subject. God asks you to yield your will, and consecrate your affections to Himself, and He asks this, whether you have any feeling or not.

Real hardness of heart, in the Bible use of the phrase, means *stubbornness of will.* So in the child, a hard heart means a will set in fixed stubbornness against doing its parent's bidding. The child may have in connection with this, either much or little emotion. His sensibilities may be acute and thoroughly aroused, or they may be dormant; and yet the stubborn will may be there in either case.

Now the hardness of heart of which God complains in the sinner is precisely of this sort. The sinner cleaves to his self-indulgence, and will not relinquish it, and then complains of hardness of heart. What would you think of a child, who, when required to do a most reasonable thing, should say — "My heart is so hard, I can't yield." "O," he says, "my will is so set to have my own way that I cannot possibly yield to my father's authority."

This complaint is extremely common. Many a sinner makes it, who has been often warned, often prayed with and wept over, who has been the subject of many convictions. And does he really mean by this plea that he finds his will so obstinate that he cannot make up his mind to yield to God's claims? Does he mean this, and does he intend really to publish his own shame? Suppose you go to the devils in hell, and press on them the claims of God, and they should reply—"O, my heart is so hard, I can't,"—what would be their meaning? Only this: I am so obstinate—my will is so set in sin that I cannot for a moment indulge the thought of repentance. This would be their meaning, and if the sinner tells the truth of himself, and uses language correctly, he must mean the same. But oh, how does he add insult to injury by this declaration! Suppose a child should plead this—I cannot find it in my heart to love my father and my mother; my heart is so hard towards them; I never can love them; I can feel pleasure only in abusing them, and trampling down their authority. *What a plea is this?* Does not this heap insult upon wrong? Or suppose a murderer arraigned before the court, and permitted before his sentence to speak, if he had ought to say why sentence should not be passed—suppose he should rise and say—"May it please the court, my heart for a long time has been as hard as a millstone. I have murdered so many men, and have been in the practice so long, that I can kill a man without the least compunction of conscience. Indeed, I have such an insatiable thirst for blood that I cannot help murdering whenever I have a good opportunity. In fact, my heart is so hard that I find I like this employment full as well as any other."

Well, how long will the court listen to such a plea? "Hold there! hold!" the judge would cry—"you infamous villain, we can hear no more such pleas! Here, sheriff, bring in a gallows, and hang the man within these very walls of justice, for I will not leave the bench until I see him dead! He will murder us all here in this house if he can!"

Now what shall we think of the sinner who says the same thing? O God, he says, my heart is so hard I never can love Thee. I hate Thee so sincerely I never can make up my mind to yield this heart to Thee in love and willing submission!

Sinners, how many of you (in this house) have made this plea—"My heart is so hard, I can't repent; I can't love and serve God!" Go, write it down; publish it to the universe—make your boast of being so hard-hearted that no claims of God can ever move you. Methinks if you were to make such a plea, you would not be half through before the whole universe would hiss you from their presence and chase you from the face of these heavens till you would cry out for some rocks or mountains to hide you from their scathing rebukes! Their voice of indignation would rise up and ring along the arch of heaven like the roar of ten thousand tornadoes, and whelm you with unutterable confusion and shame! What, do you insult and abuse the Great Jehovah? Oh! do you condemn that very God who has watched over you in unspeakable love—fanned you with His gentle zephyrs in your sickness—feasted you at His own table, and you would not thank Him, or even notice His providing hand? And then when the sympathy of your Christian friends has pressed you with entreaties to repent, and they have made you a special subject of their prayers—when angels have wept over you, and unseen spirits have lifted their warning voices in your pathway to hell—you turn up your face of brass towards Jehovah and tell Him your heart is so hard you can't repent, and don't care whether you ever do or not! You seize a spear and plunge it into the heart of the crucified One, and then cry out—"I can't be sorry, not I; my heart is hard as a stone! I don't care, and I will not repent!" What a wretch you are, sinner, if this is your plea.

But what does your plea amount to? Only this—that your heart is fully set to do evil. The sacred writer has revealed your case most clearly—"Because vengeance against an evil work is not executed speedily, therefore the heart of the sons of men *is fully set* in them to do evil." You stand before the Lord just in this daring, blasphemous attitude—fully set in your heart *to do evil.*

10. Another form of the same plea is, *My heart is so wicked I can't.* Some do not hesitate to avow this wickedness of heart. What do they mean by it? Do they mean that they are so hardened in sin, and so desperately wicked, that they will not bow? This is the only proper sense of their language, and this is the precise truth.

Since you bring this forward, sinner, as your excuse, your object must be to charge this wickedness of heart upon God. Covertly, perhaps, but really, you imply that God is concerned in creating that wicked heart! This is it, and this is the whole of it. You would feel no interest in the excuse, and it would never escape your lips but for this tacit implication that God is in fault for your wicked heart. This is only the plea of inability, coupled with its twin sister, original sin, coming down in the created blood and veins of the race, under the Creator's responsibility.

11. Another kindred plea is—*My heart is so deceitful.* Suppose a man should make this excuse for deceiving his neighbor—"I can't help cheating you. I can't help lying to you and abusing you; my heart is so deceitful!" Would any man in his senses ever suppose that this could be an apology or excuse for doing wrong? Never. Of course, unless the sinner means in this plea to set forth his own guilt and condemn himself, he must intend it as some sort of justification; and, if so, he must, in just so far, cast the blame upon God. And this is usually his intention. He does not mean sincerely to confess his own guilt; no, he charges the guilt of his deceitful heart upon God.

12. Another excuses himself by the plea, *I have tried to become a Christian.* I have done all I can do; I have tried often, earnestly, and long.

You have tried then, you say, to be a Christian; what is being a Christian? Giving your heart to God. And what is giving your heart to God? Devoting your voluntary powers to Him; ceasing to live for yourself and living for God. This is being a Christian—the state you profess to have been trying to attain.

No excuse is more common than this. And what is legitimately implied in this trying to be a Christian? A willingness to do your duty is always implied; that the heart, that is, the *will* is *right* already; and the trying refers only to the outward efforts—the executive acts. For there is no sense whatever in a man's saying that he is trying to do what he has no intention or will to do. The very statement implies that his will is not only in favor, but is thoroughly committed and really in earnest to attain the end chosen.

Consequently, if a man tries to be a Christian his heart is obedient to God, and his trying must respect his outward action. These are so connected with the will that they follow by a law of necessity unless the connection is broken: and, when this takes place, no sin attends our failure to secure the outward act. God does not hold us responsible.

Hence, the sinner ought to mean by this plea—"I have obeyed God a long time"—I have had a right heart—and I have tried sincerely to secure such external action as comports with Christian character.

Now, if this be true, you have done your duty. But do you mean to affirm all this? No, you say. Then what *do* you mean?

Suppose I should say to my son, Do this; do it, my son; why have you not done it? O, he says, "father, I have *tried*"; but he does not mean that he has ever *intended* to do it—that he has ever made up his mind to *obey* me; he only means, "I have been willing to try—I made up my mind to try to be willing"; that is all! "O," he says, I have brought myself to be willing to try to will to do it.

So you say—I have tried to get religion. And what *is* religion that you could not get it? How did you fail? You have been trying, probably, in this way. God has said, "Give me thy heart," and you turned round and asked God to do it Himself, or perhaps you simply waited for Him to do it. He commanded you to repent, and you have tried to get Him to repent for you. He said, Believe the Gospel, and you have only been thinking of getting Him to believe for you. No wonder you have tried for a long time in vain. How could it be otherwise? You have not been trying to do what God commanded you to do, but to induce God to change His system of moral government and put Himself in your place to do Himself the duty He enjoins upon you. What a miserable perversion is this.

Now, as to this whole plea of having tried to be a Christian, what is the use of it? You will easily see its use when you realize duly:

(1.) That it is utterly false when understood as you intend it.

(2.) That it is a foul implication of the character of God.

You say—Lord, I know I can't—I have tried all I can, and I know I cannot become a Christian. I am willing to get religion, but I cannot make it out.

Who, then, is to blame? Not yourself, according to your statement of your case. Where, then, is the blame? Let me ask—what would be said in the distant regions of the universe if you were believed there, when you say, I have tried with all my heart to love and serve God, but I can't?

But they never can believe such a libel on their own infinite Father! Of course they will pronounce your doom as you deserve.

13. Another excuses himself by the plea—*it will do no good to try.* And what do you mean by this? Do you mean that God will not pay well for service done Him? Or do you mean that He will not forgive you if you do repent? Do you think (as some do) that you have sinned away your day of grace?

Well, suppose you have, is this any reason why you should go on in sin? Do you not believe that God is good? O, yes. And that He will forgive you if the good of the universe admits? Most certainly. Then is the impossibility of His forgiving you any reason why you should go on in sin forever, and forever rage against a God of infinite goodness? You believe Him to be compassionate and forgiving; then should you not say, I will at least stop sinning against *such a God!* Why not say with the man who dreamed that he was just going to hell, and as he was parting with his brother—going, as his dream had it, to heaven, he said—"I am going down to hell, but I want you to tell God from me that I am greatly obliged to Him for ten thousand mercies which I never deserved; He has never done me the least injustice; give Him my thanks for all the unmerited good He has done me." At this point he awoke, and found himself bathed in tears of repentance and gratitude to his Father in heaven. O, if men would only act as reasonably as that man dreamed, it would be noble—it would be *right.* If, when they suppose themselves to have sinned away the day of grace, they would say, "I know God is good—I will at least send Him my thanks—He has done me no injustice." If they would take this course they might have at least the satisfaction of feeling that it is a reasonable and fit one in their circumstances. Sinner, will you do this?

14. Another, closely pressed, says, "*I have offered to give my heart to Christ, but He won't receive me. I have no evidence that He receives me or ever will.*" In the last inquiry meeting, a young woman told me she had offered to give her heart to the Lord, but He would not receive her. This was charging the lie directly upon Christ, for He has said—"Him that cometh to Me, I will in no wise cast out." You say, I came and offered myself and He would not receive me. Jesus Christ says, "Behold I stand at the door and knock; if *any* man"—not if some particular, some favored one—but if *any man* "hear my voice

and open the door, I will come in to him." And yet when you offered Him your heart, did He spurn you away? Did He say—*Away*, sinner, *begone*? No, sinner, He never did it, *never*. He has said He never would do it. His own words are, "Him that cometh unto Me, *I will in no wise cast out*." "He that seeketh, findeth: to him that knocketh it shall be opened." But you say, I have sought and I did not find. Do you mean to make out that Jesus Christ is a liar? Have you charged this upon Him to His very face? Do you make your solemn affirmation— "Lord, I did seek—I laid myself at Thy gate and knocked—but all in vain"? And do you mean to bring this excuse of yours as a solemn charge of falsehood against Jesus Christ and against God? This will be a serious business with you before it is done with.

15. But another says—*"There is no salvation for me."* Do you mean that Christ has made no atonement for you? But he says, He tasted death for every man. It is declared that God so loved the world that He gave His only begotten Son that *whosoever* believeth on Him shall have eternal life. And now do you affirm that there is no salvation provided and possible for you? Are you mourning all your way down to hell because you cannot possibly have salvation? When the cup of salvation is placed to your lips, do you dash it away, saying, That cannot be for me? And do you *know* this? Can you prove it even against the word of God Himself? Stand forth, then, if there be such a sinner on this footstool of God—speak it out, if you have such a charge against God, and if you can prove it true. Ah, is there no hope? none at all? Oh, the difficulty is not that there is no salvation provided for and offered to you, but that there is no heart for it. "Wherefore is there a price put into the hands of a fool to get wisdom, seeing he hath no heart for it?"

16. But perhaps you say in excuse—*"I cannot change my own heart."* Cannot? Suppose Adam had made this excuse when God called him to repent after his first sin. "Make you a new heart and a right spirit," said the Lord to him. "I cannot change my own heart myself," replies Adam. Indeed, responds his Maker, how long is it since you changed your heart yourself? You changed it a few hours ago from holiness to sin, and will you tell your Creator that you can't change it from sin to holiness?

The sinner should consider that the change of heart is a voluntary thing. You must do it for yourself or it is never done. True, there is a sense in which God changes the heart, but it is only this: God influences the sinner to change, and then the sinner does it. The change is the sinner's own voluntary act.

17. You say, again, *you can't change your heart without more conviction.* Do you mean by this that you have not knowledge enough of your duty and your sin? You cannot say this. You do know your sin and your duty. You know you ought to consecrate yourself to God. What, then, do you mean? Can't you do that which you know you ought to do?

Ah, there is the old lie — that shameless refuge of lies — that same foul dogma of *inability*. What is implied in this new form of it? This — that God is not willing to convict you enough to make it possible for you to repent. There is a work and a responsibility for God, and He will not do His work — will not bear His responsibility. Hence, you, alas, have no alternative but to go down to hell. All because God will not do His part towards your salvation. *Do you really believe that, sinner?*

18. Again, you say in excuse, *that you must first have more of the Spirit*. And yet you resist the Spirit every day. God offers you His Spirit, nay, more, God *bestows* His spirit; but you resist it. What, then, do you mean when you pretend to want more of the Spirit's influence?

The truth is, you do not want it — you only want to make it appear that God does not do His part to help you repent, and that as you can't repent without His help, therefore the blame of your impenitence rests on God. It is only another refuge of lies — another form of the old slander upon God — He has made me unable and won't help me out of my inability.

19. The sinner also excuses himself by saying — *God must change my heart*. But in the sense in which God requires you to do it, He cannot do it Himself. God is said to change the heart only in the sense of persuading you to do it. As in man's change of politics, one might say — "Such a man changed my heart — he brought me over," which, however, by no means implies that you did not change your own mind. The plain meaning is that he persuaded and you yielded. . . .

So they teach — filling the mouth of the sinner with excuses and making his heart like an adamant against the real claims of God upon his conscience.

20. The sinner pleads, again, *"I can't live a Christian life if I were to become a Christian. It is unreasonable for me to expect to succeed where I see so many fail."* I recollect the case of a man who said, "It is of no use for me to repent and be a Christian, for it is altogether irrational for me to expect to do better than others have done before me." So sinners who make this excuse come forward very modestly and tell God — "I am very humble; Thou seest, Lord, that I have a very low opinion of myself; I am so zealous of Thine honor, and so afraid that I shall bring disgrace upon Thy cause; it does not seem at all best for me to think of becoming a Christian, I have such a horror of dishonoring Thy name."

Yes; and what then? "Therefore, I will sin on and trample the blessed Gospel under my feet. I will persecute Thee, O my God, and make war on Thy cause, for it is better by far not to profess religion than to profess and then disgrace my profession." What logic! Fair specimen of the absurdity of the sinner's excuses.

This excuse assumes that there is not grace enough provided and offered to sustain the soul in a Christian life. The doctrine is, that it is irrational to expect that we can, by any grace received in this life, perfectly obey the law of God. There is not grace and help enough afforded by God! And this is taught as *Bible theology!* Away with such teaching to the nether pit whence it came!

What! is God so weak that He can't hold up the soul that casts itself on Him? Or is He so parsimonious in bestowing His gracious aid that it must be expected always to fall short of meeting the wants of His dependent and depending child? So you seem to suppose. So hard to persuade the Lord to give you a particle of grace! Can't get grace enough to live a Christian life with honor! What is this but charging God of withholding sufficient grace? . . .

So you belie the word of God, and make up a miserably slim and guilty apology for your impenitence.

21. Another excuse claims that *this is a very dark, mysterious subject.* This matter of faith and regeneration — I can't understand it.

Sinner, did you ever meet the Lord with this objection, and say, "Lord, Thou hast required me to do things which I can't understand"? You know that you can understand well enough that you are a sinner — that Christ died for you — that you must believe on Him and break off your sins by repentance. All this is so plain that "the wayfaring man, though a fool, need not err therein." Your plea, therefore, is as false as it is foul. It is nothing better than a base libel on God!

22. But you say, *"I can't believe."* You mean (do you?) that you can't believe a God of infinite veracity as you can believe a fellow man? Would you imply that God asks you to believe things that are really incredible — things so revolting to reason that you cannot admit them on any testimony that even God Himself can adduce?

And do you expect to make out this case against God? Do you even believe the first point in it yourself?

But you urge again that you can't *realize these things.* You know these things to be true, but you can't realize — you can't realize that the Bible is true — that God does offer to forgive — that salvation is actually provided and placed within your reach. What help can there be for a case like yours? What can make these truths more certain? But on your own showing, you do not want more evidence. Why not, then, act upon the known truth? What more can you ask?

Do you ever carry your case before God and say, "O Lord, Thou sayest that Christ died for me, but I can't realize that it is so; and, therefore, Lord, I can't possibly embrace Him as my Saviour"? Would this be a rational excuse?

But you also plead that *you can't repent.* You can't be sorry you have abused God. You can't make up your mind now to break off from all sin. If this be really so, then you cannot make up your mind to obey God, and you may as well make up your mind to *go to hell!* There is no alternative!

But at any rate, you can't become a Christian *now.* You mean to be converted some time, but you can't make up your mind to it *now.* Well,

God requires it now, and of course you must yield or abide the consequences.

But do you say, You can't now? Then God is very much to blame for asking it. If, however, the truth be that you can, then the lie is on your side, and it is a most infamous and abusive lie against your Maker.

III. *All excuses for sin add insult to injury.*

1. A plea that reflects injuriously upon the court or the lawgiver is an aggravation of the original crime. It is always so regarded in all tribunals. It must be preeminently so between the sinner and his infinite Lawgiver and Judge.

2. The same is true of any plea made in self-justification. If it be false, it is considered an aggravation of the crime charged. This is a case which sometimes happens, and whenever it does it is deemed to add fresh insult and wrong. For a criminal to come and spread out his lie upon the records of the court — to declare what he knows to be false; nothing can prejudice his case so fearfully. . . .

3. It is truly abominable for the sinner to abuse God and then excuse himself for it. Ah, this is only the old way of the guilty. Adam and Eve in the garden fled and hid themselves when they heard the voice of the Lord approaching. And what had they done? The Lord calls them out and begins to search them: "Adam, what hast thou done? Hast thou eaten of the forbidden tree in the centre of the garden?" Adam quailed, but fled to an excuse: "The woman whom *Thou gavest to be with me,* she gave me of the tree and I did eat." God, he says, gave him his tempter. God, according to his excuse, had been chiefly to blame in the transaction.

Next He turns to the woman: "What is that thou hast done?" She, too, has an excuse: "The serpent beguiled me and I did eat." Ah, this perpetual shuffling the blame back upon God! It has been kept up through the long line of Adam's imitators down to this day. For six thousand years God has been hearing it, and still the world is spared, and the vengeance of God has not yet burst forth to smite all His guilty calumniators to hell! O! what patience in God! And who have ever abused His patience and insulted Him by their excuses more than sinners in this house?

REMARKS

1. No sinner under the light of the Gospel lives a single hour in sin without some excuse, either tacit or avowed, by which he justifies himself. It seems to be a law of man's intelligent nature that when accused of wrong, either by his conscience or by any other agent, he must either confess or justify. The latter is the course taken by all impenitent sinners. Hence, the reason why they have so much occasion for excuses, and why they find it convenient to have so great a

variety. It is remarkable with what facility they fly from one to another, as if these refuges of lies might make up in number what they lack in strength. Conscious that not one of all the multitude is valid in point of truth and right, they yet, when pressed on one, fly to another, and when driven from all in succession they are ready to come back and fight the same ground over again. It is so hard to abandon all excuses and admit the humbling truth that they themselves are all wrong and God all right.

Hence, it becomes the great business of a Gospel minister to search out and expose the sinner's excuses; to go all round and round, and, if possible, demolish the sinner's refuges of lies, and lay his heart open to the shafts of truth.

2. *Excuses render repentance impossible.* For excuses are justifications; and who does not know that justification is the very opposite of confession and repentance? To seek after and embrace excuses, therefore, is to place one's self at the farthest possible remove from repentance.

Of course the self-excusing sinner makes it impossible for God to forgive him. He places the Deity in such a position toward himself, and I might say, places himself in such an attitude toward the government of God, that his forgiveness would be ruin to the very throne of God. What would heaven say, and hell too, and earth besides, if God were to forgive a sinner while he, by his excuses, is justifying himself and condemning his Maker?

3. *Sinners should lay all their excuses at once before God.* Surely this is most reasonable. Why not? If a man owed me, and supposed he had a reasonable excuse for not paying the debt, he should come to me and let me understand the whole case. Perhaps he will satisfy me that his views are right.

Now, sinner, have you ever done so in regard to God? Have you ever brought up one excuse before the Lord, saying, "Thou requirest me to be holy, but I can't be; Lord, I have a good excuse for not obeying Thee"? No, sinner; you are not in the habit of doing this—probably you have not done it the first time yet in all your life. In fact, you have no particular encouragement to carry your excuses before God, for you have not one yet that you yourself believe to be good for anything except to answer the purpose of a refuge of lies. Your excuses won't stand the ordeal of your own reason and conscience How then can you hope they will stand before the searching eye of Jehovah? The fact that you never come with your excuses to God shows that you have no confidence in them.

4. *What infinite madness to rest on excuses which you dare not bring before God now!* How can you stand before God in the judgment, if your excuses are so mean that you cannot seriously think of bringing one of them before God in this world? O, sinner, that coming

day will be far more searching and awful than anything you have seen yet. See that dense mass of sinners drawn up before the great white throne—far as the eye can sweep they come surging up—a countless throng; and now they stand, and the awful trump of God summons them forward to bring forth their excuses for sin.

Ho, sinners—any one of you, all—what have you to say why sentence should not be passed on you? Where are all those excuses you were once so free and bold to make? Where are they all? Why don't you make them now? *Hark!* God waits; He listens; there is silence in heaven—all through the congregated throng—for half an hour—an awful silence—that may be felt; but not a word—not a moving lip among the gathered myriads of sinners there; and now the great and dreadful Judge arises and lets loose His thunders. O, see the waves of dire damnation roll over those ocean masses of self-condemned sinners! Did you ever see the judge rise from his bench in court to pass sentence of death on a criminal? There, see, the poor man reels—he falls prostrate —there is no longer any strength in him, for death is on him and his last hope has perished!

O, sinner, when that sentence from the dread throne shall fall on thee! Your excuses are as millstones around your neck as you plunge along down the sides of the pit to the nethermost hell!

5. *Sinners don't need their excuses.* God does not ask for even one. He does not require you to justify yourself—not at all. If you needed them for your salvation I could sympathize with you, and certainly would help you all I could. But you don't need them. Your salvation does not turn on your successful self-vindication. You need not rack your brain for excuses. Better say, I don't want them—don't deserve them—have not one that is worth a straw. Better say, "I am wicked. God knows that's the truth, and it were vain for me to attempt to conceal it. *I am wicked,* and if I ever live, it must be on simple mercy!"

I can recollect very well the year I lived on excuses, and how long it was before I gave them up. I had never heard a minister preach on the subject. I found, however, by my experience, that my excuses and lies were the obstacles in the way of my conversion. As soon as I let these go utterly, I found the gate of mercy wide open. And so, sinner, would you.

6. *Sinners ought to be ashamed of their excuses, and repent of them.* Perhaps you have not always seen this as plainly as you may now. With the light now before you, it becomes you to beware. See to it that you never make another excuse, unless you intend to abuse God in the most horrible manner. Nothing can be a more grievous abomination in the sight of God than excuses made by a sinner who knows they are utterly false and blasphemous. O, you ought to repent of the insult you have already offered to God—and *now,* too, lest you find yourself thrust away from the gate of mercy.

7. *You admit your obligation, and of course are stopped from making excuses.* For if you have any good excuse, you are not under obligation. If any one of you has a good excuse for disobeying God, you are no longer under obligation to obey. But since you are compelled to admit obligation, you are also compelled to relinquish excuses.

8. Inasmuch as you do and must admit your obligation, then if you still plead excuses you insult God to His face. You insult Him by charging Him with infinite tyranny.

Now what use do you calculate to make of this sermon? Are you ready to say, "I will henceforth desist from all my excuses, now and forever; and God shall have my whole heart"? What do you say? Will you set about to hunt up some new excuse? Do you at least say, "Let me go home first—don't press me to yield to God here on the spot—let me go home and then I will"? Do you say this? And are you aware how tender is this moment—how critical this passing hour? Remember it is not I who press this claim upon you—but it is God. God Himself commands you to repent today—*this hour.* You know your duty—you know what religion is—what it is to give God your heart. And now I come to the final question—*Will you do it?* Will you abandon all your excuses, and fall, a self-condemned sinner, before a God of love, and yield to Him yourself—your heart, and your whole being, henceforth and forever? *Will you come?*

HOW TO PROMOTE A REVIVAL

"Break up your fallow ground; for it is time to seek the Lord,
till he come and rain righteousness upon you" (Hosea 10:12).

THE JEWS were a nation of farmers, and it is therefore a common thing in the Scriptures to refer for illustrations to their occupation, and to the scenes with which farmers and shepherds are familiar. The prophet Hosea addresses them as a nation of backsliders, and reproves them for their idolatry, and threatens them with the judgments of

Reprinted from Charles G. Finney, *Lectures on Revivals of Religion*, rev. ed. (New York: Fleming H. Revell Co., 1888), pp. 35–47.

God. I have showed you in my first lecture what a revival is not—what it is—and the agencies to be employed in promoting it; and in my second, when it is needed—its importance—and when it may be expected. My design in this lecture is to show,

How A Revival Is to Be Promoted

A revival consists of two parts; as it respects the church, and as it respects the ungodly. I shall speak tonight of a revival in the church. Fallow ground is ground which has once been tilled, but which now lies waste, and needs to be broken up and mellowed, before it is suited to receive grain. I shall show, as it respects a revival in the church,
1. What it is to break up the fallow ground, in the sense of the text.
2. How it is to be performed.

I. What is it to break up the fallow ground?

To break up the fallow ground, is to *break up your hearts*—to prepare your minds to bring forth fruit unto God. The mind of man is often compared in the Bible to ground, and the word of God to seed sown in it, and the fruit represents the actions and affections of those who receive it. To break up the fallow ground, therefore, is to bring the mind into such a state, that it is fitted to receive the word of God. Sometimes your hearts get matted down hard and dry, and all run to waste, till there is no such thing as getting fruit from them till they are all broken up, and mellowed down, and fitted to receive the word of God. It is this softening of the heart, so as to make it feel the truth, which the prophet calls breaking up your fallow ground.

II. How is the fallow ground to be broken up?

1. *It is not by any direct efforts to feel.* People run into a mistake on this subject, from not making the laws of mind the object of thought. There are great errors on the subject of the laws which govern the mind. People talk about religious feeling, as if they thought they could, by direct effort, call forth religious affection. But this is not the way the mind acts. No man can make himself feel in this way, merely by *trying* to feel. The feelings of the mind are not *directly* under our control. We cannot by willing, or by direct volition, call forth religious feelings. We might as well think to call spirits up from the deep. They are purely involuntary states of mind. They naturally and necessarily exist in the mind under certain circumstances calculated to excite them. But they can be controlled *indirectly.* Otherwise there would be no moral character in our feelings, if there were not a way to control them. We cannot say, "Now I will feel so and so towards such an object." But we can command our *attention* to it, and look at it in-

tently, till the involuntary affections arise. Let a man who is away from his family, bring them up before his mind, and will he not feel? But it is not by saying to himself, "Now I will feel deeply for my family." A man can direct his attention to any object, about which he ought to feel and wishes to feel, and in that way he will call into existence the proper emotions. Let a man call up his enemy before his mind, and his feelings of enmity will rise. So if a man thinks of God, and fastens his mind on any parts of God's character, he will feel—emotions will come up, by the very laws of mind. If he is a friend of God, let him contemplate God as a gracious and holy being, and he will have emotions of friendship kindled up in his mind. If he is an enemy of God, only let him get the true character of God before his mind, and look at it, and fasten his attention on it, and his enmity will rise against God, or he will break down and give his heart to God.

If you wish to break up the fallow ground of your hearts, and make your minds feel on the subject of religion, you must go to work just as you would to feel on any other subject. Instead of keeping your thoughts on everything else, and then imagine that by going to a few meetings you will get your feelings enlisted, go the common sense way to work, as you would on any other subject. It is just as easy to make your minds feel on the subject of religion as it is on any other subject. God has put these states of mind under your control. If people were as unphilosophical about moving their limbs, as they are about regulating their emotions, you would never have got here to meeting tonight.

If you mean to break the fallow ground of your hearts, you must begin by looking at your hearts—examine and note the state of your minds, and see where you are. Many never seem to think about this. They pay no attention to their own hearts, and never know whether they are doing well in religion or not—whether they are gaining ground or going back—whether they are fruitful, or lying waste like the fallow ground. Now you must draw off your attention from other things, and look into this. Make a business of it. Do not be in a hurry. Examine thoroughly the state of your hearts, and see where you are— whether you are walking with God every day, or walking with the devil — whether you are serving God or serving the devil most—whether you are under the dominion of the prince of darkness, or of the Lord Jesus Christ.

To do all this, you must set yourselves at work to consider your sins. You must examine yourselves. And by this I do not mean, that you must stop and look directly within to see what is the present state of your feelings. That is the very way to put a stop to all feeling. This is just as absurd as it would be for a man to shut his eyes on the lamp, and try to turn his eyes inward to find out whether there was any image painted on the retina. The man complains that he does not see anything! And why? Because he has turned his eyes away from the objects of sight. The truth is, our moral feelings are as much an object of consciousness as our sensations. And the way to excite them is to go on acting, and employing our minds. Then we can tell our moral feelings by consciousness, just as I could tell my natural feelings by consciousness, if I should put my hand in the fire.

Self-examination consists in looking at your lives, in considering your actions, in calling up the past, and learning its true character. Look back over your past history. Take up your individual sins one by one, and look at them. I do not mean that you should just cast a glance at your past life, and see that it has been full of sins, and then go to God and make a sort of general confession, and ask for pardon. That is not the way. You must take them up one by one. It will be a good thing to take a pen and paper, as you go over them, and write them down as they occur to you. Go over them as carefully as a merchant goes over his books; and as often as a sin comes before your memory, add it to the list. General confessions of sin will never do. Your sins were commited *one by one;* and as far as you can come at them, they ought to be reviewed and repented of one by one. Now begin; and take up first what are commonly, but *improperly,* called your

SINS OF OMISSION

1. *Ingratitude.* Take this sin, for instance, and write down under it all the instances you can remember, wherein you have received favors from God, for which you have never exercised gratitude. How many cases can you remember? Some remarkable providence, some wonderful turn of events, that saved you from ruin. Set down the instances of God's goodness to you when you were in sin, before your conversion. Then the mercy of God in the circumstances of your conversion, for which you have never been half thankful enough. The numerous mercies you have received since. How long the catalogue of instances, where your ingratitude is so black that you are forced to hide your face in confusion! Now go on your knees, and confess them one by one to God, and ask forgiveness. The very act of confession, by the laws of suggestion, will bring up others to your memory. Put down these. Go over these three or four times in this way, and you will find an astonishing amount of mercies, for which you have never thanked God. Then take another sin. Let it be,

2. *Want of love to God.* Write that down, and go over all the instances you can remember, when you did not give to the blessed God that hearty love which you ought.

Think how grieved and alarmed you would be, if you discovered any flagging of affection for you in your wife, husband, or children; if you saw somebody else engrossing their hearts, and thoughts, and time. Perhaps, in such a case, you would well nigh die with a just and virtuous jealousy. Now, God styles himself a jealous God; and have you not given your heart to other loves: played the harlot, and infinitely offended him?

3. *Neglect of the Bible.* Put down the cases, when for days, and perhaps for weeks – yea, it may be, even for months together, you had no pleasure in God's word. Perhaps you did not read a chapter, or if you read it, it was in a way that was still more displeasing to God. Many people read over a whole chapter in such a way, that if they were put under oath when they have done, they could not tell what they have been reading. With so little attention do they read, that they cannot remember where they have read from morning till evening, unless they put in a string or turn down a leaf. This demonstrates that they did not lay to heart what they read, that they did not make it a subject of reflection. If you were reading a novel, or any other piece of intelligence that greatly interested you, would you not remember what you read last? And the fact that you fold a leaf or put in a string, demonstrates that you read rather as a task, than from love or reverence for the word of God. The word of God is the rule of your duty. And do you pay so little regard to it as not to remember what you read? If so, no wonder that you live so at random, and that your religion is such a miserable failure.

4. *Unbelief.* Instances in which you have virtually charged the God of truth with lying, by your unbelief of his express promises and declarations. God has promised to give the Holy Spirit to them that ask him. Now, have you believed this? Have you expected him to answer? Have you not virtually said in your hearts, when you prayed for the Holy Spirit, "I do not believe that I shall receive it"? If you have not believed nor expected you should receive the blessing, which God has expressly promised, you have charged him with lying.

5. *Neglect of prayer.* Times when you omitted secret prayer, family prayer, and prayer meetings, or have prayed in such a way as more grievously to offend God, than to have neglected it altogether.

6. *Neglect of the means of grace.* When you have suffered trifling excuses to prevent your attending meetings, have neglected and poured contempt upon the means of salvation, merely from disrelish of spiritual duties.

7. *The manner in which you have performed* those duties – want of feeling – want of faith – worldly frame of mind – so that your words were nothing but the mere chattering of a wretch, that did not deserve that God should feel the least care for him. When you have fallen down upon your knees, and *said your prayers,* in such an unfeeling and careless manner, that if you had been put under oath five minutes after you left your closet, you could not have told what you had been praying for.

8. *Your want of love for the souls of your fellow-men.* Look round upon your friends and relations, and remember how little compassion

you have felt for them. You have stood by and seen them going right to hell, and it seems as though you did not care if they did. How many days have there been, in which you did not make their condition the subject of a single fervent prayer, or even an ardent desire for their salvation?

9. *Your want of care for the heathen.* Perhaps you have not cared enough for them to attempt to learn their condition; perhaps not even to take a Missionary paper. Look at this, and see how much you do really care for the heathen, and set down honestly the real amount of your feelings for them, and your desire for their salvation. Measure your desire for their salvation by the self-denial you practise, in giving of your substance to send them the Gospel. Do you deny yourself even the hurtful superfluities of life, such as tea, coffee, and tobacco? Do you retrench your style of living, and really subject yourself to any inconvenience to save them? Do you daily pray for them in your closet? Do you statedly attend the monthly concert? Are you from month to month laying by something to put into the treasury of the Lord, when you go up to pray? If you are not doing these things, and if your soul is not agonized for the poor benighted heathen, why are you such a hypocrite as to pretend to be a Christian? Why, your profession is an insult to Jesus Christ!

10. *Your neglect of family duties.* How you have lived before them, how you have prayed, what an example you have set before them. What direct efforts do you habitually make for their spiritual good? What duty have you *not* neglected?

11. *Neglect of social duties.*

12. *Neglect of watchfulness over your own life.* Instances in which you have hurried over your private duties, and not taken yourself to task, nor honestly made up your accounts with God. Where you have entirely neglected to watch your conduct, and have been off your guard, and have sinned before the world, and before the church, and before God.

13. *Neglect to watch over your brethren.* How often have you broken your covenant, that you would watch over them in the Lord! How little do you know or care about the state of their souls! And yet you are under a solemn oath to watch over them. What have you done to make yourself acquainted with them? How many of them have you interested yourself for, to know their spiritual state? Go over the list, and wherever you find there has been a neglect, write it down. How many times have you seen your brethren growing cold in religion, and have not spoken to them about it? You have seen them beginning to neglect one duty after another, and you did not reprove them in a brotherly way. You have seen them falling into sin, and you let them go on. And yet you pretend to love them. What a hypocrite! Would you see your wife or child going into disgrace, or into the fire, and hold your peace? No, you would not. What do you think of yourself, then, to pre-

tend to love Christians, and to love Christ, while you can see them going into disgrace, and say nothing to them?

14. *Neglect of self-denial.* There are many professors who are willing to do almost anything in religion, that does not require self-denial. But when they are called to do anything that requires them to deny themselves, Oh! that is too much. They think they are doing a great deal for God, and doing about as much as he ought to ask in reason, if they are only doing what they can do about as well as not; but they are not willing to deny themselves any comfort or convenience whatever, for the sake of serving the Lord. They will not willingly suffer reproach for the name of Christ. Nor will they deny themselves the *luxuries* of life, to save a world from hell. So far are they from remembering that self-denial is a *condition of discipleship,* that they do not know what self-denial is. They never have really denied themselves a riband or a pin for Christ, and for the Gospel. Oh, how soon such professors will be in hell! Some are giving of *their abundance,* and are giving much, and are ready to complain that others don't give more; when, in truth, they do not give anything that they *need,* any thing that they could enjoy, if they kept it. They only give of their surplus wealth; and perhaps that poor woman, who puts in twelve and a half cents at the monthly concert, has exercised more self-denial, than they have in giving thousands.

From these we turn to

SINS OF COMMISSION

1. *Worldly mindedness.* What has been the state of your heart in regard to your worldly possessions? Have you looked at them as really *yours* — as if you had a right to dispose of them as your own, according to your own will? If you have, write that down. If you have loved property, and sought after it for its own sake, or to gratify lust or ambition, or a worldly spirit, or to lay it up for your families, you have sinned, and must repent.

2. *Pride.* Recollect all the instances you can, in which you have detected yourself in the exercise of pride. Vanity is a particular form of pride. How many times have you detected yourself in consulting vanity, about your dress and appearance? How many times have you thought more, and taken more pains, and spent more time, about decorating your body to go to church, than you have about preparing your mind for the worship of God? You have gone to the house of God caring more how you appear outwardly in the sight of mortal men, than how your soul appears in the sight of the heart-searching God. You have in fact set up yourself to be worshipped by them, rather than prepared to worship God yourself. You came to divide the worship of God's house, to draw off the attention of God's people to look at your

pretty appearance. It is in vain to pretend now, that you don't care anything about having people look at you. Be honest about it. Would you take all these pains about your looks if everybody was blind?

3. *Envy.* Look at the cases in which you were envious at those who you thought were above you in any respect. Or perhaps you have envied those who have been more talented or more useful than yourself. Have you not so envied some, that you have been pained to hear them praised? It has been more agreeable to you to dwell upon their faults, than upon their virtues, upon their failures, than upon their success. Be honest with yourself, and if you have harbored this spirit of hell, repent deeply before God, or *he will never forgive you.*

4. *Censoriousness.* Instances in which you have had a bitter spirit, and spoken of Christians in a manner entirely devoid of charity and love — charity, which requires you always to hope the best the case will admit, and to put the best construction upon any ambiguous conduct.

5. *Slander.* The times you have spoken behind people's backs of their faults, real or supposed, of members of the church or others, unnecessarily or without good reason. This is slander. You need not lie to be guilty of slander — to tell the truth with the design to injure, is slander.

6. *Levity.* How often have you trifled before God, as you would not have dared to trifle in the presence of an earthly sovereign? You have either been an Atheist, and forgotten that there was a God, or have had less respect for him, and his presence, than you would have had for an earthly judge.

7. *Lying.* Understand now what lying is. Any species of *designed* deception for a selfish reason is lying. If the deception is not a design, it is not lying. But if you design to make an impression contrary to the naked truth, you lie. Put down all those cases you can recollect. Don't call them by any soft name. God calls them *lies*, and charges you with *lying*, and you had better charge yourself correctly.

How innumerable are the falsehoods perpetrated everyday in business, and in social intercourse, by words, and looks, and actions — designed to make an impression on others contrary to the truth for selfish reasons.

8. *Cheating.* Set down all the cases in which you have dealt with an individual, and done to him that which you would not like to have done to you. *That* is cheating. God has laid down a rule in the case: "All things whatsover ye would that men should do to you, do ye even so to them." That is the rule; and now if you have not done so you are a cheat. Mind, the rule is not that you should do what you might reasonably expect them to do to you. That is a rule which would admit of every degree of wickedness. But it is "As ye *would* they should do to you."

9. *Hypocrisy.* For instance, in your prayers and confessions to God.

Set down the instances in which you have prayed for things you did not really want. And the evidence is, that when you have done praying, you could not tell what you had prayed for. How many times have you confessed sins that you did not mean to break off, and when you had no solemn purpose not to repeat them? Yes, have confessed sins when you knew you as much expected to go and repeat them as you expected to live.

10. *Robbing God.* Instances in which you have misspent your time, and squandered hours which God gave you to serve him and save souls, in vain amusements or foolish conversation, reading novels, or doing nothing; cases where you have misapplied your talents and powers of mind; where you have squandered money on your lusts, or spent it for things you did not need, and which neither contributed to your health, comfort or usefulness. Perhaps some of you who are here tonight have laid out God's money for *tobacco.* I will not speak of rum, for I presume there is no professor of religion here tonight that would drink rum. I hope there is no one that uses the filthy poison, tobacco. Think of a professor of religion, using God's money to poison himself with tobacco!

11. *Bad temper.* Perhaps you have abused your wife, or your children, or your family, or servants, or neighbors. Write it all down.

12. *Hindering others from being useful.* Perhaps you have weakened their influence by insinuations against them. You have not only robbed God of your own talents, but tied the hands of somebody else. What a wicked servant is he that loiters himself, and hinders the rest! This is done sometimes by taking their time needlessly; sometimes by destroying Christian confidence in them. Thus you have played into the hands of Satan, and not only showed yourself an idle vagabond, but prevented others from working.

If you find you have committed a fault against an individual, and that individual is within your reach, go and confess it immediately, and get that out of the way. If the individual you have injured is too far off for you to go and see him, sit down and write him a letter, and confess the injury, *pay the postage,* and put it into the mail immediately. I say, pay the postage, or otherwise you will only make the matter worse. You will add to the former injury, by making him a bill of expense. The man that writes a letter on his own business, and sends it to another without paying the postage, is dishonest, and has cheated him out of so much. And if he would cheat a man out of a sixpence or shilling, when the temptation is so small, what would he not do were the temptation greater, if he had the prospect of impunity? If you have defrauded anybody, send the money, the full amount and the interest.

Go thoroughly to work in all this. Go *now.* Don't put it off; that will only make the matter worse. Confess to God those sins that have been committed against God, and to man those sins that have been committed against man. Don't think of getting off by going round the stumbling blocks. Take them up out of the way. In breaking up your fallow ground, you must remove every obstruction. Things may be left that you may think little things, and you may wonder why you do not feel as you wish to in religion, when the reason is that your proud and carnal mind has covered up something which God required you to confess and remove. Break up all the ground and turn it over. Do not balk it, as the farmers say; do not turn aside for little difficulties; drive the plow right through them, beam deep, and turn the ground all up, so that it may all be mellow and soft, and fit to receive the seed and bear fruit a hundred fold.

When you have gone over your whole history in this way, thoroughly, if you will then go over the ground the second time, and give your solemn and fixed attention to it, you will find that the things you have put down will suggest other things of which you have been guilty, connected with them, or near them. Then go over it a third time, and you will recollect other things connected with these. And you will find in the end that you can remember an amount of your history, and particular actions, even in this life, which you did not think you should remember in eternity. Unless you do take up your sins in this way, and consider them in detail, one by one, you can form no idea of the amount of your sins. You should go over it as thoroughly and as carefully, and as solemnly, as you would if you were just preparing yourself for the judgment.

As you go over the catalogue of your sins, be sure to resolve upon present and entire reformation. Wherever you find anything wrong, resolve at once, in the strength of God, to sin no more in that way. It will be of no benefit to examine yourself, unless you determine to amend in *every particular* that you find wrong in heart, temper, or conduct.

If you find, as you go on with this duty, that your mind is still all dark, cast about you, and you will find there is some reason for the Spirit of God to depart from you. You have not been faithful and thorough. In the progress of such a work you have got to do violence to yourself, and bring yourself as a rational being up to this work, with the Bible before you, and try your heart till you *do* feel. You need not expect that God will work a miracle for you to break up your fallow ground. It is to be done by means. Fasten your attention to the subject of your sins. You cannot look at your sins long and thoroughly, and see how bad they are, without feeling, and feeling deeply. Experience abundantly proves the benefit of going over our history in this way. Set yourself to the work now; resolve that you never will stop till you find you can *pray.* You never will have the spirit of prayer, till you examine yourself, and confess your sins, and break up your fallow ground. You never will have the Spirit of God dwelling in you, till you have unraveled this whole mystery of iniquity, and spread out your sins before God. Let there be this deep work of repentance, and full confession, this breaking down before God, and you will have as much of the spirit of prayer as your body can bear up under. The reason why so few Christians know anything about the spirit of prayer, is because they never would take the pains to examine themselves properly, and so never knew what it was to have their hearts all broken up in this way.

You see I have only begun to lay open this subject tonight. I want to lay it out before you, in the course of these lectures, so that if you will begin and go on to do as I say, the results will be just as certain as they are when the farmer breaks up a fallow field, and mellows it, and sows his grain. It will be so, if you will only begin in this way, and hold on till all your hardened and callous hearts break up.

REMARKS

1. It will do no good to preach to you while your hearts are in this hardened, and waste, and fallow state. The farmer might just as well sow his grain on the rock. It will bring forth no fruit. This is the reason why there are so many fruitless professors in the church, and why there is so much outside machinery, and so little deep-toned feeling in the church. Look at the Sabbath-school for instance, and see how much machinery there is, and how little of the power of godliness. If you go on in this way, the word of God will continue to harden you, and you will grow worse and worse, just as the rain and snow on an old fallow field makes the turf thicker, and the clods stronger.

2. See why so much preaching is wasted, and worse than wasted. It is because the church will not break up their fallow ground. A preacher may wear out his life, and do very little good, while there are so many stony-ground hearers, who have never had their fallow ground broken up. They are only half converted, and their religion is rather a change of opinion than a change of the feeling of their hearts. There is mechanical religion enough, but very little that looks like deep heart-work.

3. Professors of religion should never satisfy themselves, or expect a revival, just by starting out of their slumbers, and blustering about, and making a noise, and talking to sinners. They must get their fallow ground broken up. It is utterly unphilosophical to think of getting engaged in religion in this way. If your fallow ground is broken up, *then* the way to get more feeling, is to go out and see sinners on the road to hell, and talk to them, and guide inquiring souls, and you will get more feeling. You may get into an *excitement* without this breaking up; you may show a kind of zeal, but it will not last long, and it will not take hold of sinners, unless your hearts are broken up. The reason is,

that you go about it mechanically, and have not broken up your fallow ground.

4. And now, finally, will you break up your fallow ground? Will you enter upon the course now pointed out, and persevere till you are thoroughly awake? If you fail here, if you do not do *this,* and get prepared, you can go no further with me in this course of lectures. I have gone with you as far as it is of any use to go, until your fallow ground is broken up. Now, you must make thorough work upon this point, or all I have further to say will do you little good. Nay, it will only harden and make you worse. If, when next Friday night arrives, it finds you with unbroken hearts, you need not expect to be benefited by what I shall say. If you do not set about this work immediately, I shall take it for granted that you do not mean to be revived, that you have forsaken your minister, and mean to let him go up to battle alone. If you do not do this, I charge you with having forsaken Christ, with refusing to repent and do your first work. But if you will be prepared to enter upon the work, I propose, God willing, next Friday evening, to lead you into the work of saving sinners.

HINDRANCES TO REVIVALS

"I am doing a great work, so that I cannot come down. Why should the work cease, whilst I leave it, and come down to you" (Nehemiah 6:3).

THIS SERVANT OF GOD had come down from Babylon to rebuild the temple and reestablish the worship of God at Jerusalem, the city of his fathers' sepulchres. When it was discovered by Sanballat and certain individuals, his allies, who had long enjoyed the desolations of Zion, that now the temple, and the holy city were about to be rebuilt, they raised a great opposition. Sanballat and the other leaders tried in several ways to divert Nehemiah and his friends, and prevent them from going forward in their work; at one time they threatened them,

Reprinted from Charles G. Finney, *Lectures on Revivals of Religion,* rev. ed. (New York: Fleming H. Revell Co., 1888), pp. 263–93.

and then complained that they were going to rebel against the king. Again, they insisted that their design was not pious but political, to which Nehemiah replied by a simple and prompt denial, "There are no such things done as thou sayest, but thou feignest them out of thine own heart." Finally, Sanballat sent a message to Nehemiah, requesting him to meet in the plain of Ono, to discuss the whole matter amicably and have the difficulty adjusted, but designed to do him mischief. They had found that they could not frighten Nehemiah, and now they wanted to come round him by artifice and fraud, and draw him off from the vigorous prosecution of his work. But he replied, "I am doing a great work, so that I cannot come down: why should the work cease, whilst I come down to you?"

It has always been the case, whenever any of the servants of God do anything in his cause, and there appears to be *a probability that* they will succeed, that Satan by his agents regularly attempts to divert their minds and nullify their labors. So it has been during the last ten years, in which there have been such remarkable revivals through the length and breadth of the land. These revivals have been very great and powerful, and extensive. It has been estimated that not less than *two hundred thousand* persons have been converted to God in that time.

And the devil has been busy in his devices to divert and distract the people of God, and turn off their energies from pushing forward the great work of salvation. In remarking on the subject, I propose to show,

I. That a Revival of Religion is a great work.

II. To mention several things which may put a stop to it.

III. Endeavor to show what must be done for the continuance of this great revival.

I. I am to show that a Revival of Religion *is a great work.*

It is a great work, because in it are *great interests involved.* In a Revival of Religion are involved both the glory of God, so far as it respects the government of this world, and the salvation of men. Two things that are of *infinite* importance are involved in it. The greatness of a work is to be estimated by the greatness of the consequences depending on it. And this is the measure of its importance.

II. I am to mention several things which *may put a stop to a revival.*

Some have talked very foolishly on this subject, as if nothing could injure a genuine revival. They say, "If your revival is a work of God, it cannot be stopped; can any created being stop God?" Now I ask if this is common sense? Formerly, it used to be the established belief that a revival could not be stopped, because it was the work of God. And so they supposed it would go on, whatever might be done to hinder it, in the church or out of it. But the farmer might just as well reason so, and think he could go and cut down his wheat and not hurt the crop, because it is God that makes grain grow. A revival is the work of God, and so is a crop of wheat; and God is as much dependent on the use of means is one case as the other. And therefore a revival is as liable to be injured as a wheat field.

1. A revival will stop whenever the *church believe it is going to cease.* The church are the instruments with which God carries on this work, and they are to work in it voluntarily and with their hearts. Nothing is more fatal to a revival than for its friends to predict that it is going to stop. No matter what the *enemies* of the work may say about it, predicting that it will all run out and come to nothing, and the like. They cannot stop it in this way; but the friends must labor and pray in faith to carry it on. It is a contradiction to say they are laboring and praying in faith to carry on the work, and yet believe that it is going to stop. If they lose their faith, it will stop, of course. Whenever the friends of revivals begin to prophesy that the revival is going to stop, they should be instantly rebuked, in the name of the Lord. If the idea once begins to prevail, and if you cannot counteract it and root it out, the revival will infallibly cease; for it is indispensable to the work, that Christians should labor and pray in faith to promote it, and it is a contradiction to say that they can labor in faith for its continuance, while they believe that it is about to cease.

2. A revival will cease *when Christians consent that it should cease.* Sometimes Christians see that the revival is in danger of ceasing, and that if something effectual is not done, it will come to a stand. If this fact distresses them, and drives them to prayer, and to fresh efforts, the work will not cease. When Christians love the work of God and the salvation of souls so well that they are distressed at the mere apprehension of a decline, it will drive them to an agony of prayer and effort. If it does not drive them to agony and effort to prevent its ceasing; if they see the danger, and do not try to avert it, or to renew the work, *they consent that it should stop.* There are at this time many people, all over the country, who see revivals declining, and that they are in great danger of ceasing altogether, and yet they manifest but little distress, and seem to care but little about it. Whole churches see their condition, and see what is coming unless there can be a waking up, and yet they are at ease, and do not groan and agonize in prayer, that God would revive his work. Some are even predicting that there is now going to be a great reaction, and a great dearth come over the church, as there did after Whitefield's and Edwards' day. And yet they are not startled at their own forebodings; they are cool about it, and turn directly off to other things. *They consent to it.* It seems as if they were the devil's trumpeters, sent out to scatter dismay throughout the ranks of God's elect.

3. A revival will cease whenever *Christians become mechanical in their attempts to promote it.* When their faith is strong, and their

hearts are warm and mellow, and their prayers full of holy emotion, and their words with power, then the work goes on. But when their prayers begin to be cold and without emotion, and their deep-toned feeling is gone, and they begin to labor mechanically, and to use words without feeling, then the revival will cease.

4. The revival will cease whenever Christians get the idea that *the work will go on without their aid*. The church are coworkers with God in promoting a revival, and the work can be carried on just as far as the church will carry it on, and no farther. God has been for one thousand eight hundred years trying to get the church into the work. He has been calling and urging, commanding, entreating, pressing and encouraging, to get them to take hold. He has stood all this while ready to *make bare his arm* to carry on the work with them. But the church have been unwilling to do their part. They seem determined to leave it to God alone to convert the world, and say, "If he wants the world converted, let him do it." They ought to know that this is impossible. So far as we know, neither God nor man can convert the world without the co-operation of the church. Sinners cannot be converted without their own agency, for conversion *consists in* their voluntary turning to God. No more can sinners be converted without the appropriate moral influences to turn them; that is, without truth and the reality of things brought full before their minds either by direct revelation or *by men*. God cannot convert the world by physical omnipotence, but he is dependent on the moral influence of the church.

5. The work will cease when the church prefer to attend to their own concerns rather than God's business. I do not admit that men *have* any business which is properly *their own*, but they think so, and in fact prefer what they consider as their own, rather than to work for God. They begin to think they *cannot afford* sufficient time from their worldly employments to carry on a revival. And they pretend they are obliged to give up attending to religion, and let their hearts go out again after the world. And the work must cease, of course.

6. When Christians get proud of their great revival, it will cease. I mean those Christians who have before been instrumental in promoting it. It is almost always the case in a revival, that a part of the church are too proud or too worldly to take any part in the work. They are determined to stand aloof, and wait, and see what it will come to, and see how it will come out. The pride of this part of the church cannot stop the revival, for the revival never rested on them. It began without them, and it can go on without them. They may fold their arms and do nothing but look on and find fault; and still the work may go on. But when that part of the church *who work*, begin to think what a great revival they have had, and how they have labored and prayed, and how bold and how zealous they have been, and how much good they have

done, then the work will be likely to decline. Perhaps it has been published in the papers what a revival there has been in that church, and how much engaged the members have been, and they think how high they shall stand in the estimation of other churches, all over the land, because they have had such a great revival. And so they get puffed up, and vain, and then they can no longer enjoy the presence of God, and the Spirit withdraws from them, and the revival ceases.

7. The revival will stop when the church gets exhausted by labor. Multitudes of Christians commit a great mistake here in time of revival. They are so thoughtless, and have so little judgment, that they will break up all their habits of living, neglect to eat and sleep at the proper hours, and let the excitement run away with them, so that they overdo their bodies, and are so imprudent that they soon become exhausted, and it is impossible for them to continue in the work. Revivals often cease, and declension follows, from negligence and imprudence, in this respect, on the part of those engaged in carrying them on.

8. A revival will cease when the church begins *to speculate about abstract doctrines*, which have nothing to do with practice. If the church turn off their attention from the things of salvation, and go to studying or disputing about abstract points, the revival will cease, of course.

9. *When Christians begin to proselyte.* When the Baptists are so opposed to the Presbyterians, or the Presbyterians to the Baptists, or both against the Methodists, or Episcopalians against the rest, that they begin to make efforts to get the converts to join their church, you soon see the last of the revival. Perhaps a revival will go on for a time, and all sectarian difficulties are banished, till somebody circulates a book, privately, to gain proselytes. Perhaps some overzealous deacon, or some mischief-making woman, or some proselyting minister, can not keep still any longer, and begins to work the work of the devil, by attempting to gain proselytes, and so stirs up bitterness, and raising a selfish strife, grieves away the Spirit, and drives Christians all into parties. No more revival there.

10. When Christians *refuse to render to the Lord according to the benefits received.* This is a fruitful source of religious declensions. God has opened the windows of heaven to a church, and poured them out a blessing, and then he reasonably expects them to bring in the tithes into his storehouse, and devise and execute liberal things for Zion; and lo! they have refused; they have not laid themselves out accordingly to promote the cause of Christ, and so the Spirit has been grieved and the blessing withdrawn, and in some instances a great reaction has taken place because the church would not be liberal, when God has been so bountiful. I have known churches who were evidently cursed with barrenness for such a course. They had a glorious revival,

and afterwards perhaps their meeting-house needed repairing, or something else was needed which would cost a little money, and they refused to do it, and so for their niggardly spirit God gave them up.

11. When the church, in any way, *grieve the Holy Spirit*.

(1.) When they *do not feel their dependence on the Spirit*. Whenever Christians get strong in their own strength, God curses their blessings. In many instances, Christians sin against their own mercies, because they get lifted up with their success, and take the credit to themselves, and do not give to God all the glory. As he says, "If ye will not hear, and if ye will not lay it to heart, to give glory unto my name, saith the Lord of hosts, I will even send a curse upon you, and, I will curse your blessings: yea, I have cursed them already, because ye do not lay it to heart." There has been a great deal of this in this country, undoubtedly. I have seen many things that looked like it, in the papers, where there seemed a disposition in men to take credit for success in promoting revivals. There is doubtless a great temptation to this, and it requires the utmost watchfulness, on the part of ministers and churches, to guard against it, and not grieve the Spirit away by vaingflorying in men.

(2.) The Spirit may be grieved *by a spirit of boasting of the revival*. Sometimes, as soon as a revival commences, you will see it blazed out in the newspapers. And most commonly this will kill the revival. There was a case in a neighboring state, where a revival commenced, and instantly there came out a letter from the pastor, telling that he had a revival. I saw the letter and said to myself, That is the last we shall hear of this revival. And so it was. In a few days, the work totally ceased. And such things are not uncommon. I could mention cases and places, where persons have published such things as to puff up the church, and make them so proud that little or nothing more could be done for the revival.

Some, under pretence of publishing things to the praise and glory of God, have published things that savored so strongly of a disposition to exalt themselves, have made their own agency to stand out so conspicuously, as was evidently calculated to make an unhappy impression. At the protracted meeting held in this church, a year ago last fall, there were five hundred hopefully converted, whose names and places of residence we knew. A considerable number of them joined this church. Many of them united with other churches. Nothing was said of this in the papers. I have several times been asked why we were so silent upon the subject. I could only reply, that there was such a tendency to self-exaltation in the churches, that I was afraid to publish anything on the subject. Perhaps I erred. But I have so often seen mischief done by premature publications, that I thought it best to say nothing about it. In the revival in this city, four years ago, so much was said in the papers, that appeared like self-exaltation, that I was afraid

SERMONS · *Hindrances to Revivals*   377

to publish. I am not speaking against the *practice itself,* of publishing accounts of revivals. But the *manner* of doing it is of vast importance. If it is done so as to excite vanity, it is always fatal to the revival.

(3.) So the Spirit is grieved *by saying or publishing things* that are calculated to *undervalue the work of God.* When a blessed work of God is spoken lightly of, not rendering to God the glory due to his name, the Spirit is grieved. If anything is said about a revival, give only the plain and naked *facts* just as they are, and let them pass for what they are worth.

12. A revival may be expected to cease, *when Christians lose the spirit of brotherly love.* Jesus Christ will not continue with people in a revival any longer than they continue in the exercise of brotherly love. When Christians are in the spirit of a revival, they feel this love, and then you will hear them call each other brother and sister, very affectionately. But when they begin to get cold, they lose this warmth and glow of affection for one another, and then this calling brother and sister will seem silly and contemptible and they will leave it off. In some churches they never call each other so, but where there is a revival, Christians naturally do it. I never saw a revival, and probably there never was one, in which they did not do it. But as soon as this begins to cease, the Spirit of God is grieved, and departs from among them.

13. A revival will decline and cease, unless *Christians are frequently reconverted.* By this I mean, that Christians, in order to keep in the spirit of a revival, commonly need to be frequently convicted, and humbled, and broken down before God, and reconverted. This is something which many do not understand, when we talk about a Christian's being reconverted. But the fact is that in a revival the Christian's heart is liable to get crusted over, and lose its exquisite relish for divine things; his unction and prevalence in prayer abates, and then he must be converted over again. It is impossible to keep him in such a state as not to do injury to the work, unless he pass through such a process every few days. I have never labored in revivals in company with anyone who would keep in the work and be fit to manage a revival continually, who did not pass through this process of breaking down as often as once in two or three weeks. Revivals decline, commonly, because it is found impossible to make the church feel their guilt and their dependence, so as to break down before God. It is important that ministers should understand this, and learn how to break down the church, and break down themselves when they need it, or else Christians will soon become mechanical in their work, and lose their fervor and their power of prevailing with God. This was the process through which Peter passed, when he had denied the Saviour, and by which breaking down, the Lord prepared him for the great work on the day of Pentecost. I was surprised, a few years since, to find that the phrase *"breaking down"* was a stumbling block to certain ministers

and professors of religion. They laid themselves open to the rebuke administered to Nicodemus, "Art thou a master in Israel and knowest not these things?" I am confident that until some of them know what it is to be "broken down," they will never do much more for the cause of revivals.

14. A revival cannot continue *when Christians will not practice self-denial.* When the church have enjoyed a revival and begin to grow fat upon it, and run into self-indulgence, the revival will soon cease. Unless they sympathize with the Son of God, who gave up all to save sinners; unless they are willing to give up their luxuries, and their ease, and lay themselves out in the work, they need not expect the Spirit of God will be poured out upon them. This is undoubtedly one of the principal causes of personal declension. Let Christians in a revival *beware,* when they first find an inclination creeping upon them, to shrink from self-denial, and to give in to one form of self-indulgence after another. It is the device of Satan, to bait them off from the work of God, and make them dull and gross, and lazy, and fearful, and useless, and sensual, and drive away the Spirit and destroy the revival.

15. A revival will be stopped *by controversies about new measures.* Nothing is more certain to overthrow a revival than this. But as my last lecture was on the subject of new measures, I need not dwell longer on the subject now.

16. Revivals can be put down *by the continued opposition of the Old School, combined with a bad spirit in the New School.* If those who do nothing to promote revivals continue their opposition, and if those who are laboring to promote them allow themselves to get impatient, and get into a bad spirit, the revival will cease. When the Old School write their letters in the newspapers, against revivals or revival men, and the New School write letters back again, against them, in an angry, contentious, bitter spirit, and get into a jangling controversy, revivals will cease. *Let them keep about their work,* and not talk about the opposition, nor preach, nor print about it. If others choose to publish their slang and stuff, let the Lord's servants keep to their work, and all the writing and slander will not stop the revival, while those who are engaged in it mind their business, and keep to their work. It is astonishing how far this holds true in fact.

In one place where there was a revival, certain ministers formed a combination against the pastor of the church, and a plan was set on foot to ruin him, and they actually got him prosecuted before his Presbytery, and had a trial that lasted six weeks, right in the midst of the revival, and the work still went on. The praying members of the church laid themselves out so in the work, that it continued triumphantly throughout the whole scene. The pastor was called off, to attend his trial, but there was another minister that labored among the people, and the members did not even go to the trial, generally, but kept praying and laboring for souls, and the revival rode out the storm. In many other places, opposition has risen up in the church, but a few humble souls have kept at their work, and a gracious God has stretched out his naked arm and made the revival go forward in spite of all opposition.

But whenever those who are actively engaged in promoting a revival get excited at the unreasonableness and pertinacity of the opposition, and feel as if they could not have it so, and they lose their patience, and feel as if they must answer their cavils and refute their slanders, then they get down into the plains of Ono, and the work must cease.

17. *Any diversion of the public mind* will hinder a revival. Anything that *succeeds* in diverting public attention, will put a stop to a revival. In the case I have specified, where the minister was put on trial before his Presbytery, the reason why it did not ruin the revival was, that the praying members of the church *would not suffer* themselves to be diverted. They did not even attend the trial, but kept praying and laboring for souls, and so public attention was kept to the subject, in spite of all the efforts of the devil.

But whenever he succeeds in *absorbing* public attention on any other subject, he will put an end to the revival. No matter what the subject is. If an angel from heaven were to come down, and preach, or pass about the streets, it might be the worst thing in the world for a revival, for it would turn sinners all off from their own sins, and turn the church off from praying for souls, to follow this glorious being, and gaze upon him, and the revival would cease.

18. *Resistance to the Temperance Reformation* will put a stop to revivals in a church. The time has come that it can no longer be innocent in a church to stand aloof from this glorious reformation. The time was when this could be done ignorantly. The time has been when ministers and Christians could enjoy revivals, notwithstanding ardent spirit was used among them. But since light has been thrown upon the subject, and it has been found that the use is only injurious, no church member or minister can be innocent and stand neutral in the cause. They must speak out and take sides. And if they do not take ground on one side, their influence is on the other. Show me a minister that has taken ground against the temperance reformation who has had a revival. Show me one who now stands aloof from it who has a revival. Show me one who now temporizes upon this point who does not come out and take a stand in favor of temperance who has a revival. It did not use to be so. But now the subject has come up, and has been discussed, and is understood, no man can shut his eyes upon the truth. The man's hands are *red with blood* who stands aloof from the temperance cause. And can he have a revival?

19. Revivals are hindered when ministers and *churches take wrong ground in regard to any question involving human rights*. Take the

subject of *slavery*, for instance. The time was when this subject was not before the public mind. John Newton continued in the slave trade after his conversion. And so had his mind been perverted, and so completely was his conscience seared, in regard to this most nefarious traffic, that the sinfulness of it never occurred to his thoughts until some time after he became a child of God. Had light been poured upon his mind previously to his conversion, he *never could* have been converted without previously abandoning this sin. And after his conversion, when convinced of its iniquity, he could no longer enjoy the presence of God, without abandoning the sin forever. So, doubtless, many slave dealers and slave holders in our own country have been converted, notwithstanding their participation in this abomination, because the sinfulness of it was not apparent to their minds. So ministers and churches, to a great extent throughout the land, have held their peace, and borne no testimony against this abominable abomination, existing in the church and in the nation. But recently, the subject has come up for discussion, and the providence of God has brought it distinctly before the eyes of all men. Light is now shed upon this subject, as it has been upon the cause of temperance. Facts are exhibited, and principles established, and light thrown in upon the minds of men, and this monster is dragged from his horrid den, and exhibited before the church, and it is demanded of them, "*Is this sin?*" Their testimony *must* be given on this subject. They are God's witnesses. They are sworn to tell "the truth, the whole truth, and nothing but the truth." It is impossible that their testimony should not be given, on one side or the other. Their silence can no longer be accounted for upon the principle of ignorance, and that they have never had their attention turned to the subject. Consequently, the silence of Christians upon the subject is virtually saying *that they do not* consider slavery as a sin. The truth is, it is a subject upon which they cannot be silent without guilt. The time has come, in the providence of God, when every southern breeze is loaded down with the cries of lamentation, mourning and woe. Two millions of degraded heathen in our own land stretch their hands, all shackled and bleeding, and send forth to the church of God the agonizing cry for help. And shall the church, in her efforts to reclaim and save the world, deafen her ears to this voice of agony and despair? God forbid. The church cannot turn away from this question. It is a question for the church and for the nation to decide, and God will push it to a decision.

It is in vain for the churches to resist it for fear of distraction, contention, and strife. It is in vain to account it an act of *piety* to turn away the ear from hearing this cry of distress.

The church must testify, and testify "the truth, the whole truth, and nothing but the truth," on this subject, or she is perjured, and the Spirit of God departs from her. She is under oath to testify, and ministers and churches who do not pronounce it sin bear false testimony for God. It is doubtless true that one of the reasons for the low state of religion at the present time is that many churches have taken the wrong side on the subject of slavery, have suffered prejudice to prevail over principle, and have feared to call this abomination by its true name.

20. Another thing that hinders revivals is *neglecting the claims of missions.* If Christians do not feel for the heathen, neglect the monthly concert, and confine their attention to their own church, do not even read the *Missionary Herald,* or use any other means to inform themselves on the subject of the claims of the world, and reject the light which God is throwing before them, and will not do what God calls them to do in this cause, the Spirit of God will depart from them.

21. *When a church reject the calls of God upon them for educating young men for the ministry,* they will hinder and destroy a revival. Look at the Presbyterian church, look at the 200,000 souls converted within ten years, and means enough to fill the world with ministers, and yet the ministry is not increasing so fast as the population of our own country, and unless something more can be done to provide ministers, we shall become heathen ourselves. The churches do not press upon young men the duty of going into the ministry. God pours his Spirit on the churches, and converts hundreds of thousands of souls, and if then the laborers do not come forth into the harvest, what can be expected but that the curse of God will come upon the churches, and his Spirit will be withdrawn, and revivals will cease. Upon this subject no minister, no church should be silent or inactive.

22. *Slandering revivals* will often put them down. The great revival in the days of President Edwards suffered greatly by the conduct of the church in this respect. It is to be expected that the enemies of God will revile, misrepresent and slander revivals. But when *the church* herself engages in this work, and many of her most influential members are aiding and abetting in calumniating and misrepresenting a glorious work of God, it is reasonable that the Spirit should be grieved away. It cannot be denied that this has been done, to a grievous and God-dishonoring extent. It has been estimated that in one year, since this revival commenced, *one hundred thousand souls* were converted to God in the United States. This was undoubtedly the greatest number that were ever converted in one year, since the world began. It could not be expected that, in an excitement of this extent, among *human beings,* there should be nothing to deplore. To expect perfection in such a work as this, of such extent, and carried on by human instrumentality, is utterly unreasonable and absurd. Evils doubtless did exist and have existed. They were to be expected of course, and guarded against, as far as possible. And I do not believe the world's history can furnish one instance in which a revival, approaching to

this in extent and influence, has been attended with so few evils, and so little that is honestly to be deplored.

But how has this blessed work of God been treated? Admitting all the evils complained of to be real, which is far from being true, they would only be like spots upon the disc of the glorious sun; things hardly to be thought of, in comparison of the infinite greatness and excellence of the work. And yet how have a great portion of the Presbyterian church received and treated this blessed work of God? At the General Assembly, that grave body of men that represent the Presbyterian Church, in the midst of this great work, instead of appointing a day of thanksgiving, instead of praising and glorifying God for the greatness of his work, we hear from them the voice of rebuke. From the reports that were given of the speeches made there, it appears that the house was filled with complainings. Instead of devising measures to forward the work, their attention seemed to be taken up with the comparatively trifling evils that were incidental to it. And after much complaining, they absolutely appointed a committee, and sent forth a "Pastoral Letter" to the churches, calculated to excite suspicions, quench the zeal of God's people, and turn them off from giving glory to God for the greatness of the blessing, to finding fault and carping about the evils. When I heard what was done at that General Assembly, when I read their speeches, when I saw their pastoral letter, my soul was sick, an unutterable feeling of distress came over my mind, and I felt that God would "visit" the Presbyterian church for conduct like this. And ever since, the glory has been departing, and revivals have been becoming less and less frequent — less and less powerful.

And now I wish it could be known whether those ministers who poured out those complainings on the floor of the General Assembly, and who were instrumental in getting up that pastoral letter, have since been blessed in promoting revivals of religion — whether the Spirit of God has been upon them, and whether their churches can witness that they have an unction from the Holy One.

23. *Ecclesiastical difficulties* are calculated to grieve away the Spirit, and destroy revivals. It has always been the policy of the devil to turn off the attention of ministers from the work of the Lord to disputes and ecclesiastical litigations. President Edwards was obliged to be taken up for a long time in disputes before ecclesiastical councils; and in our days, and in the midst of these great revivals of religion, these difficulties have been alarmingly and shamefully multiplied. Some of the most efficient ministers in the church have been called off from their direct efforts to win souls to Christ, to attend day after day, and in some instances week after week, to charges preferred against them, or their fellow-laborers in the ministry, which could never be sustained.

Look at Philadelphia: what endless and disgraceful janglings have distracted and disgraced the church of God in that city, and through the length and breadth of the land. And in the Presbyterian church at large these ecclesiastical difficulties have produced evils enough to make creation weep. Brother Beman was shamefully and wickedly called off from promoting revivals, to attend a trial before his own presbytery, upon charges which, if true, were most of them ridiculous, but which could never be sustained. And since that time a great portion of his time has, it would seem necessarily, been taken up with the adjustment of ecclesiastical difficulties. Brother Duffield, of Carlisle, Brother Barnes, of Philadelphia, and others of God's most successful ministers, have been hindered a considerable part of their time for years by these difficulties. Oh, tell it not in Gath! When will those ministers and professors of religion who do little or nothing themselves, let others alone, and let them work for God?

24. Another thing by which revivals may be hindered is *censoriousness on either side*, and *especially in those who have been engaged in carrying forward a revival*. It is to be expected that the opposers of the work will watch for the halting of its friends, and be sure to censure them for all that is wrong, and not unfrequently for that which is right in their conduct. Especially is it to be expected that many censorious and unchristian remarks will be made about those that are the most prominent instruments in promoting the work. This censoriousness on the part of the *opposers* of the work, whether in or out of the church, will not, however, of itself put a stop to the revival. While its promoters keep humble, and in a prayerful spirit, while they do not retaliate, but possess their souls in patience, while they do not suffer themselves to be diverted, to recriminate, and grieve away the spirit of prayer, the work will go forward; as in the case referred to, where a minister was on trial for six weeks in the midst of a revival. There the people kept in the dust, and prayed, not so much for their minister, for they had left him with God, but with strong crying and tears pleading with God for sinners. And God heard and blessed them, and the work went on. . . .

III. I proceed to mention some things *which ought to be done*, to continue this great and glorious revival of religion, which has been in progress for the last ten years.

1. *There should be great and deep repentings on the part of ministers. We*, my brethren, must humble *ourselves* before God. It will not do for us to suppose that it is enough to call on the *people* to repent. We must repent, we must take the lead in repentance, and then call on the churches to follow.

Especially must those repent who have taken the lead in producing the feelings of opposition and distrust in regard to revivals. Some ministers have confined their opposition against revivals and revival measures to their own congregations, and created such suspicions among their own people as to prevent the work from spreading and prevailing among them. . . .

Others have been more public, and aimed at exerting a wider influence. Some have written pieces for the public papers. Some men in high standing in the church have circulated letters which never were printed. Others have had their letters printed and circulated. There seems to have been a system of letter-writing about the country calculated to create distrust. In the days of President Edwards, substantially the same course was pursued, in view of which he says in his work on revivals:

"Great care should be taken that the press should be improved to no purpose contrary to the interests of this work. We read that when God fought against Sisera, for the deliverance of his oppressed church, *they that handle the pen of the writer* came to the help of the Lord in that affair (Judges 5:14). Whatever sort of men in Israel they were that were intended, yet as the words were indited by a Spirit that had a perfect view of all events to the end of the world, and had a special eye in this song, to that great event of the deliverance of God's church, in the latter days, of which this deliverance of Israel was a type, it is not unlikely that they have respect to authors, those that should fight against the kingdom of Satan with their pens. Those therefore that publish pamphlets to the disadvantage of this work, and tending either directly or indirectly to bring it under suspicion, and to discourage or hinder it, would do well thoroughly to consider whether this be not indeed the work of God, and whether, if it be, it is not likely that God will go forth as fire, to consume all that stand in his way, and so burn up those pamphlets; and whether there be not danger that the fire that is kindled in them will scorch the authors." . . .

There are ministers in our day, I say it not in unkindness but in faithfulness, and I would that I had them all here before me while I say it, who seem to have been engaged much of their time for years in doing little else than acting and talking and writing in such a way as to create suspicion in regard to revivals. And I cannot doubt that their churches would, as President Edwards says, be better with no minister at all, unless they will repent, and regain his blessing.

2. *Those churches which have opposed revivals* must humble themselves and repent. Churches which have stood aloof or hindered the work must repent of their sin, or God will not go with them. Look at those churches now, who have been throwing suspicion upon revivals. Do they enjoy revivals? Does the Holy Ghost descend upon them, to enlarge them and build them up? There is one of the churches in this city, where the session have been publishing in the newspapers what they call their "Act and Testimony," calculated to excite an unreasonable and groundless suspicion against many ministers who are laboring successfully to promote revivals. And what is the state of that church? Have they had a revival? Why it appears from the official

report to the General Assembly, that it has dwindled in one year twenty-seven per cent. And all such churches will continue to dwindle, in spite of everything else that can be done, unless they repent and have a revival. They may pretend to be mighty pious, and jealous for the honor of God, but God will not believe they are sincere. And he will manifest his displeasure, by not pouring out his Spirit. If I had a voice loud enough, I should like to make every one of these churches and ministers that have slandered revivals, hear me, when I say, that I believe they have helped to bring the pall of death over the church, and that the curse of God is on them already, and will remain unless they repent. God has already sent leanness into their souls, and many of them know it.

3. *Those who have been engaged in promoting the work* must also repent. Whatever they have done that was wrong must be repented of, or revivals will not return as in days past. Whenever a wrong spirit has been manifested, or they have got irritated and provoked at the opposition, and lost their temper, or mistaken Christian faithfulness for hard words and a wrong spirit, they must repent. Those who are opposed could never stop a revival alone, unless those who promote it get wrong. So we must repent if we have said things that were censorious, or proud, or arrogant, or severe. Such a time as this is no time to stand justifying ourselves. Our first call is to repent. Let each one repent of his own sins, and not fall out, and quarrel about who is most to blame.

4. *The church must take right ground in regard to politics.* Do not suppose, now, that I am going to preach a political sermon, or that I wish to have you join and get up a *Christian party* in politics. No, I do not believe in that. But the time has come that Christians must vote for honest men, and take consistent ground in politics, or the Lord will curse them. They must be honest men themselves, and instead of voting for a man because he belongs to their party Bank or Anti-Bank, Jackson, or Anti-Jackson, they must find out whether he is honest and upright, and fit to be trusted. They must let the world see that the church will uphold no man in office, who is known to be a knave, or an adulterer, or a Sabbath-breaker, or a gambler, or a drunkard. Such is the spread of intelligence and the facility of communication in our country, that every man can know for whom he gives his vote. And if he will give his vote only for honest men, the country will be obliged to have upright rulers. All parties will be compelled to put up honest men as candidates. Christians have been exceedingly guilty in this matter. But the time has come when they must act differently, or God will curse the nation, and withdraw his spirit. As on the subject of slavery and temperance, so on this subject, the church must act right or the country will be ruined. God cannot sustain this free and blessed country, which we love and pray for, unless the church will take right ground. Politics are a part of religion in such a country as this, and

Christians must do their duty to the country as a part of their duty to God. It seems sometimes as if the foundations of the nation were becoming rotten, and Christians seem to act as if they thought God did not see what they do in politics. But I tell you, he does see it, and he will bless or curse this nation, according to the course they take.

5. *The churches must take right grounds on the subject of slavery.* And here the question arises, what is right ground? And *first* I will state some things that should be avoided.

(1.) First of all, *a bad spirit* should be avoided. Nothing is more calculated to injure religion, and to injure the slaves themselves, than for Christians to get into an angry controversy on the subject. It is a subject upon which there needs to be no angry controversy among Christians. Slave-holding professors, like rum-selling professors, may endeavor to justify themselves, and may be angry with those who press their consciences, and call upon them to give up their sins. Those proud professors of religion who think a man to blame, or think it is a shame to have a black skin, may allow their prejudices so far to prevail, as to shut their ears, and be disposed to quarrel with those who urge the subject upon them. But I repeat it, the subject of slavery is a subject upon which Christians, praying men, *need not* and *must not* differ.

(2.) Another thing to be avoided is *an attempt to take neutral ground* on this subject. Christians can no more take neutral ground on this subject, since it has come up for discussion, than they can take neutral ground on the subject of the sanctification of the Sabbath. It is a great national sin. It is a sin of the church. The churches by their silence, and by permitting slaveholders to belong to their communion, have been consenting to it. All denominations have been more or less guilty, although the Quakers have of late years washed their hands of it. It is in vain for the churches to pretend it is merely a political sin. I repeat it, it is the sin of the church, to which all denominations have consented. They have virtually declared that it is lawful. The very fact of suffering slaveholders quietly to remain in good standing in their churches, is the strongest and most public expression of their views that it is not sin. For the church, therefore, to pretend to take neutral ground on the subject, is perfectly absurd. The fact is that she is not on neutral ground at all. While she tolerates slaveholders in her communion *she justifies the practice.* And as well might an enemy of God pretend that he was neither saint nor sinner, that he was going to take neutral ground, and pray "good Lord and good devil," because he did not know which side would be most popular.

(3.) Great care should be taken *to avoid a censorious spirit on both sides.* It is a subject on which there has been, and probably will be for some time to come, a difference of *opinion* among Christians, as to the best method of disposing of the question. And it ought to be treated with great forbearance on both sides. A denunciatory spirit, impeaching each other's motives, is unchristian, calculated to grieve the Spirit of God, and to put down revivals, and is alike injurious to the church, and to the slaves themselves.

In the *second* place, I will mention several things, that in my judgment the church are imperatively called upon to do, on this subject:

(1.) Christians of all denominations, should lay aside prejudice and *inform themselves* on this subject, without any delay. Vast multitudes of professors of religion have indulged prejudice to such a degree, as to be unwilling to read and hear, and come to a right understanding of the subject. But Christians cannot pray in this state of mind. I defy anyone to possess the spirit of prayer, while he is too prejudiced to examine this, or any other question of duty. If the light did not shine, Christians might remain in the dark upon this point, and still possess the spirit of prayer. But if they *refuse to come to the light*, they cannot pray. Now I call upon all you who are here present, and who have not examined this subject because you were indisposed to examine it, to say whether you have the spirit of prayer. Where ministers, individual Christians, or whole churches, *resist truth* upon this point now, when it is so extensively diffused and before the public mind, I do not believe they will or can enjoy a revival of religion.

(2.) Writings, containing temperate and judicious discussions on this subject, and such developments of facts as are before the public, should be quietly and extensively circulated, and should be carefully and prayerfully examined by the whole church. I do not mean by this, that the attention of the church should be so absorbed by this, as to neglect the main question, of saving souls in the midst of them. I do not mean that such premature movements on this subject should be made, as to astound the Christian community, and involve them in a broil; but that praying men should act judiciously, and that, as soon as sufficient information can be diffused through the community, the churches should meekly, but *firmly* take decided ground on the subject, and express before the whole nation and the world, their abhorrence of this sin. . . .

Perhaps no church in this country has had a more severe trial upon this subject than this. They were a church of young and for the most part inexperienced Christians. And many circumstances conspired, in my absence, to produce confusion and wrong feeling among them. But so far as I am now acquainted with the state of feeling in this church, I know of no ill will among them on this subject. The Lord has blessed us, the Spirit has been distilled upon us, and considerable numbers added to our communion every month since my return. There are doubtless in this church those who feel on this subject in very different degrees. And yet I can honestly say that I am not aware of the least difference *in sentiment* among them. We have from the beginning, *previous* to my going on my foreign tour, taken the same ground on the subject of slavery that we have on temperance. We have excluded slaveholders and all concerned in the traffic from our communion. By some out of this church this course has been censured as unwarrantable and uncharitable, and I would by no means make my own judgment, or the example of this church, a rule for the government of other ministers and churches. Still, I conscientiously believe that the time is not far distant when the churches will be united in this expression of abhorrence against this sin. If I do not baptize slavery by some soft and Christian name, if I call it *sin*, both consistency and conscience conduct to the inevitable conclusion, that while this sin is persevered in, its perpetrators cannot be fit subjects for Christian communion and fellowship.

To this it is objected, that there are *many ministers* in the Presbyterian church who are slaveholders. And it is said to be very inconsistent that we should refuse to suffer a slaveholder to come to our communion, and yet belong to the same church with them, sit with them in ecclesiastical bodies, and acknowledge them as ministers. To this I answer, that I have not the power to deal with those ministers, and certainly I am not to withdraw from the church because some of its ministers or members are slaveholders. My duty is to belong to the church, even if the devil belong to it. Where I *have authority*, I exclude slaveholders from the communion, and I always will as long as I live. But where I have no authority, if the table of Christ is spread, I will sit down to it, in obedience to his commandment, whoever else may sit down or stay away.

I do not mean, by any means, to denounce all those slaveholding ministers and professors as hypocrites, and to say that they are not Christians. But this I say, that while they continue in that attitude, the cause of Christ and of humanity demands, that they should not be recognized as such, unless we mean to be partakers of other men's sins. It is no more inconsistent to exclude slaveholders because they belong to the Presbyterian church, than it is to exclude persons who drink or sell ardent spirits. For there are a great many rum-sellers belonging to the Presbyterian church.

I believe the time has come, and although I am no prophet, I believe it will be found to have come, that the revival in the United States will continue and prevail, no farther and faster than the church take right ground upon this subject. The church are God's witnesses. The fact is that slavery is, preeminently, the *sin of the church*. It is the very fact that ministers and professors of religion of different denominations hold slaves, which sanctifies the whole abomination, in the eyes of ungodly men. Who does not know that on the subject of temperance every drunkard in the land will skulk behind some rum-selling deacon, or wine-drinking minister? It is the most common objection and refuge of the intemperate, and of moderate drinkers that it is practised by professors of religion. It is *this* that creates the imperious necessity for excluding traffickers in ardent spirit, and rum-drinkers from the communion. Let the churches of all denominations speak out on the subject of temperance; let them close their doors against all who have anything to do with the death-dealing abomination, and the cause of temperance is triumphant. A few years would annihilate the traffic. Just so with slavery.

It is the church that mainly supports this sin. Her united testimony upon this subject would settle the question. Let Christians of all denominations meekly but firmly come forth, and pronounce their verdict; let them clear their communions, and wash their hands of this thing; let them give forth and write on the head and front of this great abomination, *sin!* and in three years a public sentiment would be formed that would carry all before it, and there would not be a shackled slave, nor a bristling, cruel slave-driver in this land.

Still it may be said, that in many churches, this subject *cannot be* introduced without creating confusion and ill will. This may be. It has been so upon the subject of temperance, and upon the subject of revivals too. In some churches, neither temperance nor revivals can be introduced without producing dissension. Sabbath-schools, and missionary operations, and everything of the kind have been opposed, and have produced dissensions in many churches. But is this a sufficient reason for excluding these subjects? And where churches have excluded these subjects for fear of contention, have they been blessed with revivals? Everybody knows that they have not. But where churches have taken firm ground on these subjects, although individuals and sometimes numbers have opposed, still they have been blessed with revivals. Where any of these subjects are carefully and prayerfully introduced; where they are brought forward with a right spirit, and the true relative importance is attached to each one of them; if in such cases, there are those who will make disturbance and resist, *let the blame fall where it ought.* There are some individuals, who are *themselves* disposed to quarrel with this subject, who are always ready to exclaim, "Do not introduce these things into the church, they will create opposition." And if the minister and praying people feel it their duty to bring the matter forward, they will themselves create a disturbance, and then say, "There, I told you so; now see what your introducing this subject has done; it will tear the church all to pieces." And while they are themselves doing all they can to create division, they are charging the division upon the subject, and not upon themselves. There are some such people in many of our churches. And neither Sabbath-schools, nor missions, nor revivals, nor anti-slavery, nor anything else that honors God or benefits the souls of men, will be carried in the churches, without these careful souls being offended by it.

These things, however, have been introduced, and carried, one by one, in some churches with more, and others with less opposition, and perhaps in some churches with no opposition at all. And as true as God is the God of the church, as certain as that the world must be converted, this subject must be considered and pronounced sin by the church. There might, infinitely better, be no church in the world, than that she should attempt to remain neutral or give a false testimony on a subject of such importance as slavery, especially since the subject has come up, and it is impossible from the nature of the case, that her testimony should not be in the scale, on the one side or the other.

Do you ask, "What shall be done — shall we make it the all-absorbing topic of conversation, and divert attention from the all-important subject of the salvation of souls in the midst of us?" I answer, No. Let a church express her opinion upon the subject, and be at peace. So far as I know, *we* are entirely at peace upon this subject. We have expressed our opinion; we have closed our communion against slaveholders, and are attending to other things. I am not aware of the least unhealthy excitement among us on this subject. And where it has become an absorbing topic of conversation in a place, in most instances I believe it has been owing to the pertinacious and unreasonable opposition of a few individuals against even granting the subject a hearing.

6. If the church wishes to promote revivals, *she must sanctify the Sabbath.* There is a vast deal of Sabbath-breaking in the land. Merchants break it, travelers break it, the Government breaks it. A few years ago an attempt was made in the western part of this State, to establish and sustain a Sabbath-keeping line of boats and stages. But it was found that the *church* would not sustain the enterprise. Many professors of religion would not travel in these stages, and would not have their goods forwarded in canal boats that would be detained from travelling on the Sabbath. At one time, Christians were much engaged in petitioning Congress to suspend the Sabbath mails, and now they seem to be ashamed of it. But one thing is most certain, that unless something is done, and done speedily, and done effectually, to promote the sanctification of the Sabbath by the church, the Sabbath will go by the board, and we shall not only have our mails running on the Sabbath, and post offices open, but by and by our courts of justice and halls of legislation will be kept open on the Sabbath. And what can the church do, what will this nation do, *without any Sabbath?*

7. The church must take right ground on the subject of Temperance and Moral Reform, and all the subjects of practical morality which come up for decision from time to time.

There are those in the churches who are standing aloof from the subject of Moral Reform, and who are afraid to have anything said in the pulpit against lewdness. On this subject the church need not expect to be permitted to take neutral ground. In the providence of God, it is up for discussion. The evils have been exhibited, the call has been made for reform. And what is to reform mankind but the truth? And who shall present the truth if not the church and the ministry? Away with the idea that Christians can remain neutral and keep still, and yet enjoy the approbation and blessing of God.

In all such cases, the minister who holds his peace is counted among those on the other side. Everybody knows that it is so in a revival. It is not necessary for a person to rail out against the work. If he only keeps still and takes neutral ground, the enemies of the revival will all consider him as on their side. So on the subject of temperance. It is not needful that a person should rail at the cold water society, in order to be on the best terms with drunkards and moderate drinkers. Only let him plead for the moderate use of wine, only let him continue to drink it as a luxury, and all the drunkards account him on their side. If he refuses to give his influence to the temperance cause, he is claimed of course by the other side as a friend. On all these subjects, when they come up, the churches and ministers must take the right ground, and take it openly and stand to it, and carry it through, if they expect to enjoy the blessing of God in revivals. They must cast out from their communions such members, as in contempt of the light that is shed upon them, continue to drink or traffic in ardent spirits.

8. *There must be more done for all the great objects of Christian benevolence.* There must be much greater efforts for the cause of missions, and education, and the Bible, and all the other branches of religious enterprise, or the church will displease God. Look at it. Think of the mercies we have received, of the wealth, numbers and prosperity of the church. Have we rendered unto God according to the benefits we have received, so as to show that the church is bountiful and willing to give their money and to work for God? No. Far from it. Have we multiplied our means and enlarged our plans, in proportion as the church has increased? Is God satisfied with what has been done, or has he reason to be? Such a revival as has been enjoyed by the churches of America for the last ten years! We ought to have done ten times as much as we have for missions, Bibles, education, tracts, free churches, and in all the ways designed to promote religion and save souls. If the churches do not wake up on this subject, and lay themselves out on a larger scale, they may expect the revival in the United States will cease.

9. If Christians in the United States expect revivals to spread, and prevail, till the world is converted, they must give up writing letters and publishing pieces *calculated to excite suspicion and jealousy in regard to revivals,* and must take hold of the work themselves. If the whole church as a body had gone to work ten years ago, and continued it as a few individuals, whom I could name, have done, there would not now have been an impenitent sinner in the land. The millennium would have fully come in the United States before this day. Instead of standing still, and writing letters from Berkshire, let ministers who think we are going wrong, just buckle on the harness and *go forward,*

and show us a more excellent way. Let them teach us by their example how to do better. I do not deny that some may have made mistakes, and committed errors. I do not deny that there are many things which are wrong done in revivals by some persons. But is that the way to correct them, brethren? So did not Paul. He corrected his brethren by telling them kindly that he would show them a more excellent way. Let our brethren take hold and go forward. Let us hear the cry from all their pulpits. To *the work.* Let them lead on, where the Lord will go with them and make bare his arm, and I, for one, will follow. Only let them *go on,* and let us have the United States converted to God, and let all minor questions cease.

If not, and if revivals do cease in this land, the ministers and churches will be guilty of all the blood of all the souls that shall go to hell in consequence of it. There is no need that the work should cease. If the church will do all her duty, the millennium may come in this country in three years. But if this writing letters is to be kept up, filling the country with suspicions and jealousies, if it is to be always so, that two-thirds of the church will hang back and do nothing but find fault in time of revival, the curse of God will be on this nation, and that before long.

REMARKS

1. It is high time there should be *great searchings of heart* among Christians and ministers. Brethren, this is no time to resist the truth, or to cavil and find fault because the truth is spoken out plainly. It is no time to recriminate or to strive, but we must search *our own* hearts, and humble ourselves before God.

2. We must repent and forsake our sins, and amend our ways and our doings, or the revival will cease. Our ecclesiastical difficulties *must cease,* and all minor differences must be laid aside and given up, to unite in promoting the great interests of religion. If not, revivals will cease from among us, and the blood of lost millions will be found in our skirts.

3. If the church would do all her duty, she would soon complete the triumph of religion in the world. But if this Act and Testimony warfare is to be kept up, and this system of espionage, and insinuation and denunciation, not only will revivals cease, but the blood of millions who will go to hell before the church will get over the shock, will be found in the skirts of the men who have got up and carried on this dreadful contention.

4. Those who have circulated slanderous reports in regard to revivals, must repent. A great deal has been said about heresy, and about some men's denying the Spirit's influence, which is wholly groundless, and has been made up out of nothing. And those who have made up the reports, and those who have circulated them against their

brethren, must repent and pray to God that they may receive his forgiveness.

5. We see the *constant tendency there is* in Christians to declension and backsliding. This is true in all converts of all revivals. Look at the revival in President Edwards' day. The work went on till 30,000 souls had been converted, and by this time so many ministers and Christians got in such a state, by writing books and pamphlets, on one side and the other, that they carried all by the board, and the revival ceased. Those who had opposed the work grew obstinate and violent, and those who promoted it lost their meekness and got ill-tempered, and were then driven into the very evils that had been falsely charged upon them.

And now, what shall we do? This great and glorious work of God seems to be indicating a decline. The revival is not dead—blessed be God for that—it is not dead! No, we hear from all parts of the land that Christians are reading on the subject and inquiring about the revival. In some places there are now powerful revivals. And what shall we do, to lift up the standard, to move this entire nation and turn all this great people to the Lord? We must *do right*. We must all have a better spirit, we must get down in the dust, we must act unitedly, we must take hold of this great work with all our hearts, and then God will bless us, and the work will go on.

What is the condition of this nation? No doubt, God is holding the rod of *war* over the heads of this nation. He is waiting before he lets loose his judgments, to see whether the church will do right. The nation is under his displeasure, because the church has conducted in such a manner with respect to revivals. And now suppose war should come, where would be our revivals? How quickly would war swallow up the revival spirit. The spirit of war is anything but the spirit of revivals. Who will attend to the claims of religion, when the public mind is engrossed by the all-absorbing topic of war. See now, how this nation is, *all at once*, brought upon the brink of war. God brandishes his blazing sword over our heads. Will the church repent? It is *the church* that God chiefly has in view. How shall we avoid the curse of war? Only by a reformation in the church. It is in vain to look to politicians to avert war. Perhaps they would generally be in favor of war. Very likely the things they would do to avert it would run us right into it. If the church will not feel, will not awake, will not act, where shall we look for help? If the church absolutely *will not* move, will not tremble in view of the just judgments of God hanging over our heads, we are certainly nigh unto cursing, as a nation.

6. Whatever is done *must be done quickly*. The scale is on a poise. If we do not go forward, we must go back. Things cannot remain as they are. If the church do not come up, if we do not have a more powerful revival than we have had, very soon we shall have none at all. We

have had such a great revival, that now small revivals do not interest the public mind. You must act as individuals. *Do your own duty.* You have a responsibility. Repent quickly. Do not wait till another year. Who but God knows what will be the state of these churches, if things go on *another year* without a great and general revival of religion?

7. It is common, when things get all wrong in the church, for each individual to find fault with the church, and with his brethren, and overlook his own share of the blame. Do not let anyone spend his time in finding fault with that abstract thing, "The Church." But as individual members of the church of Christ, let each one act, and act right, and get down in the dust, and never speak proudly, or censoriously. *Go forward.* Who would leave such a work, and go to writing letters, and go down into the plain of Ono, and see if all these petty disputes cannot be adjusted, and let the work cease. Let us mind our work, and let the Lord take care of the rest. Do our duty, and leave the issue to God.

Since these lectures were delivered great progress has been made in all benevolent enterprises in this country. Time has settled the question of the purity and inestimable value of those revivals, against which so much mistaken opposition existed in the Presbyterian church. It is now known that the great and disastrous reaction predicted by opposers has not been witnessed. It must now be admitted that the converts of those revivals have composed the strength of the churches, and that their Christian influence has been felt throughout the land. No revivals have ever existed the power and purity of which have been more thoroughly established by time and experience, than that great and blessed work of God, against which such a storm of opposition was raised. The opposition was evidently a great mistake. Let it not be said that the opposition was demanded by the great evils attending that work, and that those evils and errors were arrested and corrected by that opposition. The fact is that the supposed errors and evils that were made the justification of the opposition, never existed to any such extent as to justify alarm or opposition. I have written a narrative of those revivals, in which I have considered this question more fully. The churches did take hold of temperance and other branches of reform to such an extent as to avoid those evils against which they were warned. Upon the question of slavery the church was too late in her testimony to avoid the war. But the slaveholders were much alarmed and exasperated by the constantly growing opposition to their institution throughout all that region of the north where revival influences had been felt. They took up arms to defend and perpetuate the abomination, and by so doing abolished it.

FOR ADDITIONAL INFORMATION ABOUT CHARLES FINNEY:

Beardsley, Frank G. *A Mighty Winner of Souls.* New York: American Tract Society, 1937.

Cheesbro, Roy Alan. "The Preaching of Charles G. Finney." Ph.D. dissertation, Yale University Divinity School, 1948.

Day, Richard E. *Man of Like Passions.* Grand Rapids: Zondervan Publishing House, 1942.

Edman, Victor Raymond. *Finney Lives On.* New York: Fleming H. Revell Co., 1951.

Finney, Charles G. *Charles G. Finney, The American Revivalist* (autobiography). London: Simpkin, Marshall, Hamilton, Kent & Co., n.d.

_____. *Lectures on Revivals of Religion.* Oberlin, Ohio: E. J. Goodrich, 1868.

_____. *Memoirs of Rev. Charles G. Finney.* New York: Fleming H. Revell Co., 1903.

Harding, William H., ed. *Finney's Life and Lectures.* Grand Rapids: Zondervan Publishing House, 1943, 1956.

FOR OTHER SERMONS BY CHARLES FINNEY:

God's Love for a Sinning World. Grand Rapids: Kregel Pub., 1966.

So Great Salvation. Grand Rapids: Kregel Pub., 1965.

Also: *True Saints* (1967), *Victory Over the World* (1966), *Sermons on Gospel Themes* (1876).